Mobilizing the Press: Defending the First Amendment in the Supreme Court

Eric B. Easton

Vandeplas Publishing LLC
United States of America

Mobilizing the press: defending the first amendment in the supreme court

Easton, Eric B.

Published by:

Vandeplas Publishing LLC – November 2012

801 International Parkway, 5th Floor
Lake Mary, FL. 32746
USA

www.vandeplaspublishing.com

ISBN 978-1-60042-182-2

PREFACE

Following a 20-year career as reporter, editor, and publisher, I was invited to join the legal academy because of the skills I had developed as a journalist. For the past two decades, I have been teaching prospective lawyers to write clearly, concisely, and accurately at the University of Baltimore School of Law. And my reward for those labors, aside from a tenured professorship, has been the opportunity to study, teach, and write about media law.

A few years ago, with retirement looming not too far away, I felt the need for a capstone project that would allow me to join my two great loves – journalism and law – in a useful way. The Philip Merrill College of Journalism at the University of Maryland, College Park, gave me that opportunity, and this book is the culmination, not only of my graduate study there, but also of my entire academic career. For that reason, I ask the reader to indulge the presumptuous sweep of this study.

That said, the book must stand on its own as original, insightful, and significant. I hope it will do that and more. I hope it will show that the press has participated constructively, if not always decisively, in shaping First Amendment doctrine. I hope it will engender a new appreciation for an important function of the press in our democracy. And I hope it will stimulate other journalism and media law scholars to probe even more deeply into the process by which the press defends and tries to advance its First Amendment values through litigation.

ACKNOWLEDGEMENTS

I wish to thank the four persons I interviewed at some length for this book. Professor Earl Caldwell of the Hampton University provided invaluable and otherwise unavailable insights into the landmark case known to all as *Branzburg v. Hayes*, but which I will forever think of as *Caldwell v. United States*. Dean Lucy Dalglish of the Philip Merrill College of Journalism at the University of Maryland was executive director of the Reporters Committee for Freedom of the Press when I interviewed her. She opened a window on the mechanisms through which today's media defense bar, of which she has been a leading member, organizes for battle. Attorney Donald Brobst of Rosenn, Jenkins & Greewald, L.L.P., spent valuable hours with me, filling the gaps in my understanding of the *Bartnicki v. Vopper* litigation. And Professor Jane Kirtley, of the Silha Center for the Study of Media Ethics and Law, University of Minnesota, my teacher and mentor, and Dean Dalglish's predecessor at RCFP, met with me early on to guide and encourage me in this venture.

However much I would have enjoyed speaking with some of the actors in *Near v. Minnesota*, alas, my research was necessarily archival. The Brandeis papers in the Library of Congress afforded a glimpse of that great jurist's thoughts as *Near* was being decided. And Eric Gillespie of the Robert R. McCormick Research Center at Cantigny enabled me to relive McCormick's day-to-day efforts to mobilize the press to support the *Near* litigation.

I must also thank my good friend Albert Copland, for his careful proofreading at two different stages in the process, and my research assistants Hae-In Lee, for helping me collect the many *Branzburg* documents that eluded digitization; Amanda Wargo, for her help with the *Bartnicki* documents; and Steve Waddy, for his help with the bibliography; and most recently Heather Cobun, who did the laborious indexing work and was a great help with formatting. Of course, any mistakes that might be found in this manuscript are mine alone.

Others at the University of Baltimore School of Law to whom I am indebted include Gilbert Holmes and Phillip Closius, the two deans who supported this research with sabbatical time, summer research stipends, and research assistants; Law Library Director Will Tress and his staff, for whom no request of mine was too burdensome; and, of course, the many colleagues with whom I discussed various aspects of this project.

Most of the work on this book was completed while I was studying for a belated doctoral degree at the Philip Merrill College of Journalism, and I am indebted to the faculty there for their generous and patient support. Thanks to Dr. Carol Rogers, who gave me a valuable seat at the table, despite the fact that I would never repay the College with many productive years in journalism education. Thanks to John Cordes – who, along with Dr. Kalyani Chadha, undertook the impossible task of teaching me statistics – for assisting me with the simple statistical work in the concluding chapter of this dissertation. And to Dr.

Linda Steiner, Director of Research and Doctoral Studies, who encouraged and facilitated my work by permitting me to publish the principal chapters of this dissertation as law review articles during the course of my doctoral study. This rather unorthodox approach has enabled me to fulfill the requirements of my "day job" while working on my degree.

Of course, I am eternally grateful to my dissertation committee. To Dr. Christopher Hanson, whose brief exposure to legal education provided a unique empathy. To Dr. Wayne McIntosh, of the Department of Government and Politics, who opened the door to a body of scholarship about the law that I might otherwise never have encountered. To Dr. Elliot King, of Loyola Univeersity-Maryland, friend and adviser for many years now, who initially inspired me to pursue this degree. To Professor Emeritus Ray Hiebert, whom I have known and worked with since the newsletter days of the 1980s, and who has never failed to encourage my work.

I especially want to thank the chair of my committee, Professor Emerita Maurine Beasley, whom I first met in China in 1994, where she led a group of journalism educators as president of the AEJMC. As teacher, mentor, and friend, she has guided me through this process with wisdom, humor, and the occasional well-deserved rap on the knuckles.

Finally, I thank my loving wife Susan, without whose patience with my mid-life crisis, this project could never have been started, much less completed.

TABLE OF CONTENTS

Chapter 1 – Introduction: A Hypothetical

Washington, D.C., April 1, 2014 – The Department of Justice today announced that a federal grand jury here handed up a multi-count indictment against Julian Assange for violations of the Espionage Act. Assange is the founder of the Wikileaks web site, which has published thousands of classified military and diplomatic documents since 2007.

Today's indictment involves documents published by Wikileaks in 2010 concerning U.S. operations in Iraq and Afghanistan. Bradley Manning, then a private first class in the U.S. Army, was convicted last year of leaking those documents, and thousands more, to Wikileaks. The indictment accuses Assange of conspiring with Manning to obtain the documents and illegally publishing them.

The National Council for Press Freedom denounced the indictment as a frontal assault on press freedoms. "Assange did what any journalist would do upon receiving information the government would keep secret," said Martin Browning, executive director. "He published what the people need to know. That's their right and our duty under the First Amendment."

"Assange is no journalist," said Linda Conrad, managing editor of the New York *Herald*. "He broke the law to obtain the information and, therefore, had no legal right to publish it. To call him a 'journalist' is to make a mockery of all we do." Conrad lamented that Wikileaks' conduct could seriously jeopardize constitutional protection for the responsible press.

* * *

Wikileaks, Julian Assange, and Bradley Manning are real, of course;[1] Martin Browning and Linda Conrad are not. But Browning and Conrad represent real views of the Wikileaks controversy within the American media establishment.[2] Should this scenario come to pass, we will see these views, and others, debated in news rooms and journalism schools, on editorial pages and Sunday talk shows, and, perhaps most importantly, in the courtroom itself.

Today's institutional press plays an active role in defining its own legal rights as a political actor and constitutional litigator. But it was not always so. For more than two centuries, the press in America was largely an adjunct to other political actors, albeit an important one.

That role of the press in American politics has been the subject of extensive study since Alexis de Tocqueville wrote that the press "makes political life circulate in every corner of this vast land."[3] Tocqueville also wrote about the "vital connection between [political] associations and newspapers,"[4] but never saw the institutional press emerge as a political association in its own right.[5]

By the early twentieth century, however, the press had begun to organize itself for its own political ends,[6] and by the end of that century the organizations that represent the news media were fully engaged in political action. In a 1947 case, for example, the Supreme Court absolved a journalist of criminal contempt for criticizing a Texas county judge, partly on the ground that judicial officers are insulated from public opinion. In a rather bitter dissent, Justice Jackson referred to the growing power of the press:

> It is doubtful if the press itself regards judges as so insulated from public opinion. In this very case the American Newspaper Publishers Association filed a brief *amicus curiae* on the merits after we granted certiorari. Of course, it does not cite a single authority that was not available to counsel for the publisher involved, and does not tell us a single new fact except this one: "This membership embraces more than 700 newspaper publishers whose publications represent in excess of eighty per cent of the total daily and Sunday circulation of newspapers published in this country. The Association is vitally interested in the issue presented in this case, namely, the right of newspapers to publish news stories and editorials on cases pending in the courts."[7]

Yet the press as player for its own account has hardly been studied at all.[8] One might suggest several interrelated reasons for this relative obscurity:

1. The essence of the press's self-image is public service.[9] The press does not think of itself, nor does it care to be known, as a political actor. Indeed, such a role would strike most working journalists as a conflict of interest: how can the press cover political institutions with detached objectivity while it seeks favor from those same institutions?

2. Accordingly, the press does not generally interact with either the executive or legislative branches in the same way that other interest groups do. While the press is not above lobbying Congress for legislation it wants – copyright protection, favorable postal rates, open meetings and records laws, and so on – it is not especially comfortable doing so. "As a general rule," wrote *Newsweek's* Jonathan Alter to begin a recent column arguing for a federal shield law, "journalists shouldn't be in the business of lobbying Congress."[10]

3. By contrast, the press campaigns vigorously in the courts for its most important institutional interests, but the scholars that one might expect to monitor their efforts are AWOL. Media law specialists in law and journalism schools are usually focused on substantive law (outputs), rather than political action (inputs),

and many political scientists who study the courts have apparently been distracted by theories that ignore institutional dynamics altogether.

How does one explain the active role of the press in court? The simple answer is that the press is often, perhaps usually, the defendant in a lawsuit and has no other choice. For example, allegations of libel or invasion of privacy bring publishers and broadcasters to court quite against their will. Even when the press brings a lawsuit seeking access to courtrooms, meetings, and records, the reason is arguably necessity, since the alternative is abdication of journalistic responsibility.

But that theory loses much of its explanatory power beyond the trial or intermediate appellate stage. The exigencies of daily or hourly journalism will rarely justify filing a petition for review by the United States Supreme Court years after the fact. Moreover, it is never "necessary" to spend time and money to file a friend of the court brief. A much more compelling explanation for that kind of activity lies in the press's largely hidden role as "lobbyist" for its own regulatory interests.

Conventional wisdom holds that the press in the United States is not regulated at all; that is, with a few notable exceptions,[11] American journalism is largely free from government supervision. Credit for this remarkable state of affairs goes to the First Amendment to the United States Constitution and its brief, but clarion press clause: "Congress shall make no law abridging the freedom of… the press…."[12]

Although the amendment's language appears to be anything but regulatory in nature, the meaning of constitutional language is not to be found in the words alone, but in the interpretive decisions of the United States Supreme Court. Notwithstanding the position of a few "absolutist" judges, like Justices Hugo Black and William O. Douglas,[13] those interpretive opinions "regulate" press behavior just as surely – if far more benignly – as the tax code or environmental laws regulate other business behaviors.

For over two centuries, no more than nine men and women, and often far fewer, have told us what laws of Congress and the states may inhibit the press from gathering and publishing the news without unconstitutionally "abridging" its freedom. Their decisions were not reached in a vacuum, of course; constitutional doctrine must be created in the context of a real case.[14] Two or more interested and antagonistic parties present a set of facts that raises an unanswered legal question. Each party tries to obtain the most favorable outcome, as do others with more abstract or remote interests whose self-interest is minimally disguised by the title amicus curiae or friend of the court. And all are represented by counsel well-schooled in the ambiguities of existing doctrine and the techniques of judicial persuasion.

The decisions that emerge from the Court typically comprise simple outcomes – liable or not, access granted or denied – accompanied by complex rationales. Together, these set the boundaries within which the press may operate.

So it is reasonable to think of the press as subject, for better or worse, to the regulatory environment created by the Supreme Court.

This book argues that we must also think of the press as a participant in the process, influencing the creation of constitutional doctrine by initiating, defending, or otherwise joining cases that raise First Amendment questions. It may be difficult to think of the press as an interest group, "lobbying" to influence regulatory decisions. The press *reports* on interest groups; to *be* an interest group seems at odds with its fundamental purpose. Yet in more than 100 Supreme Court cases that have reached a decision, the press has played an active role, as party litigant or friend of the court, in the process of shaping First Amendment doctrine. This book aims to explore why it took so long to mobilize the press, how mobilization first came about, how the process has worked historically, how it operates today, and what that has meant for journalism, media law, and the First Amendment.

More specifically, this book explores how, when, and why the press emerged as a constitutional litigator, and how the press's approach to constitutional litigation evolved from emergence to the present. I have measured how successful the press has been in persuading the Court to its own view of the First Amendment, and, finding a significant disparity between publishing and newsgathering cases, tried to explain why that is so.

My conclusions are stated more fully in the last chapter, but this is not a novel with a surprise ending. I have found that the press emerged as a constitutional litigator only after the press began to view itself as a commercial, rather than political enterprise, with an ethos based on objectivity, rather than partisanship, and the Supreme Court allowed it to challenge states laws through the Fourteenth Amendment. Even after those requirements were realized, around 1930, the approach of the press to constitutional litigation changed dramatically, from reluctant and parsimonious litigator before 1970, to well organized and professional afterwards.

Although I am unable to prove that the press's involvement "caused" the Supreme Court to rule one way or another in any particular case, the totality of this litigation has resulted in unparalleled protection for publishing, both from prior restraints and from subsequent punishment. Unfortunately, the results are more modest for newsgathering. Scholars have long recognized this disparity, and I summarize representative views as to why this is so. I have also added my own suggestion that the press itself is partly to blame, by inconsistently and at times speciously invoking the First Amendment privilege.

I have chosen to structure this book around three detailed case studies that seem to illustrate these points better than any others. The first of these discusses the 1931 case of *Near v. Minnesota*,[15] which represents the first, halting efforts of the institutional press to mobilize in support of a First Amendment principle: the freedom to publish without answering in advance to censors, even judicial censors.[16] Success in *Near* paved the way for many more publishing cases to come, including both prior restraint and subsequent punishment cases. Causation is always elusive, but there is no doubt that *Near* would never have reached the Supreme Court without the single-minded efforts of Col. Robert McCormick and his *Chicago Tribune* lawyers, Weymouth Kirkland and Howard Ellis.

Unfortunately, the legacy of *Near* did not extend to newsgathering cases. Accordingly, the second case study discusses the seminal newsgathering case of *Branzburg v. Hayes*,[17] some forty years after *Near*.[18] *Branzburg* shows the institutional press far better organized for litigation than it had been in Col. McCormick's time, although still far from unified as to the issue before the Court: a testimonial privilege for journalists. How much the division within the press contributed to the adverse outcome in *Branzburg* is debatable, although it may be telling that *Branzburg* catalyzed the formation of one of the press's most vigorous litigators: the Reporters Committee for Freedom of the Press. Nevertheless, the result in that case unquestionably stunted any First Amendment protection for gathering the news that lower courts had already found.

The third case study brings together aspects of both the restrictive constitutional doctrine that pertains to newsgathering and the expansive constitutional doctrine that pertains to publishing. Another 30 years after *Branzburg*, *Bartnicki v. Vopper*[19] challenged the Supreme Court to determine whether broadcasting the content of an illegally intercepted telephone conversation could be punished by federal and state law.[20] What began as a local labor dispute, with local lawyers representing both parties, attracted the support of a highly organized press bar, with nationally known media attorneys representing the defendant broadcaster and friends of the court that supported him. Again, one cannot know for certain whether that representation accounted for the press's victory, but the outcome would seem to bode well for the future.

To set the stage for these three case studies, the next three chapters in the book survey the state of American media law and advocacy in the eighteenth century, the nineteenth century, and twentieth century before *Near*. Following the case study of *Near* in Chapter 5, the sixth chapter surveys the prior restraint cases that flowed directly from *Near*. After looking more closely at *Grosjean v. American Press*, in which the same Court expanded the principles articulated in *Near* to apply to subsequent punishment cases as well, the chapter continues its survey of publishing cases to include contempt, libel, and privacy cases before 1972.

Chapter 7 examines the legacy of *Branzburg* in newsgathering cases involving access to judicial and executive branch processes and information, as well as other newsgathering cases not so easily categorized, except that they bear the burden imposed by *Branzburg*, each in their own way.

Bartnicki, as yet, has left no legacy to speak of, but the final section of Chapter 8 reflects on its impact over the past decade and speculates as to how the Court might answer some of the questions that case leaves unresolved. Chapter 9 examines the role of the press in shaping the Court's regulation of commercial, sexual, and other so-called "low-value" speech, while Chapter 10 profiles today's leading media lawyers who continue to shape First Amendment doctrine in the service of a free press.

Chapter 2: Press Law and Advocacy in the 18th century

A. Andrew Hamilton: The First Media Lawyer?

Andrew Hamilton might justifiably be called the first American media defense lawyer by virtue of his 1735 representation of John Peter Zenger, the iconic hero of pre-Revolutionary War notions of press freedom.[1] The *Zenger* case was far from typical. There were relatively few seditious libel cases in the colonies, perhaps not more than half a dozen, and the *Zenger* case was the last of its kind under the royal judges.[2] Arguably, its very uniqueness accounts for the extraordinary publicity given the case throughout the period;[3] today, it appears in virtually every media law textbook or casebook used in journalism and law schools.[4] Still, it seems an appropriate place to begin any story about the use of litigation to shape the law affecting the press, not because Hamilton was successful in changing the law – he was not – but because he tried.

Zenger was a German immigrant who came to America as a teenager.[5] He was apprenticed to New York City's leading printer, William Bradford, then struck out on his own at age twenty-one. After working in Maryland for a few years, he returned to New York as Bradford's partner then went out on his own in 1726.[6] In 1732, the colony received a new royal governor, William Cosby, whose principal purpose in the colonies was to make his fortune.[7] In pursuit of that aim through the courts, Cosby sacked Lewis Morris, Sr., chief justice of the colony, and appointed his own man, young James De Lancey, as chief justice.[8]

Morris did not take all of this lying down, and, with his son Lewis Morris, Jr., and a very bright lawyer named James Alexander, started his own virulently anti-Cosby political faction.[9] They wanted an outlet for their own political ideas, and Bradford was too afraid of losing his government contracts to print them. So they financed Zenger, who had previously left Bradford and set up shop on his own.[10]

Zenger became the chief propagandist for a new anti-Cosby, Morrisite party. Alexander became the behind-the-scenes editor of Zenger's newspaper, the *Journal*, which competed with Bradford's pro-Cosby *Gazette*.[11] De Lancey tried and failed to get an indictment against Zenger and offered rewards for proof that Alexander, Morris and the others (who wrote anonymously) were responsible for the attacks on Cosby in the *Journal*... all to no avail.[12] Finally, Zenger was arrested and prosecuted on a criminal information, i.e., without a grand jury indictment.[13]

Zenger would be prosecuted by the attorney general of New York, Richard Bradley, who had sworn out the information against him. Morrisite lawyers James Alexander and William Smith launched their defense of Zenger by objecting to De Lancey's presiding at the trial. De Lancey's response was to disbar the two lawyers and appoint John Chambers as Zenger's defense counsel.[14] Alexander retaliated by engaging Andrew Hamilton of Philadelphia, perhaps the best trial lawyer in the colonies. Hamilton and Alexander had worked together before,[15] and Hamilton had had a long-standing feud with Andrew Bradford, whose father, William Bradford, had become Zenger's principal rival.[16]

Bradley opened with the charge that Zenger "did falsely, seditiously and scandalously print and publish... a certain false, malicious, seditious, scandalous libel, entitled *The New York Weekly Journal, containing the Freshest Advices, Foreign and Domestic*; in which libel (of and concerning His Excellency the said Governor, and the ministers and officers of our said lord the King, of and for the said Province) among other things herein contained are these words (two articles):

> [The people of New York] think as matters now stand that their liberties and properties are precarious, and that slavery is like to be entailed on them and their posterity if some past things be not amended....
>
> I think the law itself is at an end: We... see men's deeds destroyed, judges arbitrarily displaced, new courts erected without consent of the legislature... by which, it seems to me, trials by juries are taken away when a governor pleases, men of known estates denied their votes contrary to the received practice....[17]

Hamilton replied with a bombshell: "I cannot think it proper for me (without doing violence to my own principles) to deny the publication of a complaint which I think is the right of every free-born subject to make when the matters so published can be supported with truth; and therefore, I'll save Mr. Attorney the trouble of examining his witnesses to that point; and I do (for my client) confess that he both printed and published the two newspapers set forth in the information, and I hope in so doing he has committed no crime."[18]

As far as Bradley, De Lancey, and English law at the time were concerned, Hamilton's admission was the end of the matter. Hamilton had confessed to the only question of fact that the jury was supposed to decide. Truth was not relevant under the prevailing law,[19] and Bradley was quick to point that out: "Indeed sir, as Mr. Hamilton has confessed the printing and publishing these libels, I think the jury must find a verdict for the King; for supposing they were true, the law says that they are not the less libelous for that; nay indeed the law says their being true is an aggravation of the crime."[20]

Hamilton condemned the Star Chamber proceedings on which Bradley relied for his statement of the law and urged the court not to consider those doctrines as binding in the colonies. He also argued that the jury was entitled to decide, not merely the factual question of publication, but also the legal question of whether the writings were seditious.

Bradley called Hamilton's arguments irrelevant, which they were; but Hamilton wasn't finished. He pointed out that the charges under which Zenger was being tried specifically called the alleged libels "false" and offered to confess to sedition if Bradley could prove the attacks on Cosby were false. Bradley asked how he could prove a negative, so Hamilton offered to prove them true.[21] That was too much for De Lancey, who could not let Hamilton parade forth witness after witness attesting to Cosby's (his patron's) misdeeds. "You cannot be admitted, Mr. Hamilton, to give the truth of a libel in evidence. A libel is not to be justified; for it is nevertheless a libel that it is true."[22]

Hamilton tried one more argument. If a true libel is worse than a false one, he said, then the punishment must be more severe. If that were the case, evidence pertaining to truth or falsity must be admissible, or else how could a judge render a just sentence.[23] De Lancey did not buy that for a minute,[24] so Hamilton turned to the jury. Calling on them to use their own knowledge of the situation, urged that

> the facts which we offer to prove were not committed in a corner; they are notoriously known to be true; and therefore in your justice lies our safety. And as we are denied the liberty of giving evidence to prove the truth of what we have published, I will beg leave to lay it down as a standing rule in such cases, that the suppressing of evidence ought always to be taken for the strongest evidence....[25]
>
> [T]he question before the Court and you gentlemen of the jury is not of small nor private concern, it is not the cause of a poor printer, nor of New York alone, which you are now trying: No! It may in its consequence affect every freeman that lives under a British government on the main of America. It is the best cause. It is the cause of liberty; and I make no doubt but your upright conduct this day will not only entitle you to the love and esteem of your fellow citizens; but every man who prefers freedom to a life of slavery will bless and honor you as men who have baffled the attempt of tyranny; and by an impartial and uncorrupt verdict, have laid a noble foundation for securing to ourselves, our posterity, and our neighbors that to which nature and the laws of our country have given us a right – the liberty – both of exposing and opposing

> arbitrary power (in these parts of the world at least) by speaking and writing truth.[26]

The jury's acquittal was greeted with "three huzzas in the hall," and Hamilton would be honored by the Common Council of New York City.[27] He would later be called "The Day-Star of the American Revolution" by Gouverneur Morris for his triumph.[28]

Significantly, the law did not change. In law, if not necessarily in practice,[29] the prevailing rule remained the Blackstonian precept that "liberty of the press, properly understood, ... consists in laying no previous restraints upon publications, and not in freedom from censure for criminal matter when published."[30] On the very eve of the American Revolution, the formal law of England and the colonies was little different from that enforced by the Court of Star Chamber.[31] It was not until 1792 (nearly sixty years after the Zenger trial) that English law changed to allow juries to consider both fact and law in libel cases,[32] and it was 1843, some fifty years later still, that truth became a defense in a criminal libel case.[33]

The *Zenger* case was as pure an example of jury nullification as one can find. The law of the day was clear: Zenger was guilty, and Hamilton's arguments were irrelevant. That Zenger won was attributable, not to any change in the prevailing law, but to dissatisfaction with the nature of Cosby's governance and Hamilton's clever exploitation of it. But if it is wrong to attribute any dramatic legal breakthrough to Zenger and Hamilton, it is equally wrong to dismiss the case as meaningless. As one historian put it, "Hamilton may be said to have conducted the case according to the law of the future, and thus to have helped to make that law."[34]

For the rest of the eighteenth century, however, the press was no more successful in changing the immediate regulatory environment through the courts than Hamilton and Zenger had been. Levy points out that, prior to the Revolutionary War, the most aggressive antagonists of the press were not the courts at all, but colonial legislatures, which needed neither judges nor juries to fine and imprison printers who criticized them.[35] The last prosecution of a colonial printer, Alexander McDougall, was thwarted in 1770 when the key witness against him died before trial; according to Levy, McDougall's imprisonment "did more to publicize the cause of liberty of the press than any event since Zenger's trial."[36]

B. From Revolution to Constitution

That is not to say that the press did nothing to bring about the legal regime that would ultimately govern its operations. Indeed, Parliament's Stamp Tax Act of 1765, "towards defraying the expenses of defending, protecting, and securing, the British colonies and plantations in America,"[37] and subsequent Townshend Revenue Act of 1767,[38] galvanized the colonial press behind the coming American

Revolution.[39] Opposition to the stamp tax was so severe that the Act was repealed within a year,[40] but the damage had been done. Newspapers all over the colonies (there were 24 at the time) went to press with heavy black mourning rules or skulls and crossbones to symbolize the death of the free press.[41] Many defied the law outright, and many lined up behind the Sons of Liberty and other radicals to spread the revolutionary fever.[42]

After the Revolution, the memory of the stamp taxes lingered, and fear that the new central government might try to impose a tax on newspapers was a cornerstone of the anti-federalists' arguments for a bill of rights in general and a clause guaranteeing freedom of the press in particular. The Federal Farmer's famous aphorism, "a power to tax the press at discretion is a power to destroy or restrain the freedom of it," comes from this period.[43]

Another anti-federalist pamphlet declared that "Congress have power to lay all duties of whatever kind, and although they could not perhaps directly bar the freedom of the Press, yet they can do it in the exercise of the powers that are expressly decreed to them. Remember there are such things as stamp duties and that these will effectually abolish the freedom of the press as any express declaration."[44] To be sure, the anti-federalists may have been more interested in defeating the Constitution itself, or at least the federal taxing power, than in freedom of the press. But the result was the same.

The federalists won that battle, arguing that the new Constitution would not give Congress the right to restrain the press; as a result, the document contained no bill of rights.[45] During the ratification struggle, federalist leader Alexander Hamilton argued forcefully, in *Federalist 84*, that a bill of rights would even be dangerous because it would lead people to believe that the new government did indeed have the power to invade individual liberties not specifically protected.[46] As for taxing newspapers, Hamilton said, freedom of the press clauses in nine of the thirteen state constitutions could not stop the legislatures from imposing taxes; why should a federal press clause be any different?[47]

At the height of the ratification campaign, the Supreme Court of Pennsylvania handed down an opinion that demonstrated how little the prevailing view of the law had changed in the half-century since the Zenger trial, notwithstanding the Revolutionary War and the Constitution. One Andrew Browne had sued Eleazer Oswald, printer and publisher of the anti-federalist *Independent Gazateeer*. When a dispute regarding bail arose, Oswald published an extended diatribe against Browne and the court, which found Oswald in contempt. Jonathan D. Sergeant, a former attorney general of Pennsylvania, unsuccessfully defended Oswald; from the court's decision, it appears that the defense was based at least partly on press freedom clauses in the British Declaration of Rights ("That the freedom of the press shall not be restrained")[48] and the Pennsylvania Constitution ("that the printing presses shall be free to every person who undertakes to examine the proceedings of the legislature, or any part of the government").[49] The court's response was remarkably hostile:

> However ingenuity may torture the expressions, there can be little doubt of the just sense of these sections; they give to every citizen a right of investigating the conduct of those who are entrusted with the public business, and they effectually preclude any attempt to fetter the press by the institution of a licenser. ... But is there anything in the language of the constitution (much less in its spirit and intention) which authorizes one man to impute crimes to another...? Can it be presumed that the slanderous words, which, when spoken to a few individuals, would expose the speaker to punishment, become sacred, by authority of the constitution when delivered to the public in the more permanent and diffusive medium of the press? ... The futility of any attempt to establish a construction of this sort, must be obvious to every intelligent mind.[50]

In any event, when several state ratifying conventions adopted recommendations for a bill of rights in order to obtain the necessary votes for ratification, the first Congress obliged. Surely now, with a Constitution and a Bill of Rights that explicitly guaranteed freedom of the press, that freedom could be deemed secure. Yet, within the decade, prompted by a viciously partisan newspaper press, Congress would enact the most onerous incursion on press freedoms in American history. The 1790s saw the Federalist press, such as John Fenno's *Gazette of the United States* and William Cobbett's *Porcupine's Gazette*, virtually at war with the Republican press, such as Philip Freneau's *National Gazette* and Benjamin Franklin Bache's *Aurora*.[51]

C. A Failure of Constitutional Consciousness

When Federalist John Adams was elected president in 1796, his party and Thomas Jefferson's Republicans were deeply divided on both domestic and foreign policy issues. In the continuing European hostilities, for example, Republicans sentimentally and philosophically leaned toward the French, while the Federalists benefited from strong economic ties with Britain. Both European powers harassed the new American nation, but the Federalists controlled all three branches of government and had reached a modus vivendi with England. By 1798, partly because of clumsy French diplomatic intrigues, and partly because the Hamilton wing of the party willed it, the Federalists in Congress eagerly anticipated war with France.

In the wake of that expectation, as well as concerns that the common law of seditious libel might not apply in federal courts, the Federalist Congress enacted four statutes known collectively today as the Alien and Sedition Acts. [52] One of them, the Sedition Act, levied a fine of up to $2,000 and imprisonment for as long as two years on anyone convicted of writing, publishing, or speaking anything "false, scandalous, and malicious" against the U.S. government, the president or either house of Congress, or "to excite against them the hatred of the good people of the United States... "; or of entering into unlawful combinations to oppose the execution of national laws, or aiding or attempting "any insurrection, riot, unlawful assembly, or combination."[53]

The principal target of the Act was the Republican newspaper press, which not only maintained a steady drumbeat of criticism against President Adams and his policies, but also promised to become a formidable political weapon in the election of 1800. The Act was vigorously enforced under the leadership of Secretary of State Timothy Pickering.[54] Authorities differ slightly on the statistics, presumably because some actions were also brought under other federal acts or the common law, but at least twenty-five persons, including the editors of leading Republican newspapers, were arrested; from fourteen or fifteen indictments, ten or eleven Republicans were convicted and jailed. Eight of the convictions involved newspapers. There were also several convictions for seditious libel under common law in state courts.[55]

Bache was the first casualty of the Federalists' animus toward Republican editors; even before the Sedition Act was enacted, Bache was arrested and charged with libeling President Adams and the government but died of yellow fever before he could be tried.[56] Other notable Republicans who were victimized by the act were Matthew Lyon, John Daly Burk, Thomas Cooper, James Thomson Callender, Anthony Haswell, David Brown, William Duane, Charles Holt, Abijah Adams, and Luther Baldwin.[57] Not a single Federalist editor was indicted under the act.[58]

Cooper, the editor of a Republican newspaper in Western Pennsylvania, the *Sunbury and Northumberland Gazette*, left us a verbatim account of his trial, which involved his ill-advised broadside against President Adams in response to an article published anonymously by Pickering in Fenno's *Gazette* for the sole purpose of ensnaring Cooper. [59] Cooper was prosecuted by a Federalist prosecutor, tried before two Federalist judges, and heard by a jury chosen by a Federalist marshal. He could call no witnesses to testify to the factual truth of the opinions he had expressed, as required by the Act and the court. His defense consisted of a futile plea to a Federalist jury; he was convicted and imprisoned for six months.

Our 21st century sensibilities might lead us to think of these convictions as opportunities to ask a Supreme Court to strike down the Sedition Act as a flagrantly unconstitutional violation of the recently adopted First Amendment. We might also be tempted to think of the newspaper press, Federalist or Republican, rising as one to support this assault on freedom of speech and press that threatens their very existence. But this was the eighteenth century, not the 21st.

Most of the Sedition Act trials did not even take place until 1800;[60] by the time any appeal could have been heard, Jefferson would be president and the Act would have expired by its own terms. Even if that had not been the case, the Supreme Court and the entire judiciary were dominated by Federalists, most of whom firmly believed that the kind of robust debate that has come to be associated with the First Amendment was useful only to incite the masses.[61] Indeed, Supreme Court Justices like Samuel Chase and William Paterson presided over Sedition Act trials while riding circuit; John Marshall's biographer called Chase a "holy terror" as a trial judge.[62]

And the United States Supreme Court would not assert the authority to strike down federal laws as unconstitutional, which Republicans had urged at the various Sedition Act trials,[63] until 1803, when the Court under Marshall decided *Marbury v. Madison.*[64] Instead, the Republican reaction was to take the Federalist "reign of terror" into the political arena, with Madison and Jefferson leading Virginia and Kentucky, respectively, to issue resolutions asserting the power of the states to nullify unconstitutional laws.[65] Congressional Republicans also made futile attempts to repeal the Sedition Act, but it expired by its own terms in 1801, and newly elected President Jefferson pardoned all those imprisoned under the statute and cancelled all remaining trials. Forty years later, Congress repaid all the fines levied under the act.[66]

Finally, there was no question of Federalist newspapers joining their Republican counterparts to fight the Act. Stone points out that "Federalist newspapers pressed for vigorous enforcement of the Sedition Act, evincing no inkling of understanding that in the long run they might be placing their own liberties in jeopardy."[67] The press would exhibit the same myopia in sedition cases after 1918. While the early twentieth century press would mobilize to lobby or litigate for pocket-book issues[68] – an aspect of interest-group behavior that can probably be traced back to unity in opposition to Stamp Act taxes – unity on other press freedom issues would only begin to emerge with *Near v. Minnesota.*

If the Sedition Act had one saving grace, it was the insight provided by the congressional debates as to the meaning of the First Amendment, at least according to the Act's Federalist proponents and their Republican antagonists. The Federalists offered a Blackstonian view of liberty of the press guaranteed by First Amendment, arguing that no one could assume the amendment was meant to do away with seditious libel. The Republicans argued that such legislation could only be justified if necessary to save the country from a President paralyzed by the abuse of the press – a kind of early "clear and present danger" theory – to which the Federalists replied that it was indeed necessary under the present circumstances.[69]

Federalists also argued that the Sedition Act was consistent with state law, which generally permitted prosecution for seditious libel despite constitutional guarantees of a free press. Republicans answered that the ratification debates in the states revealed an understanding that the power to prosecute for seditious libel resided exclusively in state courts and that the Constitution did not give Congress the power to enact any laws on the subject.[70]

In the end, of course, the "meaning" of the First Amendment was not resolved by the debates in Congress. But some important doctrinal details were. As Geoffrey Stone points out, the act provided that malicious intent was a necessary element of seditious libel, that truth was a defense, and that juries could decide not only the factual question of publication, but also the legal question of whether the speech or writing was seditious – all in contrast to the common law of the time.[71] Thus, the very doctrine urged by Andrew Hamilton in the *Zenger* case was finally embodied in the Sedition Act that the Federalists pushed through Congress.

The Sedition Act may have also provided certain members of the bar with some on-the-job training in First Amendment litigation. In the trial of James Callender, for example, attorney William Wirt tried and failed to win permission from Justice Chase to argue the constitutionality of the Sedition Act.[72] Men like George Hay and Philip Nicholas, who also represented Callender, Alexander Dallas, who advised Cooper and represented both Bache and William Duane, Bache's successor as editor of *Aurora,* and Moses Levy, who also represented Bache, could be viewed as precursor to a media defense bar. Even Federalist attorneys, such as Cooper's prosecutor William Rawle, Callender's prosecutor Thomas Nelson, and Duane's prosecutor Jared Ingersoll had to deal with the constitutional argument. Indeed, the first important media case after Jefferson's victory saw Ur-Federalist Alexander Hamilton himself leading the defense.

Chapter 3 – Press Law and Advocacy in the 19th century: From Politics to Commerce

To think of Zenger's counsel Andrew Hamilton as a "media lawyer" requires a bit of imagination and a lot of historical flexibility. To think of founding father Alexander Hamilton as a "media lawyer" invites psychotherapy. And yet, the beginning of the nineteenth century finds Alexander Hamilton – former aide to General Washington, Secretary of the Treasury, and Major General of the Army – defending a Federalist editor in a New York state court against a charge of seditious libel sanctioned by President Thomas Jefferson.[1]

Harry Croswell, editor of *The Wasp* in Hudson, N.Y., had accused Jefferson of, among other things, paying Republican propagandist James T. Callender to slander Washington, Adams, and other prominent Federalists.[2] New York Attorney General Ambrose Spencer secured an indictment for seditious libel under the common law, and the case was tried before Chief Justice Morgan Lewis in the Columbia County Circuit Court. Hamilton, who had argued for liberalizing the Sedition Act, but supported it as amended,[3] joined the defense *pro bono* and argued that the trial be postponed until Callender could be brought to New York to testify as to the truth of the matter.[4] Lewis refused to postpone the trial, which proceeded on the documentary evidence.[5]

At the close of the case, Lewis charged the jury that "it was no part of the province of a jury to inquire or decide on the intent of the defendant; or whether the publication in question was true, or false, or malicious; that the only questions for their consideration and decision were, first, whether the defendant was the publisher of the piece charged in the indictment; and, second, as to the truth of the innuendoes…."[6] The jury found Croswell guilty as charged.[7]

On appeal, seeking a new trial, Hamilton argued that the trial should have been postponed, that the articles were not libelous, and, most importantly, that the jury instructions were wrong. Asserting that "the liberty of the press consists in the right to publish, with impunity, truth, with good motives, for justifiable ends, though reflecting on government, magistracy, or individuals,"[8] Hamilton argued that truth was admissible, though not dispositive, and that the jury was the arbiter of both law and fact, including the defendant's intent and the tendency of the article.

Federalist Judge James Kent wrote an opinion in support of Hamilton's argument, which Republican Judge Smith Thompson joined; Republican Chief Judge Morgan Lewis, who presided at trial, wrote against Hamilton and was joined by Republican Judge Brockholst Livingston. The evenly divided court meant that Hamilton and Croswell lost their bid for a new trial on Feb. 13, 1804, but the following year, the New York legislature enshrined Hamilton's arguments in statute[9] and the court ordered a new trial on its own initiative.[10] Hamilton never lived to see the victory; on July 12, 1804, he died of wounds suffered in a duel with Aaron Burr.[11]

In his opinion, Kent mentioned the Federal constitutional guarantee of a free press as authority for the proposition that American law was not English law, but not much more than that.[12] More particularly, he pointed out that both the Sedition Act and the constitutions of Pennsylvania and Ohio provided that truth could be admitted as evidence in seditious libel prosecutions.[13] No one else even alluded to the First Amendment, a fact that presaged the dominant role that state common law, rather than Federal constitutional law, would play in nineteenth century press cases. Freedom of the press was simply not treated as a constitutional question in the nineteenth century, and there are no United States Supreme Court decisions on press freedom issues.

That is not to say that freedom of the press was not an issue in nineteenth century cases; newspaper publishers raised it – as Kent had suggested – as a "barrier against unfavorable common-law doctrines."[14] As Gleason points out in his survey of nineteenth century libel and contempt by publication cases, "nineteenth-century freedom of the press cases were resolved in common law."[15] To defend against common law libel suits, publishers argued for expansive interpretations of common law privileges. They grounded their arguments in a theory of press freedom based on the value of the press to society – the "watchdog" concept that drove Gleason's research – rather than based on the inherent right of the speaker to speak.[16]

The *Croswell* case also marked the beginning of a gradual, century-long decline in the number of seditious or criminal libel prosecutions as the principal focus of press-related litigation.[17] No federal sedition legislation was sought or enacted during the War of 1812,[18] despite widespread hostility to the war, although some dissident newspapers were famously suppressed by violence or martial law.[19] Like Madison in 1812, Lincoln eschewed resort to a federal sedition act during the Civil War,[20] although both abolitionist and Copperhead newspapers felt the wrath of the mob and anti-Union editors were subject to military arrest. The law remained unchanged. By the end of the century, the operational definition of freedom of the press remained much as Hamilton formulated it in *Croswell.*

Members of the mainstream press were principal actors in the legal conflicts that arose throughout the Civil War period. Still, their influence on the evolution of First Amendment law was minimal. As indicated above, issues involving free speech and free press were generally resolved on common law principles, without resort to the Constitution,[21] and, during wartime, at least, by martial law.[22] Moreover, political differences among newspapers remained stronger than any institutional affinity they might have had for each other, further weakening any influence they might have had on the law. As in the previous century, when Federalist newspapers encouraged the prosecution of Republican editors under the Sedition Act with little thought to their own free press interests, few mainstream newspapers condemned the confiscation of abolitionist literature by the Post Office[23] and Republican newspapers demanded that the government suppress the "organs of treason" with Southern sympathies.[24]

Those attitudes began to change after the Civil War, as commercial interests displaced partisan ones, and the press began to see itself more as an institution unto itself. The dramatic post-war industrialization affected the newspaper industry much as it did the entire economy,[25] and publishers began to see themselves more as captains of commercial enterprises than as spokesmen for political causes.

The emergence of the press as a self-conscious, self-interested political association is closely tied to the demise of the partisan press, the rise of the commercial press, the adoption of an objectivity norm in American journalism, and incorporation of the First Amendment into the due process clause of the Fourteenth Amendment to the United States Constitution. Scholars who have looked at these phenomena have not always agreed on when they occurred or why.

The standard date given for the birth of the penny press is Sept. 3, 1833, with the founding of Benjamin Day's *New York Sun*.[26] To be sure, the partisan press was still around then,[27] but putting newspapers on a sound commercial footing would have been a prerequisite for establishing a presence independent of financial support from political parties. Scholars may disagree as to how fast or completely the transition occurred,[28] but there is little doubt that the trend through the rest of the nineteenth century and into the twentieth century was away from partisanship and toward commercialization.

In her persuasive empirical study of American newspapers between 1865 and 1920, Maria Petrova shows that the local profitability of advertising was instrumental in the increasing independence of newspapers.[29] "In areas with faster-growing advertising markets, newspapers were more likely to be independent[,] both through the entry of new newspapers and through changes in the affiliation of existing newspapers."[30] Petrova points out that political decisions, such as parties' failure to subsidize newspapers more aggressively, also contributed to commercialization.[31]

The process of commercialization was critical to the press's emergence as an interest group, because no common ideology among newspapers could emerge as long as their first ideological allegiance was to their party sponsors. Schudson notes that the transitional period was accompanied by the evolution of a common culture among working reporters.[32]

The ideology that ultimately emerged, objectivity, may have come about because of changes in the technology – specifically the use of telegraphy in the transmission of news – that occurred during the nineteenth century. The Emerys attribute the acceptance of an "'objective' method of reporting" to the "terse style dictated by high transmission costs" and the need to "keep their personal values out of stories and to stick to verifiable facts."[33]

Schudson rejects the idea that objectivity was economically motivated, that the "appearance of fairness was important to owners and editors trying to gain their share of a growing readership and the resulting advertising revenues."[34] Instead, he asserts that "professional allegiance to a separation of facts and values awaited, first, the rising status and independence of reporters relative to their employers, a change in journalism that developed gradually between the 1870s and the First World War, and second, the emergence of serious professional discussion about 'objectivity,' which came only after the First World War." Schudson also ascribes the "eventual triumph of professional journalism" to Progressive political reforms of the 1920s, which included a decline in party influence generally.[35]

The significance of this unifying ideology for this study is clear. Five of the nine journalism-related associations most active in litigating First Amendment claims were formed during this period: the American Newspaper Publishers Association (now the Newspaper Association of America) in 1887, the Magazine Publishers of America in 1919, the American Society of Newspaper Editors in 1922, the National Association of Broadcasters in 1923, and the Associated Press Managing Editors Association in 1931.

ANPA was formed to bring the daily newspaper publishers together to confront the many and varied challenges the new post-Civil War economic order would bring. Most of its early legal interests were strongly business related, involving such matters as labor relations, taxes, postal rates, and copyright,[36] and it was "largely oblivious to free press issues prior to the 1920s."[37] ANPA was not above raising press freedom as a justification for favorable treatment.[38] Some issues – advertising regulation and libel law – were even more directly tied to free press ideas, although they too had concrete business implications. For example, at ANPA's 1895 convention, K.G. Cooper, manager of the Denver *Republican*, complained that his paper had been sued for $1.2 million over the past fourteen years and had paid out $650 in damages and $25,000 in lawyers' fees.[39]

ANPA's founder, William H. Brearley of the Detroit *Evening News*, had urged the association to lobby for uniform state libel laws at the 1890 annual meeting, and a committee on libel law formed in 1893 was charged with drafting a model state libel law patterned on Minnesota's statute.[40] But the 1895 convention resolved that this was a matter for the various state editorial associations that had formed in the post-war years, rather than for ANPA itself, because libel was a state law issue.[41]

That would change dramatically in approximately sixty years,[42] facilitated by the most important nineteenth century development in the law of the press: the 14th

Amendment to the Constitution. For the first time, the press could challenge state laws on First Amendment grounds, culminating in the landmark prior restraint case of *Near v. Minnesota* in 1931.

Chapter 4: 20th Century Before *Near*: Incorporation and the Free Speech Precedents

The nineteenth century brought two related developments that were indispensable to the emergence of the institutional press as a constitutional litigator on its own behalf: the transition from partisan support to commercial independence and the evolution of objectivity as a unifying ideology. During the first third of the twentieth century, a new and expansive reading of the First Amendment by the U.S. Supreme Court became available to the press to challenge state laws. Ironically, the mainstream press was not directly involved in either expanding protection for speech or making it applicable to the states, yet these phenomena made constitutional litigation not only desirable, but also possible.

A. Incorporation

Most of the provisions of the Bill of Rights were "incorporated" by the U.S. Supreme Court, that is, made enforceable against the states, through the Due Process Clause of Fourteenth Amendment, a direct consequence of the Civil War. Until the First Amendment's incorporation, usually attributed to *Gitlow v. New York*[1] in 1925, it could not be invoked against state libel or other press laws; only Congress was precluded from abridging freedom of the press under the federal Constitution.[2]

Madison's proposed draft of the First Amendment had not been so constrained on that point: "The people shall not be deprived or abridged of their right to speak, to write, or to publish their sentiments; and the freedom of the press, as one of the great bulwarks of liberty, shall be inviolable."[3] That language appears to have passed in the House, but the Senate changed the subject of the sentence to "Congress." Paul Starr points out, however, that without a record of the discussion, there is no way to know whether the change was meant to be substantive.[4]

Madison had even proposed another amendment explicitly prohibiting the states from abridging freedom of speech. "[I]f there was any reason to restrain the government of the United States from infringing upon these essential rights, it was equally necessary they should be secured against the state governments."[5] That, too, passed the House, but not the Senate. As adopted, the First Amendment protected freedom of speech and freedom of the press from encroachment only by the new national government.[6]

Other provisions of the Bill of Rights were not so clearly drawn; the "takings clause" of the Fifth Amendment, for example, never mentions Congress. Using the passive voice, it says only, "nor shall private property be taken for public use, without just compensation."[7] So when a Baltimore wharf owner sued the city for destroying the value of his property, he not unreasonably claimed just compensation under the Fifth Amendment.[8] But when *Barron v. Baltimore* reached the U.S. Supreme Court in 1833, Chief Justice Marshall found the question presented "of great importance, but not of much difficulty."

> The constitution was ordained and established by the people of the United States for themselves, for their own government, and not for the government of the individual states. Each state established a constitution for itself, and, in that constitution, provided such limitations and restrictions on the powers of its particular government as its judgment dictated. The people of the United States framed such a government for the United States as they supposed best adapted to their situation, and best calculated to promote their interests. The powers they conferred on this government were to be exercised by itself; and the limitations on power, if expressed in general terms, are naturally, and, we think, necessarily applicable to the government created by the instrument. . . .
>
> If these propositions be correct, the fifth amendment must be understood as restraining the power of the general government, not as applicable to the states.[9]

Marshall reinforced the logical argument with a reference to the prohibitions on bills of attainder and *ex post facto* laws imposed on Congress in Article I, Section 9, and expressly imposed on the states in Section 10.

> If the original Constitution, in the ninth and tenth sections of the first article, draws this plain and marked line of discrimination between the limitations it imposes on the powers of the general government, and on those of the states; if in every inhibition intended to act on state power, words are employed which directly express that intent; some strong reason must be assigned for departing from this safe and judicious course in framing the amendments, before that departure can be assumed.
>
> We search in vain for that reason.[10]

Finally, Marshall turned to constitutional history. It was "universally understood," he said, that the Constitution was not ratified without "immense opposition."[11] He noted that nearly every ratifying convention recommended amendments against abuse of power, against "encroachments of the general government—not against those of the local governments."

> In compliance with a sentiment thus generally expressed, to quiet fears thus extensively entertained, amendments were proposed by the required majority in congress, and adopted by the states. These amendments contain no expression indicating an intention to apply them to the state governments. This court cannot so apply them.[12]

Although some constitutional thinkers, particularly more radical abolitionists, would express the view that states were nevertheless required to guarantee some or all of the rights enumerated in the first eight amendments, particularly freedom of speech and of the press, they justified their arguments on grounds other than direct application of the amendments.[13] *Barron v. Baltimore* was never seriously challenged.[14]

Thus, even had the press been ready to emerge as a constitutional litigator in its own interest – which it decidedly was not – it would have had no First Amendment shield against most of the regulations to which it was susceptible. Between the expiration of the Alien and Sedition Acts of 1798 and the Civil War, the most onerous of these would have been the laws enacted by slaveholding states criminalizing the expression of abolitionist views, as well as unsuccessful attempts to enact similar statutes in the North.[15] The extent to which the Republican reaction against those laws influenced the adoption of the Fourteenth Amendment after the war is a matter of considerable debate.

With the First Amendment now securely incorporated, it is easy enough to look back on that debate as a historical curiosity with little practical relevance today. Still, no understanding of incorporation can be complete without appreciating why that constitutional "work-around" was necessary. At the very least, it may explain why the Supreme Court seems to have incorporated the First Amendment so casually, without the detailed explication one would expect to accompany such an important shift in constitutional doctrine.

The Fourteenth Amendment says, in pertinent part, "No State shall make or enforce any law which shall abridge the privileges or immunities of citizens of the United States; nor shall any State deprive any person of life, liberty, or property, without due process of law." [16] The plain language of the first clause, the "privileges or immunities clause," seems more than adequate to deny to states the right to abridge the freedom of the press guaranteed by the First Amendment.

Was the Fourteenth Amendment designed by its framers and understood by its ratifiers to enable the national government to enforce the rights enumerated in the first eight amendments against the states through the privileges or immunities clause?[17] The leading advocate for the affirmative position was Justice Hugo Black:

> My study of the historical events that culminated in the Fourteenth Amendment, and the expressions of those who sponsored and favored, as well as those who opposed its submission and passage, persuades me that one of the chief objects that the provisions of the Amendment's first section, separately, and as a whole, were intended to accomplish was to make the Bill of Rights, applicable to the states. With full knowledge of the import of the *Barron* decision, the framers and backers of the Fourteenth Amendment proclaimed its purpose to be to overturn the constitutional rule that case had announced. This historical purpose has never received full consideration or exposition in any opinion of this Court interpreting the Amendment.[18]

In his dissenting opinion in *Adamson v. California*, Justice Black proffered a scathing indictment of the failure of the Court in the *Slaughter-House* cases[19] and their progeny to consider the legislative history of the Fourteenth Amendment. In *Slaughter-House*, the first cases on point to reach the Supreme Court after ratification, the Court effectively made a constitutional nullity of the privileges or immunities clause. A contemporary historian restates that view more emphatically with respect to the First Amendment.

> Justice Miller [who wrote the majority opinion in *Slaughter-House*] leaves out the entire history of suppression of civil liberties of white opponents of slavery, including Republicans, in the South before the Civil War. He is silent about the suppression of free speech in the South for Republicans as well as abolitionist. . . . He fails to note that Black Codes abridged privileges including free speech . . . . The struggles for free speech about slavery before the Civil War show that Justice Miller's constricted reading of the privileges-or-immunities of citizens of the United States secured by the Fourteenth Amendment was seriously mistaken.[20]

On the other side of the issue, writing two years after Justice Black's *Adamson* dissent, Stanley Morrison called Black's position "fatally weak" and based on flawed historical research.[21] "In the absence of any adequate support for the incorporation theory, the effort of the dissenting judges in *Adamson v. California* to read the Bill of Rights into the Fourteenth Amendment amounts simply to an effort to put into the Constitution what the framers failed to put there."[22] Morrison's position is supported by his Stanford colleague Charles Fairman in a companion article laying out a detailed legislative history of the Amendment.[23]

There is no need to resolve this debate here, even if that were possible, but even Morrison suggests that Black and his fellow dissenters in *Adamson* may have been logically correct with respect to the First Amendment. "Once the basic principle of substantive due process had been established, there was no reason why liberty of speech and religion should not be protected by that doctrine against arbitrary legislation, just as economic liberty was protected."[24] Still, as Justice Oliver Wendell Holmes, Jr., famously said, "[t]he life of the law has not been logic: it has been experience."[25] And it would be more than a half-century after ratification before the Supreme Court would apply the Fourteenth Amendment to strike down a state law censoring the press.

In the relevant cases that followed *Slaughter-House*, the Court consistently rejected any contention that specific rights enumerated in the first eight amendments could be enforced against contrary state law.[26] The "first intimation from any justice of the Supreme Court that the Fourteenth Amendment might be considered to incorporate the Bill of Rights"[27] came in Justice Harlan's dissenting opinion in *O'Neil v. Vermont*,[28] an 1892 cruel and unusual punishment case:

> [S]ince the adoption of the Fourteenth Amendment, no one of the fundamental rights of life, liberty or property, recognized and guaranteed by the Constitution of the United States, can be denied or abridged by a State in respect to any person within its jurisdiction. These rights are, principally, enumerated in the earlier Amendments of the Constitution.[29]

Five years later, Harlan wrote a majority opinion stating in *dicta* that due process required just compensation in a state takings case, although Morrison calls *Chicago, Burlington & Quincy R.R. v. Chicago*[30] a substantive due process case, rather than an incorporation case.[31] The incorporation argument was rejected again in 1900[32] and 1908.[33]

Notwithstanding the failure of the general incorporation doctrine to win Supreme Court approval, the idea that substantive due process might provide the rationale for enforcing the First Amendment guarantees against the states was beginning to capture some legal and scholarly imaginations. The radical International Workers of the World or Wobblies advanced that argument during the early years of the century when their legendary "free speech fights" provoked arrest and trial.[34] That, in turn, evoked a backlash from the press itself. One editorial referred to "the arrogant assumption of the street orators that they were 'exercising a constitutional privilege' – a deliberate misinterpretation" of the First Amendment, which leaves the states the power "to abridge the right of free speech" as they see fit.[35]

But one chronicler of the period, B.F. Moore, a staff member of the Commission on Industrial Relations, was not so sure. Writing in 1915, Moore noted that the Supreme Court had interpreted the due process clause of the Fourteenth Amendment as prohibiting state "infringement of property rights rather than personal rights" but indicated the possibility that the Amendment extended to guarantees of free speech and press as well. "[I]t is not positively known at present just what protection is given to certain personal rights by certain clauses of the U.S. Constitution, especially the Fourteenth Amendment."[36]

Although the notion gained no traction whatsoever in the Supreme Court, prominent scholars of the pre-World War I era, whom Mark Graber has called "the conservative libertarians,"[37] continued to move the idea forward even as they began to discard the laissez-faire economics supported by substantive due process. Thomas Cooley, for example, considered both freedom of speech and freedom of contract among the fundamental rights protected by the due process clause of the Fourteenth Amendment.[38] Theodore Schroeder and Ernst Freund, on the other hand, believed that speech rights were protected by the due process clause, but that freedom of contract stood on a different (and lesser) footing.[39] Henry Schofield maintained the view that First Amendment freedoms should apply to the states through the privileges or immunities clause.[40]

Thus, on the eve of World War I, a growing body of scholarly literature favored enforcing the First Amendment guarantees against the states. And although the Supreme Court had effectively eliminated the privileges or immunities clause as a mechanism for such enforcement, the logic of substantive due process provided a promising alternative. It would be some years, though, before the issue again reached the Court; the earliest wartime cases dealt with violations of the new federal Espionage and Sedition Acts[41] and thus raised no challenge to state law.

In the first case that arguably raised the issue, *Gilbert v. Minnesota*,[42] the Court upheld a conviction under a state law against discouraging enlistments without "deciding or considering" it.[43] In his dissenting opinion in *Gilbert*, Justice Brandeis also saw "no occasion to consider whether [the Minnesota law] violate[d] also the Fourteenth Amendment," but, in an obvious attack on substantive due process, said he could not believe that "the liberty guaranteed by the Fourteenth Amendment includes only liberty to acquire and to enjoy property."[44] Two years later though, Justice Brandeis joined a majority opinion that asserted "neither the

Fourteenth Amendment nor any other provision of the Constitution of the United States imposes upon the States any restrictions about 'freedom of speech'. . . ."[45]

In 1923, the Court struck down a state statute prohibiting the teaching of foreign languages in school on due process grounds, citing the acquisition of useful knowledge as a protected liberty interest.[46] In 1925, the Court inched even closer to resolving the issue, assuming if not quite deciding, "that freedom of speech and of the press – which are protected by the First Amendment from abridgement by Congress – are among the fundamental personal rights and 'liberties' protected by the due process clause of the Fourteenth Amendment from impairment by the States."[47] The Court brushed off its 1922 dictum in *Prudential* and cryptically cited several authorities, only some of which tended to support its proposition.[48]

Notwithstanding its now famous assumption in *Gitlow v. New York*, the Court affirmed Gitlow's conviction under New York's criminal anarchy statute over the dissent of Justices Holmes and Brandeis, who also acknowledged the application of the Fourteenth Amendment.[49] It may be that the Court made its assumption solely in order to acquire jurisdiction over the case and uphold the New York statute,[50] but the Court never looked back on that question again. Two years later, in *Whitney v. California*,[51] the Court upheld a similar statute that had been challenged on the same ground. In his concurring opinion, Justice Brandeis wrote:

> [I]t is settled that the due process clause of the Fourteenth Amendment applies to matters of substantive law as well as to matters of procedure. Thus all fundamental rights comprised within the term liberty are protected by the federal Constitution from invasion by the states. The right of free speech, the right to teach and the right of assembly are, of course, fundamental rights.[52]

In *Fiske v. Kansas*,[53] also in 1927, the Court reversed a conviction under a similar Kansas statute for insufficient evidence, holding the particular application of the statute unconstitutional.

Finally, in 1931, the Court struck down a state law prohibiting the display of an anarchist red flag. In *Stromberg v. California*, Chief Justice Hughes cited *Gitlow*, *Whitney*, and *Fiske* for the proposition "that the conception of liberty under the due process clause of the Fourteenth Amendment embraces the right of free speech."[54] Incorporation was complete, providing the indispensable condition for *Near v. Minnesota* later that same term.

B. Expanding Freedom of Speech

Although incorporation made it possible to employ the First Amendment as a shield against repressive state laws, it said nothing about the scope or substance of the First Amendment rights that could be asserted. When *Gitlow* was decided in 1925, the prevailing view of the First Amendment, reflected in the majority opinion in that case, held that "a State in the exercise of its police power may punish those who abuse [the First Amendment] freedom by utterances inimical to the public welfare, tending to corrupt public morals, incite to crime, or disturb the public peace...."[55] This so-called "bad tendency" doctrine, however, was already in its death throes by then.

The outbreak of World War I in 1914 and the inexorable movement toward American involvement prompted Congress to enact the Espionage Act of June 15, 1917.[56] Among other provisions, the act prohibited anyone from making, during wartime, false statements with intent to interfere with American military success or to promote the success of our enemies.[57] It also prohibited the mailing of any newspaper, magazine, or other literature containing such statements.[58]

Almost immediately following enactment, Thomas G. Patten, postmaster of New York City, declared "unmailable" the August issue of a magazine known as *The Masses* on the ground that four cartoons and four articles in that issue were intended to obstruct recruiting, cause insubordination, or otherwise interfere with military success.[59] The Masses Publishing Co. applied to the U.S. District Court for the Southern District of New York for a preliminary injunction forbidding Patten from refusing to accept the magazine for the mail.[60]

District Judge Learned Hand granted the injunction, first, because he found the text and cartoons to be opinion, not false statements of fact, and within the "right to criticize... which is normally the privileged of the individual in countries dependent upon the free expression of opinion as the ultimate source of authority."[61] As to the act's prohibition on "willfully causing insubordination" and worse, Hand conceded that text and cartoons might do that. But interpreting the word "cause" so broadly as to suppress all hostile criticism "is so contrary to the use and wont of our people" that Congress would have to make its intention to do that crystal clear.[62]

> If one stops short of urging upon others that it is their duty or their interest to resist the law, it seems to me one should not be held to have attempted to cause its violation. If that be not the test, I can see no escape from the conclusion that under this section every political agitation which can be shown to be apt to create a seditious temper is illegal. I am confident that by such language Congress has no such revolutionary purpose in view.[63]

Finding that none of the challenged material satisfied such a test, Hand next considered whether the magazine "willfully obstruct[ed] the recruiting or enlistment service" or "advocate[ed] forcible resistance" to the draft.[64] In keeping with the first two conclusions, Hand construed both of these prohibitions as limited to direct advocacy of resistance and, finding none, again rejected the postmaster's reading.[65]

Thus, Hand based his granting the injunction squarely on statutory grounds; the postmaster's position was simply unsupported by the language of the statute. But although he had undertaken no obvious constitutional analysis – indeed, his opinion never mentions the First Amendment – his statutory interpretation was grounded in a rejection of the "bad tendency" doctrine that then permeated First Amendment jurisprudence. Specifically, he characterized the postmaster's position as impermissibly "based… upon the doctrine that the general tenor and animus of the paper as a whole were subversive to authority and seditious in effect."[66]

Hand stayed his order pending appeal, and the stay was affirmed by a second circuit judge named Charles Merrill Hough, who, while procedurally deferential, expressed skepticism as to the propriety and substance of Hand's decision.[67] The appeal was heard by Circuit Judges Henry Wade Rogers and Henry Galbraith Ward and District Judge Julius Marshuetz Mayer, then Hand's colleague on the bench of the Southern District of New York and later his predecessor on the Second Circuit.[68]

The Court of Appeals set the bar very high for overturning the Postmaster's decision. "[I]f the Postmaster General has been authorized and directed by Congress not to transmit certain matter by mail, and is to determine whether a particular publication is nonmailable under the law, he is required to use judgment and discretion in so determining, and his decision must be regarded as conclusive by the courts unless it appears to be completely wrong."[69] Except for one cartoon, the court found either that the Postmaster was correct or that the court could not say he was incorrect.[70]

The Court of Appeals flatly rejected any First Amendment violation, citing Blackstone for the proposition that liberty of the press consists "in laying no previous restraint upon publication, and not in freedom from censure for criminal matter when published."[71] And it quickly dismissed Hand's formulation of what might constitute a seditious crime: "This court does not agree that such is the law." Rather, the court reiterated the "bad tendency" doctrine that was, in fact, the prevailing view of the law at the time:

> If the natural and reasonable effect of what is said is to encourage resistance to a law, and the words are used in an endeavor to persuade to resistance, it is immaterial that the duty to resist is not mentioned, or the interest of the persons addressed in resistance is not suggested.[72]

Thus was Hand's oblique contribution to an expansive reading of the First Amendment overturned. But Vincent Blasi, building on the work of Gerald Gunther,[73] makes the compelling case that Hand's opinion in *Masses* and his subsequent correspondence with Oliver Wendell Holmes Jr. and Zechariah Chafee established the foundation of modern First Amendment doctrine.[74] According to Blasi, it was not so much Hand's specific test, but rather the structure of reasoning he employed that informed "such landmark precedents of the first amendment tradition as *Near v. Minnesota*...."[75] Hand was, Blasi writes, "the first judge to hold that speech integral to the democratic process must be protected even when it may cause substantial harm."[76]

Neither the Congress nor the U.S. Supreme Court was ready to adopt that principle. One year after *Masses* was decided, Congress amended the Espionage Act with the Sedition Act of 1918 to criminalize, in wartime, the writing or publishing of "any disloyal, profane, scurrilous or abusive language about the form of government of the United States" or the Constitution, military or naval forces, flag, or the uniform or any language intended to bring these ideas or institutions "into contempt, scorn, contumely, or disrepute...."[77] The following year, the Supreme Court heard *Schenck v. United States*, best known for the introduction of Holmes's "clear and present danger" test.[78]

Charles Schenck was the general secretary of the Philadelphia Socialist Party who, with Elizabeth Baer and other members, printed and distributed some 15,000 antiwar leaflets urging young draft inductees to resist the draft, join the party, and work for repeal of the draft law. They also denounced the war as a ruthless adventure serving the interests of Wall Street. The circulars charged that conscription violated the 13th Amendment, which prohibited slavery, and urged conscripts to assert their rights.

They were indicted and convicted on three Espionage Act counts, sentenced to six months in prison, and appealed on First Amendment grounds. Affirming the convictions, Holmes wrote for the Court that "in many places and in ordinary times," such leaflets might have been protected by the First Amendment.

> But the character of every act depends upon the circumstances in which it is done. The most stringent protection of free speech would not protect a man in falsely shouting fire in a theatre and causing a panic. ... The question in every case is whether the words used are used in such circumstances and are of such a nature as to create a clear and present danger that they will bring about the substantive evils that Congress has a right to prevent.[79]

A week later, Holmes again wrote the majority opinion that affirmed the Espionage Act convictions and ten-year sentences of Eugene Debs,[80] one of the nation's leading socialists, and Jacob Frohwerk, publisher of the *Missouri Staats Zeitung*,[81] both for interference with the recruitment effort. Holmes dismissed their First Amendment arguments with the merest references to *Schenck*.[82] If "clear and present danger" meant anything at all, it seemed to mean no more than "bad tendency" or "natural and reasonable effect" had meant in *Masses* and earlier cases.

What happened next, that is, at the beginning of the next term, in November 1919, is a matter of great scholarly interest. Reaffirming his decisions in *Schenck, Frohwerk,* and *Debs*, Holmes dissented in an arguably indistinguishable case, *Abrams v. United States*.[83] In *Abrams*, the Court upheld the Espionage and Sedition Act convictions and 20-year sentences of five New York radicals who distributed some 5,000 pamphlets condemning American military intervention in Russia.[84] The majority opinion echoed Holmes in the previous cases: *Schenck* had disposed of the First Amendment question.

But Holmes was elsewhere. In a dissenting opinion joined by Justice Louis Brandeis, Holmes invoked a metaphor derived from John Stuart Mill,[85] suggesting that the Constitution was premised on the belief that "the ultimate good desired is better reached by free trade in ideas – that the best test of truth is the power of the thought to get itself accepted in the competition of the market.... [W]e should be eternally vigilant against attempts to check the expression of opinions that we loathe and believe to be fraught with death, unless they so imminently threaten immediate interference with the lawful and pressing purposes of the law that an immediate check is required to save the country."[86]

Scholars have long debated whether Holmes had a change of heart on the First Amendment and, if so, why; or whether he truly distinguished the cases on their facts.[87] Contributing to that debate is beyond the scope of this book, but it is beyond cavil that Hand's opinion in *Masses* and his relationship with Holmes during 1918-19 influenced that part of the *Abrams* dissent that began the process of reinterpreting the First Amendment in free speech and free press jurisprudence.

Abrams was followed by more Holmes and Brandeis opinions, such as the dissents in *Schaeffer v. United States,*[88] *Pierce v. United States,*[89] and *Gitlow,*[90] and the concurrence in *Whitney v. California.*[91] By the 1930s, similar positions began appearing, not in dissents, but in majority opinions of the Charles Evans Hughes Court: *Stromberg v. California,*[92] *Herndon v. Lowry,*[93] *DeJonge v. Oregon.*[94]

After World War II, however, when sedition reared its ugly head again with the Smith Act[95] the dissents of Justices Hugo Black and William O. Douglas in *Dennis v. United States*[96] would carry the legacy of *Masses* to mid-century, though Hand himself had written the Second Circuit opinion affirming the convictions of the Communist Party organizers in that case.[97] Subsequent Smith Act cases were decided in favor of free speech,[98] and, eventually, the law of political advocacy would be settled in *Brandenburg v. Ohio*[99] along lines combining the most protective aspects of *Masses* and the *Abrams* dissent.[100] Henceforth, advocacy could only be punished "where such advocacy is directed to inciting or producing imminent lawless action and is likely to incite or produce such action."[101]

While the mainstream press would ultimately benefit from this rethinking of the First Amendment, beginning with *Near v. Minnesota*, it had little or nothing to do with these monumental changes in the law. To the extent that the press was involved at all, it was the German language press, the labor press, the dissident press, the minority press that moved the doctrine forward.[102] The mainstream, institutional press buried its head in the sand and, if anything, had a negative influence on the evolution of First Amendment law. As Margaret Blanchard pointed out in the introduction to her detailed study of dissident speech,

> [M]ost studies of press freedom ignore the somewhat contradictory role that the press has played in terms of overall freedom of expression. Evidence suggests that the institutional press frequently has aligned itself with the forces seeking to suppress dissident speech in this country. As the press became a larger, more institutionalized force in American society, its leaders have had a greater vested interest in preserving the status quo. Thus journalistic opposition to the rights of workers to organize or anarchists to plead for their cause, for instance, dot the pages that follow. Much more research into this particular subject is needed, but press antagonism toward the

> expressive activities of dissidents historically has led to substantial problems for the development of divergent opinions on the United States.[103]

Thus, by the time the predicament of Jay Near and his *Saturday Press* reached the offices of *The Chicago Tribune's* Col. Robert R. McCormick, all of the factors favoring a landmark constitutional decision were in place. The press had largely freed itself of its partisan roots and had become financially dependent on advertising. A unifying philosophy of objectivity emerged that, for the most part, transcended political differences among publishers, at least with regard to reporting the news. Incorporation of the First Amendment through the Fourteenth made it possible to challenge repressive state laws on federal constitutional grounds. And the U.S. Supreme Court was well on its way to adopting a more expansive reading of the First Amendment than ever before. The time was right for *Near v. Minnesota.*

Chapter 5 – *Near v. Minnesota*: Mobilizing the Press

"The mere statement of the case makes my blood boil."

So wrote Weymouth Kirkland to his most illustrious client, Col. Robert R. McCormick of *The Chicago Tribune* ("*Tribune*") on Sept. 14, 1928.[1] The prominent Chicago attorney was writing about a case then styled *Minnesota ex rel. Olson v. Guilford*,[2] but which would make history as *Near v. Minnesota*[3] when it reached its conclusion in the United States Supreme Court nearly three years later. Both McCormick and Kirkland were to become principal players in *Near*, and together they created a role for the institutional press as constitutional litigator shaping the First Amendment doctrine.

As noted in the previous chapter, the American Newspaper Publishers Association had routinely lobbied and litigated on behalf of their members' business interests.[4] But constitutional litigation by the institutional press to avoid or create doctrinal precedent under the First Amendment really began with the appointment of Col. Robert R. McCormick to head the ANPA's Committee on Freedom of the Press in the spring of 1928 and his involvement in *Near v. Minnesota* beginning that fall.[5]

A. The Press as Public Nuisance

The story of *Near v. Minnesota* begins, not with Jay Near and Howard Guilford, Near's partner in sleaze, but with John L. Morrison, a highly religious, crusading prude with a venomous pen who waged a one-man crusade against the purveyors of liquor and prostitutes in the wild and wooly iron mining town of Duluth, Minnesota, in the mid-1920s.[6]

Morrison's muck-raking newspaper, the Duluth *Rip-saw*, also went after the politicians who protected Duluth's rather crude entertainment industry. They were not amused and took their pique to the state legislature. In 1925, the Minnesota legislature – with some drafting help by Minneapolis newspapers, no less[7] – enacted a Public Nuisance Law, or "gag" law, that provided for abatement as a public nuisance of any "malicious, scandalous and defamatory newspaper, magazine or other periodical."[8]

University of Minnesota historian Paul L. Murphy attributes enactment of the gag law to "public exasperation" with the yellow journalism of the time and the "emergence of a number of cheap, ephemeral scandal sheets, which were used for extortion, blackmailing petty crooks, or pressuring concessions from venal public officials."[9] Murphy points out that "Minnesota's experiment quickly drew warm national approval" as a practical alternative to censorship by an administrative agency, which would have been too costly, or civil or criminal libel actions, which had proved ineffective.[10]

Although Murphy does not discuss the importance of the *Rip-saw* to its adoption, a target of that paper, then-State Sen. Michael J. Boylan, came to be known as the "father" of the gag law.[11] In any event, Publisher Morrison died of a blood clot in the brain before he could be prosecuted under the law. Of course, there was no shortage of scandalous newspapers in that era;[12] Near and Guilford were ready targets down in Minneapolis.[13] Near was not nearly as self-righteous (or righteous at all, for that matter) as Morrison but was a complete scoundrel and bigot: anti-Semitic, anti-black, anti-labor,[14] and unfailingly hostile to Minneapolis area officials.

In 1927, Near and Guilford launched *The Saturday Press*, a scurrilous rag that, among other things, alleged that Jewish gangsters were responsible for bootlegging, gambling, and racketeering in Minneapolis (which probably didn't bother anyone), and that certain law enforcement officials – especially Hennepin County Prosecutor Floyd B. Olson – were letting the gangsters run amok (which surely bothered those so accused).[15]

Olson undertook to put Near out of business and filed a complaint on Nov. 21, 1927, alleging multiple instances of defamation.[16] Describing the newspaper as "malicious, scandalous, and defamatory," the "magic words" of the Public Nuisance Law, Olson sought an injunction under that act.[17] A temporary restraining order was issued the same day, enjoining Near and Guilford from publishing *The Saturday Press* or anything like it.[18] *The Saturday Press* never recovered, but that order, which lasted more than a year,[19] became the predicate for the most important press freedom case in American history up to that date.

At first, Near was represented only by local counsel, Thomas Latimer, a prominent Minneapolis attorney and, in Fred Friendly's words, a "self-appointed Legal Aid Society."[20] When Near finally got to court in December 1927, Latimer argued that the Public Nuisance Law was a "subterfuge" to avoid the state constitution and the requirements of its libel law.[21] Although he compared it to laws in fascist Italy and communist Russia, his argument fell on deaf ears. Judge Mathias Baldwin, who had himself been a target of *The Saturday Press*, refused to lift the restraining order but did certify the case to the Minnesota Supreme Court.[22]

On May 25, 1928, the Minnesota Supreme Court unanimously upheld the validity of the statute as an exercise of the state's police powers.[23] "A business that depends largely for its success upon malice, scandal and defamation can be of no real service to society," wrote Chief Justice Samuel Bailey Wilson for a unanimous court. "It is not a violation of the liberty of the press or of the freedom of speech for the Legislature to provide a remedy for their abuse."[24] Four and a half months later, Judge Baldwin made the temporary restraining order a permanent injunction,[25] prohibiting Near and Guilford from publishing until they agreed to publish only the truth, "with good motives and for justifiable ends."[26]

As outrageous as the Minnesota Supreme Court's opinion might seem today, the journalism of the day may have been even more outrageous. Murphy points out that, "with the rise of the tabloid, 1920's journalism offended many older, more serious Americans, who were still guided by a vigorous Victorian-Progressive morality and decorum."[27] Indeed, "[t]he national student debate topic for 1930 was: Resolved: That the Minnesota Nuisance Law should be adopted by every state in the Union."[28]

By then, however, word of the case had reached New York and the American Civil Liberties Union, which had been formed in 1920.[29] Although the ACLU announced that it would take the case to the United States Supreme Court, there were doubts about the group's financial wherewithal, and its involvement in the case was ultimately minimal.[30] Word also reached Chicago and Col. McCormick, who sent the case file on to Weymouth Kirkland.

B. The Colonel Takes Command

When Kirkland received the *Near* file from McCormick, his response was unequivocal:

> I think the decision in this case is utterly at variance with all of our Institutions . . . and most certainly establishes a dangerous precedent to a free press. Whether the articles are true or not, for a judge, without a jury, to suppress a newspaper by writ of injunction is unthinkable, and is just another step, along with the Volstead Injunction, to do away with jury trials. The remedies of civil action and criminal action were open to the State's Attorney and if the Jewish race or the grand jury was slandered, criminal libel could be invoked. If this decision stands, any newspaper in Minnesota which starts a crusade against gambling, vice, or other evils may be closed down, all of which without a trial by jury. Of course, newspapers which are habitually slanderous and defamatory should not be allowed to run, but they should be stopped only in accordance with law. We should not have criminals running the streets at large, but they are, nevertheless, entitled to a jury trial.[31]

Kirkland noted that the ACLU planned to carry the case up to the Supreme Court and expressed the hope that the decision would be reversed there. If not, Kirkland mused, it would be easy for a governor in Illinois or some other state to push a similar statute through the legislature. "I wonder if there is some way we could get in touch with the people appealing to see that their briefs are properly prepared," he mused.[32] McCormick seemed to have something more in mind.

McCormick was no stranger to hardball litigation. Early in his career, the *Tribune* had successfully defended a series of libel suits by Mayor William "Big Bill" Thompson in 1917 and 1918 seeking $1.3 million for criticizing Thompson's pro-German attitude during the war.[33] The first major libel case that involved McCormick directly arose from an editorial that he did not write, but approved, in 1916, titled "Henry Ford is an Anarchist." The editorial took Ford to task for criticizing the Mexican "troubles" and threatening the jobs of any Ford worker who volunteered for service when the National Guard was called out.[34]

Weymouth Kirkland defended the *Ford* case; Philip Kinsley, who later wrote *Liberty and the Press* hailing the *Tribune*'s role,[35] covered for the *Tribune*. The trial was vicious, with Ford portraying McCormick as having a corrupt interest in the Mexican war, and McCormick making Ford out to be something close to a traitor.[36] The trial went from mid-May to mid-August, with Ford ultimately winning six cents in damages. McCormick refused to pay, and Ford never collected.[37]

By December 1920, the animosity between McCormick and Thompson had reached the breaking point. Thompson sued the *Tribune* (and the *Daily News*) for $10 million, claiming his administration had been libeled by exposés of municipal corruption. It was the largest libel action ever filed in the U.S. at that time.[38] The suit was ultimately dismissed in October 1921:

> [W]ith a ringing affirmation of a free press as 'the eyes and ears of the world. . .the advocate constantly pleading before the alter of public opinion. It holds up for review the acts of our officials and those men in high places who have it in their power to advance peace or endanger it.'[39]

McCormick had been named chairman of the ANPA Committee on Freedom of the Press shortly after the association's 1928 annual meeting in April[40] by ANPA President Edward H. Butler of the *Buffalo Evening News*.[41] So, the day after Kirkland opined on the *Near* file, McCormick wrote his old friend Samuel Emory Thomason of the *Tampa Morning Tribune* and *Chicago Journal* and *Daily Times*. Thomason was a former law partner of McCormick's, one-time business manager of the *Tribune*, and a member of McCormick's committee.[42] "I have written to the editors of several of the largest newspapers in the state of Minnesota and asked their opinion on [the case]," wrote McCormick.

> I have referred the records in the case to my own lawyer. It may be that we should intervene in the appeal to the Supreme Court of the United States. If the freedom of the

> press is in jeopardy I don't think we should leave it to any outside organization to fight our battle.[43]

Thomason readily agreed that the ANPA should intervene in the Minnesota case and offered to bring the matter up at a board of directors meeting in New York. "It might be a good idea if you would write a note to the Board and suggest, as chairman of the committee on the Freedom of the Press, that this step be taken, and then I'll follow it through."[44] McCormick did write the directors on Sept. 21, warning that "there is but little chance of there being a reversal of the case unless the ANPA or some other similar public-spirited association takes over the litigation."[45] According to Friendly, however, their response was minimal.

Nevertheless, when Judge Baldwin reconvened the trial court on Oct. 10, *Tribune* lawyers William Symes and Charles Rathbun had joined Latimer at Near's table.[46] As it happened, the additional firepower was useless. Following a largely perfunctory hearing, Olson asked Baldwin to issue a permanent injunction, and Baldwin told him to prepare the order.[47] Three months later, Baldwin signed the order for a permanent injunction: "Let said nuisance be abated."[48]

That final order set the stage for a new appeal to the Minnesota Supreme Court, but it also seemed to embarrass the Minnesota legislature, and the *Tribune*'s coverage shifted from the court battle to an effort to repeal the gag law. On Feb. 27, 1929, the *Tribune* reported that State Representative R. R. Davis had introduced a bill in the House to repeal the law.[49] The article reported that the *Tribune* had criticized the gag law since it was first enacted but made no mention of any involvement in the litigation. In fact, it incorrectly reported that the "[American] Civil Liberties [U]nion has entered the fight and has taken the case of the *Saturday Press* to the United States Supreme [C]ourt in an effort to prove the law unconstitutional."[50]

The support of the press in general remained tepid. "I have written to approximately ten publishers of leading newspapers and magazines in the United States," the *Tribune* quotes Davis. "The replies, which are beginning to come back to me, are *almost* unanimous for repeal of the law."[51] The *Tribune*, however, kept up the drumbeat. On March 5, it covered a speech Davis made before a House legislative committee condemning the gag law. Davis noted that, in addition to the *Tribune*, the *St. Paul Pioneer Press*, and *Editor & Publisher* had editorialized against the law.[52]

The *Tribune* continued its thorough coverage of the Minnesota hearings throughout March, at one point partially correcting the record regarding the pending litigation. "Now an appeal to the United States Supreme [C]ourt from this decision is being undertaken by the publisher of *The Chicago Tribune*. The American Civil Liberties league also has interested itself in repeal of the law."[53] The article also noted that the ANPA had taken the position that the Minnesota law "is a dangerous precedent to permit on court records in a nation which has prided itself on its freedom of press and speech."[54] But most Minnesota editors, the article said, had "failed to take a serious interest in the law, contenting themselves with the idea that 'decent newspapers will not be affected by the law.'"[55]

The next day, the *Tribune* editorialized against the gag law under the headline "A Monkey State Candidate" – an unstated reference to the Scopes evolution trial in Tennessee.[56] In the editorial, the *Tribune* formally announced that it "will challenge the law in behalf of the *Saturday Press* before the United States Supreme [C]ourt."[57] That editorial, and others, were quoted extensively by Rep. Davis when the hearings continued on March 25.[58] Also testifying against the gag law then were S.M. Williams, editor of the *St. Paul Pioneer Press and Dispatch*; Sam Haislett, secretary of the Minnesota Editorial Association; and Prof. Bruce McCoy of the University of Minnesota Journalism School.[59]

It was all to no avail, however, as the committee voted 11-3 to recommend postponing action on the repeal bill indefinitely, and the House adopted the committee report, 86-30.[60] Opposition to the bill was led by Rep. C.A. Peterson, who said supporters of repeal suffered from "hallucinations" with regard to threats to freedom of the press.[61] "If you repeal this bill," Peterson said, "there is an army of persons waiting to begin publication of scandal sheets."[62] The *Tribune*'s editorial response was scathing and classic McCormick. In "Minnesota Joins the Monkey States," the *Tribune* declared:

> The defeat of the repeal bill is a disgrace to the state of Minnesota. When the law was enacted in 1925 it had attracted relatively little attention, and its passage could be interpreted charitably as an oversight. Today the significance of the law is plain and the refusal to repeal it indicates beyond all question that the enactment of the law was a deliberate attempt to strangle criticism in a way which enlightened men have rejected as unsound politically and morally for nearly 300 years.
>
> Minnesota joins hands with Tennessee, and of the two Minnesota may justly claim to be the more ridiculous. After all, it is less than a hundred years since intelligent men discarded the traditional biological notions found in the Bible.[63]

The day that editorial appeared, the *Tribune* legal team submitted a voluminous 377-page brief to the Minnesota Supreme Court surveying 2,300 years of censorship, from Socrates to the present, mentioning such exemplary "critics of government" as Christ and Savonarola, Zenger and Vallandigham.[64] The brief was signed by Weymouth Kirkland, Louis Caldwell, Charles Rathbun, and Edward Caldwell of the Kirkland firm. The Latimers were listed as associate counsel. The brief argued that affirming the gag law

> would put a precedent on the books which hereafter would be used by an entrenched minority to escape ouster from office and opprobrium.
>
> It is unconstitutional to issue an injunction stifling a newspaper even after hearing and trial; to issue a temporary injunction before hearing and without any trial whatsoever is a despotic act which the American people always have thought could be characteristic only of a czar or the inquisition, and inconceivable in a democracy.[65]

On this trip to the Minnesota Supreme Court, Near had not only the full attention of McCormick, his *Tribune*, and its law firm, but also, at long last, the organized support of the publishers. When L.B. Palmer asked McCormick on March 6 for a report of his Freedom of the Press Committee for the ANPA annual meeting,[66] set for April 24, in New York City, McCormick had the law firm prepare a summary of the Minnesota case. Kirkland's associate, Howard Ellis, sent a draft to McCormick on March 19. Ellis summarized the case through May 25, 1928, when the Minnesota Supreme Court affirmed the restraining order and remanded the case:

> It was at this point that *The Chicago Tribune* became aware of the revolutionary effect of this decision upon the liberties of the people and of the press. By agreement with the defendants, the attorneys for [*The*] *Chicago Tribune* became additional council (sic) in the case with instructions to present, if possible, the illegality of the statute under the Fourteenth Amendment to the Federal Constitution.[67]

Ellis went on to discuss the trial and expressed the hope that, if the Minnesota Supreme Court reaffirmed its previous holding, "the Supreme Court of the United States can review the whole matter; and a sincere effort will be made to obtain a review by the Supreme Court of the United States."[68] Under the heading, "Some Objections to the Statute," Ellis outlined the substantive case in detail, then appealing to the publishers through their wallets, considered "The Effect of the Statute on Newspaper Values":

> Needless to say, if this statute is held valid, the value of newspaper properties throughout the country will be greatly diminished. If the law is valid in Minnesota it is valid in other states. There is always the possibility of similar legislation being adopted elsewhere. Newspapers can be suppressed at the will of the legislature and a single judge sitting without a jury and, if a preliminary injunction is granted, before notice to the newspaper or hearing. No legitimate business can stand up under such a load. No legitimate business has ever been subjected to such a burden . . . .
>
> The possibility that such a law could legally be adopted and enforced would cause newspaper properties everywhere to decline in value.[69]

The report seems to have had the desired effect. On the opening day of the ANPA convention, the publishers accepted the report that Ellis prepared for McCormick and adopted a resolution pledging a united front against the Minnesota law.[70] The following day, New York City's three leading dailies lent their editorial support to the fight. The *World* said the law was "the most extreme attempt to fetter journalism made anywhere in the country since civil war days," while the *Herald-Tribune* said the law "authorize[s] capital punishment of a newspaper by the fiat of a single judge."[71] The *Times* praised McCormick's "effective struggle against the statute" and said publishers who heard his committee report "were amazed that any state legislature in the Union could have passed such a law."[72] A few days later, the *Herald-Tribune* editorial was reprinted in full in McCormick's *Tribune* as its "Editorial of the Day."[73]

McCormick had also garnered the moral support of the American Society of Newspaper Editors, which met in Washington on April 18 shortly before the ANPA convention in New York City. President Walter M. Harrison, editor of the *Daily Oklahoman* and the *Oklahoma City Times*, urged ASNE to "lend every assistance possible" to support McCormick's campaign to overturn the Minnesota statute.[74]

> No larger club could be held over the newspaper profession by the judiciary. Under such a tyrannical statute a corrupt judge might silence any fair comment about his derelictions and kill a newspaper by a temporary writ that would ruin a going business before the editor might have an opportunity to prove his case during his day in court.[75]

Harrison praised McCormick effusively as "the first to raise his voice" against what Harrison called "a medieval invasion of the freedom of the press guaranteed in our bill of rights."[76] McCormick was a member of ASNE as well as ANPA and served on ASNE's committee on legislation and freedom of the press, along with Edward S. Beck of his own *Chicago Tribune* and Samuel Williams and R. J. Dunlap of the *St. Paul Pioneer Press and Dispatch*.[77] Notwithstanding Harrison's call, there is no indication that ASNE ever contributed any money to the litigation campaign.[78]

Oral arguments before the Minnesota Supreme Court were scheduled for May 23, but were postponed until Oct. 1, at Kirkland's request, then postponed again until Dec. 2. When the court finally heard the case, Friendly writes, the event "more resembled a procedural ceremony than a legitimate clash of arguments."[79] Having found the gag law constitutional once, there was little chance the court would change its mind and nothing the *Tribune*'s "dream team" did seemed to have any contrary influence. Near's frustration boiled over, and on Dec. 14, even before the Supreme Court decision came down, he wrote a truly grotesque letter to McCormick, complaining about Ellis's handling of the case, including delays since the spring and his attraction to "Minnesota moonshine."[80]

> This case means everything to me. It is I who am deprived of a chance to make a living, of my property. True, I am defying court orders and inviting a jail sentence for writing for the Beacon, but I have got to live and Mr. McCormick, if I'm going to be made an ass of by Mr. Ellis and the laughing stock of the city because of his actions while here – I'm not and I don't believe you expect me to. [81]

In all likelihood, nothing Ellis could have done would have affected the outcome of the case. As expected, the Minnesota Supreme Court once again upheld the gag law in a perfunctory opinion. "The record presents the same questions upon which we have already passed. . . . Upon authority [of the earlier opinion], wherein our views have been more fully expressed, the judgment herein is affirmed."[82] But the decision touched off a flurry of activity from McCormick and Kirkland to enlist support from the publishers to take the case to the United States Supreme Court.[83]

A draft letter from McCormick to Harry Chandler, president of the *Los Angeles Times*, dated Dec. 23, 1929, served as the model.[84] "The question now arises, – shall the case be taken to the United States Supreme Court? It may be taken on three grounds, – violation of the First Amendment to the Constitution, violation of the Fourteenth Amendment to the Constitution, and violation of the First Amendment to the Constitution of Minnesota."[85]

McCormick then reiterated the appeal Ellis had made to the publishers' financial interests and offered the best- and worst-case scenarios:

> It is obvious that if we appeal the case and win it, such cloud as has been placed upon our titles will have been removed. The chances appear to be very much in favor of our winning the case, but in the event of our failure to win the case, I imagine we might expect the legislatures of the various States to enact similar legislations, which then would be probably held up by the Supreme Courts of most, if not all, the States. Free press in this country would disappear.
>
> The other alternative is to wait quietly and trust that the Minnesota case with the Minnesota statute will not be copied in other jurisdictions, or if it is copied in other States and upheld by the other Supreme Courts, then take the fight to Washington. I think it is obvious that the Supreme Court of the United States would be less likely to reverse two or more States [sic] Supreme Courts than to reverse one.[86]

Finally, McCormick makes a plea for solidarity among the publishers, presumably more for symbolic than financial purposes.

> This matter is of vital interest to all of us. I do not feel that I should definitely take action which will be binding upon all the newspapers of the country. I am writing this letter to all the members of the Committee on the Freedom of the Press, soliciting their views. It may be that they will be sufficiently unanimous and positive to enable us without a further meeting to make a recommendation to the Directors. If not, I will endeavor to obtain a meeting of the Committee, as time will not permit our awaiting the annual Convention without losing our right of appeal.[87]

McCormick sent this draft to Kirkland, who suggested a change in the paragraph that involved grounds for taking the case to the United States Supreme Court.[89] McCormick changed the letter the same day and sent it off via teletype to Chandler. The paragraph now read: "It may be taken on two grounds. Does the statute violate the Fourteenth Amendment to the United States Constitution or does it violate the Free Speech Amendment to the Constitution of Minnesota, which is virtually the same as the First Amendment to the United States Constitution?"[90]

Kirkland also advised McCormick that, after a long talk with Ellis, he and Ellis were both "quite confident . . . that the Supreme Court of the United States will not uphold this statute."[91] But he warned that waiting to see if other states might enact similar legislation could have a negative influence on the High Court.[92]

McCormick added Kirkland's observations to the committee letter and, on Dec. 26, asked his secretary, Genevieve Burke, to remove any remarks specific to Chandler and prepare the letter for all committee members and ANPA President Butler.[93] The letters went out on Dec. 27.[94]

Butler wrote back on Dec. 30, 1929, agreeing with McCormick's proposal to take the matter to the United States Supreme Court "along the grounds outlined in your letter."[95] But Butler said he did not think he had authority, as ANPA president, to "direct this action without the consent of the Board."[96] Butler asked McCormick to send him copies of the responses he received from the committee members, "and I, in turn, will immediately take a mail vote on the proposition from the members of the Board in order that this matter will not be delayed unduly, for, as you say, there is danger in delay."[97] Dewart also wrote back on Dec. 30, recommending the case be taken up on state constitutional grounds.[98] Thomason agreed.

> Because I can not imagine that the United States Supreme Court would sustain the opinion of the Supreme Court of Minnesota, and because I think it is wise to get this matter settled while we know that the preparation of the briefs and arguments is in the hands of capable lawyers, I am for taking the case to the United States Supreme Court now.[99]

> Chandler's response was dated Jan. 1, 1930,[100] and he counseled wait[ing] a little before proceeding . . . and see[ing] in the interval if any disposition manifests itself on the part of other states to enact similar legislation.
>
> I have heard of none and I should say the chances are somewhat against any considerable movement in this direction. In many, in fact most states, I am inclined to believe that the combined influence of the newspapers would prevent such enactments, if attempted.

> The policy is frankly that of letting sleeping dogs lie. If we go to the Supreme Court now and that tribunal upholds the Minnesota court, we will have stirred up the matter to a point strongly conducive to similar legislation in other states. If so formidable a movement develops as to make it necessary ultimately to go before the Supreme Court, I do not believe we will be any worse off than we are now. I note the objection of Mr. Kirkland to this delay. While I am not a lawyer, it seems to me likely that if the Supreme Court should knock out the Minnesota statute because of its faulty wording, as Mr. Kirkland suggests, this would not prevent another state from drawing a similar law but avoiding the errors made in Minnesota.
>
> This is merely an offhand opinion. The matter is certainly worthy of the very best consideration we can give it.[101]

There is a pencil annotation on Thomason's letter, "send copy of each to each," and a follow-up letter to each member dated Jan. 16, 1929, confirms that the Dewart, Thomason, and Chandler letters were sent to each of them.[102] In that follow-up letter, McCormick noted that he had also received many newspaper clippings and found them to be "practically unanimous" in their strong opposition to the Minnesota decision.[103]

> It seems to me desirable that we take the appeal at this time both because we will lose our rights if we delay and because this is the most advantageous way in which to mobilize the press of the country in defense of its rights.
>
> Acting in unison, I strongly believe we can defend this essential principle of our form of government. Without united action I am afraid that we will be destroyed piecemeal, and with us the Republican form of government.[104]

On Jan. 18, McCormick wrote Butler suggesting that the ANPA Board of Directors recommend taking the case to the Supreme Court and asking for approval of the entire membership by mail ballot:

> In this way, I think you will put practically every newspaper in America actively behind our movement. At

> the same time you will have aroused the newspapers of the country to such an extent that wherever similar legislation is proposed the newspapers of the state will be ready to organize against it.[105]

James Kerney finally responded on Jan. 21. "On the whole, while there is some force in Mr. Chandler's arguments, I agree with you that the considerations on the other side of the question are much more important, and that an immediate appeal should be taken to the United States Supreme Court."[106]

McCormick then turned his attention to Near's frustration. He sent some of Near's correspondence to Kirkland on Jan. 23, including a letter asking for money to expand and promote a new *Saturday Press*.[107] "I take it that this Johnny is trying to shake us down," McCormick told Kirkland.[108] "I think you draw the right conclusion," replied Kirkland.[109] "You will remember that some time last fall I told you we had a request from him for money which you very properly refused to grant. Ellis transmitted this information to him and since then he has had no use for Ellis."[110]

Kirkland asked to see McCormick as soon as possible – McCormick was wintering in Florida[111] – "because I am under the impression that whether we take up the case or not, Near will have someone do it and with his lack of means it will probably be very poorly briefed."[112] Later, Kirkland condemned the Minnesota gag law in a speech to the Legal Club.[113]

Meanwhile, McCormick's efforts to enlist the support of the other publishers was having mixed results, receiving praise for his efforts but no financial backing.[114] The ANPA board met on Feb. 8, 1930, and, according to Lincoln Palmer, was "in full accord with Colonel McCormick's suggestion that [taking the case to the Supreme Court] was the proper course to follow."[115] In a letter to Thomason, however, Palmer pointed out that the association had been "under unusually heavy expense during the past year."[116]

> In view of these heavy expenses already incurred the Board naturally hesitates to incur additional heavy expense, and so I have been asked to write to you to express the hope of the Board that you will discuss the matter with Colonel McCormick who is, I understand, in Florida at this time, with a view toward learning in what manner the expense of carrying this case through to a conclusion may be met.[117]

Thomason forwarded Palmer's letter to McCormick, along with his own summary of the Board's position.

> They did not feel that they had any right to ask you to bear the expense of the Freedom of the Press case any further, but they assigned to me the delicate task of saying to you that the Association would be glad to cooperate in every way if the Tribune would bear the legal burden.[118]

McCormick was more interested in polling the ANPA membership than in any financial contribution, telling his secretary to inform committee members he would be glad to bear the expense if a substantial majority favored the appeal.[119] He wired Thomason especially to explain that the poll would "have the effect of thoroughly arousing the membership which is just as important as the appeal itself."[120] He asked Thomason whether he thought he could get the idea adopted, and Thomason wired back to say he would try and believed he could succeed.[121]

The next day, McCormick wrote Thomason that he had instructed Kirkland to "perfect the appeal to the Supreme Court of the United States."[122] He also provided a longer, more detailed explanation of his overall strategy.

> It seems to me highly desirable that the members of the A.N.P.A. should be polled as to their favoring this procedure. In this manner we will arouse them to the peril of the situation as we cannot in any other way, and will have them prepared to resist any injunction laws proposed in other States or in Washington. Unless we do arouse the Publishers in time, I am afraid that the politicians will begin knocking them off State by State until they have shown they can get away with it and then will pass injunction laws throughout the Union.
>
> It is to be borne in mind that the Courts were never favorable to the Freedom of the Press. The press attained its freedom by legislative action. On the other hand, our Supreme Court is more favorable to Constitutional rights than it was when Taft was Chief Justice, and may be more favorable now than it will be when some of the present Judges, notably Brandeis and Holmes, have passed on.
>
> I hope the Board of Directors will act before the next meeting of the Association in New York.[123]

Thomason wrote back to tell McCormick that he had written to Butler to ask for an immediate poll, but that Butler had gone south for the winter. So he wired Palmer asking for a telegraphic vote of the directors authorizing the referendum. "I think you are entirely right in your conclusion," he told McCormick, "and I will keep after Palmer and the directors with a view to getting a referendum before the New York meetings."[124]

Having received assurances from Kirkland that there was time to conduct the referendum before the right of appeal expired,[125] Palmer sent McCormick a draft of the referendum letter. The letter hailed McCormick as an "ardent champion" of freedom of the press, "so seriously challenged" by the Minnesota law. The letter said McCormick had retained counsel and perfected an appeal in the case and

> is prepared to continue this fight through to a United States Supreme Court decision to the end that newspapers may be protected from suppression by injunction, provided the membership is in accord with such action. A referendum vote has been ordered by President Butler and you are requested to record your vote.[126]

McCormick found the letter "entirely satisfactory."[127]

In March, McCormick stepped up the campaign to bring the publishers on board in anticipation of the ANPA annual convention the following month. He wrote to M.V. Atwood, secretary of the New York State Society of Newspaper Editors, asking him to "suggest to the members of your State Association that they vote in the affirmative" on the referendum.[128] He also reported the ANPA referendum in the *Tribune*, summarizing the case "[f]or the information of editors and other readers who have not had the [case] brought to their attention."[129] And he wired Palmer suggesting the press be given results of the referendum on a weekly basis, mailed out as "news matter," not merely put in the ANPA *Bulletin* as Palmer had suggested.[130] At the time, the vote was 275-5 in favor of the appeal.[131]

McCormick was very eager for the annual convention, as well as for a meeting of his Freedom of the Press committee. Palmer wrote McCormick, noting the difficulty in scheduling a meeting the previous year and asking whether he wanted one this year.[132] "Of course we will have a meeting . . .," McCormick replied. "As far as I am concerned, I will put it ahead of any other meeting."[133] McCormick also asked Palmer for fifteen minutes "to put my views before the convention. I don't care when."[134] Palmer wrote back to say he had arranged for McCormick to address the convention during the first session and had scheduled a meeting of the committee.[135] He also told McCormick that the poll stood at 331-6 in favor of intervention.

That eagerness, however, did not extend to preparing a committee report. Palmer had asked for a report by April 10 so that it could be published in the preconvention *Bulletin*. He told McCormick the report would be of "outstanding interest to our Convention."[136] McCormick replied that he couldn't make a report "until the vote of the members is in and until the Board of Directors has taken some action upon our recommendation." He suggested Palmer "might phrase a report of the situation to date" and he would "be glad to sign it."[137]

Before receiving McCormick's response, Palmer again asked for the report in another letter.[138] Noting that their correspondence was crossing, McCormick repeated his unwillingness to submit a report, this time telling Palmer that the editorial assistant he had assigned to collect material for the report had left the *Tribune*. "I believe you could write a report on this one subject, the Minnesota case, which we could submit to our committee . . . . Next year I will have somebody on [t]he *Tribune* compile a comprehensive report on the subject for the following meeting." [139]

Palmer sent a draft report to McCormick's secretary on April 11, suggesting that she forward one copy to Kirkland.[140] The report, which was to be signed by the committee members, found "no attempts to abridge [freedom of the press] by state or federal legislation, and . . . few attempts on the part of the courts."[141] One of those attempts involved an Ohio court that sentenced two editors to thirty days and $500 in fines for publishing editorials criticizing a judge for sitting on a trial in a case in which the judge had an interest.[142] The convictions were overturned on appeal to the Ohio Appeals Court,[143] and Palmer quoted from the opinion of Judge Willis Vickery:

> We live in an age of pitiless publicity! We live in an age when freedom of speech and freedom of press are paramount issues. People should be allowed to say what they please, and newspapers to print what they please, always making themselves liable under the laws of slander or the laws of libel . . . .[144]
>
> In other words, it is better that the press be free, that speech be free . . . [and] that the right to air our views be free, than it is that they be uttered in fear and trembling . . . .
>
> A free people must have a free press and they must have the right to speak freely their thoughts.[145]

Palmer also reported on the Minnesota case referendum, which now stood at 375-8. "The Chicago Tribune's attorneys, therefore, are perfecting the appeal to the United States Supreme Court, and your Committee feels that there is every indication of a successful termination of the issue involved."[146]

McCormick forwarded the draft to all of the members of the committee.[147] Kerney sent back a lengthy letter, thanking McCormick and congratulating him on his vigilance. "It is fine and I am proud to have my name signed to it, although I have contributed nothing. You are doing a great job."[148]

> As I see it, the biggest danger to American institutions comes from the arrogance of the courts, which undertake to assume all the functions of the three departments of government. Perhaps a large part of the blame rests with the press, which has been too indulgent, or too timid, in pointing out the infringement on liberty by stupid judges.[149]

Kerney added that the quotation from Judge Vickery "should be pasted in the hat of every editor and every judge in America."[150] Dewart wrote the same day, "It suits me."[151]

Meanwhile, a formal resolution had been drafted for adoption by the ANPA convention. McCormick sent a copy to Kirkland, and Ellis suggested revised language:

> Be it resolved that Chapter 285, Session Laws of 1925 of the State of Minnesota, popularly known as the 'Gag Law', (sic) is a violation of the first and fourteenth amendments to the Constitution of the United States, a peril to the right of property and a menace to republican institutions;
>
> Be it further resolved that this association condemn this statute as a dangerous and vicious invasion of personal liberties;
>
> Be it further resolved that this association and its members cooperate to cause its annullment [sic] and to prevent the enactment of similar legislation.[152]

The 1930 ANPA convention saw Harry Chandler replace Edward Butler as president and also, apparently, experience a change of heart regarding the financing. Chandler had written to McCormick back in March suggesting the membership "share expenses pro rata with The Chicago Tribune."[153] On April 19, the ANPA directors actually voted to "meet the cost incurred in connection with taking an appeal."[154] Chandler had told the directors immediately after the convention that he would communicate with McCormick to get some idea of the costs involved, but illness prevented Chandler from following through until late May. "If you have any approximate idea of what the appeal cost will be I should like to have it in order to make Mr. Palmer's records as complete as possible," Chandler wrote.[155]

McCormick asked Kirkland to "kindly supply the important and interesting information" that Chandler had requested.[156] Kirkland estimated the total cost, including oral argument, at $25,000.[157] McCormick forwarded the information to Chandler, adding, "[a]ny sum that the A.N.P.A. sees fit to pay will be satisfactory to me."[158] In the end, ANPA contributed $5,000 to the appeal.[159]

Meanwhile, Kirkland's legal team had been working on a brief for the Supreme Court. McCormick monitored the process closely and freely offered his advice. At one point, for example, he advised Kirkland that Justice Louis D. Brandeis was "a fairly orthodox Jew, and it may not be wise to greatly emphasize the crucifixion in the appeal . . . ."[160] Later, he advised Kirkland, "I think we should point out that the Government in Washington is the outcome of a fight for free government of which freedom of the press was an integral part."[161] That advice came in a cover letter for a document McCormick entitled "Comments on the Minnesota Brief," which contained sixteen suggestions for changes in the draft:

> 1. I have never read JUNIUS. I understand it was very bitter and was anonymous. Can't you argue that if anonymous publications are forced by law, they will be much more bitter and defamatory than established publications? . . . .
>
> 3. Page 55: It seems as though it might be more convincing to present an instance or two of the prosecutions instituted after the expiration of licensing: were they not against political opponents rather than against scandalous, lewd, or malicious publications? ....
>
> 5. Page 74: It appears you might profitably continue the quotation from Madison where he shows how the executive, judiciary and legislature are curtailed by the first amendment.
>
> 6. Page 87: Might we comment that the Minnesota statute does not give the defendant even such protection as the sedition act was supposed to afford through a jury and

> therefore is much worse than this greatly reprobated statute? ....
>
> 10. Page 175: Of course the decision that the jury and not the judge should decide the libelous nature of a writing is a precedent against letting a judge make the decision through the expedient of an injunction.[162]

McCormick's suggestions continued in letter after letter to Kirkland. "I wonder if the old laws against scolds are in any way relevant to the injunction case," he wrote in one.[163] Kirkland assured McCormick that "most of your ideas can and will be incorporated in the brief," but cautioned that, "while the brief in the Supreme Court of Minnesota was 377 pages in length, the brief in the Supreme Court of the United States cannot be permitted to run over 75 pages." Pointing out that the Court had "recently dismissed several briefs merely on account of the length," Kirkland told McCormick that "[s]uch of your suggestions that cannot be incorporated in the brief can undoubtedly be worked into oral argument."[164]

That admonition seemed to have little or no effect on McCormick. "Would the best way to fix the court's mind upon the essential issue be – to start off with a quotation of the First amendment to the Constitution?" he asked in another letter, which he drafted at least twice.[165] In that letter, he urged Kirkland to use an extended quotation from Richard Brinsley Sheridan on the power of the press to overcome even the most corrupt government that is now carved in the entry hall of the *Tribune* building in Chicago.[166]

McCormick's attention during the summer of 1930 was necessarily focused on the murder of *Tribune* crime reporter Jake Lingle and revelation of Lingle's all-too-close relationship with the Capone gang.[167] Still, McCormick and the *Tribune* remained active in the *Near* case and other press freedom issues.[168] Among the more interesting issues to surface that summer was the fifteen percent annual tax on newspaper advertising proposed by Louisiana Gov. Huey P. Long, which would later become the central issue in another landmark Supreme Court decision, *Grosjean v. American Press, Inc.*[169] McCormick had received a letter from Philip Schuyler of *Publishers' Service Semi-Monthly* in New York "wondering" what his committee was going to do about the tax.[170] McCormick said the committee had "asked all the newspapers of America to oppose the newspaper tax bill in Louisiana" and had been advised by the *Item-Tribune* in New Orleans "that the opposition is proving effective."[171]

By the fall of 1930, the *Near* case was back in the news as the gag law's initial sponsor, Minnesota State Sen. George Lommen, announced that he would support repeal in the Minnesota legislature.[172] Soon thereafter, Floyd B. Olson, the former district attorney who had filed for the injunction against Near's *Saturday*

Press, was elected governor of Minnesota and, in his inaugural address in January 1931, expressed support for the repeal. Olson explained that, although he remained convinced of the statute's constitutionality, he now believed "that the possibilities for abuse make it an unwise law," a position he could not take as prosecutor.[173] The *Tribune*'s editorial in support of repeal fell far short of embracing Olson, claiming credit instead for having initiated the court challenge.[174] The *St. Louis Post-Dispatch* was more charitable toward Olson, and the *Tribune* duly carried its editorial the following day.[175]

Bills to repeal the gag law were introduced in both the Minnesota House and Senate on Jan. 15[176] and approved by the House on Feb. 4 by a vote of 68-58 after two days of intense debate.[177] Perhaps anticipating the demise of the gag law one way or the other,[178] one Minnesota state senator began drafting a draconian new criminal libel law that provided prison terms of one to three years.[179] But prospects for the legislation's clearing the Senate had begun to dim,[180] and, at one point, its chief sponsor, Sen. Lommen, agreed to allow the bill to lie dormant in committee pending a "speedy" decision by the United States Supreme Court.[181] In the end, the bill died in the crush of other legislative business when sponsors failed to win a special order giving it priority consideration.[182]

But the machinations of the Minnesota legislature had no effect on the legal process through which *Near v. Minnesota* finally reached the United States Supreme Court. Near's jurisdictional statement had reached the Court on May 17, 1930,[183] and the Court had noted probable jurisdiction on Oct. 20.[184] Kirkland filed Near's brief on Dec. 12,[185] and Minnesota Attorney General Henry N. Benson filed the state's reply brief on Jan. 19, 1931.[186] Oral arguments were scheduled for Jan. 30.

C. Before the Supreme Court

After describing the statute as interpreted and applied by the Minnesota courts, Kirkland's seventy-page brief defined "freedom of the press" as broader than Supreme Court "precedents passing upon that right under the First Amendment."[187] Rather, Kirkland asserted that precedents defining the right under state constitutions and the common law are also apposite.[188] Averring that all such authorities, from Blackstone to the present, agree with the proposition that freedom of the press prohibits prior restraints,[189] Kirkland proceeded to offer the court a veritable library of precedents supporting that position.[190] He acknowledged a handful of cases where an injunction had been granted affecting freedom of speech or of the press but distinguished the lot as aimed at preventing unlawful conduct and having only an incidental effect on the right of free speech and press.[191]

Having established that the statute violated freedom of the press, Kirkland next set out to show that freedom of the press is protected by both the due process and privileges or immunities clauses of the Fourteenth Amendment.[192] For the former proposition, Kirkland pointed to *Gitlow v. New York*[193] and subsequent cases; by 1930, that issue had been all but conclusively decided,[194] and Kirkland's case was strong and focused. Precedents for the latter proposition were more general, with only a tenuous link to freedom of the press; the *Slaughter-House Cases*[195] had gutted the privileges or immunities clause, and Kirkland could not resurrect it here.[196] No matter, he concluded; freedom of the press "is probably a right of such magnitude that it would exist even in the absence of the Fourteenth Amendment."[197]

Minnesota's brief began by limiting the issue to the due process clause, which the state conceded *arguendo* might protect Near's liberty interest in freedom of the press (although not without a skeptical footnote).[198] But that freedom, the brief asserted, "does not include the free and unrestricted right to publish obscene, scandalous or defamatory matter."[199] Minnesota relied heavily on the World War I Espionage and Sedition Act cases for the proposition that freedom of speech is not absolute, then concentrated on showing that the injunction against Near was a valid exercise of the state's police power to abate a real nuisance, not an injunction against mere libel as Kirkland had characterized it.[200]

There is no transcript of the oral argument, but Friendly reconstructs it from newspaper accounts.[201] "The words were delivered by counsel," Friendly says, "but the rhetoric was vintage McCormick."[202] Kirkland spoke for fifty-four minutes, interrupted by Justice Pierce Butler's reminders that "the *Saturday Press* was a hate sheet which regularly published defamatory articles . . . "[203] Butler asked "if it wasn't 'fanciful' to prevent a state such as Minnesota from enforcing a decree to prevent further publication of malicious articles."[204] Friendly reports Kirkland responding that "the proper remedy for persons feeling themselves defamed was to seek indictments and criminal trials before juries . . . . The Minnesota gag law [was] a remedy worse than the evil it attempted to cure . . . ."[205]

Deputy Attorney General James E. Markham argued for the state that the statute did not violate the federal Constitution "because it provided for due process of law as commanded by the Fourteenth Amendment."[206] Chief Justice Charles Evans Hughes interrupted to steer Markham away from any Fourteenth Amendment argument, citing *Gitlow* to establish conclusively that freedom of the press is a fundamental right. He then asked Markham to address the prior restraint question. Markham denied that the injunction amounted to a prior restraint, calling it a "punishment for an earlier wrong."[207] He also defended the statute as "beneficial to newspapers because it would 'have the effect of purifying the press.'"[208]

Both Friendly's account and the *Tribune*'s coverage emphasize the questioning of Justice Louis D. Brandeis. It is evident from Brandeis's own papers that he had been preparing for this case for some time. One note to a clerk, H. Thomas Austern, dated Oct. 14, 1930, for example, says "let me know as early as possible" whether the case has been discussed in any newspapers, trade magazines, or law reviews.[209] Two days later, Brandeis asked Austern to check the house organs and annual reports of the ANPA and ASNE for anything they might have said about the case.[210] Other notes showed that Austern tracked coverage of the case in *Editor & Publisher, Printers Ink*, the *Minneapolis Journal*, and the *Minnesota Law Review*, among others.[211]

Brandeis's papers also contain handwritten and typed copies of a *Minneapolis Journal* editorial supporting the gag law and the Minnesota Supreme Court's second affirmation of it.[212] Some segments of the press had supported the law, and *Minneapolis Journal* editors had even helped draft it.[213] Brandeis also collected clips from *The Washington Post* and the newspaper *Labor* on efforts to repeal the gag law.[214]

At oral argument, Brandeis told Markham that it was "difficult to see how one is to have a free press and the protection it affords a democratic community without the privilege this act seems to limit."[215] He led Markham like an experienced cross-examiner to admit that the kind of collusion between gangsters and public officials reported in the *Saturday Press* was "privileged" as "'a matter of prime interest to every American citizen.'"[216] When Markham replied, "'[a]ssuming it to be true,'" Brandeis "snapped back: 'No. A newspaper cannot always wait until it gets the judgment of a court.'"[217]

According to Friendly, Markham looked to Justice Oliver Wendell Holmes, Jr., to rescue him from Brandeis's embrace, noting Holmes's majority opinion in *Patterson v. Colorado*,[218] which upheld a contempt charge against a newspaper publisher. Friendly quotes Holmes as replying, "I was much younger when I wrote that opinion than I am now, Mr. Markham. If I did make such a holding, I now have a different view."[219]

Near, at least, reacted favorably to the oral arguments. On Feb. 4, 1931, he wrote to McCormick expressing the view that the case seemed to be won but also complaining that, for him, the victory would be a Pyrrhic one because he was jobless and broke.[220] Near had been working off and on for a paper called the *Beacon* and, in April 1930, was acquitted of criminal libel charges stemming from his reporting there.[221] Now, he wanted McCormick to "underwrite the Saturday Press for a few months" and help Near turn it into a "national publication with wide influence and certain financial success."[222] McCormick apparently ignored him.

It is far from clear, however, why Near was so confident that the case would be won. From the oral arguments, he could be reasonably certain of support from Justices Brandeis and Holmes and probably Harlan Fiske Stone. He could also be sure that Justice Butler would vote the other way, and probably carry the other three conservatives: Willis Van Devanter, James McReynolds, and George Sutherland – who came to be known as the "four horsemen."[223] The other votes, however, were not so easily predicted.

Less than a year earlier, on March 8, 1930, then-Chief Justice (and former president) William Howard Taft (who had resigned a month earlier) and Associate Justice Edward T. Sanford died within five hours of each other. Had they not left the Court when they did, *Near v. Minnesota* might well have gone the other way.[224] As it was, the new appointees, Chief Justice Charles Evans Hughes and Owen J. Roberts, were no sure bets, but both were more liberal than the men they replaced, and Roberts would eventually provide "the switch in time that saved nine" – putting an end to President Roosevelt's so-called "court-packing" scheme.[225]

Taft had led a solid six-vote conservative bloc consisting of Butler, Van Devanter, McReynolds, Sutherland, and Sanford. The dissenters were typically Holmes, Brandeis, and Stone.[226] With a few personnel changes, this was essentially the ultra-conservative Court that ruthlessly enforced sedition laws against WWI dissenters and would go on to block Roosevelt's New Deal reforms.

Hughes had been nearing the end of his second term as governor of New York in 1910 when then-President Taft offered him a seat on the Supreme Court upon the death of Justice David J. Brewer.[227] Hughes accepted and served as associate justice until 1916, when he accepted the Republican nomination for the presidency.[228] While on the bench, Hughes earned a reputation as a great liberal, supporting (usually in dissent) the use of state police powers to protect the public health and welfare against the conservative juggernaut that was substantive due process and liberty of contract, and use of the Fourteenth Amendment's equal protection clause to protect blacks and aliens insofar as the times permitted.[229]

Hughes lost the election of 1916 to Woodrow Wilson[230] and practiced law – including waging a campaign in support of five Socialists who had been expelled from the New York State Assembly.[231] In 1918, Hughes was a featured speaker at the ANPA annual banquet.[232] When the Harding administration came into power in 1921, Hughes became Secretary of State, but he resigned from the Cabinet in 1925. Returning to the practice of law, Hughes also served on international tribunals from 1926 to 1930.[233] When Taft retired as Chief Justice because of ill health, President Hoover immediately nominated Hughes to succeed him.[234] Despite his liberal record on the Court, Hughes was vigorously opposed by Senate progressives and populists, but in the end, Hoover's allies prevailed 52-26.[235] Hughes assumed the office of Chief Justice on Feb. 24, 1930, and retained the position until his retirement in 1941.[236]

Roberts had been a successful corporate lawyer and taught at the University of Pennsylvania Law School. He had not been very active politically, although he had served the government in the Teapot Dome cases, and his views were not very well known. He was not, in fact, Hoover's first choice to succeed Sanford. But Judge John J. Parker, whose name was first submitted, was rejected by the Senate for his having voted to uphold "yellow dog" contracts while a U.S.

Circuit Court judge.[237] Roberts joined the Court in June 1930, and the *Near v. Minnesota* Court was complete.

D. "The Essence of Censorship"

The decision was announced on June 1, 1931, with Hughes, Roberts, Holmes (who would retire the following year), Brandeis, and Stone in the majority, and the "four horsemen" – Butler, McReynolds, Sutherland, and Van Devanter – in dissent.

Hughes began his opinion with an unadorned description of the state nuisance statute under which Near was enjoined and which, by the end of the opinion, Hughes would declare unconstitutional.[238] Hughes quoted directly from the first section of the act, which provides for the abatement of "obscene, lewd and lascivious" or "malicious, scandalous and defamatory" publications and establishes the defense of "truth . . . published with good motives and for justifiable ends."[239] He paraphrased the second and third sections, which outline the act's enforcement procedures and the penalty for violation of not more than $1,000 or one year in the county jail.[240]

Hughes next began a chronology of the case against Near with a description of the complaint and its principal allegations.[241] His recitation was remarkably dry, considering that it encompassed a number of very colorful articles, which are extensively quoted in the dissenting opinion. Drier still were the procedural details that followed, even though the route from temporary injunction to final appeal included two trips to the Minnesota Supreme Court, which twice affirmed the statute's constitutionality. Nothing in the early paragraphs of the opinion betrayed the direction Hughes's opinion would take, unless it is the absence of any reaction whatsoever to Near's outrageous brand of journalism.

Quite the contrary, Hughes all but ignored the *Saturday Press* as he proceeded to take aim at the Minnesota nuisance act. Calling it "unusual, if not unique," Hughes found that it raised questions of "grave importance" that transcended local concerns.[242] Awkwardly, with a pair of double negatives, he reminded the reader that liberty of the press is safeguarded against infringement by state laws and that state police powers are limited. Noting that liberty of the press is also limited and that states can punish abuses, Hughes finally revealed his analytical direction: "[T]he inquiry is as to the historic conception of the liberty of the press and whether the statute under review violates the essential attributes of that liberty."[243]

Hughes seemed to digress from his historical course to consider assertions from both parties that Near's constitutional challenge was facial, that is, focused on the statute itself, not on its application to the *Saturday Press*. Hughes ignored the fact that this was a peculiar stance for an aggrieved party – though a rational strategic choice where the goal is to shape doctrine – and agreed that the Court's proper concern went beyond any errors of the trial court to the "purpose and effect" of the statute as construed by the state's highest court.[244] Accordingly, he launched into a four-part description of purpose and effect that reads more like an indictment.

First, Hughes wrote, the statute does not redress private wrongs but aims to protect public welfare.[245] Second, the statute targets not merely private libels but also publication of "charges against public officers of corruption, malfeasance in office, or serious neglect of duty."[246] Third, the object of the statute is not punishment, but suppression.[247] And fourth, the statute operates not only to suppress the offending newspaper, but "to put the publisher under an effect of censorship."[248] The words of the statute evoke, not "the historic conception of the liberty of the press," Hughes wrote, but the very conditions that liberty was supposed to ameliorate.[249]

"If we cut through mere details of procedure,"[250] Hughes concluded, public authorities may bring a publisher before a judge for exposing their own dereliction and, unless the publisher proves truth published with good motives and justifiable ends, the newspaper is suppressed and further publication is punishable as contempt. "This is the essence of censorship."[251]

Then, as abruptly as he digressed, Hughes returned to the historical inquiry with Blackstone's classic definition: "The liberty of the press is indeed essential to the nature of a free state; but this consists in laying no *previous* restraints upon publications, and not in freedom from censure for criminal matter when published."[252] Quoting Madison and citing an 1825 Massachusetts case, he asserted that the historical immunity from previous restraints applies to legislative as well as executive action, and to false statements as well as true.[253]

Acknowledging that Blackstone had been criticized, Hughes pointed out that the critics did not object to the prohibition on previous restraints but rejected the presumption that liberty of the press stands for that and nothing more. Defending both civil and criminal libel laws, Hughes brought the analysis back to Jay Near: "For whatever wrong the appellant has committed or may commit, by his publications, the state appropriately affords both public and private redress by its libel laws."[254]

Other critics, Hughes noted, believe the prohibition on previous restraints has been stated too broadly.[255] Hughes agreed, excluding "actual obstruction to its recruiting service or the publication of the sailing dates of transports or the number and location of troops," obscenity, incitement, and speech acts from its purview.[256] But "these limitations are not applicable here," Hughes continued.[257] To the contrary, "[t]he exceptional nature of its limitations places in a strong light the general conception that liberty of the press, historically considered and taken up by the Federal Constitution, has meant, principally although not exclusively, immunity from previous restraints or censorship."[258]

Hughes reinforced the message with additional quotations from Madison and the Massachusetts case, this time emphasizing the value of prior restraints in stifling criticism of public officials.[259] The conviction that such restraints would violate constitutional rights, he said, is evinced by the almost complete absence of any attempts to restrain "publications relating to the malfeasance of public officers" in 150 years.[260] Even where honorable officers are recklessly assaulted, subsequent punishment is the "appropriate remedy, consistent with constitutional privilege."[261]

Turning finally to Minnesota's arguments, Hughes rejected the state's assertion that the statute dealt not with publications per se but rather with the business of publishing defamation. "Characterizing the publication as a business, and the business as a nuisance," he wrote, "does not permit an invasion of the constitutional immunity against restraint."[262] Nor is that immunity lost, he continued, when the alleged official malfeasance would be punishable as crimes.[263]

Hughes found the defense of truth, "published with good motives and for justifiable ends," inadequate to justify the Minnesota statute.[264] Finding such a law constitutionally valid would be to recognize "the authority of the censor against which the constitutional barrier was erected."[265] Equally unavailing is the state's insistence that the statute was designed to preserve the public peace, he wrote, citing an early condemnation of what would come to be called the "heckler's veto" by a New Jersey court.[266] "If the township may prevent the circulation of a newspaper for no reason other than that some of its inhabitants may violently disagree with it . . . there is no limit to what may be prohibited," that court had opined.[267] For all of these reasons, Hughes concluded, the Minnesota statute infringed the liberty of the press guaranteed by the Fourteenth Amendment.[268]

Writing for the four dissenting justices, Associate Justice Pierce Butler accused the majority of giving press freedom "a meaning and a scope not heretofore recognized . . . ."[269] Conceding that the Court had previously interpreted the Fourteenth Amendment to protect press freedom from abridgment by the states, Butler asserted that the *Near* decision imposed an unprecedented restriction on the states.[270]

In contrast to Hughes and both litigants, Butler insisted that the record required the Court to consider the statute, not facially, but as applied to Near's "malicious, scandalous and defamatory" articles.[271] And, in contrast to Hughes's restrained description of the *Saturday Press*, Butler reprinted its virulently anti-Semitic articles verbatim, presumably to facilitate the as-applied analysis.[272]

After retracing the procedural history of the case against Near, Butler began his analysis with the assertion that the statute at issue was enacted as an exercise of the state's police power, that is, for the preserving of the peace and good order. "The publications themselves disclose the need and propriety of the legislation," he wrote, relating some of the unsavory history of Near and Guilford and their criminal journalism.[273] States must be free to "employ all just and appropriate measures" to prevent such abuses, Butler insisted.[274]

Butler quoted Justice Joseph Story's famous treatise on the Constitution for the proposition that the First Amendment is not absolute.[275] Such a supposition, Story had said, is "too wild to be indulged by any rational man."[276] Butler rebutted Hughes's reliance on Blackstone by arguing that the previous restraints against which Blackstone railed were those that "subjected the press to the arbitrary will of an administrative officer," not a judge acting pursuant to duly enacted legislation as the Minnesota statute provides.[277]

Asserting that the existing libel laws were "inadequate effectively to suppress evils resulting from the kind of business" in which Near engaged, Butler concluded that the doctrine against previous restraints, if imposed in cases like Near's, would

> expose[] the peace and good order of every community and the business and private affairs of every individual to the constant and protracted false and malicious assaults of any insolvent publisher who may have purpose and sufficient capacity to contrive and put into effect a scheme or program for oppression, blackmail or extortion.[278]

E. Denouement

By a single vote, Butler's limited view of freedom of the press was relegated to an historical footnote, and the principle that prior restraints are anathema to the Constitution has been a bulwark of the legal system ever since. McCormick was jubilant:

> The decision of Chief Justice Hughes will go down in history as one of the greatest triumphs of free thought. The Minnesota gag law was passed by a crooked legislature to protect criminals in office and supported by a state court as feeble in public spirit as it was weak in legal acumen.
>
> We must not blind ourselves to the fact that subversive forces have gone far in this country when such a statute could be passed by any legislature and upheld by any court, and must be on guard against further encroachments.

> The newspapers of America will realize the responsibilities devolving upon them under this decision and will maintain and increase the high principles which have guided them since the inception of a free press.[279]

The June 2 *Tribune* carried a full banner headline, DECISION ENDS GAG ON PRESS, with a full column on the front page and nearly two full pages inside.[280] The story included the full text of the opinion and dissent, the full text of ANPA's resolution, and an individual photograph of every Supreme Court justice.[281] Favorable reaction was reported from Minnesota Governor Floyd B. Olson[282] and the National Editorial Association, meeting in convention in Atlanta.[283] And, of course, McCormick's statement was run in full, although modestly positioned between the Olson and NEA reaction stories.[284]

Coverage continued on June 3 with the favorable reaction of various members of Congress,[285] an analysis of the recent "liberalization" of the Supreme Court by Washington correspondent Arthur Sears Henning,[286] and an editorial expressing the hope that the decision would "arrest, if it does not end, the efforts to cripple the guarantee of a free press . . . ."[287] More editorials followed.[288]

So did the congratulatory messages. Dewart wired McCormick the day after the decision came down: "Congratulations on the decision of the Supreme Court upholding your contention that the freedom of the press is not a political plaything. Since you did all the work, you deserve all the credit."[289] To *Seattle Times* publisher Col. C.B. Blethen, who had also sent a congratulatory wire on June 2, McCormick wrote: "As a five to four decision, we just squeezed through. If Taft were still occupying Hughes' place, we would have been beaten."[290]

Perhaps the most important message came from ACLU president Roger Baldwin. The ACLU had been an early supporter of the *Near* litigation and, shortly before the decision came down, circulated a pamphlet declaring: "Scandal and Defamation! The Right of Newspapers to Defame/Unique Minnesota law empowers judges to suppress papers by injunction/First such use of judicial power in American history/Chicago Tribune takes the case to the U.S. Supreme Court, where it awaits decision."[291] Baldwin sent the pamphlet "To the Editor" with a cover letter urging editors to comment on the case and "the larger issues of freedom of speech and of the press on which the American Civil Liberties Union bases its activity."[292]

Now Baldwin reminded McCormick of ACLU's early role in the case and expressed "delight[] with the outcome in the Supreme Court, even by so narrow a margin."[293]

> On behalf of our entire Board, our liveliest appreciation of the service you have rendered the cause of a 'free press' in this country by thus backing the appeal. It was a victory by a dangerously narrow margin, but, I have

> no doubt, a victory that is decisive against the abuse of the injunctive process.[294]

McCormick wrote back thanking Baldwin for the letter and condemning the Minnesota legislation as "merely another step in the demolition of private rights. . ."[295]

> If the press had not acted when it did and with substantial unanimity, I am afraid the law would have been enacted in one State after the other and would probably have been held Constitutional first by the State Supreme Courts and afterwards when the law seemed so well established, by the United States Supreme Court.
>
> Let us hope that the Supreme Court decision in this case marks the turning of the tide.[296]

Perhaps McCormick's worst fears were exaggerated, but *Near v. Minnesota* still stands as one of the great landmarks of First Amendment law to this day. Few people – journalists or lawyers – are aware of the vital role that Col. Robert R. McCormick played in shaping the prior restraint doctrine established by that opinion. And fewer still realize that he was instrumental in mobilizing the mainstream press to litigate, not only in their narrow commercial interests, but also in pursuit of their most fundamental rights to gather and publish the news.

Chapter 6 – *Near's* Legacy: The Publishing Cases

The press wasted little time in consolidating the gains of *Near*. If there were any remaining doubts about the incorporation of the First Amendment, the commitment of the national press to constitutional litigation, and the application of free press protection beyond prior restraints, they were quickly put to rest by the unanimous decision in *Grosjean v. American Press Co.*[1] Although *Grosjean* raised a constitutional challenge to a punitive tax on newspapers, its importance extended far beyond mere business matters or even the prior restraint issue in *Near*.

This chapter examines the legacy of *Near*, beginning with a wide variety of prior restraint cases. Then, following a more detailed summary of *Grosjean*, we will survey two other lines of cases – libel and privacy – that demonstrate the overwhelming success of the institutional press in shaping First Amendment doctrine through constitutional litigation – but only with respect to the right to publish without censorship or fear of abusive punishment. The chapter concludes with a preview of the newsgathering cases, which more often than not ended in failure.

A. The Prior Restraint Cases

For the first 35 years after *Near v. Minnesota*, no prior restraint cases related to the news media reached the U.S. Supreme Court. The press had played no role, as litigant or amicus, in prior restraint cases like *Lovell v. City of Griffin*[2] in 1938, in which the Court struck down a local Georgia ordinance prohibiting pamphleteering without a permit, or *Freedman v. Maryland*[3] in 1965, in which the Court so burdened the Maryland State Board of [Motion Picture] Censors that it was effectively eliminated. The year after *Freedman*, however, the first press-related case that did reach the Court was – in form, if not in substance – a subsequent punishment case. The offending material had already been published and the editor arrested. Neither the Court nor amici made a prior restraint argument, and neither even mentioned *Near v. Minnesota*. But for all that, the true gravamen of *Mills v. Alabama*[4] was prior restraint: a state anti-corruption statute that was held to forbid a newspaper, on pain of criminal punishment, from publishing an editorial on election day that advocated a particular outcome, one way or the other. Perhaps the case was so clear to Justice Black, who wrote the opinion for a Court that was unanimous as to the judgment, that no parsing of constitutional doctrine was necessary. "It is difficult to conceive of a more obvious and flagrant abridgment of the constitutionally guaranteed freedom of the press," Black wrote.[5] But throughout the opinion, Black characterized the act as suppressing the press, muzzling the press, silencing the press, and restricting a newspaper editor's freedom to publish. And if the act had not stopped the *Post-Herald* from publishing an election day editorial, it had stopped others. In a separate opinion, Justice Douglas, joined by Justice Brennan, noted that, according to amici Alabama Press Association and Southern Newspaper Publishers Association, editorial comment on election day had been nonexistent in Alabama since enactment.[6] Prior restraint or not, the Court reversed the Alabama Supreme Court and held the act – at least as applied in this case – unconstitutional.

Today, *Mills* might be called a "no brainer"; the next prior restraint case to reach the Supreme Court was anything but. In *New York Times v. United States*,[7] better known as The Pentagon Papers case, the Court was called upon to prevent the *Times* and *The Washington Post* from publishing an analysis of America's involvement in the Vietnam War commissioned by then-Secretary of Defense Robert McNamara.[8] The Pentagon Papers, which were classified "top secret," had been leaked to the newspapers by Daniel Ellsberg, a Rand Corp. analyst who worked on the project before his change of heart regarding the war.[9]

Ellsberg delivered a copy of the secret "History of U.S. Decision-Making Process on Vietnam Policy" to *Times* reporter Neil Sheehan, who spent three months editing documents and writing accompanying stories under highly secret conditions.[10] When first published on June 13, 1971, the Justice Department asked William Rehnquist, the newly appointed assistant attorney general in charge of the Office of Legal Counsel, to evaluate the Nixon administration's options. According to David Rudenstine, Rehnquist, who would later become Chief Justice of the United States, was principally guided by *Near v. Minnesota* and the limited exceptions to its prohibition of prior restraints.[11] Rehnquist advised that the administration could stop the *Times* from publishing additional articles if it could persuade the courts that continued publication threatened national security in the same way that publishing battlefield information – one of *Near*'s explicit exceptions – would do.[12]

When Justice notified the *Times* that it would take legal action if the paper did not suspend publication, *Times* executives, editors, and in-house counsel met to decide whether to comply or not.[13] As soon as the decision was made to proceed with publication, the *Times's* in-house counsel, James Goodale, began assembling a legal team: Yale law professor Alexander Bickel and Wall Street lawyer Floyd Abrams.[14] Assistant U.S. Attorney Michael D. Hess was tapped to present the government's case in the U.S. District Court in Manhattan before Judge Murray Gurfein, an experienced attorney, newly appointed to the bench, hearing his very first case as a judge.[15]

Gurfein granted the government a temporary restraining order on Tuesday, June 15,[16] and scheduled a public hearing for Friday, June 18.[17] In the meantime, *The Washington Post* had obtained a copy of the documents from Ellsberg and published its first story on that same Friday morning.[18] That afternoon, the government asked the U.S. District Court in Washington, D.C., to restrain the *Post* from further publication, but Judge Gerhard A. Gesell refused.[19] Later that night,

Gesell was reversed by a panel of three judges on the U.S. Court of Appeals for the D.C. Circuit. The court remanded the case to Gesell to give the government an opportunity to substantiate its claim that publication would threaten national security.[20] Judge J. Skelly Wright dissented. "This is a sad day for America," Wright wrote. "Today, for the first time in the 200 years of our history, the executive department has succeeded in stopping the presses. It has enlisted the judiciary in the suppression of our most precious freedom."[21]

In New York, however, Gurfein would reach the opposite conclusion. On Saturday, June 19, he dissolved the temporary restraining order and denied the government's motion for an injunction. Relying heavily on *Near* for his First Amendment rationale, Gurfein wrote:

> The security of the nation is not at the ramparts alone. Security also lies in the value of our free institutions. A cantankerous press, an obstinate press, a ubiquitous press must be suffered by those in authority in order to preserve the even greater values of freedom of expression and the right of the people to know.[22]

The government appealed immediately to the U.S. Court of Appeals for the Second Circuit, which stayed Gurfein's order until June 21, then reversed on a 5-3 vote on Tuesday, June 22. [23] The Second Circuit continued the restraining order and remanded the case to Gurfein to determine whether any of the documents "pose such grave and immediate danger to the security of the United States as to warrant their publication being enjoined."[24]

In Washington, Gesell had convened a second hearing on June 21 and announced his decision later that afternoon. Declaring that the government had failed to prove that publication would harm national security in any of the particulars that the government had claimed, Gesell denied injunctive relief.[25] This time, Gesell's decision was affirmed on a 7-2 vote by the D.C. Circuit in a per curiam opinion on June 23.[26] The case was ready to proceed to the United States Supreme Court.

The *Times* petitioned for a writ of certiorari on Thursday, June 24, as well as an emergency petition with Justice John M. Harlan, who was circuit justice for the second circuit, both seeking to reverse the court of appeals' order for a new hearing before Judge Gurfein. The government also sought Supreme Court review to reverse the D.C. Circuit's decision in favor of the *Post*. The following day, the Supreme Court granted both petitions and set oral argument for Saturday, but barred both newspapers from publishing any further material from the Papers.[27]

In the Supreme Court, Bickel argued the case for the *Times*, William Glendon of Royall, Koegell, and Wells, for the *Post*, and Solicitor General Erwin N. Griswold for the United States. Amicus briefs were filed by the American Civil

Liberties Union, the National Emergency Civil Liberties Committee, and First Amendment Scholar Thomas I. Emerson for 27 members of Congress who supported the *Times*. There were no briefs from other members of the press or its associations, although the Reporters Committee for Freedom of the Press – which would become one of the industry's principal litigators in years to come – had been organized the previous year.[28]

Citing *Near* and two other cases, the Supreme Court issued a brief per curiam opinion, holding that

> 'Any system of prior restraints of expression comes to this Court bearing a heavy presumption against its constitutional validity.' The Government 'thus carries a heavy burden of showing justification for the imposition of such a restraint.' The District Court for the Southern District of New York in the *New York Times*case and the District Court for the District of Columbia and the Court of Appeals for the District of Columbia Circuit in the *Washington Post* case held that the Government had not met that burden. We agree.[29]

Six justices joined the opinion; three dissented. Astoundingly, the justices wrote nine separate opinions in the case, ranging from the absolutist positions of Justices Hugo Black and William Douglas – who declared that "[e]very moment's continuance of the injunctions against these newspapers amounts to a flagrant, indefensible, and continuing violation of the First Amendment"[30] – to the outrage of Justice Harry A. Blackmun – who warned the newspapers that "the nation's people will know where the responsibility... rests" for the dire consequences predicted by the government if publication were allowed to continue.[31]

Near v. Minnesota was cited in every significant argument and every significant opinion in the Pentagon Papers case. Most of the judges who heard the case agreed that the government had failed to meet the standard for prior restraint established by *Near*, but none could say exactly what that standard was. How close to "actual obstruction to its recruiting service or the publication of the sailing dates of transports or the number and location of troops" does classified, national security information have to come before falling within the *Near* exception? After the Pentagon Papers case, we know only that historical analysis is not close enough.

Throughout his chronicle of the case, Rudenstine faults the government for seeking to resolve the case on the broadest possible terms, that is, as near as possible to a blanket proscription against publishing classified information – regardless of the true dimensions of the threat.[32] The government got nothing for its efforts; the press won a smashing reaffirmation of the Constitution's disapproval of prior restraints, with the bar now set at a very high level: classified government secrets, leaked to the press in colorable violation of federal law,[33] could not, without more particularized evidence of the threat, be suppressed by injunction.

The case also made bona fide media defense bar stars of James Goodale and Floyd Abrams, both of whom would continue to influence cases for decades.[34] By the time the next important prior restraint case reached the Supreme Court five years after the Pentagon Papers case, the media defense bar would be well prepared to participate. Much of that development would occur in the wake of the 1972 case of *Branzburg v. Hayes*,[35] the principal focus of Chapter 6, so the difference in that regard between the Pentagon Papers case in 1971 and *Nebraska Press Association v. Stuart*[36] in 1976 is striking.

Ironically, it was the press that sought a blanket rule on prior restraints in *Nebraska Press* – a kind of mirror image of the blanket rule sought by the government in Pentagon Papers. The Court did not oblige, but gave the press a powerful victory that remains in force to this day.

The case began on Oct. 19, 1975, when a sociopath named Erwin Charles Simants killed six members of the Henry Kellie family in Sutherland, Neb., then confessed to anyone who would listen.[37] The crimes, which included the rape of a ten-year-old girl, was widely publicized by the local media in Sutherland, a town of 840 people, as well as statewide and national media. Simants was arraigned in Lincoln County court in North Platte, population 24,000, and both the defense and prosecution asked the court to restrict what could be reported about the preliminary hearing in view of the intense coverage.[38] Judge Ronald Ruff called a hearing for the evening of Tuesday, Oct. 21, to consider the request and invited representatives of the local media to attend,[39] without revealing the existence of the formal motion to restrict reporting.[40]

Scherer recounts at some length how the local media mobilized in response to Ruff's invitation and the suggestion that he might restrict their reporting. Two of the media representatives contacted, G. Woodson Howe, executive assistant to the president of the *Omaha World-Herald*, and Joe R. Seacrest, editor of the *Lincoln Journal*, were members of the Nebraska Joint Press/Bar Committee on Free Press/Fair Trial. That group had been formed some years before by the Nebraska State Bar Association and the Nebraska Press Association. Howe and Seacrest were also active in Media of Nebraska, a lobbying organization that represented print and broadcast outlets throughout the state. According to Scherer, Media of Nebraska would become the primary conduit for the collection and distribution of funding for the litigation that would ensue.[41] The group's first order of business was retaining North Platte attorney Harold Kay to represent the media at Ruff's hearing that night.[42]

Kay was instructed to oppose any sort of gag order on coverage of the preliminary hearing and, failing that, to seek more time to prepare a case against such an order. In the meantime, he was to assure the judge that the press would voluntarily comply with the "Nebraska Bar-Press Guidelines for Disclosure and Reporting of Information Relating to Imminent or Pending Criminal Litigation," established in 1970 to deal with free press/fair trial issues. Among other things, the guidelines provided that reporting the existence of a confession was inappropriate.[43]

The following morning, Wednesday, Oct. 22, just before the preliminary hearing was set to begin, Ruff issued his ruling: the press would be prohibited from publishing any testimony or evidence adduced at the hearing or anything else about the case "other than as set forth in" the guidelines – effectively making the voluntary guidelines mandatory.[44]

Even as the preliminary hearing proceeded, the press was debating their options. On Thursday, Oct. 23, the Nebraska Press Association, along with the Nebraska Broadcasters Association, members of both organizations and the two wire services, Associated Press and United Press International, applied to be heard in Lincoln County District Court, a higher court also in North Platte, regarding Ruff's order.[45] Judge Hugh Stuart, who had been assigned to preside over Simants's trial, convened a hearing that night, but Omaha attorney Stephen McGill, who joined in Kay in representing the press before Judge Stuart, made a tactical error in arguing that he would rather let a guilty defendant go free than "deny freedom of speech."[46]

Three days later, on Oct. 27, Stuart issued an opinion finding a clear and present danger to Simants' right to a fair trial from pretrial publicity, that is, publicity about the proceedings before a jury could be empaneled. He terminated the Ruff order and substituting his own, explicitly adopting the voluntary guidelines as a formal court order, and specifically barring the press from reporting essentially all of Simants's inculpatory statements and any detail regarding the sexual assaults. The press was permitted to report the existence of the gag order, but not its substance.[47] For days later, on Oct. 31, the press filed notice of appeal to the Nebraska Supreme Court and petitioned that court for a writ of mandamus rescinding the gag order.[48]

The state supreme court, however, was in no rush to take the case and told the media lawyers that it would not even consider their documents until Dec. 1. On Nov. 5, the lawyers filed an emergency application for a stay of Stuart's order to the U.S. Supreme Court.[49] Justice Blackmun was circuit justice for the Eighth Circuit, however, and he had famously dissented in the Pentagon Papers case. Following an unusually rancorous exchange of orders between Washington and Lincoln, Blackmun issued a partial stay of Stuart's gag order on Nov. 20.[50] Blackmun rejected the application of the press-bar guidelines, but retained Stuart's prohibition on publishing Simants's confession and other inculpatory statements.[51] The following day, the media lawyers asked the entire U.S. Supreme Court to vacate so much of Blackmun's order as would prohibit publication of information learned in open court or from public records.[52]

In Lincoln, meanwhile, the Nebraska Supreme Court heard arguments in the appeal on Nov. 25, and five days later, on Dec. 1, issued its own version of the gag order. Focusing on dicta in *Branzburg v. Hayes* to the effect that reporters "may be prohibited from attending or publishing information about trials" if necessary to ensure a fair trial, the court prohibited publication of Simants's confessions to law enforcement, his "admissions against interest," and "other information strongly implicative of the accused as the perpetrator of the slayings"[53] – whatever that meant.

As Blackmun's order expired on its own terms as soon as the Nebraska Supreme Court acted, the media lawyers, McGill and James L. Koley, filed an application with the U.S. Supreme Court to stay the Nebraska gag order and asked the Court to treat all previously filed papers as a petition for certiorari.[54] After a brief delay, the Court granted certiorari on Dec. 12, although it denied the media's request for a stay or expedited consideration.[55] As a result, there would be no decision until Simants's trial was over; the gag order would remain in effect until a jury was empanelled.[56]

To present the case before the Supreme Court, the Nebraska Press Association had retained E. Barrett Prettyman, Jr., an experienced Supreme Court litigator who was already involved in this case through amicus curiae Reporters Committee for Freedom of the Press (RCFP). Within days of Ruff's original gag order, RCFP – now five years old – had sent a lawyer, Larry Simms, to Omaha to work with the media lawyers there.[57] RCFP initially hired Prettyman to write its amicus brief to the high court, but it made more sense for him to serve as co-counsel with McGill and Koley. Prettyman would present the oral arguments for the Nebraska press, with Floyd Abrams arguing for the National Broadcasting Co. and the 60 or so national media organizations that filed amicus briefs in the case.[58] Although Abrams had worked on the Pentagon Papers case, this would be his first oral argument before the Supreme Court.[59] Seven amicus briefs were filed, representing the ACLU and groups of media organizations led by ANPA, RCFP, The Tribune Co., The Washington Post Co., and the National Press Club.[60] All of the amicus briefs supported the press, although Solicitor General Erwin Griswold joined the brief for the state of Nebraska.

Notwithstanding the apparent unanimity of the press at this stage of the proceedings, RCFP was criticized for its aggressive role in the *Nebraska Press* case by none other than Fred Friendly, who would become the leading chronicler of *Near v. Minnesota*.[61] Friendly, who had been with Edward R. Murrow at CBS and was then teaching at Columbia University and a consultant for the Ford Foundation, called for "reasonable people to work out differences" that had resulted in the gag order.[62] With Ford support, Friendly had launched a series of television broadcasts about media cases that emphasized mediation and compromise, putting him at odds with the "absolutist" approach of RCFP Executive Director Jack Landau and others in the organization. Floyd McKay points out that the conflict between Friendly's neutrality and RCFP's strident support for the press cost the organization Ford Foundation funding in the mid-1970s.[63]

There are several accounts of the Court's deliberations in the *Nebraska Press* case,[64] and they differ in several particulars. Scherer says all of the justices thought the Nebraska gag order was unconstitutional;[65] Woodward and Armstrong say Justice Rehnquist initially disagreed.[66] At least three justices – Brennan, Stewart and Marshall – and perhaps five – Stevens and White – initially supported the press position that all gag orders restricting reports of criminal proceedings should be held impermissible under the First Amendment.[67] But Chief Justice Burger was adamant that the Court should not issue a blanket declaration that all gag orders were per se unconstitutional.[68] Blackmun, Rehnquist and Powell supported the Chief, who had assigned the opinion to himself. Ultimately, White gave Burger the fifth vote, while Stevens concurred in the judgment only.[69]

Even though the press did not get the blanket ruling they sought, the test that Burger's opinion established for gag orders has proved to be adequate to prevent such a case from ever reaching the Supreme Court again. To begin, Burger borrowed a formulation of the "clear and present danger" test applied by Judge Learned Hand in the *Dennis v. United States*: "whether the gravity of the evil, discounted by its improbability, justifies such invasion of free speech as is necessary to avoid the danger."[70] Then he translated that formula into a three-factor analysis that lower courts must follow before issuing a gag order. Specifically, he said, a court must consider in express findings the nature and extent of pretrial news coverage; whether other measures would be likely to mitigate the effects of unrestrained pretrial publicity; and how effectively a restraining order would operate to prevent the threatened danger.[71] While the prohibition was not absolute, no trial court has been able to meet that test.

Simants, incidentally, was convicted, but his conviction was overturned because a sheriff improperly fraternized with the sequestered jury;[72] on retrial, he was found not guilty by reason of insanity.[73]

If *Nebraska Press* was the last "classic" prior restraint case involving the press to reach the Court, there have been others that arguably involved prior restraints. For example, the Court refused to prohibit a reporter from publishing his own secret grand jury testimony after the grand jury's term had ended, despite a state law to the contrary.[74] More recently, and much more significantly, the Court struck down Federal Election Commission regulations that restricted certain campaign expenditures on the ground that they essentially restricted free speech in the controversial *Citizens United v. FEC.*[75] With the support of some press amici,[76] particularly broadcasters, Justice Kennedy cited *Near v. Minnesota* to liken the rules to a prior restraint.

> This regulatory scheme may not be a prior restraint on speech in the strict sense of that term, for

> prospective speakers are not compelled by law to seek an advisory opinion from the FEC before the speech takes place. As a practical matter, however, given the complexity of the regulations and the deference courts show to administrative determinations, a speaker who wants to avoid threats of criminal liability and the heavy costs of defending against FEC enforcement must ask a governmental agency for prior permission to speak. These onerous restrictions thus function as the equivalent of prior restraint by giving the FEC power analogous to licensing laws implemented in 16th- and 17th-century England, laws and governmental practices of the sort that the First Amendment was drawn to prohibit. Because the FEC's "business is to censor, there inheres the danger that [it] may well be less responsive than a court – part of an independent branch of government-to the constitutionally protected interests in free expression." When the FEC issues advisory opinions that prohibit speech, "[m]any persons, rather than undertake the considerable burden (and sometimes risk) of vindicating their rights through case-by-case litigation, will choose simply to abstain from protected speech-harming not only themselves but society as a whole, which is deprived of an uninhibited marketplace of ideas." Consequently, "the censor's determination may in practice be final." [citations omitted][77]

On the other hand, the Court prohibited a newspaper from publishing confidential information it received through the discovery process, although it conceded that the same information was fair game if acquired through conventional reporting.[78] The Court also upheld the authority of Congress to prohibit the press from publishing color reproductions of U.S. currency,[79] and it permitted a high school principal to censor articles on pregnancy and divorce, where the student newspaper involved was part of the journalism curriculum.[80]

Prior restraint may also be implicated in so-called "compelled speech" cases. For example, the Court struck down a state statute giving candidates a right of reply to adverse newspaper editorials at least partly because such "compelled speech" would constrain the paper from publishing what it wanted to publish.[81] Broadcasting, however, was – and continues to be – treated differently. The Court had previously upheld a federal regulation requiring the same kind of right of reply with respect to radio and television stations, and would later uphold a federal statute requiring broadcasters to sell airtime to candidates for federal office.[82]

However, the Court also held that broadcasters could not be required to accept paid issue advertising if they chose not to as a matter of policy,[83] and it struck down an FCC rule prohibiting public broadcasting stations from editorializing.[84]

The role of press amici in the "right of reply" cases is worth further examination here. In *Red Lion Broadcasting Co. v. Federal Communications Commission,* [85] the broadcast "right of reply" case, the Court reviewed and affirmed an FCC decision requiring a Pennsylvania broadcaster to give an author free airtime to respond to accusations of communist tendencies in a syndicated broadcast under a policy known as the "Fairness Doctrine." At the same time, it heard a constitutional challenge to the rules by the Radio and Television News Directors Association (RTNDA), which had been successful in the U.S. Court of Appeals for the Seventh Circuit.[86] CBS and NBC filed separate briefs as joint respondents with the RTNDA, but the ACLU, the AFL-CIO, and a coalition of religious organizations filed amicus briefs supporting the right of reply.[87] There was no participation by the print media in either case. When their ox was being gored in *Miami Herald Publishing Co. v. Tornillo,* [88] however, the print press came out in force to oppose Florida's newspaper "right of reply" statute, supported by the broadcasters and the ACLU. [89] To be completely fair, the press's inclination and ability generally to mobilize for litigation had grown exponentially between 1969 and 1974, but there is no question that the print and broadcast industries did not always see their interests as identical.[90]

In all of these cases, as in *Near v. Minnesota*, the government tried to prevent the press – directly or indirectly – from publishing. That the press succeeded in defeating these efforts more often than not is a testament to the legacy of *Near* and the efforts of Col. McCormick and those journalists and lawyers who followed his example. But success in these cases also reflects the disfavor with which courts have viewed prior restraint cases since Blackstone.[91] To see how the legacy of *Near* extended constitutional protection beyond prior restraints and into the realm of subsequent punishment – conceding that those categories are fluid at the margins – we have to return to the 1930s.

B. The Bridge to Subsequent Punishment: *Grosjean v. American Press*

Louisiana Gov. Huey Long's first attempt to stifle the newspapers that opposed his absolute control over Louisiana politics occurred two years after his election and one year before *Near* was decided by the U. S. Supreme Court. In June 1930, Long had two bills introduced in state legislature: one, similar to the Minnesota "gag law," permitted courts to enjoin the publication of any newspaper deemed "malicious, scandalous, or defamatory" by the government or private individuals; the other imposed a fifteen percent tax on the newspapers' gross advertising revenues.[92] With McCormick's committee leading the national response,[93] ANPA denounced the bills as "the boldest and most flagrant measures ever aimed at the freedom of American newspapers."[94]

Both bills died in committee;[95] the gag law could never be resurrected after the *Near* decision, but the tax bill was not a classic prior restraint of the sort *Near* held unconstitutional and would resurface in 1934. Long was then U.S. Senator, but his animosity toward the opposition press in Louisiana was undiminished, and he took the necessary steps to restore his power in the state legislature.[96] The Long forces introduced a bill imposing a two percent "license tax" on the gross advertising receipts of newspapers with 20,000 weekly circulation or greater, [97] affecting only the New Orleans and Shreveport dailies that were most outspoken in their opposition to the Long machine.[98] Final passage occurred on July 9, with Long standing inside the rail on the house floor exhorting his supporters to "Vote yes."[99]

Both the Louisiana Press Association and the ANPA condemned the tax, with *Editor & Publisher* calling for carrying the case all the way to the U.S. Supreme Court if necessary.[100] The affected dailies began coordinating their legal efforts as soon as the tax became law, retaining a battery of prominent lawyers to plan strategy.[101] Eberhard P. Deutch, who represented the New Orleans *Item-Tribune* crafted the First Amendment argument, relying heavily on *Near* as "the leading decision in the country, if not the world, on freedom of the press."

> [I]ts general language is so enlightening on the general principle of the freedom of the press, that it cannot help but have an important bearing on the decision in the instant case, since it holds, in effect, that any slight infringement, direct or indirect, of the freedom of the press will invalidate legislation.... [There] can be no proper discussion of any point involving the freedom of the press without including the foregoing decision.[102]

Although Deutsch overstated *Near's* import somewhat, he correctly identified its indispensability to the First Amendment argument. Perhaps even more important in the end was Deutsch's historical analysis of the use of taxation as a mechanism for control, culminating in the quotation from Chief Justice Marshall that "the power to tax is the power to destroy."[103] But Deutsch was overruled by the legal strategists, who determined that their best hope of victory lay in a provision of the Louisiana Constitution prohibiting discrimination in taxation, supported by the Equal Protection Clause of the Fourteenth Amendment to the U.S. Constitution.[104] The majority of lawyers felt *Near* was just not a strong enough precedent, but they agreed to let Deutsch develop his case further.

Significantly, Deutsch enlisted the help of ANPA and its general counsel, Elisha Hanson, in addition to several ANPA members and schools of journalism.[105] Hanson was originally retained as the Washington representative of the association in 1923 by the ANPA Committee on Federal Laws.[106] Hanson had been a Washington correspondent for the *Chicago Tribune* from 1913 to 1917, and secretary to Sen. Medill McCormick from 1917 to 1922, and, according to Emery, would come to "eclipse" Col. McCormick as "the leading exponent of freedom of the press" in his capacity as ANPA general counsel.[107] With the additional research and staff support, Deutsch persuaded his fellow Louisiana lawyers to pursue both the discrimination and press freedom issues in court.[108]

Given the improbability of a fair shake in state court, the newspapers brought their lawsuit before a three-judge district court of the type established by Congress in 1910 to hear constitutional challenges of state law.[109] The suit was styled American Press Co., a fairly neutral newspaper that Long said he would not have taxed if he could have found a way to avoid it,[110] versus Alice Lee Grosjean, Louisiana Supervisor of Public Accounts and, supposedly, Long's mistress.[111] The court issued a temporary restraining order to prevent the collection of taxes before the case could be heard[112] and scheduled a hearing for the fall.[113]

The state had outlined its case in a motion to dismiss that focused on the court's lack of jurisdiction and denied the tax was impermissibly discriminatory. Cortner points out that Charles J. Rivet, serving as a special assistant attorney general for the case, failed to mention the press freedom issue because he was unaware that *Near* had applied the First Amendment guarantees to strike down a state law.[114] The newspapers had all submitted affidavits to the courts on the discrimination issue, while affidavits of ANPA president Howard Davis of the *New York Herald Tribune* and Dean Carl. W. Ackerman of Columbia University School of Journalism concentrated on the First Amendment issue.[115]

At the Nov. 23 hearing, Rivet argued for the state; Deutsch and Esmond Phelps of the *New Orleans Times-Picayune* argued for the newspapers, with Hanson in attendance. On March 22, 1935, the court announced a decision that found for the newspapers on the discrimination issue alone.[116] Fortunately for the newspapers, the state appealed the decision to the United States Supreme Court, rather than merely amending the statute to remove the discriminatory effect.[117] Long was assassinated on Sept. 8, 1935, before the Supreme Court could hear the case, but Rivet proceeded with the case for the state.[118] Hanson, rather than Deutsch, joined Phelps to argue for the newspapers.[119]

The oral arguments proceeded along the same lines as those before the district court, and the justices were about to rule on the same ground. Sutherland wrote a majority opinion, but, according to Cortner, a concurring opinion by Benjamin Cardozo on First Amendment grounds, was so persuasive that Sutherland redrafted his opinion to incorporate most of Cardozo's language. The decision was unanimous.

After rejecting Rivet's procedural arguments, Sutherland turned to the constitutional questions.[120] Calling the First Amendment issue a "question of the utmost gravity and importance," Sutherland reaffirmed *Near's* holding on incorporation.[121] He then went into a lengthy exegesis on the history of repression through licensing and taxing the press, embodying much of Deutsch's research on those subjects.[122] Based on the framers' knowledge of that history, Sutherland said it was clear that that First and Fourteenth Amendments were meant to preclude government from adopting any form of previous restraint such as that "effected by these two well-known and odious methods."[123]

While the press is subject to ordinary forms of taxation, this was not an ordinary form of tax, "but one single in kind, with a long history of hostile misuse against the freedom of the press." The Louisiana tax, he said, is a "deliberate and calculated device in the guise of a tax to limit the circulation of information to which the public is entitled by virtue of the constitutional guaranties."[124] Finding the tax thus unconstitutional because it abridged the freedom of the press, the Court saw no reason to consider the discrimination claim.[125]

Sutherland's opinion in *Grosjean* was a complete victory for the institutional press as constitutional litigator. Its direct legacy was the 1983 case of *Minneapolis Star & Tribune Co. v. Minnesota Commissioner of Revenue*,[126] in which the Court held that a use tax on newsprint and ink violated the First Amendment simply because it singled out the press for special treatment. Unlike *Grosjean*, there was no hint of a "any impermissible or censorial motive on the part of the legislature" in the Minnesota case.[127] Knight-Ridder Newspapers and ANPA supported the publisher with amicus briefs, as did the ACLU and local civil liberties groups.[128]

The Court reached a similar conclusion four years later in *Arkansas Writers' Project, Inc. v. Ragland*,[129] striking down an Arkansas tax scheme that exempted some members of the press, but not others, based on their content. There were no amicus briefs supporting the petitioner, although a number of state governments filed briefs supporting Arkansas.[130] In 1991, however, the cable television industry protested another Arkansas tax that discriminated among media, without reference to content, but the Supreme Court rejected cable's arguments.[131]

But *Grosjean's* legacy is hardly limited to tax cases. *Grosjean* boldly took First Amendment doctrine through the door that *Near* had left open when it defined liberty of the press as "principally *although not exclusively*, immunity from previous restraints or censorship."[132]

> It is impossible to concede that by the words "freedom of the press" the framers of the amendment intended to adopt merely the narrow view then reflected by the law of England that such freedom consisted only in immunity from previous censorship; for this abuse had then permanently disappeared from English practice. …
>
> Judge Cooley has laid down the test to be applied – "The evils to be prevented were not the censorship of the press merely,

> but any action of the government by means of which it might prevent such free and general discussion of public matters as seems absolutely essential to prepare the people for an intelligent exercise of their rights as citizens..."[133]

In the next two sections, we will see how the press's constitutional litigators used that doctrine successfully to win the majority of contempt, libel and privacy cases that reached the United States Supreme Court.

C. The Contempt Cases

The earliest evidence of a dramatic change in the Supreme Court's attitude toward the First Amendment guarantees in subsequent punishment cases can be found by examining the "contempt by publication" cases that reached the Court before and after *Near*. *Near* itself was not the instrument of that change; indeed, Chief Justice Hughes acknowledged the validity of "contempt by publication" in his opinion.[134] But *Near's* conclusive recognition of incorporation and its assertion that freedom of the press is broader under the Constitution than under the common law[135] certainly contributed to the philosophical swing.

According to Blackstone, "the method, immemorially used by the superior courts of justice, of punishing contempts by attachment" included the power to punish "speaking or writing contemptuously of the court or judges acting in their judicial capacity."[136] Although, as Gleason points out, legal historians have found no sound basis for that assertion in earlier case law, contempt by publication was well established by the nineteenth century.[137]

In simplest terms, contempt by publication is a crime that is committed by criticizing a judge in a pending judicial proceeding in a manner the judge finds to be calculated to embarrass, hinder, or obstruct the court in the administration of justice or otherwise reduce its authority or dignity. This use of the contempt power was called "constructive" or "consequential" contempt, rather than "direct" contempt, because the contemptible act took place outside of the courtroom.[138]

In 1831, a striking abuse of the contempt power prompted Congress to enact a statute to remove the power of constructive contempt from federal judges by restricting the contempt power to acts "in the presence of the said courts, or so near thereto as to obstruct the administration of justice."[139] Gleason notes that, in the first half of the nineteenth century, judges' use of the contempt power was also held in check by three factors: the tradition of freedom of the press, a widespread distrust of judges and lawyers, and the threat of the power of the press.[140]

Most of the states also enacted statutes restricting contempt, with 23 of the 30 states adopting such acts by 1860,[141] and 34 of 45 by the end of the century.[142] Judges, however, often ignored those statutes as contrary to their inherent powers or interpreted them so narrowly as to be meaningless. After the Civil War, judges used the contempt power with increasing frequency against newspapers; by the end of the century, courts in seventeen states had reasserted the power to punish contempt by publication.[143]

In 1907, the Supreme Court heard *Patterson v. Colorado*,[144] the first contempt-by-publication case to reach that court. The alleged contempt was the publication of articles and a cartoon that purportedly "reflected upon the motives and conduct of the Supreme Court of Colorado in cases still pending and were intended to embarrass the court in the impartial administration of justice."[145] Attorneys for the publisher raised the common law privilege of fair comment and charged the court with ignoring the state contempt statute.[146] They also claimed a right under both the U.S. and Colorado Constitutions to prove that the allegations in the articles were true.[147] Attorneys for the state denied the authority of the legislature to limit the inherent power of the court and denied the authority of the U.S. Supreme Court even to review the decision.[148]

The state also argued:

> While freedom of the press, like that of freedom of speech, is necessary to the perpetuation of a republican form of government, this does not mean that either can be carried to such an extreme as to impede, embarrass, or unjustly influence the due and orderly administration of justice, or prejudice the rights of litigants in pending cases, for the latter would more surely impair the existence of our government than the former.[149]

Justice Oliver Wendell Holmes, writing the opinion of the court and dismissing the publisher's writ of error for lack of jurisdiction, declined to decide whether the First Amendment had been incorporated through the Fourteenth, but indicated that it would make no difference in this case. The main purpose of the constitutional provisions on freedom of speech and the press, he said, is "to prevent... previous restraints upon publication... and they do not prevent the subsequent punishment of such as may be deemed contrary to the public welfare."[150] Moreover, Holmes said, freedom from prior restraint extends "as well to the false as to the true; the subsequent punishment may extend as well to the true as to the false."[151] Writing in dissent, Justice John Marshall Harlan reiterated the incorporation argument he had made in 1897;[152] Justice Brewer would have found jurisdiction on other grounds and considered the merits.[153]

More than a decade later, in 1918, the Court granted certiorari to review a contempt conviction against the Toledo Newspaper Co. and the editor of its Toledo *News-Bee* for criticizing a federal district court's handling of a dispute involving street cars.[154] The U.S. Court of Appeals for the Sixth Circuit affirmed the lower court's decision, and the U.S. Supreme Court affirmed in turn. Chief Justice Edward D. White wrote that the 1831 act's requirement that the contemptuous behavior occur "so near" the court as to obstruct justice did not actually change the prevailing law and was thus satisfied by conduct having a tendency to obstruct the discharge of the court's duty, wherever it occurred.[155]

As to the publisher's argument that the articles in question were immune from liability for contempt because, as matters of public concern, they were protected by freedom of the press, White wrote that the argument itself contains the

> contention that the freedom of the press is the freedom to do wrong with impunity and implies the right to frustrate and defeat the discharge of those governmental duties upon the performance of which the freedom of all, including that of the press, depends. The safeguarding and fructification of free and constitutional institutions is the very basis and mainstay upon which the freedom of the press rests, and that freedom, therefore, does not and cannot be held to include the right virtually to destroy such institutions. It suffices to say that, however complete is the right of the press to state public things and discuss them, that right, as every other right enjoyed in human society, is subject to the restraints which separate right from wrong-doing.[156]

Holmes dissented on factual grounds; Brandeis concurred in Holmes's opinion.[157]

Twenty-three years went by before the next contempt by publication case reached the Supreme Court, and the Court's approach to the First Amendment had changed utterly. The change had begun with the World War I era sedition cases and the emergence of the "clear and present danger" standard in the great Holmes and Brandeis dissents.[158] *Gitlow* and *Near* had conclusively settled the incorporation question,[159] and *Grosjean* showed that the Court would no longer view freedom of the press as a mere prohibition of prior restraints.[160] In addition, the press itself had become active in First Amendment litigation.

In April 1941, the Court overruled White's holding in *Toledo Newspaper Co.*; the language "so near thereto" in the federal contempt statute would henceforth mean what it said: criminally contemptuous acts had to be in or physically near the courtroom.[161] Although none of the contempt cases to reach the High Court after *Nye* involved the federal statute, the Court applied the principle to the state contempt cases that reached the Court. On Dec. 8, the day after Pearl Harbor was attacked, the Supreme Court announced its decision in *Times-Mirror Co. v. Superior Court* and *Bridges v. California*.[162] With ANPA and the ACLU filing amicus briefs, the press would win that case and the next two, and contempt by publication would cease to be a threat to press freedom.

In *Bridges*, as the consolidated opinion is best known, the U.S. Supreme Court reviewed two contempt convictions on certiorari to the California Supreme Court. The *Los Angeles Times* had been held in contempt for three editorials about a case in progress; labor leader Harry Bridges was held in contempt for a telegram he sent to the Department of Labor regarding a pending case. Both defendants argued that their free expression rights under the First Amendment and Fourteenth Amendments had been violated. Borrowing now established doctrine from the sedition cases, Justice Black wrote for a 5-4 majority that contempt by publication could not be punished absent a "clear and present danger," that is, "the substantive evil must be extremely serious and the degree of imminence extremely high."[163]

The worst of the editorials, Black said, merely threatened future adverse criticism if the court granted probation to two union members jailed for assaulting nonunion truck drivers. The basis for punishing the publication as contempt was its "inherent tendency," said the trial court, or its "reasonable tendency," said the state supreme court, to interfere with the orderly administration of justice. Even if that were the standard, rather than "clear and present danger," Black said, it would be an exaggeration to apply it here. Given the *Times's* hostility to labor unions, such criticism would be expected anyway. [164]

Four years later, in *Pennekamp v. Florida*,[165] a unanimous court reversed the decision of the Florida Supreme Court affirming the contempt conviction of the *Miami Herald* and its associate editor for two editorials and a cartoon criticizing a trial court for being too lenient toward criminals and gambling establishments in three cases that had already been dismissed, although a new indictment had been obtained in one of them and trial was pending. Again, the ACLU filed an amicus brief. This time, however, ANPA's General Counsel, Elisha Hanson, argued the case for the *Herald*, and major newspapers throughout the country – although not *The New York Times* or *The Washington Post* – editorialized in support of the decision despite the crush of war news.[166]

Justice Reed wrote the opinion of the court, which applied the "clear and present danger" standard;[167] Justice Frankfurter, who had dissented in *Bridges*, now concurred in the opinion on factual grounds, while still resisting the standard.[168] Justices Murphy, who accepted the standard, and Rutledge, who seemed to accept it, also wrote separate concurrences.[169] There was no chief justice at the time *Pennekamp* was decided, and Justice Jackson did not participate. But Jackson would render his opinion of the press in no uncertain terms in *Craig v. Harney,*[170] the last of the press-related contempt by publication cases to reach a decision in the U.S. Supreme Court.[171]

In *Craig*, the Court reversed the Texas courts' conviction of the publisher, editorial writer, and reporter of the Corpus Christi *Caller-Times* for criticizing a Texas judge's repeatedly rejecting the jury's verdict in a civil case. Justice William O. Douglas wrote the 6-3 majority opinion, which closely tracked its predecessors, and Murphy's concurrence averred that the First Amendment "outlawed" summary contempt. Frankfurter dissented again, this time joined by Chief Justice Vinson, but it was Justice Robert H Jackson's separate dissent that revealed the growing recognition of the press as an interest group in its own right:

> It is doubtful if the press itself regards judges as so insulated from public opinion. In this very case the American Newspaper Publishers Association filed a brief *amicus curiae* on the merits after we granted certiorari. Of course, it does not cite a single authority that was not available to counsel for the publisher involved, and does not tell us a single new fact except this one: "This membership embraces more than 700 newspaper publishers whose publications represent in excess of eighty per cent of the total daily and Sunday circulation of newspapers published in this country. The Association is vitally interested in the issue presented in this case, namely, the right of newspapers to publish news stories and editorials on cases pending in the courts."
>
> This might be a good occasion to demonstrate the fortitude of the judiciary.[172]

Lofton suggests that, while the Court continued to express concern for unfair publicity, it was telling trial courts that the threat of contempt was the wrong remedy. "Not until the 1970s was the contempt citation to be significantly revived as judges again attempted to control the press by issuing restrictions against printing what they perceived would interfere with the administration of justice."[173]

D. The Libel Cases, Part 1

No expansion of First Amendment protection into what had been the exclusive province of common law is more celebrated than the constitutionalization of libel law. And no constitutional libel case is more celebrated than the 1964 case of *New York Times v. Sullivan.*[174] Part 1 briefly reviews the common law of libel and the first expansion of common law protections in the late 18th and early 19th Centuries. Then it summarizes the *Sullivan* case, again focusing on the role of the press in moving the litigation forward, and concludes with a survey of constitutional libel cases between 1964 and 1974. Part 2 brings the survey up to date.

Only two civil libel cases involving the press reached the Supreme Court before *Sullivan.* In 1909, the Court reversed the decision of the U.S. Court of Appeals for the Seventh Circuit that had affirmed a federal trial court's refusal to award damages for a libelous newspaper advertisement.[175] And 50 years later, the Court upheld the decision of the South Dakota Supreme Court that Section 315 of the Federal Communications Act immunized broadcasters from libel suits for campaign speech the broadcaster was forbidden to censor.[176] In neither case did the Court consider the constitutionality of state libel law under the First and Fourteenth Amendments.[177]

While state libel law varied in its particulars from state to state, the typical state law required the plaintiff to prove three elements: (1) that the defendant published the offending statement, (2) that the statement was "of and concerning" the plaintiff, and (3) that the statement was defamatory, that is, tended harm a person's reputation, to expose that person to distrust, hatred, contempt, ridicule, or obloquy, or to injure that person in his office, occupation, business or employment.[178] If a plaintiff could prove those three elements, the burden shifted to the defendant to prove that the statement was either true or privileged. Privileges accorded to the press – such as the privilege to accurately report government pronouncements or to criticize politicians and entertainers – were always "qualified," that is, could be defeated by a showing of malice. No showing of fault was required; falsity and injury to reputation were presumed.

It had never been seriously contended that this common law formulation violated the First Amendment, and this description essentially described the state of the law of Alabama before 1964.[179] As noted earlier, Gleason's study shows that the press's principal efforts with respect to libel law in the 19th and early 20th Centuries were directed toward expanding the common law privileges.[180] Two turn-of-the-century cases bear particular mention for their influence on the Sullivan decision: *Post Publishing Co. v. Hallam*[181] and *Coleman v. MacLennan.*[182] In *Hallam*, the U.S. Court of Appeals for the Sixth Circuit had held that criticism of public officials was privileged only if the underlying facts were true. In *Coleman*, the Supreme Court of Kansas held that facts relating to matters of public interest – honestly believed to be true – are privileged even if false, and that any comment based on those facts would also be privileged. These ideas, and the cases that followed one or the other model, would provide the inspiration for the revolution in First Amendment doctrine that Justice Brennan began in *New York Times v. Sullivan.*[183]

On March 29, 1960, *The New York Times* carried a full-page advertisement called entitled "Heed Their Rising Voices," in support of African-American students at Alabama State College in Montgomery who were trying to integrate public facilities in the face of white violence. The ad appeared over the names of sixty-four prominent persons. Among other charges, the ad accused "Southern violators" of bombing the home of Martin Luther King, arresting him for trivial offenses, and charging him with perjury.[184]

Asserting that "violators" had to mean the police, attorneys for Gov. John Patterson and for City Commissioner L.B. Sullivan, who was responsible for the police in Montgomery, wrote the *Times* demanding a retraction. Alabama law required public officials to demand a retraction before seeking punitive damages. The *Times* did print a retraction on the demand of Gov. John Patterson, but said it believed that nothing in the ad referred to Sullivan. When the *Times* asked for a clarification, Sullivan filed suit against the *Times* asking for $500,000 in damages. He also sued the four Alabama ministers whose names appeared on the ad so the case could not be removed to federal court. Patterson and two others filed similar suits, so from this ad alone, the *Times* was potentially liable for $3 million.[185] And these were not the only lawsuits filed against the *Times* and other members of the press; Lewis estimates that, by the time *Sullivan* was decided in 1964, "Southern officials had brought nearly $300 million in libel actions against the press."[186]

The *Times* was represented by Louis M. Loeb, a partner in the Wall Street firm of Lord, Day & Lord; for local counsel, the *Times* chose Birmingham lawyer T. Eric Embry. M. Roland Nachman, Jr., of Montgomery represented Sullivan. Before the trial, the *Times* tried to get off the hook by challenging the court's personal jurisdiction over the newspaper because there was insufficient nexus between the paper and the state of Alabama. It might have lost on this issue anyway, but it was facing a segregationist judge, Walter B. Jones, who was so determined to find jurisdiction that he overruled his own procedure treatise to do it.[187]

During the three-day trial, much of the testimony focused on the element of identification. Sullivan insisted that "Southern violators" implied the police, and as the elected city commissioner responsible for the police, further implicated him. Witnesses were called who testified that they thought the ad was "of and concerning" Sullivan and that, if they believed the charges, it would have lowered him in their estimation. Sullivan also put on testimony to show that the accusations the ad allegedly made against Sullivan were false, anticipating the *Times's* truth defense. Jones overruled the *Times's* objections that the ad never said that Sullivan or the police had anything to do with those things.[188]

There were mistakes in the ad, most of them as trivial as mistaking "The Star Spangled Banner" for "My Country Tis of Thee." The most serious mistake was the allegation that the dining hall of Alabama State University had been padlocked to starve the protesting students into submission.[189] The *Times's* advertising acceptability manager testified that he had not checked the facts because the ad was prepared by a reputable agency and the signatories were certified (apparently without authorization) by noted civil rights leader A. Philip Randolph.[190]

In his charge to the jury, Jones removed the issue of defamation on the ground that the challenged statements were libelous per se and thus did not require a jury decision. He also refused to let the jury consider the defense of truth; the *Times* had conceded error with respect to the padlocking and thus failed to meet its burden as a matter of law. Damages were also presumed, as was typical under the common law, so the case went to the jury with instructions that the ad was libelous, false and injurious.[191]

The jury had to decide only whether the *Times* published the ad, whether it was "of and concerning" Sullivan, and, if so, how much to award. The jury found that Sullivan had been libeled and awarded him $500,000.[192] Significantly, the jury was not asked to specify whether the award represented compensatory or punitive damages. The *Times* asked for a new trial, which Jones ultimately denied, but not before ordering the ministers' property confiscated and sold at auction because they had neglected to file a separate motion for a new trial.[193]

After Jones denied the *Times's* motion for a new trial, the *Times* appealed to the Alabama Supreme Court on a number of grounds, primarily the jurisdictional question, but also including a First Amendment argument. The Alabama Supreme Court affirmed, agreeing with Jones and the jury in every respect, and explicitly finding no First Amendment protection for libel.[194]

The question at this point was whether the case could or should be appealed to the U.S. Supreme Court on constitutional grounds; to resolve it, the *Times* enlisted the support of Prof. Herbert Wechsler of Columbia University. The *Times's* legal team had made a constitutional argument before the Alabama Supreme Court, but it had been summarily dismissed. Now Wechsler wanted to make the First Amendment argument the focus of his petition for certiorari, but, according to Lewis, the *Times* brass were hesitant. "To my amazement," Wechsler told Lewis, "the Madisonian and Jeffersonian doctrines had not penetrated to the upper reaches of *The New York Times*."[195] Publisher Orvil Dryfoos, however, apparently persuaded the *Times* executives to go along with Wechsler.[196] It would not be the last time that the *Times* was less than fully supportive of constitutional litigation.[197]

Once he had the green light, Wechsler took over the case and began preparing the petition for certiorari. Lewis says it was actually Marvin Frankel, Wechsler's former student and now colleague at Columbia, whose insight – that Alabama libel law, as used in this case, could be redefined as a sedition law – would carry the day.[198] In his petition for certiorari, Wechsler wrote:

> The decision of the Supreme Court of Alabama gives a scope and application to the law of libel so restrictive of the right to protest and to criticize official conduct that it abridges the freedom of the press, as that freedom has been defined by the decisions of this Court. It transforms the action for defamation from a method of protecting private reputation to a device for insulating government against attack. If the judgment stands, its impact will be grave – not only upon the press but also upon those whose welfare may depend on the ability and willingness of publications to give voice to grievances against the agencies of governmental power. The issues are momentous and call urgently for the consideration and determination of this Court.[199]

The Supreme Court agreed to hear the case.[200]

There was little doubt that the Court would reverse; the only question was "how?" Wechsler's brief had advanced two possibilities: that the Court require public officials to prove that they suffered a financial loss because of the libel, called "special damages"; or to prove that the defendant knew the statement was false at the time of publication, called "actual malice."[201] In one of the amicus briefs, *The Washington Post* endorsed the second alternative, urging the Court to protect otherwise defamatory statements where "honestly made in the belief that they are true."[202] *The Chicago Tribune* also filed an amicus brief, reinforcing Wechsler's fundamental argument: that the Alabama libel applied to public officials amounted to a sedition law.[203] The ACLU also filed an amicus brief in support of the *Times*.[204]

Sullivan's brief emphasized that the Constitution did not protect libelous statements, which was in accordance with every previous pronouncement by the Supreme Court, and accused "The *Times* and its powerful corporate newspaper friends" of claiming for themselves alone an "absolute privilege" to defame all public officials.[205] While the briefs of the *Times* and amici focused on newspapers, Wechsler denied at oral argument that the constitutional protection he sought was limited to the press. But he did not deny that the privilege he sought was absolute, although he argued that even a lesser privilege would require reversal.[206]

In the end, the Court divided precisely along the fault line of absolute or qualified privilege. Writing for the Court, Justice William O. Brennan fully accepted Wechsler's sedition analogy, noting that the "court of history" had found the Sedition Act of 1798 unconstitutional and that Congress had remitted all fines paid in Sedition Act convictions.[207] But instead of an absolute immunity, Brennan adopted one of Wechsler's lesser arguments, one suggested by *Coleman v. MacLennan*:

> The constitutional guarantees require, we think, a Federal rule that prohibits a public official from recovering damages for a defamatory falsehood relating to his official conduct unless he proves that the statement was made with 'actual malice' – that is, with knowledge that it was false or with reckless disregard of whether it was false or not.[208]

Brennan also declared that this new fault standard must be proved by clear and convincing evidence, a departure from the typical civil standard of proof: a preponderance of the evidence.[209] In an even greater departure, Brennan applied the new standards to the evidence adduced in the trial court and, finding it wanting, declared the *Times* not liable, rather than remanding the case for a new trial. There was no way the Court was going to allow this politically charged case to go back to Alabama.[210]

Three justices – Black, Douglas, and Arthur Goldberg – wrote separately that the immunity extended to criticism of public officials, whether intentionally false or not, should be absolute.[211] It is perhaps a great irony that, had these three great defenders of freedom of the press won the day, *New York Times v. Sullivan* might have been a brilliant repudiation of the doctrine of seditious libel – and nothing more. It is inconceivable that the Court would have extended an absolute privilege for libelous speech in any other context, and there is no compelling reason for the wholesale change in libel law that followed *Sullivan*, except perhaps to require a showing of negligence or other culpable behavior rather than holding newspapers strictly liable, even without fault, as the common law had done.

The first libel case to follow *Sullivan* gave no hint of the revolution to come. *Garrison v. Louisiana*,[212] which came eight months later, was a criminal libel case in which the flamboyant New Orleans district attorney, Jim Garrison, accused state judges of inefficiency and laziness. He was convicted under a state criminal libel law that permitted punishment of false or, if made with common law malice, that is, ill-will or spite, even truthful criticism of public officials. There were no significant constitutional issues raised by Garrison's conviction that were not already raised by the *Times* verdict in Alabama, or, for that matter, any other sedition or contempt case. The Supreme Court reversed, with Brennan applying the *Sullivan* rules to criminal libel. Black and Douglas concurred, but again wrote that all seditious libel laws were unconstitutional. Douglas suggested that, with the *Garrison* decision, the Court ought to overturn the 1952 case of *Bauharnais v. Illinois*,[213] affirming a criminal libel statute that punished hate speech; otherwise, *Garrison* is of little consequence to the story of libel and no particular consequence for the press.[214]

The next case, *Rosenblatt v. Baer*,[215] added little to the constitutional analysis except to help lower courts distinguish a public official, who was required to prove actual malice, from a mere public employee, who was not. The Court held that the question turned on whether the public has an independent interest in the qualifications and performance of the plaintiff, beyond the interest it has in all public employees.[216] The judge, not a jury, would decide that in every case,[217] and states could not exempt their own officials from the burden of actual malice by defining public official as a matter of state law.[218]

The case that began to change the common law libel doctrine significantly was not technically a libel case at all; the cause of action was, rather, a close relative called "false light," which is usually grouped with privacy cases. In *Time, Inc. v. Hill*,[219] the plaintiff did not allege that he had been defamed by a *Life* magazine story, but that the coverage showed his family's horrific story in a false light, which constituted an actionable invasion of privacy.

In 1952 the Hill family – husband, wife and five children – were held hostage in their suburban Philadelphia home by three escaped convicts. The Hills were not harmed; in fact, they were treated reasonably well by their captors. A year later, however, a book called *Desperate Hours* dramatized their experience, but added an episode of violence against the father and verbal abuse of a daughter.

The novel led to a Broadway play and ultimately a Hollywood movie starring Frederic March and Humphrey Bogart.[220] To avoid the publicity, the Hills moved from Philadelphia to Connecticut, but to no avail. The last straw was an article in *Life* magazine featuring photos of the cast of the play in the Hills's old home. One showed a convict roughing up a Hill son. Another showed a daughter biting a convict's hand to make him drop his gun. And a third showed the father throwing the gun out of a window. While none of these things actually happened to the Hills, the copy and photo captions made the connection apparent.[221]

Hill sued for false light invasion of privacy under a broadly interpreted New York privacy statute and won a $75,000 judgment. An appeals court held the award excessive and remanded for a new trial. On retrial, the Hills won $30,000, which was affirmed on appeal. Time, Inc., petitioned for certiorari on First Amendment grounds, and the Supreme Court agreed to hear the case. Writing for the Court, Justice Brennan said the "constitutional protections for speech and press precluded the application of [state privacy law] to redress false reports of matters of public interest in the absence of proof that the defendant published the report with knowledge of its falsity or reckless disregard for the truth."[222] Only three members of the 6-3 majority signed onto the actual malice standard. Two others would have held that the First Amendment rules out any false light action,[223] while the sixth would have permitted the Hills to prevail on a showing of negligence.[224] Three justices dissented.[225]

How did Brennan justify the application of the actual malice standard to this case? "The guarantees for speech and press are not the preserve of political expression or comment upon public affairs, essential as those are to healthy government," Brennan said, but – particularly where non-defamatory material is concerned – to matters of public interest generally.[226] This surgical separation of the actual malice standard and the sedition analogy opened the door for the Court to hold five months later – in two cases decided in the same opinion – that the actual malice standard applied to "public figure" libel plaintiffs as well as public official plaintiffs.

In *Curtis Publishing Co. v. Butts,*[227] the well-known Georgia football coach, Wally Butts, was awarded $60,000 in compensatory and $400,000 in punitive damages in a libel action against the *Saturday Evening Post*, which accused him of fixing a game between Alabama and Georgia. Butts was technically employed by a private corporation and was not a public official.

In *Associated Press v. Walker*, a politically prominent retired general, Edwin Walker, was awarded $500,000 in compensatory and $300,000 in punitive damages in a suit against AP for accusing him of encouraging rioters at the University of Mississippi protesting the enrollment of a black student. Butts won his case; Walker did not,[228] but the effect of the two terribly divided opinions was to extend the *Sullivan* rule to public figures as well as public officials.

Both Butts and Walker were very well known figures at the time, "household words" in some quarters, and few doubted that they were public figures. Such celebrities have come to be called "all-purpose public figures," but the standard applies as well to so-called "limited purpose public figures," comprising those plaintiffs whose position or "purposeful activity amounted to a thrusting of his personality into the 'vortex' of an important public controversy." The Court has justified the extension of the actual malice standard to public figures on several grounds: public figures often play an influential role in ordering society, public figures have ready access to mass communications media, citizens have a legitimate and substantial interest in the conduct of public figures, and public figures assume the risk of exposure to criticism.[229]

Later that year, the Court heard a little remembered case alleging that the editor of the Beckley, W.Va., *Post-Herald* libeled a candidate for public office in three editorials regarding the controversial issue of drinking water fluoridation. In a per curiam opinion in *Beckley Newspapers Corp. v. Hanks*,[230] the Court held that lower courts had woefully misinterpreted its new standard and reversed a judgment against the newspaper. The following year, the Court clarified the meaning of reckless disregard for the truth in the non-press case of *St. Amant v. Thompson.*[231] Reckless disregard can be found, the Court said, if the "defendant in fact entertained serious doubts as to the truth of his publication" but published anyway.[232]

The next libel case taken by the Supreme Court also added nothing to the new constitutional doctrine, but *Greenbelt Cooperative Publishing Association v. Bresler*[233] began to expose a fissure in the Court that would only grow worse as the decade wore on. In *Bresler*, the weekly *Greenbelt News Review* newspaper accurately reported the use of the term "blackmail" at a public meeting to describe a developer's negotiating position with the local government.

The developer had argued that, because the paper knew he had committed no such crime, the paper should be held liable for knowingly publishing a false and defamatory statement. The jury agreed, and the judgment on the verdict was affirmed by the Maryland Court of Appeals. The U.S. Supreme Court reversed, again finding that the jury was improperly instructed as to malice, but adding that use of the term "blackmail" in that context was not actionable.[234] Justice Potter Stewart wrote the opinion for the Court; Black and Douglas, as usual, concurred in the judgment while continuing to oppose the "actual malice" standard. But the most significant opinion was Justice Byron R. White's. Agreeing that the jury instructions were flawed, White concurred in the judgment, but he criticized the Court's holding on "blackmail," and, indirectly, the press itself. White took the Court to task for

> immuniz[ing] professional communicators from liability for their use of ambiguous language and their failure to guard against the possibility that words known to carry two meanings, one of which imputes commission of a

> crime, might seriously damage the object of their comment in the eyes of the average reader. I see no reason why the members of a skilled calling should not be held to the standard of their craft and assume the risk of being misunderstood – if they are – by the ordinary reader of their publications.[235]

This would be the first of a succession of increasingly hostile attacks on the press from White, which resumed early the following year with three libel decisions handed down the same day. In *Monitor Patriot Co. v. Roy*,[236] the Supreme Court reversed a New Hampshire Supreme Court decision upholding a jury verdict finding the Concord *Monitor* liable for calling a candidate for office a "former small-time bootlegger." In *Time, Inc. v. Pape*,[237] the Court reversed a decision of the U.S. Court of Appeals for the Seventh Circuit holding that *Time* magazine's failure to make clear that charges against a Chicago police official reported in the magazine were merely allegations, rather than official findings, raised a jury question as to actual malice. And in *Ocala Star-Banner Co. v. Damron*,[238] the Court reversed a Florida decision finding the newspaper liable for falsely reporting that a mayor and candidate for office had been charged with perjury.

In all three cases, Stewart wrote the majority decision, while Black and Douglas offered their usual absolutist concurrences. Harlan dissented in *Pape*, but White's concurrence in *Roy* and *Damron* could only be read as another gratuitous slap at the press.

> The First Amendment is not so construed, however, to award merit badges for intrepid but mistaken or careless reporting. Misinformation has no merit in itself; standing alone it is as antithetical to the purposes of the First Amendment as the calculated lie. Its substance contributes nothing to intelligent decisionmaking by citizens or officials; it achieves nothing but gratuitous injury.[239]

Notwithstanding White's growing irritation, the Court's most generous libel ruling came a few months later in *Rosenbloom v. Metromedia*,[240] in which a plurality of the Court applied the principle of *Time, Inc. v. Hill* to defamatory speech. Rosenbloom was a Philadelphia distributor of nudist magazines who initiated a libel suit against a local radio station for falsely describing books seized from him as "obscene" when a criminal court had ruled otherwise. Because Rosenbloom was neither a public official nor a public figure, the trial judge imposed a mere negligence standard and the jury awarded him $750,000. The U.S. Court of Appeals for the Third Circuit reversed, indicating that because the broadcast concerned matters of public interest and were made under deadline pressure, the actual malice standard applied despite Rosenbloom's status as a private citizen.

The Supreme Court affirmed, 5-3, but only a plurality of three – Brennan, who wrote for the Court, joined by Chief Justice Burger and Harry Blackmun – endorsed the Third Circuit's reasoning. Black offered his usual concurrence, although Douglas did not participate in the case. Dissenting, Marshall, Stewart, and Harlan rejected Brennan's extension of the actual malice rule to matters of public interest, which they found too burdensome on judges, and argued that states should be free to set their own standards for private figure libels so long as they did not find liability without fault – essentially, a negligence standard.[241] The dissenters differed from each other only on the issue of punitive damages.

White's concurrence in the judgment found all the opinions "displaced more state libel law than necessary," and he would have affirmed solely on the ground that this case involved the "official actions of public servants." Again, White had a word for the press:

> Some members of the Court seem haunted by fears of self-censorship by the press and of damage judgments that will threaten its financial health. But technology has immeasurably increased the power of the press to do both good and evil. Vast communication combines have been built into profitable ventures. My interest is not in protecting the treasuries of communicators but in implementing the First Amendment by insuring that effective communication which is essential to the continued functioning of our free society.[242]

The *Rosenbloom* doctrine only lasted three years. By 1974, the Court had taken a decided turn to the right. Even before *Rosenbloom*, President Nixon had replaced Earl Warren with Warren Burger and Abe Fortas with Harry Blackmun (then considered conservative). After *Rosenbloom*, Black and Harlan died, and Nixon appointed Lewis Powell and William Rehnquist to replace them. That was the posture of the Court when *Gertz v. Robert Welch, Inc.*,[243] was decided, and it quickly repudiated the *Rosenbloom* plurality opinion. The press might have been forgiven for thinking the unbroken string of libel victories would go on forever, but it stopped at *Gertz*. Even so, the Court only rolled the *Rosenbloom* standard back as far as the Marshall and Harlan dissents; most of the gains of the past decade were preserved.

Elmer Gertz was a lawyer who was hired to sue the Chicago policeman who had killed his clients' son. The right-wing John Birch Society magazine, *American Opinion*, charged Gertz with a communist-inspired conspiracy to discredit the police and, among other charges, falsely claimed Gertz had a police record. The trial court originally found for Gertz as a matter of law, leaving only the amount of damages to the jury. Then the judge changed his mind, deciding that the actual malice standard applied under the *Rosenbloom* plurality rule, and entered judgment notwithstanding the verdict for the magazine. The U.S. Court of Appeals for the Seventh Circuit affirmed, but the Supreme Court reversed.[244]

Writing for the 5-4 majority, Powell used a traditional tort law balancing analysis to conclude that actual malice should not be applied in private plaintiff/public issue cases. Public people have more access to the press for rebuttal, so the state has a greater interest in protecting private people; public people must accept certain consequences of their involvement in public affairs that private people need not accept. He also cited Marshall's dissent in *Rosenbloom* for the proposition that the Court should not be making content-based decisions on what information is relevant to self-government. Instead, Powell said, states can define the appropriate standard of liability, as long as they do not impose liability without fault, that is, any libel plaintiff must prove at least negligence on the part of the defendant. Powell also said that no compensatory damages could be awarded without proof of injury, and no presumed or punitive damages could be awarded without proof of actual malice. "In short, the private defamation plaintiff who establishes liability under a less demanding standard than [actual malice] may recover only such damages as are sufficient to compensate him for actual injury."[245]

Blackmun voted with Powell, although his sympathies were with Brennan, in order to create a 5-4 majority ruling and eliminate the uncertainty in the lower courts. Brennan and Douglas dissented; Brennan would have applied actual malice under the *Rosenbloom* doctrine, while Douglas would provide absolute immunity for matters of public interest. Burger and White also dissented, but on the ground that states should be free to adopt their own standards for private libels; both said that the jury's verdict should be reinstated. White was especially upset, and his hostility toward the press reached its zenith. Likening the relationship between the public and the press to David and Goliath, White excoriated the Court for its "evisceration of the common-law libel remedy for the private citizen," thus "remov[ing] from his legal arsenal the most effective weapon to combat assault on personal reputation by the press establishment."[246]

> I fail to see how the quality or quantity of public debate will be promoted by further emasculation of state libel laws for the benefit of the news media. If anything, this trend may provoke a new and radical imbalance in the communications process. It is not at all inconceivable that virtually unrestrained defamatory remarks about private citizens will discourage them from speaking out and

> concerning themselves with social problems. This would turn the First Amendment on its head.[247]

Since Gertz was a private figure, a new trial was required. On retrial, the jury found actual malice and awarded $100,000 in compensatory and $300,000 in punitive damages.

We pause for a moment in this discussion of the libel cases to take stock of the doctrinal changes made by the Court in the 1964-74 decade, all presumably commanded by the First Amendment, and the role of the press in shaping those changes. When the decade began, the elements of libel were three: publication, identification ("of and concerning"), and defamation. At the end of the decade, a fault requirement had been added: actual malice, by clear and convincing evidence, for public figures and anyone seeking punitive damages; and negligence or more for private citizens, at least where matters of public interest were concerned. While the Court would not explicitly say so until 1986, the fault standard implied a fifth element: falsity. If the burden was now on the plaintiff to prove fault, and no fault could be found with a true statement, the burden had already shifted to the plaintiff to prove that the statement was not true.[248] Finally, the Court added injury to the plaintiff as a sixth element to be proved where only negligence was shown.

And what role did the press play in these dramatic changes, in the constitutionalization of libel law? Apart from the seminal *Sullivan* decision itself, there were no amicus briefs filed by the press on behalf of their colleagues (or by anyone on behalf of the plaintiffs) in any of the libel decisions. Judging from the stature of the lawyers on both sides, these were not exactly low stakes cases. Among the more prominent media representatives were Bernard G. Segal of Philadelphia, who represented Metromedia in *Rosenbloom*, and also counted Bell Telephone, NBC, and RCA as clients; Don H. Reuben of Chicago, who represented Time, Inc., in *Pape*, and had been on the Tribune Co.'s brief in *Sullivan*, along with Howard Ellis; Edward Bennett Williams of Washington, D.C., who represented the Concord *Monitor* in *Roy*, and was for years the leading counsel for *The Washington Post*; Thurman Arnold of Washington, D.C., who represented Beckley Newspapers against Hanks, and who had headed Roosevelt's Antitrust Division, served on the U.S. Court of Appeals for the D.C. Circuit and founded the firm of Arnold & Porter; Herbert Wechsler of New York, who represented Curtis Publishing Co. against Butts soon after representing *The New York Times* in *Sullivan*; and William P. Rogers of New York, who represented the Associated Press against Walker, and served as Eisenhower's Attorney General and Nixon's Secretary of State. There were some very well-known attorneys on the other side of these cases as well, including Ramsey Clark, who represented Rosenbloom against Metromedia, and served as President Johnson's Attorney General; Richard M. Nixon, who represented Hill against Time, Inc., and became President of the United States; and numerous locally prominent "superlawyers."

When this series of cases began, the media defense bar was not well organized; by the end of the decade, that had changed dramatically, but *Gertz* did not directly involve the mainstream press and, in any event, the leading media organizations that might have filed briefs were far more concerned with another case that was announced the same day as *Gertz*: *Miami Herald v. Tornillo*, the "right of reply" case discussed in Part A of this chapter.[249] Indeed, White's "David and Goliath" analogy and his use of the term "press establishment" may have been inspired by the sheer number and prominence of the amicus briefs filed in that case. His concurring opinion in *Tornillo* suggested as much, even as he took another shot at *Gertz*.

> To me it is a near absurdity to so deprecate individual dignity, as the Court does in *Gertz*, and to leave the people at the complete mercy of the press, at least in this stage of our history when the press, as the majority in this case so well documents, is steadily becoming more powerful and much less likely to be deterred by threats of libel suits.[250]

We end this digression with a word about why we have focused so much on Justice White. In all of the libel opinions discussed here, White's opinions were either concurrences or dissents and of no legal significance. As we will see in the next chapter, however, White became the Court's point man on newsgathering, beginning with the 1972 case of *Branzburg v. Hayes*,[251] and at least one reason why the press fared so poorly in those cases.

E. The Libel Cases, Part 2

Following *Gertz*, the Court continued to adjust and clarify the doctrine and related procedural issues for another 17 years, with the institutional press playing a much more active role as *amicus curiae*, yet losing more than twice as many cases as it won. In *Time, Inc. v. Firestone*,[252] *Time* magazine misidentified the grounds for divorce of a wealthy, publicity-seeking heiress; *Time* won the case because the Florida courts had failed to explicitly consider the publisher's fault. Doctrinally, however, the press lost some ground when the Court declared the plaintiff a private figure because her divorce was a private, not public, controversy – notwithstanding the press conferences she held during the proceeding. In *Herbert v. Lando*,[253] CBS lost a bid to limit a public figure libel plaintiff's ability to probe deeply into the editorial process and state of mind of the journalists and editors during discovery. The opinion, reversing the U.S. Court of Appeals for the Second Circuit, exposed the actual malice rule as a double-edged sword; if the plaintiff had to prove knowing falsity or reckless disregard for the truth, Justice White wrote for the majority, he could not be deprived of the opportunity to gather that state-of-mind evidence.[254] The importance of this case was not lost on the press generally, which turned out *en masse* in a futile attempt to limit the costly discovery process in libel cases.[255]

In two 1979 cases decided the same day, ANPA and ASNE filed amicus briefs urging the Court to affirm lower court decisions declaring libel plaintiffs to be public figures and, in the absence of actual malice, granting summary judgment to the defendants; in both cases, the Court reversed. In *Hutchinson v. Proxmire*,[256] the Court held that the Speech and Debate Clause did not immunize a United States senator from liability for statements made off the Senate floor and that the senator's attack on the plaintiff's scientific research did not make the plaintiff a public figure. In *Wolston v. Reader's Digest Association*,[257] the Court held that the nephew of convicted Soviet spies was a private figure even though he had previously been convicted of contempt for failing to respond to a subpoena.

In 1984, the Court decided two libel cases raising jurisdictional issues related to libel litigation; again, the press lost both cases. In *Keeton v. Hustler Magazine, Inc.*,[258] the Court allowed a New York plaintiff to take advantage of New Hampshire's unusually long, six-year statute of limitations to file a libel suit there against a nationally circulated magazine over the objection of press amici led by CBS, Inc.[259] The same day, in *Calder v. Jones*,[260] the Court agreed with Actress Shirley Jones that the California courts had jurisdiction to hear her libel case against the *National Enquirer*, which is published in Florida but also circulated nationally. Contrary to the position advocated by amicus Reporter's Committee for Freedom of the Press,[261] the Court affirmed a state court opinion that the First Amendment had no bearing on the jurisdictional question. The following month, the press fared rather better in *Bose Corp. v. Consumers Union*,[262] in which the Court affirmed a lower court ruling that appellate courts must conduct an independent review of the entire record to determine whether the actual malice standard was met with "convincing clarity," rather than apply the "clearly erroneous" standard usually prescribed by state law. The case involved a disparaging review of the plaintiff's loudspeakers that appeared in *Consumer Reports* magazine. Floyd Abrams wrote the amicus brief for the press, led by *The New York Times*; the ACLU also filed in support of *Consumer Reports*.[263]

But the press lost a major case the following year when the Court held that *Gertz's* prohibition against the award of presumed or punitive damages without a showing of actual malice does not apply to matters of private concern – in this case, an erroneous credit report. In *Dun & Bradstreet v. Greenmoss Builders, Inc.*,[264] the Court rejected arguments to the contrary by *The Washington Post* as amicus; the *Post* had devoted most of its brief, however, to an even more futile argument that punitive damages should never be awarded in a libel case.[265] Dow Jones, publisher of *The Wall Street Journal*, also filed an amicus brief in the case,[266] fully agreeing with both the *Post's* positions. More significantly, Dow Jones, as well as the relatively new Information Industry Association,[267] argued that Dun & Bradstreet's status as a "non-media" actor whose speech was "of a commercial or economic" nature should not have a bearing on the Court's decision.[268]

The Vermont Supreme Court had concluded that the *Gertz* rule did not apply to non-media defendants, and the U.S. Supreme Court asked the parties to address the question in that form. Ultimately, however, the Court decided against making the distinction based on status, but rather on whether the information was public or private in nature. Chief Justice Burger and Justice White concurred, although both asserted that *Gertz* should be overruled altogether; Brennan, Marshall, Stevens, and Blackmun dissented. Powell's decision for the Court was joined only by Justices Rehnquist and O'Connor. What makes *Dun & Bradstreet* so problematic, however, is not merely its holding with respect to presumed and punitive damages, but the specter it raises that some future Court will hold, as at least one state court has suggested,[269] that *Gertz's* requirement that state courts impose a fault standard in all libel cases may be waived where both the plaintiff and the matters at issue are deemed private.

Sure enough, the Court added to this concern in its very next libel case. In *Philadelphia Newspapers v. Hepps*,[270] the Court held that a private figure plaintiff bore the burden of proving the falsity of links to organized crime alleged in a series of five articles that ran in *The Philadelphia Inquirer*. That plaintiffs carried such a burden had been widely taken for granted as long as a fault element was imposed, but the Pennsylvania Supreme Court held that requiring proof of fault did not necessarily imply requiring proof of falsity and that Pennsylvania's unusual statutory presumption of falsity did not offend the First Amendment. The U.S. Supreme Court reversed, giving the press an major victory. But Justice O'Connor's opinion revived the media/non-media distinction and limited the scope of the holding to media defendants and matters of public concern.[271]

Press amici – and they were legion – argued that the Pennsylvania rule would force media defendants to calculate not whether what they print is true, but rather whether they will be able to prove in court that what they print is true. They also argued that there is no rational justification for presuming the falsity of any defamatory speech, so any such presumption would violate due process;[272] that a presumption of falsity effectively nullified the *Gertz* safeguards, particularly the fault element, since, as a practical matter, juries were inclined to find negligence in any inaccurate report;[273] and that the problems raised by the Pennsylvania statute applied with even greater force to broadcasters, who were required to work under tighter deadline pressure.[274]

Two months later, the press won an important procedural decision holding that the "clear and convincing" evidentiary standard for actual malice must be considered by trial courts in deciding whether to grant summary judgment in lieu of trial. As press amici pointed out in *Anderson v. Liberty Lobby, Inc.*,[275] the actual malice standard is a "purposefully difficult standard to meet" and its proper application – including the "clear and convincing" evidentiary standard – avoids much "burdensome, punitive litigation" through pretrial disposition.[276] Ironically, Justice White wrote the opinion for the majority; Justice Brennan dissented, as did Chief Justice Burger and Justice Rehnquist separately, although for reasons having more to do with the practicalities of litigation than with First Amendment concerns.[277]

Two years later, in 1988, the Court imposed the actual malice standard in another non-libel case. Like *Time v. Hill*, more than 20 years earlier, *Hustler Magazine v. Falwell*[278] did not come to the Court as a libel case, but rather sounded in a different tort, "intentional infliction of emotional distress." Televangelist Jerry Falwell had sued *Hustler Magazine* and its iconoclastic publisher, Larry Flynt, for a mock advertisement that appeared in the magazine. The parody was modeled after a series of legitimate ads for the liqueur Campari that were in wide circulation at the time; celebrities spoke of their "first time," describing their first taste of Campari in terms that suggested their first sexual experience. In the *Hustler* ad, Mr. Falwell was the celebrity and the "first time" he recounted described sex with his mother in an outhouse. Falwell sued for libel and intentional infliction of emotional distress; the jury rejected the libel claim, specifically finding that the parody could not reasonably be construed as factual, but found *Hustler* liable for intentional infliction of emotional distress.[279]

On appeal, the U.S. Circuit Court for the Fourth Circuit affirmed, rejecting *Hustler's* argument that the First Amendment required a showing of actual malice, even where the tort is not technically libel. As urged by two amicus briefs from the press,[280] the U.S. Supreme Court reversed. Writing for a unanimous Court, at least as to the judgment, Chief Justice Rehnquist held that the First Amendment precluded public figures from recovering damages under a theory of intentional infliction of emotional distress for a publication that does not contain a false statement of fact made with actual malice.[281] Concurring in the judgment, Justice White wrote that the actual malice standard was irrelevant to the case, which could have been decided simply as a parody protected by the First Amendment.[282] White's reluctance to extend *New York Times v. Sullivan* any further than necessary, and his narrow view of the holding in *Hustler*, would be critical to the decision in *Cohen v. Cowles Media*,[283] discussed in Chapter 8.

The press would not be so fortunate in the next case. In *Harte-Hanks Communications v. Connnaughton*,[284] decided the following year, the Court reviewed a finding of actual malice in a libel case brought in federal court by a disappointed office seeker against the Hamilton, Ohio, *Journal News*, for a story accusing the candidate of "dirty tricks" in the late election. A properly instructed jury found the newspaper liable, and the U.S. Court of Appeals for the Sixth Circuit affirmed. Despite the protestation of the newspaper and press amici to the contrary,[285] a unanimous U.S. Supreme Court held that the appellate court had reviewed the trial record *de novo* as required by the *Bose*[286] case. The best the press got out of *Harte-Hanks* was a declaration from the Court that "highly unreasonable conduct constituting an extreme departure from the standards of investigation and reporting ordinarily adhered to by responsible publishers" did not, in itself, constitute actual malice, but was merely evidence of actual malice.[287] That formulation, taken from Justice Harlan's opinion for the Court in *Butts*,[288] had apparently confused the Sixth Circuit court.[289]

The following year, the press lost another libel case that turned on a misunderstood dictum from an earlier case; this time, the misleading phrase was Justice Powell's statement in *Gertz* that "there is no such thing as a false idea."[290] In *Milkovich v. Lorain Journal*,[291] a columnist for the newspaper implied that a local wrestling coach had committed perjury at an administrative hearing. Because the column was clearly styled as an opinion column, the lower courts dismissed the coach's libel suit against the newspaper. In a 6-2 opinion, the U.S. Supreme Court reversed, finding the label "opinion" inadequate to insulate the newspaper from liability. Writing for the Court, Chief Justice Rehnquist held that libel doctrine already provided enough protection for opinion that was not susceptible of proof, one way or the other, or was mere rhetorical hyperbole. However, Rehnquist wrote, a provable statement merely cast as opinion – such as, "In my opinion, Jones is a liar" – can support a libel action.[292] The national press, as well as the ACLU, argued for the formal preservation of the fact/opinion dichotomy,[293] while the Ohio press argued that the Court had no jurisdiction to reverse an Ohio Supreme Court's contrary decision regarding an opinion privilege.[294] Both arguments were futile.

In the last libel case covered by this study, *Masson v. New Yorker Magazine, Inc.*,[295] the journalism community was sharply divided, although the institutional press closed ranks behind *The New Yorker*. In an article for the magazine, journalist Janet Malcolm admittedly fabricated direct quotations purporting to have been uttered in the course of her interview with well-known psychiatrist Jeffrey Masson. Masson sued on the ground that the alleged quotations were defamatory, but the trial court granted summary judgment for *The New Yorker* on the ground that the alleged quotations were either substantially true or rational interpretations of ambiguous conversations. The U.S. Court of Appeals for the Ninth Circuit affirmed, but the U.S. Supreme Court reversed and remanded, holding that several of the fabricated quotes raised a jury question as to actual malice. The press, however, could take heart from the Court's conclusion that even

> a deliberate alteration of the words uttered by a plaintiff does not equate with knowledge of falsity for purposes of [finding actual malice] unless the alteration results in a material change in the meaning conveyed by the statement. The use of quotations to attribute words not in fact spoken bears in a most important way on that inquiry, but it is not dispositive in every case.[296]

In this case, a number of journalists and journalism professors – incensed by the notion that fabricated quotations served any First Amendment interests – urged the Court to reverse.[297] But the institutional press, arguing that journalistic standards or ethics had no place in the First Amendment analysis, urged the Court to affirm the decisions of the lower courts.[298] In the end, the institutional press probably got more out of *Masson* than many conscientious journalists and academics thought was deserved.

There were few dramatic changes in constitutional libel doctrine after *Gertz*; most of the cases involved clarification: where was that elusive line between public and private figures, how deeply could libel plaintiffs probe the editorial process during discovery, where could libel suits be filed, what were the responsibilities of reviewing courts, and how false was false enough? The one significant doctrinal question remaining after *Gertz*, and remaining today – the fault standard for private plaintiffs on matters of private concern – is irrelevant to the press as a practical matter, although the return of strict liability would be philosophically tragic. The mobilization of the press as an interest group was most impressive after *Gertz*, even if its success rate fell below fifty percent. As the next section demonstrates, the press did much better in the privacy arena.

F. The Privacy Cases

The genesis of the notion that plaintiffs ought to be able to recover for an invasion of their privacy was an 1890 *Harvard Law Review* article by Louis Brandeis and his law partner Samuel Warren.[299] The concept did not exist in English common law, and invasion of privacy is often called the only truly American tort. Dean William L. Prosser's classification scheme for the American common law privacy torts included the right of publicity or misappropriation, false light, intrusion on seclusion, and disclosure of private facts.[300] The case of *Time, Inc. v. Hill*, discussed in Section D above, was substantively a false light case, although the lawsuit was brought under a New York statute that more properly concerned the right of publicity, that is, the right to control the use of one's name or likeness for commercial purposes.[301] Apart from five cases that substantively parallel the tort of disclosure of private facts – which are the central focus of this section – only two other privacy cases involving the press ever reached the U.S. Supreme Court.

In the 1974 case of *Cantrell v. Forest City Publishing Co.*,[302] the Court upheld a jury verdict finding that a Cleveland *Plain Dealer* reporter had knowingly placed the Cantrell family in a false light through numerous inaccuracies and false statements in his article about them. And in the 1977 case of *Zacchini v. Scripps-Howard Broadcasting Co.*,[303] the Court held that an Ohio television station misappropriated the entire act of a circus "human cannonball" by filming and broadcasting his entire, 15-second act. Other than the litigants, the mainstream press did not participate in either of these cases.

Of far greater importance, however, was the series of five privacy-related cases that reached the Court between 1975 and 1989. None of these cases directly implicated the tort of public disclosure of private facts; the press rarely lost those cases in the state courts because of an absolute "newsworthiness" defense that was said to have "swallowed" the tort itself. The cases that did get to the Court, however, were all based, directly or indirectly, on statutes that criminalized the publication of truthful, but embarrassing, information. Sometimes they were characterized as prior restraints, sometimes as subsequent punishment. But as we will see in Chapter 8, the Court's decisions in these cases had a profound effect on the Court's early 21st century jurisprudence and may, just may, improve prospects for better legal treatment of newsgathering cases in the future.

On Aug. 18, 1971, Cynthia Leslie Cohn, 17, was raped and suffocated to death by six high school boys following a drinking party in Sandy Springs, Fulton County, Georgia. In April 1972, when the six perpetrators were arraigned, five pled guilty to rape, murder charges against them having been dropped, and a date was set for the trial of the youth who pled not guilty. A reporter covering the case for WSB-TV duly broadcast the story later that day, including, for the first time in any media, the name of the victim. The reporter had learned the name from personal observation of the proceedings and from the indictments, which were public records available to anyone who asked. The next month, Martin Cohn, Cynthia Cohn's father, filed a lawsuit against the Cox Broadcasting Corp., the owner of WSB-TV, for invasion of privacy and for violating a Georgia statute that prohibited the publication or broadcasting of the name of any rape victim.

The trial court held that the statute gave Cohn a private right of action against Cox, notwithstanding the broadcaster's constitutional claims, and granted Cohn summary judgment as to liability, with damages to be considered at a later jury trial. On appeal, the Georgia Supreme Court held that the statute did not give Cohn a private right of action, so summary judgment was inappropriate, but also that Cohn's common law invasion of privacy claim was not precluded by the First Amendment. On a motion for rehearing the state supreme court held that the statute was an authoritative declaration of state policy to the effect that the name of a rape victim was not a matter of public concern, so the right to disclose that information was not protected by the First Amendment. The U.S. Supreme Court reversed in *Cox v. Cohn.*[304]

Writing for a nearly unanimous Court – only Justice Rehnquist dissented – Justice White got to the heart of the matter. "Because the gravamen of the claimed injury is the publication of information, whether true or not, the dissemination of which is embarrassing or otherwise painful to an individual, it is here that claims of privacy most directly confront the constitutional freedoms of speech and press."[305] Determined to approach the constitutional balance cautiously, White largely restricted his holding to the facts at hand. "We are convinced that the State may not ... impose sanctions on the accurate publication of the name of a rape victim obtained from public records – more specifically, from judicial records which are maintained in connection with a public prosecution and which themselves are open to public inspection."[306] If the state wanted to keep such information from the press, the Court said, it would have to find some way to avoid public documentation or other exposure of private information, possibly by sealing court records containing such facts. Only Justice Douglas would have ruled on broader grounds: that "there is no power on the part of government to suppress or penalize the publication of 'news of the day.'" Rehnquist's dissent turned on jurisdiction, not the merits.[307]

While only regional media companies participated in the *Cox* case, the next privacy case to reach the Court drew the attention of the ANPA. *Oklahoma Publishing Co. v. District Court in and for Oklahoma County*[308] was not a tort case at all, but rather challenged an injunction issued by the county court prohibiting the news media from "'publishing, broadcasting, or disseminating, in any manner, the name or picture'" of an 11-year-old boy alleged to have shot and killed a railroad switchman. Reporters were able to learn his name and take his photograph during and after an open detention hearing, and they used both the in newspaper, radio, and television stories that followed. A few days later, when the boy appeared in court again for arraignment, the judge closed the proceeding and issued the injunction. On appeal, the Oklahoma Supreme Court affirmed the judge's order, but the U.S. Supreme Court stayed the order. It granted certiorari and, in the same per curiam opinion, reversed.[309]

As if to illustrate the relationship between prior restraint and privacy cases, the Court relied on both *Nebraska Press* and *Cox* to hold that "the First and Fourteenth Amendments will not permit a state court to prohibit the publication of widely disseminated information obtained at court proceedings which were in fact open to the public."[310] The Court's very brief opinion closely tracked the arguments made by ANPA in its amicus brief, but did not follow ANPA's suggestion for a general rule to avoid "a constant stream of minor fact variations which will needlessly take up the time of this Court and of the press in preventing encroachments upon the First and Fourteenth Amendments by trial judges who do not yet believe or perhaps understand the teachings of this Court …."[311] The Court continued to resist formulating a broad, general rule in the next privacy-related case the following year.

On Oct. 4, 1975, Landmark's *Virginian-Pilot* published an article that accurately reported on a pending inquiry by the Virginia Judicial Inquiry and Review Commission and identified the state judge whose conduct was being investigated. A month later, a grand jury indicted Landmark for violating a state statute by "unlawfully divulg[ing] the identification of a Judge of a Court not of record, which said Judge was the subject of an investigation and hearing" by the Commission. Landmark was convicted of a misdemeanor in a bench trial and fined $500. The Virginia Supreme Court affirmed the conviction, citing the need to protect the judge's reputation from the publicity that might attend frivolous claims; preserving public confidence in the judicial system; and protecting complainants and witnesses before the Commission. Landmark appealed to the U.S. Supreme Court, which granted certiorari.

In contrast to *Cox* and even *Oklahoma Publishing*, *Landmark Communications, Inc. v. Virginia*[312] attracted the attention of a substantial number of media companies and press associations.[313] The media companies argued that, under the Constitution, none of the purported interests cited by the Virginia Supreme Court could be protected by imposing criminal sanctions on the press, and called for a rule barring accurate reports of government affairs. The press associations similarly argued that the Constitution barred states from imposing criminal sanctions for publishing information on the public duties of public officials. As before, the Court shied away from any generalized pronouncement. Writing for a nearly unanimous Court, Chief Justice Burger found it "unnecessary to adopt this categorical approach to resolve the issue before us. …

> The narrow and limited question presented, then, is whether the First Amendment permits the criminal punishment of third persons who are strangers to the inquiry, including the news media, for divulging or publishing truthful information regarding confidential proceedings of the Judicial Inquiry and Review Commission. We are not here concerned with the possible applicability of the statute to one who secures the information by illegal means and thereafter divulges it.
>
> * * *
>
> We conclude that the publication Virginia seeks to punish under its statute lies near the core of the First Amendment, and the Commonwealth's interests advanced by the imposition of criminal sanctions are insufficient to justify the actual and potential encroachments on freedom of speech and of the press which follow therefrom.[314]

Even without propounding the general rule sought by the press, the Court had, in these three cases, begun to make clear that privacy interests – including the name of a rape victim, a juvenile offender, or even a judge merely accused of wrongdoing – would not be enough to overcome the presumptive right of the press to publish truthful information, lawfully acquired, on matters of public concern, even where the publication was otherwise prohibited by a state's legislature or its courts. In *Smith v. Daily Mail*,[315] the Court would make that rule explicit.

That 1979 case, like *Oklahoma Publishing*, involved an indictment against two West Virginia newspapers for violating state law by publishing without a court's permission the name of a 14-year-old who had shot and killed a high school classmate. In this case, however, the reporters did not obtain the name in open court, but by monitoring the police band radio frequency, going to the scene, and interviewing witnesses, police, and a prosecutor. The papers sought and won a writ of prohibition against prosecution from the West Virginia Supreme Court, which held that prosecution would be unconstitutional under recent U.S. Supreme Court decisions, but the attorney general of West Virginia filed a successful petition for certiorari on behalf of the trial judge, Robert K. Smith. Once again, the press amici came out in force to support the newspapers. Once again, the ACLU added its voice to that of the press.[316] Once again, Floyd Abrams, who had represented Landmark Communications, was representing the newspaper. And once again, the Chief Justice wrote the opinion for a nearly unanimous Court.

Because of the language of the statute requiring a court order before publishing the name of a juvenile offender, the press amici tended to characterize the statute as a prior restraint – even though the information had already been published and the case reached the Court through a criminal prosecution. Burger agreed after a fashion:

> Whether we view the statute as a prior restraint or as a penal sanction for publishing lawfully obtained, truthful information is not dispositive because even the latter action requires the highest form of state interest to sustain its validity. Prior restraints have been accorded the most exacting scrutiny in previous cases. However, even when a state attempts to punish publication after the event it must nevertheless demonstrate that its punitive action was necessary to further the state interests asserted. Since we conclude that this statute cannot satisfy the constitutional standards defined in *Landmark Communications, Inc.*, we need not decide whether, as argued by respondents, it operated as a prior restraint.[317]

But Burger went further and gave the press the general rule it had been seeking. Burger pointed out that in the previous cases – *Cox, Oklahoma Publishing,* and *Landmark Communications* – the press received the information from the government or government sources, so those cases did not directly control the outcome here, where the press gathered the information through routine reporting techniques. Asserting that it made no difference – "A free press cannot be made to rely solely upon the sufferance of government to supply it with information" – Burger said those cases "suggested" the general rule: "if a newspaper lawfully obtains truthful information about a matter of public significance then state officials may not constitutionally punish publication of the information, absent a need to further a state interest of the highest order."[318]

Articulation of a rule seemed to put an end to this kind of litigation, as Justice White had once predicted,[319] but ten years later, a similar case reached the Court. In *Florida Star v. B.J.F.,*[320] a novice reporter picked up a police report that identified sexual assault victim B.J.F. by her full name from the Jacksonville police press room. The unedited report had been left there inadvertently. When the paper ran a brief item using her full name, contrary to its own editorial policy and a Florida statute, B.J.F. sued on a theory of negligence per se. The trial judge agreed that the newspaper's violation of the statute gave rise to a negligence per se claim, and a jury awarded B.J.F. $75,000 in compensatory and $25,000 in punitive damages. That was affirmed per curiam by an intermediate court; the Florida Supreme Court declined to review. The newspaper petitioned successfully for certiorari.

Perhaps the change in court personnel over the decade – Burger, Stewart, and Powell were gone; Scalia, O'Connor, and Kennedy had arrived – made this a much tougher decision. Or perhaps it was the change in leadership from Burger to Rehnquist. On its facts, this case did not look all that different from the previous cases. But Justice White, who dissented along with Chief Justice Rehnquist and Justice O'Connor, declared that the 6-3 *Florida Star* decision was the "bottom of the slippery slope" created by the previous decisions – in each of which he had concurred.[321]

Writing for the majority, Marshall said *Cox* did not control the case because a police report is not a court document and does not carry with it the constitutionally significant notions of open trials. *Daily Mail* provided the proper rule, Marshall said, but he tweaked Burger's formulation to add a "narrowly tailored" requirement: "where a newspaper publishes truthful information which it has lawfully obtained, punishment may lawfully be imposed, if at all, only when narrowly tailored to a state interest of the highest order." And that was not the case here.[322] In an opinion that reasonably tracked the substance of the press amici briefs, which were substantial,[323] Marshall pointed out that a rape victim's privacy might be a state interest of the highest order under some circumstances, but not where the government itself provided the information, albeit inadvertently; that the statute covered only the mass media, and not other forms of dissemination, including neighborhood gossip; and that liability would attach without showing fault, making the publication of truthful information even less protected than publication of a libelous falsehood.[324]

The Supreme Court has heard one more case in this line – *Bartnicki v. Vopper*[325] –with an outcome similarly favorable to the press. Before that case was decided in 2001, however, it was not at all clear whether it would be controlled by and continue this line of cases, or whether the Court would treat it more like a newsgathering case. *Bartnicki* clearly had aspects of both and might very well have come out the other way. We explore that story at length in Chapter 8, but first turn to the newsgathering cases to see why treating *Bartnicki* as a newsgathering case would have been disastrous for the press's constitutional litigators. Chapter 7 will survey the newsgathering cases since the mid- 1970s, but we begin with a case study of the seminal newsgathering case, *United States v. Caldwell*, one of three cases the Court consolidated in 1972 under the caption *Branzburg v. Hayes*.[326]

Chapter 7 – *Branzburg v. Hayes*: The Press Divided

A. Seeking a Testimonial Privilege

1. The *Caldwell* Case

Earl Caldwell was born in Clearfield, Pa., and attended the University of Buffalo as a business major until, as an African-American, he became disillusioned by racism in the insurance industry. On returning to Clearfield, Caldwell landed a job on the local newspaper, *The Progress*, where he became sports editor. From there, he moved on to the Lancaster *Intelligencer-Journal*, and then to the Rochester, N.Y., *Democrat and Chronicle,* where he first began writing on racial issues. In 1965, he began reporting for the *New York Herald Tribune*, moving briefly to the *New York Post* when the *Herald Tribune* closed. He joined *The New York Times* in 1967.[1]

Caldwell was one of a number of black reporters hired in the mid- to late 1960s by the mainstream press to cover race relations, particularly the urban rioting that was largely inaccessible to white reporters.[2] Gene Roberts points out that, until then, only a handful of black reporters worked on white dailies – 31 in 1955, according to *Ebony* magazine.[3] Caldwell recalls the new influx of black reporters hired to cover, not only the riots, but also the dramatic changes occurring in the black community, led to the formation of the New York Association of Black Journalists, which would play a critical part in his story.[4]

In the fall of 1968, the *Times* assigned Caldwell to cover the Black Panther Party in the San Francisco Bay area, and he developed a confidential relationship with the Panthers that enabled him to write stories "that no one else in the country could have written."[5] Caldwell's stories from the period point to access to Panther headquarters and personalities that could not help but attract official attention.

> In the black room of an apartment deep in the Fillmore slum a bearded youth in an Afro hair style uncovered a stack of rifles that was only partly hidden in a dark corner. He said nothing but began wrapping the weapons in robes and old blankets, preparing to transport them to Oakland, where [Huey] Newton has been jailed for nearly a year. Some were high-powered lever action rifles. Others appeared to be automatic weapons. "The verdict [in the Newton trial] is irrelevant," the youth said. "The sky is the limit.[6]

> It is well past midnight and quiet out on Shattuck Avenue. The liquor store on the corner is empty, and the lights are already out

> in the barbecue shop next door. But up in the middle of the block, up there in the two-story brownstone that the Black Panther party occupies, a dash of yellow light slips through an upstairs window. They are still there, up there in those cluttered, noisy rooms behind windows covered with huge steel plates and walls lined with bulging, dusty sandbags.[7]

In late 1969, the FBI began calling Caldwell every day, asking him to spy on his sources. Caldwell refused to cooperate, and, on the advice of bureau chief Wallace Turner, eventually stopped answering the telephone. "They were hounding me for over a month," Caldwell says, warning "'We're not playing. This is not a game. If you won't talk to us, you'll tell it to the court.'"[8]

When the federal marshal initially came to the *Times* bureau with a subpoena, Caldwell was out. Turner urged him to destroy his files, then do some reporting from Alaska until it all blew over. Caldwell did destroy most of the files he had been saving to write a book, including information on Panthers he had not written about in the newspapers ("Panthers I keep in my pocket," he called them). But once the material was destroyed, he says, he "didn't have the heart" to go to Alaska.[9]

On Feb. 2, 1970, Caldwell was served with a subpoena *duces tecum* ordering him to appear before a federal grand jury in the Northern District of California.[10] He was told to bring his notes and recorded interviews with the Panther leadership and to testify as to the purposes and activities of the Party.[11] Caldwell believes the FBI broke into the *Times* bureau, or tapped its telephones, or both, because some of the Panthers named in the subpoena had been "in his pocket" and never written about.[12] In any event, he objected to the scope of the subpoena, and his scheduled appearance was postponed.[13] On March 16, however, he received a second subpoena, without the requirement that he produce documents.[14] Caldwell and the *Times* moved to quash on the ground that requiring Caldwell to testify before the grand jury would "suppress vital First Amendment freedoms."[15]

Caldwell was supported by a number of affidavits from *New York Times* and *Newsweek* reporters, as well as an amicus curiae brief from CBS News, with affidavits from its leading correspondents;[16] the government filed three memoranda in opposition to the motion to quash, each supported by affidavits.[17]

Behind the scenes, however, all was not nearly so harmonious. According to Caldwell, the *Times* initially hired the San Francisco law firm Pillsbury, Madison & Sutro to defend him.[18] When he met with John Bates, the attorney assigned to his case, Caldwell recalls that the lawyer told him, "We have a problem out here with law and order. I'm sure that some of your material ought to be turned over to the FBI."[19] Bates told Caldwell to bring all of his material to the office, meet with Times Co. Executive Vice President Harding Bancroft, who was flying out to oversee the case, and together they would decide what should be turned over.[20]

Determined to find his own lawyer, Caldwell sought help from the New York Association of Black Journalists. That connection led him to the NAACP Legal Defense Fund (LDF), which found the perfect lawyer for the case. Anthony G. Amsterdam had done a number of death penalty cases for LDF and, in 1969, had helped in the appeal of Black Panther Bobby Seale. He was teaching at Stanford Law School at the time, and agreed to hear Caldwell's story.[21]

Caldwell was initially reluctant to talk with another white lawyer, but he had nowhere else to turn. He called Amsterdam around midnight and drove to his home in Los Altos. When Amsterdam told Caldwell he had a "legal right to refuse" to testify, Caldwell was thrilled. Amsterdam took the case *pro bono*, and he, not Caldwell, attended the strategy meeting with Bancroft the next day. When Caldwell arrived some hours later, Bancroft indicated that he was delighted with Amsterdam and wanted to hire him. Amsterdam refused to accept money from the paper.[22]

On April 6, the District Court denied the motion to quash, but issued a protective order limiting the scope of Caldwell's testimony to information given to him for publication.[23] The court also stayed the effective date of its order pending appeal to the U.S. Court of Appeals for the Ninth Circuit,[24] but the appeal was dismissed by the Ninth Circuit "apparently on the ground that the District Court order was not appealable."[25]

Caldwell received yet a third subpoena on May 22, 1970, and the District Court again ordered attendance under the protective order.[26] Fearing for his personal safety, Caldwell refused to appear before the grand jury in secret.[27] The District Court found Caldwell in contempt, and he again appealed to the Ninth Circuit.[28]

According to Caldwell, the Times Company was furious at the appeal. The company ordered him back to New York to discuss the matter with General Counsel James Goodale. Caldwell remembers Goodale "wagging his finger in front of my face, saying 'you keep pushing it and you're going to get a bad law written.'"[29] Goodale's prediction would ultimately come true, but not in the Ninth Circuit. Caldwell, who did not attend the argument, said Amsterdam persuaded the court that ruining Caldwell's career and risking his life was too high a price for a grand jury appearance where no confidences would be revealed.[30]

The Ninth Circuit reversed on Nov. 16, 1970, ordering the contempt judgment vacated and holding that "where it has been shown that the public's First Amendment right to be informed would be jeopardized by requiring a journalist to submit to secret Grand Jury interrogation, the Government must respond by demonstrating a compelling need for the witness's presence before the judicial process properly can issue to require attendance."[31] The United States petitioned for certiorari, which was granted on May 3, 1971, along with petitions from Paul Branzburg and Paul Pappas, whose cases are discussed below.[32]

2. The *Branzburg* Case

In 1969, Paul Branzburg was a 27-year-old reporter for the Louisville *Courier-Journal*, where he served as a member of a special assignment group doing investigative journalism.[33] Branzburg had received an A.B. from Cornell University in 1963, a J.D. from Harvard Law School in 1966, and an M.S. *Cum Laude* from Columbia University Graduate School of Journalism in 1967. His investigative work on the use of narcotics and other issues had been recognized on numerous occasions, and he was nominated twice for the Pulitzer Prize based on stories dealing with drugs and agricultural subsidies.

On Nov. 15, 1969, the *Courier-Journal* carried a story by Branzburg describing his observations of two Louisville "hippies" synthesizing hashish from marijuana in a makeshift lab.[34] Branzburg wrote: "'I don't know why I'm letting you do this story,' [Larry] said quietly. 'To make the narcs (narcotics detectives) mad, I guess. That's the main reason.' However, Larry and his partner asked for and received a promise that their names would be changed."[35] The article also included a photograph of hands working with hashish.[36]

Branzburg was subpoenaed shortly thereafter by the Jefferson County grand jury; he appeared, but declined to identify the "Larry" and "Jack" of his story.[37] Branzburg's counsel, Edgar A. Zingman, argued that Kentucky's shield law[38] permitted Branzburg to protect his sources, but Judge J. Miles Pound rejected the argument and directed Branzburg to answer the question.[39] Zingman objected, citing both the shield law and the press clause of the First Amendment, and petitioned the Court of Appeals for an injunction against enforcement of Pound's order.[40] The petition urged the Court to grant relief based on the state shield law, the state constitution, and the United States Constitution "as an interference with the exercise of freedom of the press [which] would permit courts to destroy that confidential relationship which is essential to a free press...."[41]

The Court of Appeals granted a temporary restraining order the same day,[42] but a year later denied the petition over a single dissent.[43] Branzburg filed a motion to reconsider[44] based on the newly issued opinion of the United States Court of Appeals for the Ninth Circuit in *Caldwell v. United States.*[45] In January 1971, the Court of Appeals issued a revised opinion without substantive change.[46] The Court did not address the constitutional issue and *Caldwell* was never mentioned by name.[47] A further motion to stay the order pending petition for certiorari[48] was denied.[49]

Even before the revised opinion was issued, Branzburg had published two more controversial stories based on observations and interviews with Kentucky drug users.[50] Once again, he was subpoenaed, this time to appear before the Franklin County Grand Jury,[51] and once again, he refused, submitting instead a motion to quash the subpoena.[52] At the same time, he filed another petition with the Kentucky Court of Appeals for injunctive relief.[53]

Judge Henry Meigs denied the motion subject to issuance of a protective order in accordance with *Caldwell*.[54] After hearing arguments from Branzburg and the Commonwealth, Meigs issued the protective order, which limited the testimony Branzburg would be required to give to his personal observation of criminal activity. Specifically, he would not be required to reveal confidential sources or anything told him in confidence.[55]

That same day, the Kentucky Court of Appeals denied the petition for injunctive relief[56] and issued its opinion three days later.[57] The Court of Appeals went to great lengths to distinguish Branzburg's case from the new *Caldwell* decision in the Ninth Circuit on their respective facts. The court also expressed "misgivings" about the rule announced in *Caldwell* as a "drastic departure from the generally recognized rule" that journalists' sources are not privileged under the First Amendment.[58] Once again, Branzburg's motion to stay the order[59] was denied.[60] Branzburg's petition for certiorari was granted by the United States Supreme Court on May 3, 1971,[61] along with petitions in the *Caldwell* and *Pappas* cases.

3. The *Pappas* Case

The *Pappas* case also involved reporting on the Black Panther movement of the early 1970s. Paul Pappas was a television reporter and photographer for WTEV-TV in New Bedford, Mass.,[62] working out of the East Providence, R.I., office.[63] On July 30, 1970, he was called to New Bedford to cover civil disorders there from the Panther perspective. He was given an address for the Party's storefront headquarters, and, after one false start, finally threaded his way through the barricades and gained entry. There, at about 3 p.m., he recorded and photographed a prepared statement read by one of the Panther leaders.[64]

Pappas apparently took his story back to the station after receiving permission to return to Panther headquarters. He returned around 9 p.m. and was allowed to enter and remain inside the headquarters on condition that he not to disclose anything he saw or heard there. If, as the Panthers anticipated, the police raided the headquarters, Pappas would be free to report and photograph that as he wished. The raid never occurred, and Pappas wrote nothing further about the three hours he spent at Panther headquarters that night.[65]

Two months later, Pappas was summoned to appear before the Bristol County Grand Jury, where he claimed a First Amendment privilege to decline to answer any questions about his observations and conversations at Panther headquarters that night.[66] When he was again directed to appear before the grand jury a few days later, he filed a motion to quash on First Amendment grounds and because he feared "that any future possibilities of obtaining information to be used in my work would be definitely jeopardized, inasmuch as I wouldn't be trusted or couldn't gain anyone's confidence to acquire any information in reporting the news as it is."[67] Pappas also said he feared for his personal safety.[68]

The motion to quash was denied by the trial judge, who noted the absence of a shield law in Massachusetts and held there was no constitutional privilege. "Pappas does not have any privilege and must respond to the subpoena and testify to such questions as may be put to him by the Grand Jury relating to what he saw and heard, and the identity of any persons he may have seen."[69] The case was reported by the superior court directly to the Supreme Judicial Court of Massachusetts for an interlocutory ruling.[70]

Despite receiving "helpful and thorough briefs... filed by Massachusetts and New York attorneys in behalf of a number of broadcasting, television, and news gathering interests,"[71] the Supreme Judicial Court on Jan. 29, 1971, rejected *Caldwell*, on which Pappas and amici "seemed greatly to rely on." [72] To follow that opinion, the court said, would be to engage in "judicial amendment of the Constitution or judicial legislation."[73] The court concluded that the Superior Court was correct in holding that Pappas had no privilege.[74] As it did in *Branzburg* and *Caldwell*, the United States Supreme Court granted Pappas's petition for certiorari on May 3, 1971.[75]

4. In the Supreme Court

The three cases were thoroughly briefed in the United States Supreme Court, and oral arguments were conducted on Feb. 22, 1972, in *Caldwell*, and the very next day in *Branzburg* and *Pappas*. On June 28, 1972, the Court issued its opinion, with Justice Byron R. White writing for the Court.[76] The decision has been described and analyzed many times,[77] including this author's own analysis.[78] We return to the opinion in Part D; for now, it will suffice to say that the Court reversed *Caldwell* and affirmed *Branzburg* and *Pappas*, finding no testimonial privilege for reporters in the First Amendment. While Justice White acknowledged that newsgathering qualifies for some measure of First Amendment protection,[79] the Court was deeply divided as to the scope of that protection.

Writing in dissent, Justice Douglas would have found that journalists have "an absolute right not to appear before a grand jury."[80] Also in dissent, Justice Stewart, joined by Justices Brennan and Marshall, would have affirmed the balancing test in *Caldwell*.[81] Justice Powell, in a concurring opinion, interpreted Justice White's opinion for the Court as requiring courts to strike "a proper balance between freedom of the press and the obligation of all citizens to give relevant testimony with respect to criminal conduct."[82]

Although Powell's concurring opinion is sometimes seen as a fifth vote for an undefined reporter's privilege,[83] Justice White's opinion[84] is more widely viewed as a stunning defeat for the press with lasting precedential consequences. Yet mainstream media organizations initiated the litigation that led to the *Branzburg* decision. Mainstream media organizations made the decisions to appeal all of these cases to the United States Courts of Appeals and two of them to the United States Supreme Court. And mainstream media organizations provided the theoretical foundation for all the appeals through party and amicus briefs.

B. Why Litigate? Journalistic Values at Stake

In each of the cases considered in this chapter, the reporters – Earl Caldwell, Paul Branzburg, and Paul Pappas – were confronted with three choices: (1) testify before the grand jury, breaking one or more promises of confidentiality; (2) refuse to testify and risk being jailed for contempt of court; or (3) litigate the issue to avoid either testifying or going to jail. Assuming their employers would pay for litigation, the reporters' choices were not surprising. But litigation costs money, not only in attorney fees and court costs, but also in lost productivity and general distraction. The logical economic choice for their employers would be to encourage the reporters to testify. As noted above, the Times Company initially opposed Caldwell's refusal to comply with the subpoena[85] and his appeal to the Ninth Circuit, but there is no indication that financial considerations played a role in that decision. Moreover, the company ultimately joined Caldwell's motion to quash the original subpoena.[86]

In the end, all three cases were litigated, suggesting that personal and/or journalistic values were at stake here that transcended economics. Caldwell's fear for his personal safety certainly weighed heavily in his desire to litigate, rather than appear or testify, but he never believed that his employer shared that concern.[87] Nor was fear Caldwell's sole motivation; appearing before the grand jury would, at minimum, deprive him of the access he needed to fulfill his self-described "mission to tell the truth, to tell the story."[88] The briefs and oral arguments presented in the three cases suggest three core journalistic values that might be considered fundamental:

1. Satisfying the public's "right to know"
2. Upholding the reporter's ethical responsibility
3. Preventing press entanglement with government[89]

We turn to the filings to see how these three values were asserted as journalistic justifications for finding a reporter's privilege in the First Amendment.

1. Right to Know

Much has been written, pro and con, about the public's so-called "right to know."[90] Often, the question is framed as whether the First Amendment's press clause contemplates something more than the absence of governmental restriction on the right to publish the information one already knows, including an affirmative right to acquire information in the public interest. Whatever the legal soundness of that proposition, it is axiomatic that the journalistic enterprise depends utterly upon the public's right to know to justify, not only its "preferred position"[91] in our democratic society, but its very existence.[92]

In each of the three *Branzburg* cases, the argument growing out of this value goes something like this: requiring reporters to testify before grand juries would undermine any promise of confidentiality that a reporter might extend to sources of information, and thus have a chilling effect on sources' willingness to provide information that the public has a right to know. One or another version of this argument is not only present in each of the cases, it is central to all of them. Paul Branzburg's argument to the Supreme Court states the argument this way:

> A. Newsgathering activities are essential to the effective functioning of a free press, and as such are protected by the First Amendment to the Constitution of the United States. A significant portion of such newsgathering activities is the development by individual reporters of confidential informants who give information to the reporter with the understanding that some or all of the information or the source of such information will not be revealed.
>
> B. The courts below are attempting to force the Petitioner to appear before a grand jury to answer questions pertaining to the identities of such informants and unpublished information received from them. Such compelled testimony will inevitably discourage these and other informants from contacting and talking to reporters, as well as discourage the reporter from publishing information gathered from such sources. This inability of the press to be able to obtain such information, or its reluctance to use such information, is a severe abridgment of the freedom of the press protected by the First Amendment.[93]

In his brief for *The New York Times* and other amici on Caldwell's behalf, noted attorney and Yale law professor Alexander Bickel stated the case even more succinctly:

> The people's right to be informed by print and electronic news media is thus the central concern of the First Amendment's Freedom of Speech and of the Press Clause. [If] an obligation is imposed by law on a reporter of news to disclose the identity of confidential sources… the reporter's access to news, and therefore the public's access, will be severely constricted and in some circumstances shut off. The reporter's access *is* the public's access…. (emphasis in original) The issue here is the public's right to know. That right is the reporter's by virtue of the proxy which the Freedom of the Press Clause of the First Amendment

gives to the press on behalf of the public.[94]

In its brief supporting Branzburg, the American Newspaper Publishers Association (ANPA) argued similarly that "but for the assurance of confidence, many controversial issues presented in the daily newspapers of this country would otherwise never reach the typesetting stage."[95] And at oral argument, Branzburg's attorney, Edgar Zingman, insisted that "it is necessary to the functioning of the press, and it has been a part of the process of the press, that such confidences be given, and those confidences are the condition upon which information is available to the public."[96]

In *Pappas* and *Caldwell*, the argument is pressed, not only by the parties and amici, but through affidavits from prominent individual journalists. Pappas's petition for certiorari contains the following footnote:

> In an *amicus* brief filed in this case by the Columbia Broadcasting System, Inc., before the Massachusetts Supreme Judicial Court, correspondents Walter Cronkite, Eric Sevareid, Mike Wallace, Dan Rather and Marvin Kalb submitted affidavits strongly asserting the necessity of preserving confidentiality in newsgathering and demonstrating that the betrayal of news sources and private communications would seriously diminish the effectiveness of reporting and the amount and nature of news available to the public. Example after example was given, from talks with bartenders to discussions with the President of the United States, in which it was essential to preserve confidentiality.[97]

These affidavits, which were originally submitted as part of the record in *Caldwell*, along with others from *New York Times* and *Newsweek* reporters,[98] prompted the Massachusetts court to remark upon the "substantial news media pressure for adoption" of a reporter's privilege.[99] Indeed, amicus briefs supporting the three reporters in these cases were filed at one or another point in the proceedings by more than 20 major news organizations[100] – each emphasizing the "right to know" value and the threat to that value by a chilling effect on sources or self-censorship by reporters.[101]

2. Ethical Responsibility

If the "right to know" value provided the principal justification for finding a reporter's privilege in the First Amendment, the "ethical responsibility" value might be seen as a normative supplement to the instrumentalism of "right to know." As the current version of the Society of Professional Journalists (SPJ)

Code of Ethics makes clear, journalists are expected to keep their promises of confidentiality to sources.[102] Because the normative argument is far less compelling to a court, however, it is barely mentioned within the *Branzburg* advocacy documents.

The "ethical responsibility" notion does surface in the Radio Television News Directors Association (RTNDA) brief, at least in a footnote:

> Until now reporters have often risked contempt convictions in challenging compulsory process for the disclosure of confidential information; they have been encouraged to do so by a belief that there is First Amendment underpinning for their position, *as well as by moral commitments to informants*. In this manner confidential relationships have been supported by the reporter's fulfillment of his promise not to betray confidences, even though several lower courts have refused to recognized a constitutional privilege. If, however, the Supreme Court were to rule in such a way as to remove or seriously compromise the legal underpinning of *the basic ethic of journalists*, a reporter would not be so likely to guarantee confidentiality unconditionally.[103]

Notwithstanding this decidedly minimal treatment in the *Branzburg* cases, the "ethical responsibility" rationale exists independently within the journalism community. Ironically, the evidence comes from the betrayal of a confidential source the led to another Supreme Court opinion written by Justice White. In *Cohen v. Cowles Media*,[104] reporters for the *Minneapolis Star Tribune* and *St. Paul Pioneer Press*, among others, accepted an offer by Dan Cohen, a Republican campaign operative, for information concerning Marlene Johnson, the Democratic-Farmer-Laborite candidate for lieutenant governor of Minnesota, in exchange for a promise of confidentiality.[105] Cohen then provided the reporters with court records showing the candidate had two trivial arrests, leading to dismissed charges in one case and a vacated conviction in the other.

Editors at both papers independently decided to print the story, not of the candidate's indiscretions, but of Cohen's "dirty trick" and, over their reporters' protests, to identify Cohen by name.[106] As the author has previously noted:

> While the *Pioneer Press* editors buried Dan Cohen's name deep in the story, the *Star Tribune* editors featured it, apparently reasoning that the value of the story, if any, lay in Cohen's conduct, not Johnson's. The *Star Tribune* also attacked Cohen in its editorial pages, but neither paper reported that it had broken a promise of confidentiality with Cohen.[107]

Ultimately, the United States Supreme Court upheld Cohen's claim for damages against the newspapers for breaking their promise of confidentiality.[108]

From the editors' perspective, the public's "right to know" trumped the reporters' "ethical responsibility" to keep their promises. From the protesting reporters' perspective, the reverse was true. Either way, this episode shows that these values are independent, if related, and both are fundamental; the *Cohen* case is still debated in newsrooms today. *Cohen* is discussed at greater length in Chapter 7.

3. Government Entanglement

The third journalistic value found in the *Branzburg* documents is an aversion to serving as, or at least being perceived as, an agent of the government. Again, this value is not unrelated to the "right to know," but has implications beyond newsgathering to suggest an effect on reporting as well. Indeed, two of Kovach and Rosenstiel's nine "elements of journalism" stress independence: independence from faction and independence from power.[109]

As discussed in ANPA's amicus brief in *Caldwell*, "the subpoenas involved in these appeals pierce the wall traditionally separating the press and the government."[110] ANPA quoted extensively on that point from the Ninth Circuit opinion:

> If the Grand Jury may require appellant to make available to it information obtained by him in his capacity as news gatherer, then the Grand Jury and the Department of Justice have the power to appropriate appellant's investigative efforts to their own behalf – to convert him after the fact into an investigative agent of the Government. The very concept of a free press requires that the news media be accorded a measure of autonomy; that they should be free to pursue their own investigations to their own ends without fear of governmental interference; and that they should be able to protect their investigative processes.[111]

The Newspaper Guild's brief in *Caldwell* and *Pappas* also quoted the Ninth Circuit passage, and further asserted that widespread use of the press as a government agency was responsible for increasing violence against reporters by police and participants during public demonstrations.[112] "Not only does the prolific use of the subpoena impress a governmental function on the press; the practice, in addition to the destruction of communication with confidential news sources, significantly impairs the ability of the newsman to report public events of great significance."[113]

Still another danger of "government entanglement" caught the ACLU's attention: abuse of the grand jury process to harass reporters. Once conceived as a buffer between the state and the people, the civil liberties group said, grand juries have increasingly become "rubber stamps" for prosecutors and instruments for police investigation.[114]

> The prosecutor simply sits back, waits for the reporter to investigate and then causes the grand jury to issue a sweeping subpoena, regardless of the effects on the journalist's relationship to his confidential sources. Equally dangerous is the possibility that overbroad grand jury subpoenas will be used to penalize reporters who write news stories which the government finds objectionable and to deter such stories in the future.[115]

All of the foregoing demonstrates convincingly that the cases consolidated in *Branzburg v. Hayes* involved values the press considers fundamental to its constitutional role. A successful outcome in the litigation would have yielded statutory and/or constitutional interpretations that would have vindicated those values and greatly facilitated the work of all journalists. But that alone is not enough to justify the time and treasure the press put into this case. Part C examines the relative costs, benefits, and likelihood of success of the *Branzburg* litigation.

C. Why Litigate? Strategic Considerations

As noted above, the fact that these cases were litigated at all suggests that fundamental values were at stake; in this section, we posit that the decision to pursue these cases also depended on the parties' assessment of the benefits of success, the costs of failure, and the probability of either outcome. We begin by exploring the factors that may have led the media lawyers to think they could win.

1. Probability of Success

To reconstruct the participants' perception as to the probability of success or failure in the *Branzburg* cases, we will first examine precedent and related doctrine, particularly in the lower courts, where prior decisions may be binding and where respect for precedent and other canons of jurisprudence are more compelling than in the highest courts. Second, we will analyze judicial preferences, including political ideology, judicial philosophy, and attitude toward the press, from the litigants' perspective. Finally, we will look at public policy, as articulated in statutes and executive practices.

a. Precedent

As a general proposition, precedent and other jurisprudential considerations should have operated to discourage the litigants from pursuing these cases. But the *Caldwell* decision in the Ninth Circuit may well have created the impression in the Branzburg and Pappas camps that the weight of precedent could be overcome.[116] The most widely cited judicial precedent rejecting the reporter's testimonial privilege was *Garland v. Torre*,[117] an appeal from a criminal contempt holding. In the underlying case, singer Judy Garland had filed a libel claim against the Columbia Broadcasting System based on allegedly defamatory statements about her that appeared in a New York *Herald Tribune* column. The statements were attributed to an unnamed CBS executive, and columnist Marie Torres refused to identify the source of the statements when ordered to do so by the court. In an opinion authored by then Judge (later Justice) Potter Stewart, a Second Circuit panel declined to find a constitutional privilege that would protect Torres's source.[118]

The court accepted the "hypothesis that compulsory disclosure of a journalist's confidential sources of information entail an abridgment of press freedom by imposing some limitation upon the availability of news."[119] But the court pointed out that the freedom so abridged is not absolute. "What must be determined is whether the interest to be served by compelling the testimony of the witness in the present case justifies some impairment of this First Amendment freedom."[120]

Quoting Chief Justice Hughes's admonition that giving testimony is the duty of every citizen,[121] the court extended the principle to the press. "If an additional First Amendment liberty – the freedom of the press – is here involved, we do not hesitate to conclude that it too must give place under the Constitution to a paramount public interest in the fair administration of justice."[122]

Although *Garland* was not binding on any of the courts involved in the *Branzburg* cases, Judge Stewart had noted that no previous court had found a reporter's privilege in the absence of a statute.[123] While proponents of the privilege tried to distinguish *Garland*,[124] the precedents overwhelmingly favored compelling reporters' testimony, and, of course, Judge Stewart had become Justice Stewart.

The Ninth Circuit opinion in *Caldwell* was issued eleven days before the Kentucky Court of Appeals denied Paul Branzburg's motion to quash in *Branzburg v. Pound*. Ten days later, Branzburg filed a motion to reconsider that decision in light of the *Caldwell* holding.[125] The court reissued its original opinion, adding only a footnote to assert that Branzburg had abandoned his constitutional argument, rendering *Caldwell* irrelevant without mentioning it.[126]

By the time *Branzburg v. Meigs*[127] reached the Kentucky Court of Appeals, *Caldwell* had been integrated into Branzburg's case. As noted above, the court both distinguished *Branzburg* from *Caldwell* on their facts and expressed "misgivings" about the rule announced in *Caldwell*. Nevertheless, the *Caldwell* decision may well have given Branzburg's team the confidence that, in taking the case up to the Supreme Court, the weight of precedent would now be a much closer call.

In Massachusetts, meanwhile, Pappas relied on the protective order granted by the District Court in *Caldwell* to support his motion to quash.[128] Superior Court Justice Frank E. Smith noted that reliance, but otherwise did not address the new case in ruling that Pappas had no privilege. By the time the Supreme Judicial Court reviewed Smith's ruling, the Ninth Circuit opinion in *Caldwell* had been out for about six weeks. Again, as discussed above, the precedent did not move the court, but may well have encouraged Pappas to press on.

But if the favorable *Caldwell* decisions encouraged Branzburg and Pappas to appeal their cases to the Supreme Court, precedent provides no explanation for Caldwell's decision to incur a contempt judgment by refusing to appear before the grand jury under the District Court's protective order. Indeed, we know that Times Co. General Counsel James Goodale and Caldwell attorney Anthony Amsterdam looked at the same precedents and reached different conclusions. Amsterdam unequivocally told Caldwell that he had a "right" to refuse to testify, while Goodale vigorously opposed Caldwell's taking the appeal because he feared it would make "bad law." Goodale, the more experienced media lawyer, got the outcome right in the end, but Amsterdam was more in tune with his client's wishes and the case moved ahead.

b. Judicial Preferences

One possible key to Amsterdam's assertion may have been a sense that the federal courts in California would be as sympathetic as any, anywhere in the country.[129] Judge Zirpoli had been appointed by President John F. Kennedy and had served about ten years when the *Caldwell* case came up. [130] For much of his career, however, he had been a prosecutor, serving as assistant district attorney for the City and County of San Francisco from 1928-1932, and as assistant United States attorney in Northern California from 1933-1944.[131]

On the Ninth Circuit Courtof Appeals, Republican appointees held an 8 to 5 edge over Democrats in 1970.[132] The three-judge panel that Caldwell ultimately drew included Eisenhower appointee Charles Merton Merrill[133] and Johnson appointee Walter Raleigh Ely, Jr.,[134] as well as William R. Jameson,[135] a U.S. District Judge for the District of Montana, sitting by designation, another Eisenhower appointee. So if the ideology of the judges was a motivating factor, it was not predictable by party affiliation. Yet the overwhelmingly favorable opinion issued by the Ninth Circuit panel made it all but inevitable that the government would seek and the Supreme Court would grant certiorari.[136]

Presumably, both Amsterdam and Goodale considered the preferences of the Supreme Court justices at some point during the litigation. But that consideration would have been strategically valuable only on or before June 4, 1970, when Caldwell incurred the contempt judgment that formed the basis for his appeal to the Ninth Circuit. From that moment on, the decision to take the case to the Supreme Court was effectively out of his hands.

The Burger Court in 1970 was ideologically divided into three groups. On the left were Justices Hugo Black and William O. Douglas, very nearly First Amendment absolutists, and usually reliable liberals William Brennan and Thurgood Marshall.[137] On the right were Chief Justice Warren Burger and Justice Harry Blackmun, then called "The Minnesota Twins" for their matched conservatism.[138] In the center were moderate Republicans John Marshall Harlan and Potter Stewart and conservative Democrat Byron White.[139] Justices Lewis Powell and William Rehnquist, who would ultimately hear the *Branzburg* case, had not yet replaced Black and Harlan.

The justices sitting in June 1970 had voted in 16 press-related cases over the years. Of the 87 votes cast by these nine justices in those 16 cases, 61 votes or 70% of the total were cast in favor of the press's position; only 26 votes or 30% were cast against the press's position.[140] Amsterdam and Goodale were certainly aware that Black and Harlan were nearing retirement and that Richard Nixon was president, but the likelihood of success must still have looked very strong based on ideological preferences in June 1970.

Moreover, Justice White's hostility toward the press had not begun to manifest itself before June 1970. To be sure, he had written one opinion that could be interpreted as denying broadcasters of their full First Amendment rights,[141] and two separate opinions[142] expressing reservations against broadly interpreting the standards in *New York Times v. Sullivan*.[143] But the *Red Lion* decision had been unanimous against the broadcasters, and White had supported the broadcasters in another important case, *Estes v. Texas*,[144] by dissenting from the opinion that cameras in the courtroom were per se unconstitutional.[145] White had also unequivocally supported *Sullivan* itself and most of its progeny through 1970.[146] Although White's antipathy toward the press is said to date from his football days,[147] its clear expression would only come later.[148] The Court had not heard any newsgathering cases before 1970, and Caldwell's legal team could not have anticipated the strength of White's opposition to extending First Amendment protection to newsgathering activities.[149]

Ironically, Amsterdam must have counted Justice Potter Stewart among the likely opponents of the privilege. After all, he had been the author of the oft-cited *Garland v. Torre*[150] decision when he served on the Second Circuit, and there was no reason to believe he would change his mind. A reasonable head count of the then-current Supreme Court bench would have found Black, Douglas, Brennan, and Marshall solidly in favor of the privilege; Harlan, Burger, Blackmun, and Stewart solidly against; and White very probably in favor.

In short, if Amsterdam had conducted an analysis of judicial preferences before June 4, 1970, that analysis would have suggested that success was at least as likely as failure, if not more likely, and he would not have been dissuaded from taking the case further. Of course, no one could have predicted the appointments of Powell and Rehnquist to the Supreme Court, much less the pivotal role that Powell would come to play. To Caldwell, however, it was Rehnquist's appointment that was most problematic. Caldwell says the late Fred Graham, legal reporter for the *Times* and later CBS News, told him that Rehnquist had been deeply involved in his case while serving in the Department of Justice.[151] And he deeply believes that the *Times's* half-hearted support for his cause undermined Caldwell's efforts to persuade Rehnquist to recuse himself. Had he done so, the 4-4 decision would have affirmed the Ninth Circuit, although it would have no precedential value.[152]

c. Public Policy

To this point, we have suggested that Caldwell may have been encouraged to try for a better First Amendment interpretation from the appellate courts based on the liberal reputation of the Ninth Circuit Court of Appeals generally and the still liberal-leaning United States Supreme Court, which had overwhelmingly supported the press in recent years. We have further suggested that Branzburg and Pappas may well have been encouraged to seek Supreme Court review of their cases, despite the absence of compelling precedent, based on the new *Caldwell* decision in the Ninth Circuit.

To help determine how realistic those expectations might have been, we now turn to public policy considerations. Public policy is broadly defined as the expression of the people's will by the political branches of government through statutes and executive practice.[153] Here, identifying the prevailing public policy requires us to examine the prevalence of reporter's shield laws and the policies of the Department of Justice on issuing subpoenas commanding reporters to testify. The analysis will show that, while only Branzburg had a legitimate expectation based on public policy of a better deal than he got from the courts, all three journalists might have been encouraged by new Department of Justice rules governing reporters' testimony.

Perhaps the best place to begin a discussion of the relevant public policy is Wigmore's hoary dictum that "the public... has a right to every man's evidence,"[154] quoted in one form or another throughout these cases.[155] All testimonial privileges, whether grounded in statute, common law, or the Constitution, are exceptions to this general rule and, according to traditional principles of interpretation, must therefore be narrowly construed.

Of the three jurisdictions involved in this case, only Kentucky had enacted a testimonial privilege for reporters, often called a reporter's shield law.[156] That statute was the principal basis, along with constitutional arguments, for Branzburg's initial request for injunctive relief and subsequent state court appeals.[157] Ultimately, the Court of Appeals ruled that the shield law was inapplicable because it protected only the "source" of Branzburg's information and not his personal observations.[158]

The court took great pains to distinguish the "source" of any information procured by a reporter, whose identity was privileged by the statute, from the "information" itself. Here, Branzburg was not asked to reveal the identity of any informants he may have had, the court said, but rather the identity of persons he saw committing a crime.[159]

> In all likelihood the present case is complicated by the fact that the persons who committed the crime were probably the same persons who informed Branzburg that the crime would be, or was being, committed. If so, this is a rare case where informants actually informed against themselves. But in that event the privilege which would have protected disclosure of their identity as *informants* cannot be extended beyond their role as informants to protect their identity in the entirely different role as perpetrators of a crime (emphasis in original).[160]

Otherwise, the court said, a reporter who witnessed the assassination of the president or governor, or a bank robbery in progress, or a forcible rape, might not be required to identify the perpetrator.[161] Chief Justice Edward P. Hill, writing in dissent, rejected that parade of horribles and called the majority view "a strained and unnecessarily narrow construction" of the term "source."[162] Hill pointed out that the statute contained no such limitation and quoted extensively from a Pennsylvania case upholding that state's shield law.

> [I]mportant information, tips and leads will dry up and the public will often be deprived of the knowledge of dereliction of public duty, bribery, corruption, conspiracy and other crimes committed or possibly committed by public officials or by powerful individuals or organizations, unless newsmen are able to *fully and completely* protect the sources of their information. It is vitally important that this public shield against governmental inefficiency, corruption and crime be preserved against piercing and erosion.
>
> * * *
>
> The [shield law] is a wise and salutary declaration of public policy whose spiritual father is the revered Constitutionally ordained freedom of the press. The Act must therefore, we repeat, be liberally and broadly construed in order to carry out the clear objective and intent of the Legislature *which has placed the gathering and the protection of the source of news as of greater*

> *importance to the public interest and of more value to the public welfare* than the disclosure of the alleged crime or the alleged criminal (emphasis is Hill's).[163]

But Chief Justice Hill was the only state judge in all of these cases to support the privilege. In the *Pappas* case, the Massachusetts Supreme Judicial Court took pains to point out that, "unlike certain other states," Massachusetts had created no reporter's privilege.[164] The court cited opposition to the privilege in the American Law Institute's Model Code of Evidence to support the rejection of both statutory and constitutional privileges.[165] And in the Ninth Circuit, District Judge Jameson's concurring opinion also pointedly noted that Congress had not enacted a shield law as he expressed the view that Judge Zirpoli's protective order might have satisfied Caldwell's constitutional rights.[166]

On the other hand, 17 states had enacted shield laws by 1970,[167] and several of those enactments had occurred only recently.[168] One could reasonably expect that the Supreme Court might be swayed by the trend in public policy in favor of the privilege. The lawyers would also have been aware of a dramatic development within the Justice Department of President Richard Nixon.

During the oral arguments before the Ninth Circuit, counsel for the government submitted a press release from Attorney General John N. Mitchell outlining new guidelines for issuing subpoenas to the news media. As summarized by Judge Jameson, the guidelines "expressly recognized that the 'Department does not approve of utilizing the press as a spring board for investigations,'" and provided *inter alia*, that,

> There should be sufficient reason to believe that the information sought is essential to a successful investigation – particularly with reference to directly establishing guilt or innocence.... The government should have unsuccessfully attempted to obtain the information from alternative non-press sources.... [Subpoenas] should normally be limited to the verification of published information and to such surrounding circumstances as relate to the accuracy of the published information.... [S]ubpoenas should, wherever possible, be directed at material information regarding a limited subject matter, should cover a reasonably limited period of time, and should avoid requiring production of a large volume of unpublished material.[169]

While the Justice Department's announcement of the guidelines follows by two months Caldwell's critical decision on June 4, 1970, to refuse to appear, work on the guidelines was well underway before then. And although there is nothing in the record to indicate the extent of their knowledge, there is little doubt that Caldwell and Amsterdam would have known about the guidelines at the time. The guidelines were being drafted by William H. Rehnquist, who was appointed by President Nixon in 1969 to be assistant attorney general in the Office of Legal Counsel,[170] and Jack C. Landau, former Supreme Court reporter for the Newhouse News Service.[171] Landau joined the Nixon Justice Department in 1969, only to leave in April 1970 to return to Newhouse.[172] Landau had been a key figure in the early days of the Reporters Committee for Freedom of the Press, which was formed specifically to deal with the *Caldwell* case, and became executive director of the organization not long after his return to Newhouse.[173]

By the time briefs were filed in the United States Supreme Court, the guidelines were being held up by the journalists and amici as the government's recognition that grand jury inquiries could pose First Amendment problems.[174] Perhaps the most extensive use the guidelines appears in Alexander Bickel's amicus brief in *Caldwell* for *The New York Times* and other media companies. Acknowledging that the guidelines do not have the force of law, Bickel said they nevertheless "evince most authoritatively a developing consensus of what the law should be."[175]

Thus, taking three critical predictors of success – precedent, preferences, and public policy – as a whole, the press had some reason to believe that it could win the fight for a testimonial privilege under the First Amendment. The *Caldwell* decision in the Ninth Circuit seemed likely to counterbalance older, adverse precedent;[176] there seemed to be five potentially favorable votes on the Supreme Court; and public policy as articulated by several state legislatures and the Department of Justice seemed to be moving in the right direction. Additional factors, such as the strong support of amici[177] – including the American Civil Liberties Union[178] – and some of the nation's best legal talent, must have seemed sufficient to overcome the government's opposition.[179]

Even if some doubts remained about the likelihood of success, important forces within the media apparently concluded that the benefits of pursuing the cases to victory – an absolute or qualified First Amendment privilege – outweighed the costs of defeat. We turn to that cost-benefit analysis now.

2. Cost-Benefit Analysis

It is hard to overstate how devastating the *Branzburg* precedent has been for newsgathering; the Supreme Court's refusal to find a meaningful First Amendment privilege in that case has been the foundation for numerous decisions minimizing any First Amendment right to gather news.[180] Moreover, the high cost of an adverse decision in *Branzburg* was obviously apparent to Times Co. General Counsel James Goodale, who warned Caldwell that his appeal to the Ninth Circuit could make "bad law."

On the other hand, a victory in *Branzburg* must have seemed especially beneficial in light of the Nixon administration's and local prosecutors' unprecedented use of subpoenas for reporters' sources, notes, pictures, and testimony that characterized the late 1960s.[181] Particularly after the 1968 Democratic convention, subpoenas targeting the coverage of anti-Vietnam War activists and Black Power militants like Caldwell's Panthers proliferated. McKay calls the rapid increase in the number of subpoenas "staggering," citing research showing about 500 subpoenas served on reporters between 1970 and 1976, compared to about a dozen between 1960 and 1968.[182]

Of course, it is not possible to quantify and analyze the cost of a disastrous precedent in *Branzburg* versus the benefits of permanent relief from the threat of subpoenas. But it is entirely possible that a rough cost-benefit calculation, tempered by the probability of success, may have influenced the decision of most – but not all – media participants to ask the Supreme Court for a qualified, rather than absolute, testimonial privilege. An absolute privilege, going beyond the ruling of the Ninth Circuit, beyond even the benefits of most state shield laws, would have been the most desirable, yet least likely outcome in the case. Thus, prudence would have dictated a reasoned argument for a qualified privilege – a somewhat less desirable, but far more likely outcome – except for those participants who calculated that the benefits of an absolute shield outweighed the cost of losing the case altogether.

The initial response to the subpoenas by Caldwell and the *Times* – a plea in the alternative to quash the subpoenas or issue a protective order[183] – certainly reflected a degree of caution. Even after the split between Caldwell and the *Times*, Caldwell's opposition to the government's petition for certiorari suggests they were reasonably satisfied with the Ninth Circuit opinion. Caldwell's Brief in Opposition suggested the Court could best confront "the vexing and difficult First Amendment problems presented by grand jury subpoenas addressed to newsmen…after more than one lower court has grappled with them."[184]

In his brief to the Supreme Court, Amsterdam argued for a qualified privilege, but with a strong presumption of confidentiality.[185] He insisted that a "compelling state interest" was required by the First Amendment in order to force a reporter to appear before a grand jury.[186] "The elements of such a showing are at least three," he said:

> (1) The "information sought" must be demonstrably relevant to a clearly defined, legitimate subject of governmental inquiry….
>
> (2) It must affirmatively appear that the inquiry is likely to turn up material information, that is: (a) that there is some factual basis for pursuing the investigation, and (b) that there is reasonable ground to conclude that the particular witness subpoenaed has information material to it…[and]

> (3) The information sought must be unobtainable by means less destructive of First Amendment freedoms....[187]

The New York Times also insisted on a "compelling interest" standard as amicus in the Supreme Court proceeding. Joined by NBC, CBS and ABC, by the Chicago *Sun-Times* and *Daily News*, by the Associated Press Managing Editors and Broadcasters' Associations, and by the Association of American Publishers, the *Times* urged the Court to require the government to "clearly demonstrate a compelling and overriding interest in the information" before requiring a reporter to testify.[188] The *Times* went on to explain that such a standard would preclude requiring a reporter's testimony "with respect to a category of crimes that cannot be deemed 'major,' as for example crimes variously categorized as 'victimless,' 'regulatory,' and 'sumptuary.'"[189]

Other amici urged a similar standard. For example, the Chicago *Tribune* sought to limit testimony to evidence "so important that non-production thereof would cause a miscarriage of justice."[190] The Radio Television News Directors Association characterized the desired standard as "irreparable harm," rather than "compelling interest," and said "the Court should adopt a standard which in the normal situation would raise no more than the slightest possibility of later disclosure."[191] A "compelling need" standard was urged by the Authors League of America[192] and a coalition of religious groups.[193]

These groups advocated a balancing test, albeit with a very high standard, apparently because they believed that the benefits of an absolute privilege were outweighed by the cost of defeat.[194] Other media organizations reached the opposite conclusion. The American Newspaper Publishers Association, for example, openly broke with the *Times* and joint amici as to the standard required:

> Nothing short of an absolute privilege, under the First Amendment, vested in professional newsmen to refuse to testify before any tribunal about any information or source of information derived as a result of their reportorial functions will create the certainty needed to generate confidence in their promises, whether express or implied, to preserve either a source's anonymity or privacy, and thus guarantee the right of the public to be fully informed.[195]

ANPA was joined in that position by *The Washington Post* and *Newsweek*;[196] the American Society of Newspaper Editors, Dow Jones, and Sigma Delta Chi;[197] and the National Press Photographers Association.[198] Even the venerable suggested that because reporters should only be required to testify to their knowledge concerning a planned, future crime of violence, "it may be preferable for the Court to adopt something approximating an absolute privilege, leaving to another day the carving out of possible exceptions."[199]

Whether one believes that the media representatives' advocacy of an absolute or qualified privilege was a reasonable proxy for their strategic cost-benefit analyses, or sincere expressions of their views of the law, it is clear that the press was a "house divided" on the desired scope of the testimonial privilege they sought. This failure to speak with one voice may have diluted the message being sent to the Court that such a privilege, whatever its scope, was commanded by the First Amendment. It would certainly have that effect in the legislative arena.[200] In the end, *Branzburg v. Hayes* was a stunning defeat,[201] with long-lasting implications for First Amendment doctrine.

D. Disaster in Court and Congress

1. The *Branzburg* Opinion

Paul Pappas's Reply Brief before the Supreme Court quotes a then-new report by University of Michigan Law School Professor Vincent Blasi for a then-new organization called Reporters Committee for Freedom of the Press, which had been organized in response to the *Caldwell* case:[202]

> Nothing, in the opinion of every reporter with whom I discussed the matter, would be more damaging to source relationships than a Supreme Court reversal of the Ninth Circuit's *Caldwell* holding. Several newsmen told me that initially they were extremely worried about the subpoena spate of two years ago, but that now their anxieties have greatly subsided as a result of the strong stand taken by the journalism profession and the tentative victories in court. However, a Supreme Court declaration that the first amendment is in no wise abridged by the practice of subpoenaeing reporters would, these newsmen assert, set off a wave of anxiety among sources. The publicity and imprimatur that would accompany such a Court holding would, in the opinion of these reporters, create an atmosphere even more uncongenial to source relationships than that which occurred two years ago, when the constitutional question remained in doubt.[203]

Unfortunately, Blasi proved more prophetic than persuasive. With lip service to "some" First Amendment protection for newsgathering, Justice White proceeded to list all the First Amendment values that were *not* at issue in these three cases:

> [N]o intrusions upon speech or assembly, no prior restraint or

> restriction on what the press may publish, and no express or implied command that the press publish what it prefers to withhold. No exaction or tax for the privilege of publishing, and no penalty, civil or criminal, related to the content of published material.... No attempt is made to require the press to publish its sources of information or indiscriminately to disclose them on request.
>
> The sole issue before us is the obligation of reporters to respond to grand jury subpoenas as other citizens do and to answer questions relevant to an investigation into the commission of a crime.[204]

Framing the issue thus told the entire story.

Emphasizing that "'the publisher of a newspaper has no special immunity from the application of general laws,'"[205] a theme he would return to in other newsgathering cases, White further minimized the protection accorded newsgathering by undermining the "right to know" value on which it is predicated: "[T]he First Amendment does not guarantee the press a constitutional right of special access to information not available to the public generally."[206] Citing the absence of a reporter's privilege under either the common law or the "prevailing constitutional view,"[207] White noted that, while "a number of states" have provided a statutory privilege, "the majority have not done so, and none has been provided by federal statute."[208]

> On the records now before us, we perceive no basis for holding that the public interest in law enforcement and in ensuring effective grand jury proceedings is insufficient to override the consequential, but uncertain, burden on news gathering that is said to result from insisting that reporters, like other citizens, respond to relevant questions put to them in the course of a valid grand jury investigation or criminal trial.[209]

White gave particularly short shrift to Branzburg's claim of privilege. "Insofar as any reporter in these cases undertook not to reveal or testify about the crime he witnessed, his claim of privilege under the First Amendment presents no substantial question. The crimes of news sources are no less reprehensible and threatening to the public interest when witnessed by a reporter than when they are not."[210] For the others, White said, "the evidence fails to demonstrate that there would be a significant constriction of the flow of news to the public if this Court reaffirms the prior common-law and constitutional rule regarding the testimonial obligations of newsmen."[211]

Even assuming some informants will refuse to talk to reporters, White continued, "we cannot accept the argument that the public interest in possible future news about crime from undisclosed, unverified sources must take precedence over the public interest in pursuing and prosecuting those crimes reported to the press by informants and in thus deterring the commission of such crimes in the future."[212]

One by one, White rebutted and rejected each of the arguments raised by the reporters, returning finally to clarify the scope of First Amendment protection for newsgathering. "[G]rand jury investigations if instituted or conducted other than in good faith, would pose wholly different issues for resolution under the First Amendment. Official harassment of the press undertaken not for the purposes of law enforcement but to disrupt a reporter's relationship with his news sources would have no justification."[213]

That was the extent of the concession won by the press in *Branzburg v. Hayes* – far less than the Ninth Circuit opinion or even the original District Court's protective order. Even though numerous shield law bills have been introduced in Congress since *Branzburg*,[214] enactment has always been considered a long shot, and all First Amendment protections for newsgathering activities might well be stronger if *Branzburg* had never reached the United States Supreme Court.

But if *Branzburg* was a strategic miscalculation, one cannot say that pursuit of a testimonial privilege for journalists was irrational or irresponsible. From the perspective of the key actors at the time, the odds favoring success were at least even, and important segments of the press saw prospective benefits of victory as greater than the downside costs. Perhaps the best thing to come out of the case was the Reporters Committee for Freedom of the Press, which is today the premier legal information clearing house and litigator representing working journalists.

2. The Legislative Fiasco

According to Floyd McKay, principal chronicler of the Reporters Committee's early years, the *Caldwell* case was the precipitating factor in the formation of the Committee in 1970.[215] Thirty-five to 40 reporters attended a meeting at Georgetown University to discuss *Caldwell* and other cases.[216] Led by J. Anthony Lucas and Fred Graham of *The New York Times*, and Jack Nelson of the *Los Angeles Times*, the group took the name Reporters Committee for Freedom of the Press and created a steering committee of eleven colleagues.[217]

What distinguished the Reporters Committee from other media organizations that became involved in *Caldwell* and its companion cases was its insistence that working reporters, not editors or publishers, would call the shots.[218] "Reporters needed their own advocacy group," James Doyle of *The Washington Star* told McKay in an interview, "and we could not be sure publishers would do the job."[219] Indeed, the *Times* lawyers' initial reaction to the *Caldwell* case seemed indicative of a philosophical difference between working journalists and their managers, although the split over absolute versus qualified privilege had not yet broken down along those lines – at least in the Supreme Court briefs.[220]

Whatever the basis for that split, it was to prove fatal to enacting a statutory remedy for the *Branzburg* decision. By the time that decision was handed down in 1972, the Reporters Committee was being led by Jack Landau, a reporter-lawyer for Newhouse News Service, who had returned to his Supreme Court beat after a brief stint in the Nixon Justice Department.[221] Landau's aggressive advocacy for an absolute privilege in the years following the *Branzburg* decision, and his unwillingness to compromise with media organizations willing to accept some qualifications, must bear a fair portion of the blame – or credit – for Congress's failure to enact a shield law in the early 1970s, when reaction to the Nixon administration's contempt for the press and *Branzburg* made such enactment most likely.[222]

Reacting to what he called "the recent wave of broad and sweeping subpoenas which have issued from the Justice Department," Sen. Thomas H. McIntyre (D-N.H.) introduced the first testimonial privilege bill of the decade on March 5, 1970.[223] Although McIntyre's bill died in committee, Sen. James Pearson (R-Kan.) introduced another shield bill, S.1311, in the beginning of the 92nd Congress in January 1971.[224] According to Sen. Sam Ervin (D-N.C.), the most authoritative reporter of this legislative process, the Pearson bill "met with less than urgent response," with the press adopting a "'wait and see' attitude" toward the bill pending resolution of the *Caldwell* case.[225]

Ervin's Judiciary Subcommittee on Constitutional Rights held hearings on the Pearson bill in September and October 1971.[226] Months earlier, the White House and Justice Department had begun taking a more conciliatory approach to the issuance of subpoenas against reporters,[227] and Ervin recalled that "most press spokesmen who commented on the Pearson bill recommended that Congress proceed cautiously. Most urged that a statutory privilege be enacted only if the Court refused to recognize a constitutional privilege."[228] Indeed, Ervin said the subpoena problem "seemed to come last in the minds of most witnesses."[229] The bill went nowhere in 1971.[230]

When the *Branzburg* decision came down in June 1972, Sen. Alan Cranston (D-Calif.) immediately introduced legislation providing an absolute shield for journalists in both federal and state proceedings.[231] But the press was irreparably divided. The inactive Joint Media Committee was revived for the purpose of drafting new legislation embodying a qualified privilege.[232] Their bill was introduced by Sen. Walter Mondale (D-Minn.) on Aug. 17[233] and Rep. Charles Whalen (R-Ohio) on Sept. 5.[234] Ervin had introduced his own qualified privilege bill on Aug. 16.[235] No new hearings were held in the Senate, and although the House Judiciary Committee held a series of hearings in late September,[236] Congress adjourned without taking action.

Ervin noted that "public's attention was not really drawn" to the issue until two reporters were jailed in the fall of 1972 for refusing to reveal their sources.[237] "The attitude of the press began to harden," Ervin said, and more groups began urging an absolute privilege.[238] The American Newspaper Publishers Association, which supported an absolute privilege, spearheaded a new press alliance called the Ad Hoc Coordinating Committee, which tried to draft a bill acceptable to all factions.[239] The Joint Media Committee, finding that a qualified bill no longer commanded a majority of its members, issued a statement stressing the urgency of legislative relief.[240]

In November 1972, President Nixon told American Society of Newspaper Editors that he did not think federal legislation was warranted at this time, further inflaming the situation, and in December, another reporter was briefly jailed for failing to produce unpublished tapes of a confidential interview.[241] When the 93rd Congress convened in January, eight bills and one joint resolution were introduced in the Senate, and 56 bills were introduced in the House.[242] There was only one problem: "the great number of proposals demonstrated disagreement" among the legislators, and that, in turn, "only reflected the divergence in the press."[243] The Ad Hoc Coordinating Committee, created to find common ground, produce six different bills, revealing differences not only in philosophy but also in estimates of what kind of legislation could pass.[244] Even Anthony Amsterdam complicated the picture by suggesting that a judicial hearing should be required before issuing a subpoena to reporters, an "interesting" concept, said Ervin, but one that "represented a new, complicated, and untested legal innovation, which reduced its political acceptability in Congress."[245]

Ervin admitted to being conflicted himself; he introduced his own qualified privilege bill at the beginning of a new round of hearings, then found himself persuaded by Reporters Committee for Freedom of the Press, that any effective legislation would have to cover the states as well as the federal government.[246] His new bill, however, contained an exception for testimony regarding crimes committed in the reporter's presence, which drew fire from both the Reporters Committee and the Joint Media Committee.[247] Even after a dozen subpoenas were issued during the hearings to news organizations in a libel action filed by the Committee to Re-Elect the President (CREEP),[248] the "fragmented press could not coalesce" behind one approach to legislation in either the Senate or the House.[249]

"It did seem clear," Ervin said, "that unless the press groups themselves could achieve some unanimity on the issue, it was likely to fail without any effort from its opponents."[250] And so it did. The Eighth[251] and Second[252] Circuit Courts of Appeal had both declined to force reporters to reveal their confidential sources, notwithstanding *Branzburg*.[253] Now, in March 1973, Judge Charles Richey granted a motion to quash the dozen subpoenas issued to news organizations by CREEP in the Watergate matter,[254] and prosecutors around the country had begun to show some restraint.[255] Ervin noted that Watergate itself demonstrated to some previous supporters that the press could do its job without a statutory privilege.[256] Despite Rep. Robert Kastenmeier's success in forging a compromise bill in his House Judiciary subcommittee, he could not get a majority of the media representatives to support it.[257] The legislative effort crumbled.

In this chapter, we have examined *Branzburg v. Hayes* as part of a continuing exploration into the mobilization of the press to shape First Amendment doctrine through constitutional litigation. In *Branzburg*, the press failed, despite several favorable indicators, and that failure had grave implications for any First Amendment right to gather news. While it is impossible to say conclusively why a Supreme Court decision goes this way or that, we can safely suggest that differences within the press, between Earl Caldwell and *The New York Times*, indeed, between reporters and their bosses generally,[258] and between advocates of an absolute versus a qualified privilege, did not help the press make its case. The latter division proved to be even more significant when the issue moved to the legislative arena.

The tragedy of *Branzburg v. Hayes* was the failure of the Court to adopt Anthony Amsterdam's argument that, for First Amendment purposes, the distinction between newsgathering and publishing is an artificial one, advanced by the government to divide and conquer.[259] The lesson of *Branzburg v. Hayes* and its aftermath is that a "house divided" is not likely to be effective in molding constitutional doctrine or winning a legislative privilege. As the next chapter demonstrates, the failure to win constitutional recognition for newsgathering in *Branzburg* has been a persistent thorn in the side of media litigators ever since.

Chapter 8 –*Branzburg's* Legacy: The Newsgathering Cases

If *Branzburg v. Hayes* was the first bona fide newsgathering case to reach the U.S. Supreme Court, it was not the first time the Court expressed doubt that the Constitution provided much protection for gathering information. That distinction belongs to *Zemel v. Rusk.*[1] Zemel had sought to have his passport validated for travel to Cuba as a tourist. When his request was denied, he renewed it, this time asking for permission to travel "to satisfy my curiosity about the state of affairs in Cuba and to make me a better informed citizen."[2] Refused again, Zemel challenged the Secretary of State's authority to take such action. A three-judge district court granted the Secretary's motion for summary judgment,[3] and the United States Supreme Court affirmed.[4] The Court rejected Zemel's contention that the refusal to validate his passport for Cuba infringed upon his First Amendment right to inform himself.

> For to the extent that the Secretary's refusal to validate passports for Cuba acts as an inhibition . . . it is an inhibition of action. There are few restrictions on action which could not be clothed by ingenious argument in the garb of decreased data flow. . . . The right to speak and publish does not carry with it the unrestrained right to gather information.[5]

Ample reasons exist for considering Zemel as something other than a bona fide newsgathering case. State Department policy at the time contemplated exemptions for bona fide journalists, among others,[6] and Zemel's desire to "inform himself" seems as disingenuous now as it obviously did to the Court then. Still, the Court has repeatedly held that the First Amendment rights of the press and public are coextensive;[7] Zemel did not have to attend journalism school to gather news and information.

More importantly, the Court recognized that the Secretary's interference with the flow of information about Cuba was "a factor to be considered in determining whether [Zemel] has been denied due process of law."[8] As Justice Stewart would later point out in his *Branzburg* dissent, the rule at issue in *Zemel* was justified by the "weightiest considerations of national security."[9] Justice Stewart also noted that the Court's use of the word "unrestrained" to characterize unprotected newsgathering necessarily implies that "some right to gather information does exist."[10] In *Branzburg*, the Court begin to define the scope of that right.

Branzburg is appropriately characterized as a newsgathering case because the newspapers' right to publish the information their reporters had obtained, without fear of censorship or sanction, was never called into question. At issue rather was the reporters' ability to acquire the information in the first instance, and there is a dramatic difference between the Court's attitude toward publishing and its attitude toward access to information. The law can affect access to information both directly, by establishing the boundaries of secrecy within which government institutions and private actors are entitled to operate, and indirectly, by limiting the means by which reporters can gather the news without running afoul of the law. In depriving Paul Branzburg, Earl Caldwell, and Paul Pappas of a constitutional privilege to protect their confidential sources from disclosure, *Branzburg* exemplifies the indirect effect of the law on access to information. In each case, the reporter had already acquired and published the information in question, but did so through promises of confidentiality that they could not keep absent a legal privilege. The Court's refusal to recognize a constitutional privilege thus jeopardized the ability of these and other reporters to acquire more information from the same or different sources in the future. More importantly, *Branzburg* also sounds a theme underlying all newsgathering cases: that the First Amendment entitles the press as an institution only to that information available to the public generally. If a member of the public has no constitutional privilege to protect the confidences of information sources from, say, a grand jury inquiry, then neither does a reporter.

This view of the First Amendment is reflected in the direct access cases as well. Two types of direct access cases have reached the Court with some frequency: access to judicial proceedings and access to executive branch information. As early as 1959, the Court began reversing criminal convictions on the ground that trial courts failed to properly manage and or account for press coverage before or during the trials. In these cases, unlike the contempt cases, the actual conduct of the press, while often deplorable, was not found to be illegal. But the series of reversals certainly gave courts the incentive to restrict trial coverage by closing the courtrooms. Part A of this chapter looks briefly at these press coverage cases, then more closely at those cases in which the Court ultimately established the ground rules for press access to judicial proceedings. In Part B, we turn to the cases in which the press tried, and almost always failed, to use the courts to gain access to information held by the executive branch of government. In Part C, we return to the handful of newsgathering cases that, like *Branzburg*, did not involve direct access information, but rather threatened newsgathering indirectly, and in some cases, even more seriously. In Chapter 9, after studying a contemporary case in depth, we summarize what the cases tell us about the ability of the press to shape First Amendment doctrine with respect to newsgathering.

A. Access to Courtrooms

The contempt-by-publication cases discussed in Chapter 6 were not about newsgathering, of course, but the concern they expressed for the influence of news reporting and editorializing on the judicial process certainly set the stage for restricting press coverage of the courts. For example, in the contempt case of *Patterson v. Colorado*,[11] Justice Holmes took pains to point out that trial outcomes must be "induced only by evidence and argument in open court and not by any outside influence, whether of private talk or public print."[12] Similarly, in *Bridges v. California*,[13] Justice Black wrote, "Legal trials are not like elections, to be won through the use of the meeting hall, the radio, and the newspaper."[14]

In 1910, the Court entertained, but ultimately rejected, a claim that a murder conviction should be overturned because, among other things, a juror had read newspaper accounts of the case before the trial and had formed opinions as to the defendant's guilt and other jurors had read accounts of the case in the Seattle newspapers during the trial.[15] Half a century later, however, the Court was prepared to take such claims more seriously. In *Marshall v. U.S.*,[16] the Court reversed the defendant's conviction for illegally distributing amphetamines on the ground that the jurors had been improperly influenced by reading newspaper stories about Marshall's two prior convictions, one for practicing medicine without a license, which the trial judge had excluded from evidence.

Two years later, in *Irvin v. Dowd*,[17] the Court the court granted Leslie "Mad Dog" Irvin a new murder trial on the ground that nine of twelve jurors had been prejudiced by pretrial publicity, including the nickname bestowed on Irvin by the press. *Irvin* established as a principle of federal constitutional law that decisions reached by jurors who have been influenced by pretrial publicity violate the sixth amendment guarantee of trial by an impartial jury. Although *Irvin* put the burden on the defense to show specific instances of prejudice, that test was soon softened.

In *Rideau v. Louisiana*,[18] the defendant's confession to robbery, kidnapping, and murder charges was broadcast three times on local television prior to jury selection, yet the trial court denied Rideau's motion for a change of venue. Three members of the jury saw the broadcast, but Justice Potter Stewart, writing for the 7-2 majority, held that no particularized showing of prejudice was required, that drawing a jury from such a contaminated jury pool was, in itself, a deprivation of due process. That rule was applied in the next two cases as well. In *Estes v. Texas*,[19] a sharply divided Court reversed the fraud conviction of the notorious financier Billie Sol Estes. In his opinion for the Court, Justice Clark held that the massive pre-trial publicity – including two days of televised pre-trial hearings and televised portions of the trial itself – had deprived Estes of due process. And in *Sheppard v. Maxwell*,[20] the Court reversed the conviction of Sam Sheppard for allegedly murdering his wife, with Justice Clark citing the "carnival atmosphere"[21] of the trial and the utter failure of the trial judge to control media coverage.

These cases were highly publicized and attracted substantial national press attention. *Sheppard*, in particular, would exert considerable influence on the press's ability to cover the courts, with Justice Clark issuing guidance to trial judges as to how they were to protect the defendant's right to an impartial jury before and during the trial.[22] Yet only in *Estes* was the press involved as amicus curiae before the Supreme Court, and then only to plead the special case of televised trial coverage. That would change dramatically once trial judges began to slam courtroom doors shut in order to implement Justice Clark's admonition that "the presence of the press at judicial proceedings must be limited when it is apparent that the accused might otherwise be prejudiced or disadvantaged."[23]

At first, the Supreme Court seemed to endorse that practice. In *Gannett v. DePasquale*,[24] attorneys for both the prosecution and defense asked the trial judge, Daniel DePasquale, to close a pretrial suppression hearing that would determine whether certain statements and physical evidence, including a gun, were admissible in a murder trial.[25] Concerned that information about inadmissible evidence might reach prospective jurors, DePasquale agreed to close the hearing. The evidence was suppressed and the defendants pleaded guilty to a lesser charge. A Gannett reporter who had left the courtroom wrote a letter to the judge asking to see a transcript of the proceedings, and Gannett followed up with a formal motion. Ultimately, DePasquale denied the motion, balancing Gannett's First Amendment rights against the right of the defendants to a fair trial.[26] He was reversed by the intermediate appellate court, but affirmed by the Court of Appeals.[27] The U.S. Supreme Court affirmed 5-4.[28]

Justice Stewart wrote for the Court and one other justice that the defendant could waive his right to an open proceeding and the Sixth Amendment gave the press no grounds for objection.[29] If the First Amendment provided any such ground, it was limited, and Judge DePasquale fulfilled his obligation by giving the press a hearing.[30] Chief Justice Burger limited his concurrence to pretrial proceedings,[31] while Justice Powell suggested formal guidelines for weighing the press's First Amendment interests in such cases.[32] Only Justice Rehnquist, among the majority, held that there was no First Amendment interest in open proceedings at all.[33] The dissenters, led by Justice Blackmun, would have held that the Sixth Amendment requires at least a hearing before any proceeding is closed, giving "full and fair consideration" to "the public's interest... in open trials."[34] In other words, the dissent would have found that the Sixth Amendment right to an open trial belongs not only to the defendant, but also to the public. They would have put the burden on defendant to show sufficient potential prejudice to overcome the qualified right of the public.[35]

Press support for Gannett was substantial, both with respect to the firm's petition for certiorari[36] and on the merits of the case.[37] Gannett had argued the case first on First Amendment grounds,[38] as did ANPA and ASNE,[39] and then on Sixth Amendment grounds,[40] as did RCFP and NAB.[41] The New York Times Co. emphasized the importance of pre-trial proceedings,[42] while SPJ/SDX urged the Court to adopt a *Nebraska Press*-like test for closing courtrooms.[43] The ACLU, which had tended to favor reversing convictions in the pretrial publicity cases, argued here in support of Gannett on both First and Sixth Amendment grounds.[44]

Ultimately, the Court would accept the argument that the right of the public to attend judicial proceedings controlled the question, but it would set that right squarely in the First Amendment, rather than the Sixth.

That was the analytical approach adopted in *Richmond Newspapers v. Virginia*,[45] in which the trial court had granted defendant's motion to close a criminal trial to the press and public. John Paul Stevenson's first conviction had been reversed, and the next two attempts to try him ended in mistrials.[46] On the fourth attempt, the court granted the motion to close the trial, without a hearing, under a state law allowing a trial judge to exclude anyone whose presence might impair the conduct of a fair trial. [47] Richmond Newspapers filed a motion claiming the constitutional right of the public to attend trials, arguing the judge erred by not first determining whether alternative measures could not guarantee a fair trial.[48] The Virginia Supreme Court denied the papers' motion, citing *Gannett v. DePasquale*, as had many other courts since that decision, and Stevenson was acquitted in a closed trial. Again, the press strongly supported Richmond Newspapers,[49] but this time the outcome in the U.S. Supreme Court was much more favorable.

In his opinion for the 7-1 majority, Chief Justice Burger traced the history of open trials from before the Norman conquest, and cited its "community therapeutic value" in earning "public acceptance of both the process and its results."[50] Today, he said, the media acts as surrogates for the public. "We are bound to conclude that a presumption of openness inheres in the very nature of the criminal trial under our system of justice."[51] Burger said that the First Amendment can be read as protecting the right of everyone to attend trials so as to give meaning to the explicit guarantees of speech, press, assembly and petition. "Free speech carries with it some freedom to listen," he said.[52] The amendment prohibits government from limiting the stock of information available to the public, Burger said, and prohibits the government from summarily closing doors which had long been open to the public at the time that amendment was adopted.[53] Noting that the trial judge had made no findings to support closure, no inquiry as to whether alternative solutions would have met the need to ensure fairness, and no recognition of any First Amendment right for the press and public to attend trials, Burger said that, absent an overriding interest articulated in findings, the trial of a criminal case must be open to the public.[54]

Six different opinions were written in the case. Justices White[55] and Blackmun,[56] concurring, continued to express the belief that the public's right to an open trial was grounded in the Sixth Amendment, and Justice Rehnquist, dissenting, continued to believe that neither the First nor the Sixth Amendment provided any such right.[57] Justice Stewart, concurring, cautioned that the right of the press and public to attend trials was not absolute,[58] and the concurring opinion of Justice Brennan, joined by Justice Marshall, noted that, in determining whether a particular proceeding should be open, the courts needed to take into account both the history of that proceeding and the function that it serves.[59] These points would ultimately be incorporated into the rule that was fine-tuned over the next four cases and now governs all closed courtroom situations.

In *Globe Newspaper Co. v. Superior Court, County of Norfolk*,[60] the Court held that a Massachusetts law requiring the closing of courtrooms during the testimony of certain sex crime victims violated the First Amendment. Despite the lack of history of openness in this kind of trial, the Court found that the state interests asserted to support the restriction would be best served by case-by-case consideration.[61] Once again, the press amici were out in force.[62] Two years later, in *Press-Enterprise Co. v. Superior Court of California, Riverside County* (*Press-Enterprise I*),[63] the Court held that the examination of prospective jurors known as *voir dire* must be conducted in the open unless convincing evidence shows closure is needed to ensure a fair trial. Chief Justice Burger, writing for the majority, wrote that "the presumption of openness may be overcome only by an overriding interest based on findings that closure is essential to preserve higher values and is narrowly tailored to serve that interest."[64] Here, too, the press amici were well represented.[65] The same year, in *Waller v. Georgia*,[66] the Court held that pre-trial suppression hearings can be closed over the defendant's objections only if there are compelling reasons to do so and only after considering alternative remedies.[67] This was considered a purely Sixth Amendment case, and the press did not participate. These two cases were held to be controlling in a 2010 case reversing a criminal conviction because the press and public were excluded from *voir dire*, a position supported in an amicus brief filed by Reporters Committee for Freedom of the Press.[68]

The last case in this line to refine the doctrine regarding assess to courtrooms, a second *Press-Enterprise Co. v. Superior Court of California, Riverside County* (*Press-Enterprise II*),[69] pulled together all of the rules established in the preceding cases and, without explicitly over-ruling *Gannett v. DePasquale*, consigned it to a jurisprudential footnote. In *Press-Enterprise II*, Defendant Robert Diaz was charged with 12 counts of murder for administering overdoses of lidocaine in his capacity as a nurse. Diaz moved to exclude the public from the preliminary hearing, and the prosecutor, who was seeking the death penalty, did not oppose the motion. The magistrate judge granted the motion on the ground that the case had attracted national publicity and "only one side may get reported in the media."[70] The hearing lasted forty-one days; Diaz was bound over for trial and the record was sealed. Both the state and the *Press-Enterprise* petitioned for release of the transcript, but Diaz opposed release and the Superior Court denied the motion based on a "reasonable likelihood of substantial prejudice" to Diaz's fair trial.[71] Although Diaz ultimately waived his right to a jury and transcripts of the preliminary hearing were released, the state appellate courts essentially affirmed the decision below, holding that there was no generalized First Amendment right of access to preliminary hearings and that the burden was on the press to prove no reasonable likelihood of prejudice.[72] Again, there was no lack of advice from the press.[73]

Over a dissent by Justice Stevens, joined by Justice Rehnquist, [74] Chief Justice Burger established a two-part rule for judges to follow whenever the issue of closure arises. Borrowing from Justice Brennan's concurrence in *Richmond Newspapers*, Burger posited a "qualified First Amendment right of access" to any judicial proceeding that has historically been open to the public and where access contributes positively to its proper functioning.[75] Once that test is met, he said, *Press-Enterprise I* dictates that the presumption of openness can be rebutted only by findings that closure is essential to an overriding governmental interest and is narrowly tailored to serve that interest.[76] As to this particular case, Burger held that the California preliminary hearing – which is often as dispositive as a trial – meets both the history and function prongs of the preliminary test. He also held that the "reasonable likelihood" test applied in the lower court was inadequate. Where the asserted interest is the defendant's fair trial, Burger said closure is permissible only where there is a "substantial probability" that the defendant's right to a fair trial will be prejudiced and that reasonable alternatives to closure cannot adequately protect the defendant's fair trial rights.[77] The Court some years later applied that rule to preliminary hearings in Puerto Rico in response to a newspaper's lawsuit,[78] but no other general closure cases have reached the Supreme Court.

On the issue of televising judicial proceedings, moreover, the Court has reversed itself since *Estes* was decided in 1965. In *Estes*,[79] Chief Justice Warren, joined by Justices Douglas and Goldberg,[80] and Justice Harlan,[81] concurring separately, agreed with Justice Clark's majority opinion that Estes's conviction had to be reversed,[82] but Harlan's concurring opinion was at least equivocal as to whether televising a criminal trial would forever be an inherent deprivation of due process.[83] Justices White, Stewart, Black, and Brennan dissented, writing that televising trials was neither inherently prejudicial nor specifically prejudicial in this case.[84] Brennan took pains to point out that, given Harlan's equivocation, the decision in *Estes* fell short of a constitutional rule against televising trials.[85] That may have been some comfort to the NAB and the RTNDA, who argued as amici that courtroom reporting by broadcast media – properly controlled by the court – does not deprive a defendant of due process of law.[86] In that assertion, they were joined only by the State Bar Association of Texas; the ACLU and American Bar Association supported the majority.[87]

The constitutional issue – although not the lingering question of desirability – was resolved in *Chandler v. Florida*.[88] In that case, the Court upheld a Florida program that allowed trial courts, under controlled conditions, to televise portions of a burglary trial in which the defendants were convicted and their convictions affirmed on appeal. Writing for a unanimous Court, at least with regard to the outcome, Chief Justice Burger referred specifically to Justice

Harlan's equivocal concurring opinion in *Estes* and declared that *Estes* created no per se constitutional rule against televising criminal trials.[89] He further held that nothing in the Florida rule or its application in this particular case deprived the defendants of their due process rights.[90] The decision vindicated the earlier arguments of the NAB and RTNDA, who were joined this time by a broad array of press amici.[91]

Although lower courts continue to close hearings and even portions of trials from time to time, today's constitutional doctrine clearly favors access to judicial proceedings for the press and the public. Most of the decisions that created this very favorable doctrine resulted from cases that were instigated by the press in the first instance and, in most cases, the media plaintiffs were strongly supported by the rest of the industry through the filing of amicus briefs at the certiorari phase and on the merits. Unfortunately, as we will see in the next section, the result was exactly the opposite when the press tried to gain access to executive branch information.

B. Access to Executive Branch Information

> The press is free to do battle against secrecy and deception in government. But the press cannot expect from the Constitution any guarantee that it will succeed. There is no constitutional right to have access to particular government information, or to require openness from the bureaucracy. The public's interest in knowing about its government is protected by the guarantee of a Free Press, but the protection is indirect. The Constitution itself is neither a Freedom of Information Act nor an Official Secrets Act.
>
> The Constitution, in other words, establishes the contest, not its resolution. Congress may provide a resolution, at least in some instances, through carefully drawn legislation. For the rest, we must rely, as so often in our system we must, on the tug and pull of the political forces in American society.[92]

Justice Potter Stewart's assessment of the constitutional status of newsgathering *vis a vis* the executive branch of government is as accurate today as it was in November 1974 when he included those words in an address to the Yale Law School Sesquicentennial Convocation. Only two years earlier, the Court had offered as dictum in *Branzburg v. Hayes* the proposition that "the First Amendment does not guarantee the press a constitutional right of special access to information not available to the public generally."[93] And less than six months earlier, the Supreme Court had issued its first opinion directly on point, with Justice Stewart writing for the 5-4 majority.

Pell v. Procunier[94] was the first of three Supreme Court decisions involving access to prisons, and that trio has been remarkably influential ever since. The second case, *Saxbe v. Washington Post*,[95] was decided the same day and, for all practical purposes, the same way. Both cases involved regulations – state regulations in *Pell*, federal regulations in *Saxbe* – that prohibited reporters from interviewing specific prisoners. The institutional press strongly supported the individual journalists who, along with the prisoners they wished to interview, brought suit against the California Department of Corrections in *Pell*. In three amicus briefs, they argued that the public had a right to know what went on the prisons, that the prisoners' own First Amendment rights could only be vindicated by granting press access, and that allowing the press to interview specific inmates would not cause any particular problems for the system.[96] A three-judge U.S. District Court found the rules violated the prisoners' rights, although not the media's,[97] but the U.S. Supreme Court found no First Amendment violation at all. The fact that the press could tour the facilities, along with the general public, and interview inmates at random, was enough to satisfy the First Amendment; the regulations were merely reasonable time, place, and manner restrictions, a category long held to pass constitutional muster.[98] Justices Powell, Douglas, Brennan, and Marshall dissented; in *Pell*, Powell agreed with the Court that the California rules did not violate the prisoners' First Amendment rights, but agreed with press and the other dissenters in both cases that the California regulations "impermissibly restrain[ed] the ability of the press to perform its constitutionally established function of informing the people on the conduct of their government."[99]

In his extensive dissenting opinion in *Saxbe*, Powell pointed out that working reporters and academic journalists testified as experts at the trial level.[100] Unlike the experience in *Pell*, the press was successful at trial in *Saxbe*, and that favorable opinion was affirmed by the U.S. Court of Appeals for the D.C. Circuit. The only additional amicus brief filed in *Saxbe* came from Reporters Committee for Freedom of the Press,[101] but it hardly mattered. The majority saw *Saxbe* as a carbon copy of *Pell* and ruled accordingly.

The third case in the prison access trio, *Houchins v. KQED*,[102] involved media access to portions of the Alameda County, Calif., jail and the prisoners it housed, beyond the limited public tours that were offered after the case was filed. A federal district court had enjoined the sheriff from denying the press reasonable access to the facilities and inmates, including the use of cameras and sound equipment; the U.S. Court of Appeals for the Ninth Circuit affirmed.[103] On a 4-3 vote, the Supreme Court reversed, without a majority opinion. Writing for the Court and joined by Justices White and Rehnquist, Chief Justice Burger held it was the province of the political branches to determine the extent to which the jail should be open to the press and public.[104] Justice Stewart wrote separately, concurring in the judgment, to assert that, once the doors of the jail had been opened to the public, reasonable and "effective" access to the press was required.[105] Justice Stevens, joined by Justices Brennan and Powell, and supported by press amici,[106] wrote in dissent that the press and public could not be excluded from meaningful access to the jail without violating the First Amendment.[107] There have been no Supreme Court decisions regarding newsgathering in prisons since *Houchins*, and Dienes points out that these three cases continue to control the disposition of prison cases in the lower courts.[108]

The Watergate scandal provided another opportunity for the press and the government to square off in the U.S. Supreme Court over access to government-held information. The first Watergate-related case to reach the High Court was a rare victory for the press's position, but principally because the press and the Congress found themselves on the same side. In *Nixon v. Administrator of General Services*,[109] the Court upheld the constitutionality of the Presidential Recordings and Materials Preservation Act,[110] which vested control over former President Nixon's presidential records – including the infamous Watergate tapes – with the General Services Administration, abrogating an agreement Nixon had made with GSA that would likely have led to the destruction of the most incriminating of those materials. Ironically, the only First Amendment argument raised in the case was Nixon's assertion that the Act violated his freedom of speech and association.[111] Reporters Committee for Freedom of the Press, which was allowed to intervene at the District Court level, pointed out that the First Amendment "was conceived in 'the struggle . . . to establish and preserve the right of the English people to full information in respect to the doings and misdoings of their government,'" [112] but did not frame that as a First Amendment "right-to-know" argument.

The *GSA* decision had no effect on First Amendment doctrine, but the second Watergate-related case was argued and decided, in part, on First Amendment grounds. *Nixon v. Warner Communications, Inc.*,[113] is often classified as a case involving access to judicial proceedings, rather than access to executive information.[114] However it is framed, the decision was a clear defeat for the broadcast media specifically and for the press in general.

When the Watergate tapes were played in open court at the obstruction of justice trial of former Nixon advisers, including former Attorney General John Mitchell, the jury, press and public received printed transcripts. But the Court refused requests to copy the tapes and broadcast and sell the copies submitted by ABC, CBS, NBC, PBS, RTNDA, and, separately, Warner Communications, even after the trial had ended. Noting that the defendants planned to appeal, Judge John Sirica held that the public's "right to know" did not outweigh the possible prejudice to the defendants' appeals from commercial exploitation of the tapes.[115] The U.S. Court of Appeals for the District of Columbia reversed Sirica's decision, stressing the importance of the public's common law right of access to the tapes and First Amendment limits on the use of the tapes once released to the press and public.[116] The U.S. Supreme Court reversed.

Writing for the majority, Justice Powell held that the common law right of access to judicial records was trumped by the Presidential Recordings and Materials Preservation Act, which established a procedure for releasing the tapes to the public.[117] Any First Amendment right of access or Sixth Amendment right to a public trial was satisfied by the fact that reporters could attend the trial, listen to the tapes, and report what they heard. "The contents of the tapes were given wide publicity by all elements of the media," Powell wrote. "There is no question of a truncated flow of information to the public."[118] Justices White and Brennan dissented in part, but only on a technical point regarding the reach of the statute;[119] Justices Marshall[120] and Stevens[121] dissented on the merits, but neither raised a constitutional issue. Interestingly, there was no press participation in this case outside the broadcast and cable industry respondents, who, nevertheless, were well represented by Floyd Abrams and Edward Bennett Williams, superlawyers generally associated with *The New York Times* and *The Washington Post*, respectively.

The last Watergate-related newsgathering case to reach the U.S. Supreme Court, *FBI v. Abramson*,[122] was decided on purely statutory grounds. Because the statute construed in that case was the federal Freedom of Information Act,[123] it bears some mention here. The Freedom of Information Act, or FOIA, as it is often called, was enacted in 1966 as an amendment to the public information section of the then-20-year-old Administrative Procedure Act.[124] By its terms, it provides for public access to all records created or obtained by a federal agency that do not fall within one of nine discretionary exemptions, which are to be narrowly construed by the courts. Over the years, different administrations have offered varying guidance to executive officers over how FOIA should be applied, but the press has lost almost every case in which it fought for access all the way up to the U.S. Supreme Court. Even though the focus of this dissertation is constitutional litigation, that fact alone warrants a very brief description of the FOIA cases in order to give a more complete picture of the Court's treatment of newsgathering.

In the first FOIA newsgathering case to reach the Supreme Court, *Kissinger v. Reporters Committee for Freedom of the Press*,[125] the Court refused to order production of notes and transcripts of telephone conversations of Henry Kissinger while National Security Adviser and Secretary of State – requested by journalist William Safire, RCFP, and others – finding those documents were not agency records governed by FOIA.[126] In the Watergate-related case, *Abramson*, journalist Howard Abramson sought information on the extent to which the Nixon White House used FBI files to collect derogatory information about political opponents beginning in 1969.[127] Reversing the U.S. Court of Appeals for the District of Columbia, and disregarding press amici,[128] the Court held 5-4 that the records fell under the law enforcement exemption, even though the only records sought were being used for other purposes.[129]

The same day that *Abramson* was decided, the press lost another FOIA case, *Department of State v. Washington Post*,[130] in which the *Post* sought documents indicating whether two Iranian nationals, prominent figures in the revolutionary government, were American citizens. Despite the objections of press amici,[131] the Court reversed both courts below to hold unanimously that the records represented a clearly unwarranted invasion of privacy and were thus exempt from FOIA.[132] In *Department of Justice v. Reporters Committee for Freedom of the Press*,[133] the court again rejected press amici[134] and the D.C. Circuit to hold unanimously that FBI criminal histories (rap sheets) were protected under the law enforcement exemption, even though individual arrest records were publicly available documents.[135] Finally, in 2004, the Court ruled against press amici in one FOIA and one closely related case. In the FOIA case, *National Archives and Records Administration v. Favish*,[136] the press amici found themselves on the same side as one of their harshest critics, the former associate counsel for Accuracy in Media, Allan J. Favish. The Court rejected Favish's FOIA request, in his own name, for release of copies of photographs showing the condition of Clinton White House aide Vince Foster's body at the scene of his apparent suicide over the objections of Foster's family. [137] In the non-FOIA access case, *Cheney v. U.S. District Court*,[138] the Court declined to apply the disclosure requirements of the Federal Advisory Committee Act to proceedings of the Vice President's National Energy Policy Development Group.[139]

The Court also declined to force the Federal Open Market Committee to release its Domestic Policy Directives without the customary delay;[140] refused to force the Air Force to disclose statements made during an aircraft accident investigation;[141] upheld Los Angeles Police Department rules restricting dissemination of arrestee addresses;[142] and upheld federal legislation limiting states' right to disseminate driver's license information without the driver's consent.[143]

While the press lost all of these cases, press involvement in FOIA and other access litigation has not been futile. In its most recent effort, *John Doe #1 v. Reed*,[144] press amici helped to persuade the Court to affirm a decision allowing Washington state to release petitions filed in a gay marriage referendum under its Public Records Act. Reporters Committee for Freedom of the Press and others have also filed amicus briefs on the winning side in many Supreme Court cases that involved access to information where the newsgathering interests were not immediately obvious. For example, the Court has held that federal district court orders and opinions received by the Department of Justice in litigating tax cases could all be obtained through FOIA, greatly easing the cost and effort of the nonprofit magazine that sought them;[145] that FOIA's inter- and intra-agency memorandum exemption did not apply to documents submitted by Indian tribes to the Department of Interior;[146] that having students grade each others' papers did not violate the Federal Educational Records Privacy Act (FERPA),[147] and, separately, that FERPA violations did not create a private cause of action[148] that the information dissemination requirements of sex offender notification statutes were not unconstitutional *ex post facto* laws,[149] and, separately, that they did not violate due process;[150] that actual injury must be shown to collect damages for a Privacy Act violation;[151] and that litigation by one FOIA requester does not necessarily preclude claims by another for the same documents.[152] RCFP has also been successful in many cases filed in state courts and lower federal courts.[153]

Thus far, we have seen that the Court has generally been responsive to press demands for access to judicial proceedings, but far less responsive to demands for access to executive branch information. Why the discrepancy? If we analyze the question using the "history-function" test of Justice Brennan's *Richmond Newspapers* concurrence, we can readily see that the courts traditionally have been more open to the public than have executive agencies. Likewise, we can acknowledge that the degree of secrecy required for the executive to function properly is far greater overall than that required by the judiciary. We can also understand that the Court is more comfortable setting the boundaries of secrecy for the judiciary than for another, co-equal branch of government. This appears to be so even where the Court's function involves setting boundaries for state courts, over which it exercises no supervisory authority, or interpreting the boundaries set by the legislature in the Freedom of Information Act and other statutes.

What is not apparent is any particular difference in the support of the institutional press for constitutional litigation to enhance access to judicial and executive information. In both spheres, the press has pursued access as party litigants and amici with the same resources and talent that it put into the publishing cases.

C. Indirect Impact Cases

The preceding sections have explored in some detail those cases applying the principle, firmly established in *Branzburg*, that the First Amendment rights of the press regarding direct access to information are co-extensive with the rights of the general public. We now focus on those cases, of which *Branzburg* was the exemplar, which have inhibited newsgathering by indirectly curtailing access to information. These cases all sound a similar theme, phrased somewhat differently, but to the same effect: that the press, like the public at large, is bound to comply with laws of general applicability that do not single out the press for special treatment or are otherwise aimed at suppressing freedom of speech.

After *Branzburg* itself, the first of these cases was *Zurcher v. Stanford Daily*.[154] Following a student demonstration to protest the firing of a black janitor by the Stanford University Hospital, which included a sit-in and, later, a violent confrontation with local police, the Santa Clara County District Attorney obtained a search warrant to search the offices of the *Stanford Daily*, which had published a special edition of the student newspaper containing articles about and photographs of the demonstration.[155] The stated purpose of the warrant was to find photographs of students who may have assaulted police officers and committed other felonies during the confrontation. The warrant was served by four officers in the presence of the *Daily* staff; they found nothing that had not already been published and left empty-handed.[156] The *Daily* and various members of its staff subsequently sued officials responsible for the search claiming their rights under the First, Fourth, and Fourteenth Amendments had been violated. The U.S. District Court held that the Fourth and Fourteenth Amendments "forbade the issuance of a warrant to search for materials in possession of one not suspected of crime unless there is probable cause to believe, based on facts presented in a sworn affidavit, that a subpoena *duces tecum* would be impracticable."[157] The court also held that where the object of the search is a newspaper, the First Amendment allowed such a search "only in the rare circumstance where there is a *clear showing* that (1) important materials will be destroyed or removed from the jurisdiction; *and* (2) a restraining order would be futile."[158] The Court of Appeals for the Ninth Circuit affirmed per curiam, and the U.S. Supreme Court granted certiorari.[159]

Although 1971 was still relatively early for the massive mobilization of press amici that became more common by the end of the decade, there was respectable support for the *Daily* in the form of an amicus brief filed by Reporters Committee for Freedom of the Press and others.[160] The press's brief focused on the First Amendment issue, supporting the position of the District Court, including its ruling that $47,000 in legal fees was appropriate in this case. Arrayed against the press were briefs filed by the United States, several individual states, and organizations representing district attorneys and police departments.[161] Only the criminal defense attorneys supported the lower court's holding,[162] and then only on the Fourth Amendment issue. No matter; the Supreme Court reversed both prongs of the decision.

On the First Amendment question, Justice White, writing for the 5-3 majority, rejected all five arguments offered by the press in support of the First Amendment rule propounded by the District Court:

> First, searches will be physically disruptive to such an extent that timely publication will be impeded. Second, confidential sources of information will dry up, and the press will also lose opportunities to cover various events because of fears of the participants that press files will be readily available to the authorities. Third, reporters will be deterred from recording and preserving their recollections for future use if such information is subject to seizure. Fourth, the processing of news and its dissemination will be chilled by the prospects that searches will disclose internal editorial deliberations. Fifth, the press will resort

> to self-censorship to conceal its possession of information of potential interest to the police.[163]

Pointing out that the framers of the Fourth Amendment did not see fit to provide any special consideration for the press, White wrote, "[p]roperly administered, the preconditions for a warrant – probable cause, specificity with respect to the place to be searched and the things to be seized, and overall reasonableness – should afford sufficient protection against the harms that are assertedly threatened by warrants for searching newspaper offices."[164] White cited his own opinion in *Branzburg* to support his assertion that newsroom searches would neither dry up sources nor result in self-censorship.

Concurring, Justice Powell took the opportunity to clarify his concurring opinion in *Branzburg*, noting that it did not "support the view that the Fourth Amendment contains an implied exception for the press, through the operation of the First Amendment. That opinion noted only that in considering a motion to quash a subpoena directed to a newsman, the court should balance the competing values of a free press and the societal interest in detecting and prosecuting crime."[165] Dissenting, Justice Stewart, joined by Justice Marshall, sought to distinguish *Branzburg*. In that case, Stewart wrote, the Court was concerned that important evidence might be lost by extending the privilege; here, the Court is only concerned with "whether any significant societal interest would be impaired if the police were generally required to obtain evidence from the press by means of a subpoena rather than a search."[166] Stevens also dissented,[167] on Fourth Amendment grounds, and Brennan took no part in the case.

Toward the end of his majority opinion, White echoed his *Branzburg* decision by inviting Congress to enact statutory protection if appropriate. "Of course," he wrote, "the Fourth Amendment does not prevent or advise against legislative or executive efforts to establish nonconstitutional protections against possible abuses of the search warrant procedure."[168] This time, Congress took White up on his offer, enacting the Privacy Protection Act of 1980.[169] The act, which applies to federal, state and local law enforcement agencies, protects the work product and documentary materials of persons engaged in First Amendment activities from search warrants unless there is probable cause to believe that a journalist is using them to commit a crime or seizure is necessary to prevent death or serious injury. Even then, seizure is only permissible if there is reason to believe they would be destroyed in response to a subpoena or have not been handed over in response to a court order.[170]

If the press was united behind the *Stanford Daily*, it was splintered again by the next case in this line, *Cohen v. Cowles Media,*[171] perhaps even more than it had been in *Branzburg*. Dan Cohen was a Minneapolis public relations executive associated with the 1982 gubernatorial campaign of Independent-Republican Wheelock Whitney.[172] In late October 1982, just six days before the general election, Cohen contacted a number of journalists in the St. Paul- Minneapolis area, offering to give them information concerning a Democratic-Farmer-Laborite (DFL) candidate in exchange for a promise of confidentiality.[173] Among the journalists accepting the offer were reporters for the St. Paul *Pioneer Press* and the Minneapolis *Star Tribune*.[174]

Cohen provided the reporters with public court records showing that Marlene Johnson, the DFL candidate for Lieutenant Governor, had previously been arrested for unlawful assembly and petit theft. The unlawful assembly charges, which grew out of a civil rights demonstration, were ultimately dismissed. The candidate had been convicted on the theft charge, which involved a minor shoplifting offense while she had been emotionally distraught, but the conviction was later vacated.[175]

Editors at both the *Pioneer Press* and the *Star Tribune* independently decided to print the story and, over their reporters' protests, to include the name of the source. While the *Pioneer Press* editors buried Dan Cohen's name deep in the story, the *Star Tribune* editors featured it, apparently reasoning that the value of the story, if any, lay in Cohen's conduct, not Johnson's. The *Star Tribune* also attacked Cohen in its editorial pages, but neither paper reported that it had broken a promise of confidentiality with Cohen. [176]

When the story broke, Cohen lost his job[177] and later sued the newspapers' publishers alleging fraudulent misrepresentation and breach of contract. Overcoming the publishers' First Amendment claims, Cohen won $200,000 in compensatory damages and $500,000 in punitive damages at trial.[178] The Minnesota Court of Appeals struck down the punitive damage award after finding that Cohen had failed to establish a fraud claim.[179] The Minnesota Supreme Court struck down the compensatory damage award, holding a contract action "inappropriate" under the circumstances.[180]

During oral argument before the Minnesota Supreme Court, one of the justices had asked a question about "estoppel," a cause of action in equity that might serve as an alternative to Cohen's contract claim in enforcing the reporters' promises.[181] Addressing that issue in its opinion, the court found it necessary to "balance the constitutional rights of a free press against the common law interest in protecting a promise of anonymity."[182] In this case, the court said, enforcing the promise would violate the newspapers' First Amendment rights. The United States Supreme Court granted certiorari "to consider the First Amendment implications of this case."[183]

Writing for a five to four majority,[184] Justice White rejected the newspapers' argument that this case was controlled by the line of cases holding that "if a newspaper lawfully obtains truthful information about a matter of public significance then state officials may not constitutionally punish publication of the information, absent a need to further a state interest of the highest order."[185] Instead, Justice White said, the case was controlled "by the equally well-established line of decisions holding that generally applicable laws do not offend the First Amendment simply because their enforcement against the press has incidental effects on its ability to gather and report the news."[186]

Justice White proceeded to list a number of cases – starting with *Branzburg v. Hayes* – purporting to demonstrate that enforcement of general laws against the press is not subject to any stricter scrutiny than would be applied to enforcement against other persons or organizations. Finding Minnesota's doctrine of promissory estoppel just such a "law of general applicability," Justice White had no problem applying it to the press. He even suggested that the newspapers' breaking their promises might serve as a predicate for finding their conduct unlawful, thus arguably negating First Amendment protection for the information itself.

Justice White further distinguished Cohen's situation from that of a plaintiff seeking to avoid the strict requirements for establishing a libel claim by stating an alternative cause of action. Specifically citing *Hustler Magazine, Inc. v. Falwell*, where the Court denied a claim for intentional infliction of emotional distress without a showing of actual malice,[187] Justice White pointed out that Cohen had not sought damages for injury to his reputation or state of mind, but rather for the loss of his job and his lowered earning capacity.

Finally, Justice White tackled the argument that allowing the promissory estoppel claim would inhibit the press from disclosing the identity of a confidential source when, as in Cohen, that information is newsworthy. If true, he said, the "chilling effect" would be "no more than the incidental, and constitutionally insignificant, consequence of applying to the press a generally applicable law that requires those who make certain kinds of promises to keep them."[188]

Writing for Justices Marshall and Souter in dissent, Justice Blackmun argued that *Hustler* should have controlled the outcome in this case, that First Amendment protection applies to published speech regardless of the cause of action asserted. Blackmun saw no meaningful distinction between the types of damages sought by Jerry Falwell and those sought by Daniel Cohen.[189] Justice Souter also filed a separate dissenting opinion, joined by Justices Marshall, Blackmun, and O'Connor, that rejected White's reliance on the doctrine of "generally applicable laws," denying any "talismanic quality" in such laws. Souter would have found the state's interest in protecting the promise of confidentiality insufficient to outweigh the value of the information revealed in this case.[190] Nevertheless, the case was remanded to the Minnesota Supreme Court, which reversed its previous position and held the newspapers liable for Cohen's damages on a theory of promissory estoppel.[191]

In his account of this case, Cohen's lawyer, Elliot Rothenberg, called the decision "the worst defeat the media had ever suffered in the Supreme Court."[192] Even allowing for some self-indulgent boasting, Rothenberg was not far off the mark. How had the press, as constitutional litigator, blown such a big one? Clearly, there was no lack of legal talent applied to the case. Both newspapers brought in new legal teams for the Supreme Court contest – "heavy artillery," Rothenberg called them. Supreme Court specialist Stephen M. Shapiro became lead counsel for the *Pioneer Press*, and eight lawyers signed its brief. Minneapolis lawyer John French – Harvard Law School and clerk for Justice Felix Frankfurter – took over the *Star Tribune* campaign, and four lawyers signed its brief. Rothenberg's description of the press amici is particularly apt:

> Shapiro and French were not the only blue-ribbon lawyers joining the case on the other side. In fact, a battalion of the nation's leading lawyers and most prominent media organizations entered the Supreme Court appeal supporting the *Star Tribune* and *Pioneer Press*. Nineteen attorneys from leading law firms in New York, Washington, and Los Angeles filed a third brief opposing mine. Their amicus curiae brief represented the big leagues of American media....[193]

Nor were the press's arguments off track. Indeed, they paralleled, if not influenced, the arguments of the four dissenting justices. Apart from Rothenberg himself, there was no outstanding opposition to the press's position; heavy hitters like the United States and the ACLU did not have a dog in the hunt, and even those in or involved with the media who thoroughly disapproved of the newspapers' conduct stayed out of the Supreme Court action.

Nevertheless, it is not difficult to identify reasons why the press lost this case. Arguably, the case should have ended with the first state supreme court opinion; the state court rejected Cohen's contract claim, and Cohen had not raised promissory estoppel. The First Amendment question, essential to getting the case to the U.S. Supreme Court, need never have been reached. Timing, too, was a problem for the press. Justice Brennan retired just before the case was heard, and although his successor, Justice Souter, also supported the press's position, Brennan's voice would have been a far more powerful counterweight to Justice White's hostility. But perhaps the most serious problem of all was the nature of the case itself and the dissension it engendered within the media establishment.

In *Cohen*, the press was forced to argue that promises of confidentiality to sources were not serious enough to be considered contracts – without weakening the central argument in *Branzburg* that such promises deserved constitutional protection. If not altogether untenable, the press's position was at best precarious. It was also highly contentious. Rothenberg quotes University of Minnesota journalism professor Ted Glasser as characterizing the trial as more "between reporters and editors" than between plaintiff and defendants,[194] and urged reporters to oppose the newspapers in any appeal.

> To claim to have a First Amendment right to renege on a reporter's promise not only places the press above the law but denies reporters the very freedom they need to operate in the day-to-day world of journalism. Reporters have every reason to file a friend-of-the-court brief on behalf of Cohen.[195]

There was no reporters' brief at any level, and the Reporters Committee for Freedom of the Press did not sign on to the press's amicus brief. *The Washington Post* also declined to join, as did a number of other media companies who might otherwise have been expected to participate. Rothenberg's petition for certiorari had capitalized on that dissension by quoting star media lawyer Floyd Abrams calling the newspapers' conduct in breaking their reporters' promises of confidentiality "reprehensible and damaging to all journalists."[196] Shortly before the decision came down, Abrams again spoke out publicly in a speech and op-ed column, charging that the newspapers

> acted in a fashion contrary to core principles of journalistic ethics. They also invited the lawsuit now awaiting decision by the Supreme Court, one that offers enemies of the press a particularly inviting target. What the Minnesota newspapers did was wrong; they should have said so. Why is any defender of the press unwilling to say as much.[197]

There is no direct evidence that the division within the press over the *Cohen* case had a significant or even marginal influence on the outcome. Nor was there any direct evidence that differences among media organizations played a significant role in the Court's rejection of constitutional protection for confidential sources in *Branzburg v. Hayes*, although those differences certainly weakened the campaign for federal shield legislation. There is no doubt, however, that the two most important newsgathering cases ever to reach the U.S. Supreme Court did not show the press in the best light as a constitutional litigator.

The last two cases of indirect influence on newsgathering were reported the same day in 1998. Both *Wilson v. Layne*[198] and *Hanlon v. Berger*[199] were Fourth Amendment cases, and while both restricted that newsgathering technique known as "ride-alongs," neither had any influence on First Amendment doctrine. In *Wilson*, a *Washington Post* reporter and photographer accompanied federal and local law enforcement officers in serving an arrest warrant at the Maryland home of a fugitive; in *Hanlon*, a CNN crew accompanied federal agents serving a search warrant at the Berger ranch in Montana, where the owner was suspected of illegally killing protected eagles. The Wilsons did not sue *The Washington Post*, which never published the photographs;[200] the Supreme Court denied CNN's petition for certiorari,[201] so only the cases against the officers reached the U.S.

Supreme Court. A unanimous Court held that, by inviting the press along to cover the events, the officers involved violated the Fourth Amendment rights of the Wilson and Berger families against unreasonable searches and seizures.[202]

The principal interest of the institutional press in both cases was to reverse the decision of the U.S. Court of Appeals for the Ninth Circuit in *Hanlon* that such "ride-alongs" were per se unconstitutional, that they always and necessarily violated the Fourth Amendment. In a brief filed in both cases, the press amici argued that the Court should affirm the decision of the U.S. Court of Appeals for the Fourth Circuit in *Wilson* that declined to reach the Fourth Amendment issue because the officers were immune from liability.[203] CNN argued separately in *Hanlon* that its conduct did amount to a search or seizure, but that even if the Fourth Amendment applied, the Bergers' privacy interests were outweighed by the public interest in coverage, specifically "enabling public oversight of law enforcement, deterring crime, and curbing potential police misconduct and danger to police."[204]

Writing for the Court in *Wilson*, Chief Justice Rehnquist gave short shrift to the press arguments.

> Surely the possibility of good public relations for the police is simply not enough, standing alone, to justify the ride-along intrusion into a private home. And even the need for accurate reporting on police issues in general bears no direct relation to the constitutional justification for the police intrusion into a home in order to execute a felony arrest warrant... [And w]hile it might be reasonable for police officers to themselves videotape home entries ... such a situation is significantly different from the media presence in this case.
>
> The *Washington Post* reporters in the Wilsons' home were working on a story for their own purposes. They were not present for the purpose of protecting the officers, much less the Wilsons. A private photographer was acting for private purposes, as evidenced in part by the fact that the newspaper and not the police retained the photographs. Thus, although the presence of third parties during the execution of a warrant may in some circumstances be constitutionally permissible, the presence of these third parties was not.[205]

Rehnquist may not have articulated a per se rule, but it was just about as close as he could have come. "We hold that it is a violation of the Fourth Amendment for police to bring members of the media or other third parties into a home during the execution of a warrant when the presence of the third parties in the home was not in aid of the execution of the warrant."[206]

Whatever the reason or combination of reasons for the disparity between publishing and newsgathering cases, the third and final extended case study in this exploration puts the Court's jurisprudence in these two areas on a dramatic collision course. Although it was decided a decade ago, *Bartnicki v. Vopper*[207] is still the most recent case to significantly alter First Amendment doctrine as it pertains to the press. The next chapter examines *Bartnicki* in detail, not only for its doctrinal development, but for what it can tell us about the press today in its role as constitutional litigator.

Chapter 9 – *Bartnicki v. Vopper:* Pulling It All Together

How many different ways can one approach a First Amendment press clause analysis? What influences a court to select one analytical approach over another? And what is the long-term effect of choosing one over another? In *Bartnicki v. Vopper*,[1] a case in which the United States Supreme Court considered federal and state statutes prohibiting the disclosure of illegally intercepted telephone conversations,[2] we are privileged to have a small laboratory through which to study the first two questions. And, of course, we can always make some speculative predictions as to the third.

In *Bartnicki*, the United States Supreme Court held that the First Amendment gave the news media a right to publish truthful information on matters of public concern, even if unlawfully acquired, provided the publisher did not participate in the unlawful conduct.[3] How the Court ultimately reached that conclusion is one principal focus of this chapter, precisely because the story of this litigation reveals so much about alternative First Amendment analyses and the efforts exerted by the press to influence the courts' choices among those analyses.

In this one case, the district court framed the issue as a battle between conflicting and potentially controlling precedents.[4] The circuit court selected a doctrinal formula called "intermediate scrutiny," and applied it in textbook fashion to reach a conclusion.[5] And the United States Supreme Court resorted to an "ad hoc balancing" of interests in personal privacy versus publicly significant information, ultimately ruling in favor of the latter.[6]

Even more interesting are the reasons why the courts made the decisions they did. Did they track the arguments of the party litigants? How influential was the United States government's intervention to defend the federal statute at issue? And what role did the press itself play? *Bartnicki* provides an excellent opportunity to study the press's increasing sophistication in helping to shape First Amendment doctrine through litigation in the Supreme Court.

Some 70 years earlier, the press's first serious effort in *Near v. Minnesota*[7] established the supremacy of the right to publish.[8] Forty years later, the disastrous decision in *Branzburg v. Hayes*[9] stunted any First Amendment right to gather news and revealed the need for coordinated media attention to doctrinal litigation.[10] Now, after another 30 years, the *Bartnicki* case brought publishing and newsgathering issues together, and this time the press proved to be up to the challenge.

As interesting as this case may be from analytical and strategic perspectives, the implications of *Bartnicki's* contribution to First Amendment doctrine are difficult to discern. The Court allowed a law-abiding press to publish with impunity truthful, important information, regardless of its initial unlawful acquisition, but did it significantly expand the public's right to receive newsworthy information?

The question actually presented by this case was whether the broadcaster could, consistent with the First Amendment, be punished for his dissemination of publicly significant information initially acquired from an unknown person who had illegally intercepted a private telephone conversation.[11] Both federal and state statutes provided a civil cause of action for, not only the interception, but also the further disclosure of the intercepted conversation.[12]

In declaring the disclosure provision unconstitutional as applied, however, the Court declined to abstract its holding to a legal principle. The ambiguity of the decision suggests that a different balance could be struck if the subject matter of the disclosure were, say, national security rather than labor relations matters. The conclusion of this chapter looks to the contemporary WikiLeaks.com controversy to illuminate this issue.

Part A of this chapter recounts the underlying facts of the *Bartnicki* case and its procedural posture up to certiorari. Part B examines the two contending precedents initially asserted by the parties and accepted as the basis for analysis in the district court. Part C looks at the shift to doctrinal analysis in the Court of Appeals, prompted at least in part by the federal government's entry into the case. Part D studies the proceedings before the United States Supreme Court, with emphasis on the participation and analytical approach of prominent media lawyers. Part E dissects the opinion and the shift to an ad hoc balancing approach, particularly in light of the press arguments, while Part F ventures some predictions about the significance of the decision with the WikiLeaks.com controversy as a backdrop.

A. "Blow Off Their Front Porches"

The Wyoming Valley of Pennsylvania encompasses the cities of Scranton, Pittston, and Wilkes-Barre,[13] and numerous smaller towns, including the boroughs of Courtdale, Edwardsville, Forty Fort, Larksville, Luzerne, Plymouth, Pringle, Kingston, and Swoyersville. These towns, all hard by Interstate Highway 81 and just a little northwest of Wilkes-Barre, are served by the Wyoming Valley West School District.[14] The district boasts seven elementary schools, a middle school, and a high school, with about 5,000 students altogether.[15]

From mid-1992 until November 1993, the district was torn by a contract dispute between the Wyoming Valley West School Board and the Wyoming Valley West Education Association, the union representing the district's 341 teachers. Five months of hard bargaining for a new teachers' contract turned nasty in October 1992, when the board decided to warn teachers that they might be subject to furlough a week before the next scheduled bargaining session.[16] By March 1993, the teachers had halted all volunteer work, including chaperoning school activities,[17] and in May the union threatened to strike in early June unless its salary demands were met.[18]

The union was asking for six percent increases each year for the next three years, raising the average salary from $40,000 to $47,640 in 1994.[19] The board was standing firm at three percent per year for three years.[20] The teachers' health insurance plan was also in dispute.[21] At 10:30 p.m. on May 27, 1993, the union delivered a strike notice to Superintendent Dr. Norman Namey,[22] and, on June 4, the teachers launched their first strike in the 27-year history of the district.[23]

The timing of that strike was the subject of one particular cellular telephone conversation between Gloria Bartnicki and Anthony Kane, Jr., sometime in May.[24] Bartnicki was employed by the Pennsylvania State Education Association (PSEA) and assigned as a negotiator in the Wyoming Valley West School District contract dispute.[25] Kane was a teacher at Wyoming Valley West High School and president of the PSEA local, the Wyoming Valley West Education Association.[26]

But it was another remark by Kane that captured the attention of the public – and the legal system – when the conversation was broadcast several months later: "If they're not going to move for three percent, we're gonna have to go to their, their homes ... to blow off their front porches, we'll have to do some work on some of those guys...."[27] How the public came to know of this conversation forms the factual predicate of this case.

The contentious contract negotiations prompted the formation of a citizens' group called the Wyoming Valley West Taxpayers' Association to oppose the teachers' union proposals.[28] Sometime after the conversation took place, still during the spring of 1993, the president of that organization, Jack Yocum, allegedly found a five-minute tape of the conversation in his mailbox.[29] Yocum claimed not to know who made the tape or why,[30] but he listened to it, identified the voices, played it for some school board members, and gave copies of the tape to Frederick W. Vopper.[31] Vopper had a news and public affairs talk show under the name "Fred Williams" that was broadcast on WILK Radio and simulcast on WGBI-AM.[32]

By all accounts, Vopper did nothing with the tape until late September.[33] By then, contract negotiations had completely broken down, the dispute had been submitted to non-binding arbitration, the arbitrator had sided with the teachers' union, and the school board had rejected the arbitrator's decision.[34] About the same time, Vopper, who had been critical of the teachers' union in the past.[35] began airing the tape repeatedly, while adding bomb-like sound effects.[36] Intended or not, the tapes had the effect of further inflaming the contract dispute,[37] and the Luzerne County District Attorney launched an investigation at the behest of the school board.[38] In the end, neither his investigation nor another undertaken by the PSEA could determine who actually made the tape.[39] According to Vopper's first attorney, Donald Brobst, the question remains unanswered to this day.[40]

The contract dispute was ultimately settled in November after the school board offered salary increases of 4% per year over four years,[41] but the controversy over Vopper's broadcasts continued; in August 1994, Bartnicki and Kane filed a complaint in the U.S. District Court for the Middle District of Pennsylvania against Vopper and the parent companies of the stations that carried his show (the "media defendants") under civil suit provisions of Federal and state wiretap laws.[42] The unknown persons who intercepted the conversation were also named as John Doe and Jane Doe.[43]

The media defendants retained Donald H. Brobst of the Wilkes-Barre law firm Rosenn, Jenkins & Greenwald, L.L.P., to represent them in district court. Brobst had long represented WILK and its then-parent company, Keymarket of NEPA (Northeastern Pennsylvania), Inc., and this was neither the first nor the last case he had involving Fred Vopper. In addition to his defamation and other media law work, Brobst specialized in employment law cases, and he both initiated and defended cases brought under Section 1983 of the U.S. Code, which gives plaintiffs a federal cause of action when deprived of a constitutional right under color of state law.

The media defendants filed their answer in September.[44] The following February, they consented to Plaintiffs' amending their complaint to add Yocum as a defendant.[45] Yocum answered on June 30, 1995.[46] After extensive discovery, plaintiffs and defendants moved for summary judgment, with both defendants asserting a First Amendment right to disclose the conversation.[47] By Memorandum and Order dated June 17, 1996, the District Court denied both motions, ruling that the circumstances of the interception and the defendants' knowledge of them represented genuine issues of material fact, but that imposing liability on the defendants would not violate the First Amendment.[48]

The court denied defendants' subsequent motion to reconsider in November, and in January 1998 certified that its orders were appealable.[49] On Jan. 14, the Media Defendants filed an appeal in the U.S. Court of Appeals for the Third Circuit with the concurrence of the other parties to the litigation.[50] The Third Circuit granted the petition on Feb. 26,[51] and after receiving briefs from the parties[52] and the PSEA as amicus curiae,[53] heard arguments on Oct. 5. The United States, which intervened as of right and at the invitation of the court to defend the constitutionality of the federal statute,[54] filed a brief on Nov. 17, 1998, but to no avail. On Dec. 27, 1999, the Third Circuit reversed the District Court,[55] and the United States Supreme Court granted certiorari on June 26, 2000.[56]

B. In the District Court

In his motion for summary judgment, Brobst had argued for the media defendants that Bartnicki and Kane could not prove that their telephone conversation had been illegally, that is, intentionally and not inadvertently, intercepted, or that Vopper knew or had reason to know that the telephone conversation was illegally intercepted.[57] He also argued that Bartnicki had no reasonable expectation of privacy in the conversation, which took place on a cellular telephone that she acknowledged was susceptible of interception.[58] Brobst later conceded that neither of these factual arguments was persuasive, and that he staked everything on the First Amendment argument from the beginning.[59] Brobst's First Amendment argument relied almost exclusively on *Landmark Communications v. Virginia* and the line of constitutional privacy cases beginning with *Cox Broadcasting v. Cohn* and ending with *Florida Star v. BJF.*[60] Those cases held that "where the media lawfully obtains truthful information about a matter of public significance or concern, government officials may not constitutionally punish the publication of that information absent the need to further a government interest of the highest order."[61] Brobst later said he focused on *Landmark* in particular because the governmental interests there – maintaining the reputation of the judges and the institutional integrity of the courts – were far greater than the privacy interests protected in this case.[62]

To United States District Court Judge Edwin M. Kosik, however, the *Bartnicki* case essentially countered Brobst's *Landmark* rule with another well-established First Amendment principle: that "generally applicable laws 'do not offend the First Amendment, simply because their enforcement against the press has incidental effects on its ability to gather and report the news.'" Kosik referred to this principle as the *Cohen* doctrine, after *Cohen v. Cowles Media*, the only case cited for that proposition in his opinion,[63] despite much earlier origins.[64]

For the District Court, the conflict between *Landmark* and *Cohen* was easily resolved. According to the court, which completely misread the precedent cases, *Landmark* only applies where "a state actor attempted to place a prior restraint on specified speech or where the intentional interception was legal but the disclosure was illegal."[65] Here, the court said without further explanation, "there exist no statutory provisions specifically designed to chill free speech."[66]

One could try to supply the logical steps left out of the court's conclusory analysis. If by "prior restraint on specified speech" the court meant suppression of speech because of its message, rather than merely its source, there is no classic prior restraint here. To be sure, it is easier to regulate speech selected because of its source, rather than its message, but one expects rather more scrutiny than this court applied.[67]

And if "interception was legal" means no laws were broken in the newsgathering process, then this case is certainly *different* from the cases relied upon by the media defendants.[68] One might question, however, where the *distinction* comes from; the precedent cases explicitly avoid addressing the issue of illegally acquired information.[69]

In any event, the District Court found *Landmark* inapplicable and *Cohen* controlling. "In reviewing both the federal and the state electronic surveillance laws, we conclude that both acts are matters of general applicability."[70] In his motion for reconsideration, Brobst argued that the court's reliance on *Cohen* was misplaced and that *Landmark* did not involve a prior restraint.[71] The Virginia statute at issue in *Landmark* was "generally applicable" and did not "single out the press," yet the Supreme Court reversed the newspaper owner's conviction on First Amendment grounds. This case, Brobst argued, is indistinguishable. Moreover, he said, by breaking its promise to Cohen, the press arguably obtained its information unlawfully; here, there was no question that the press obtained its information lawfully from Yocum, whatever might have happened earlier.[72] Perhaps recognizing that engaging in a serious analysis of the issue before it on a motion for summary judgment was probably a waste of time and effort, the District Court denied Brobst's motion and kicked the can down the road. Brobst asked Judge Kosik to certify the case up to the Third Circuit and he agreed.

While Brobst might have taken the case to trial instead of appealing Kosik's denial of his motion, he acknowledges that there would have been no point in going that route. Apart from the constitutional claim, Brobst says, "We didn't have much [in the way of another] defense in this case. They had us dead to rights on what we did. We clearly had broadcast the tape many times. There was no doubt about that. It was pretty hard for us to claim that we didn't know that it had been a surreptitiously recorded tape." In fact, Brobst says, "we had a settlement agreement with the other side that the outcome of the appeal would decide the outcome of the case because there was no sense going to trial.... If we win [on the constitutional issue], we don't have to pay them anything, obviously, and if they win, it was a fixed amount of money that we would pay them." While the agreement reserved the right of either party to petition the Supreme Court for review, Brobst said neither side really expected the case to go that far.[73]

C. In the Third Circuit

On appeal, the parties agreed that no factual issues barred the Third Circuit from resolving the legal issues,[74] which boiled down to one: Does the First Amendment bar the imposition of liability for publishing truthful information of public significance, where both the acquisition and publication of that information are prohibited by statute and where the publisher was not involved in the unlawful acquisition?

As might be expected, Appellants continued to rely on the *Landmark* doctrine and related cases, asserting that the government's interest in the privacy of cellular telephone communications is "significantly less[]" than the interest at stake in *Landmark*.[75] In that case, the interest at issue was the confidentiality of state judicial review commission proceedings, the disclosure of which were prohibited by the state constitution and statutes.[76]

Appellants also cited a remarkably similar case in which the U.S. District Court for the Northern District of Texas ruled that the First Amendment protected the press from civil liability for reporting the contents of an illegally recorded telephone conversation of a school board trustee, where the tape had been recorded anonymously, delivered to certain school board members, and played at a public school board meeting.[77]

Perhaps even more interesting was Appellants' attempt to distinguish *Cohen* by reciting many of the arguments used against the media companies in that case: that the newspapers determined the scope of their own legal obligations by contract, that any restriction on publication was thus self-imposed, and that the newspapers may not have acted lawfully in acquiring the information by reneging on a promise of confidentiality.[78] Appellants also argued that the impact of enforcing the disclosure provisions of the wiretapping statutes would be far greater than "incidental," as required to impose the *Cohen* doctrine.[79]

Appellees also framed the case as a contest between the *Landmark* and *Cohen* principles, although of course they asserted that *Cohen* applies to this case.[80] Appellees also found a similar case in which a state trial court had distinguished the *Landmark* line on two grounds: (1) that the information in those cases had been properly part of the public record, albeit protected by statutory confidentiality; and (2) that the information in this case had been a private conversation, rather than governmental records.[81] That case never mentioned the *Cohen* doctrine at all, but the Appellees devoted a section to amplifying the District Court's assertions.[82]

Appellees added some new arguments as well. First, they asserted that the *Landmark*-related holdings were very narrow and limited to their specific facts.[83] Specifically, Appellees pointed to the famous footnote 8 in *Florida Star* in which the Court declined to address the question of "unlawfully" acquired information,[84] suggesting the Appellants' reliance on those cases was therefore "misplaced."[85] Appellants, of course, would find that footnote irrelevant, since they committed no unlawful act in acquiring the information.

But even if the strict scrutiny of *Landmark* controlled, Appellees argued, the wiretapping statutes would pass muster because they were narrowly tailored to protect privacy rights of the highest order.[86] Drawing on legislative history, the Appellees asserted that Congress was aware of and increasingly concerned about the impact of modern communications technology on personal privacy and the law's failure to keep up with that technology.[87]

Appellant Yocum had claimed the status of news gatherer in his less-than-coherent brief to the Third Circuit, citing *Branzburg v. Hayes* for the proposition that he was therefore entitled to First Amendment protection.[88] Appellees pointed out that, if anything, *Branzburg* stands for the proposition that news gatherers enjoy very limited protection, supporting their argument based on the *Cohen* principle, and that in any case Yocum's case would succeed or fail on the same grounds as the other Appellants' case.[89]

The only amicus brief in the Third Circuit was filed by the PSEA on behalf of Appellees, and that brief largely echoed the Appellees' analysis. It raised – and criticized – another new decision based on similar facts,[90] and it added another rather spurious argument analogizing the imposition of civil liability for violation of copyright law and for violation of the wiretap law's disclosure provisions.[91] Two aspects of the PSEA brief, however, bear mention because of their emphasis in the government's brief and the Third Circuit opinion. Unlike either the district court opinion or the Appellees' brief, the PSEA brief put particular emphasis on the wiretap statute's prohibition of "uses" of the intercepted materials other than disclosure to show its more general applicability[92] and characterized the *Landmark* line as involving "heightened scrutiny" dependent upon the lawfulness of information's initial acquisition.[93] Both of these arguments would be substantially amplified in the federal government's brief and addressed, albeit negatively for the most part, in the Third Circuit opinion.

There were no amicus briefs supporting Vopper's position. Brobst does not know why there was no support from other media organizations at this stage – "they certainly would have been aware of the case" – but he acknowledges that he did not solicit any amicus briefs from those organizations. Given the outcome in the Third Circuit, there was no apparent need for such support.

Following oral argument before the Third Circuit, the United States filed a brief – signed by the Assistant Attorney General for the Justice Department's Civil Division, the U.S. Attorney for the Middle District of Pennsylvania, and two staff appellate attorneys – defending the constitutionality of the wiretap statute's disclosure provision against Appellants' as-applied challenge.[94] Under federal law, the United States has the right to defend the constitutionality of any federal statute challenged on constitutional grounds.[95] Although Brobst argued that his "as-applied" challenge did not rise to that level,[96] the Third Circuit saw the case otherwise, and immediately after the argument, duly issued a letter inviting the government to file a post-argument brief in this case. The government's brief points out that its filing was both "at the invitation of the Court" and pursuant to its motion to intervene as of right under the law to defend the constitutionality of the wiretap statute.[97]

As previously discussed, the United States can be something of an 800-pound gorilla when it litigates or intervenes in a constitutional challenge. In this case, the United States framed the issue, less in terms of competing precedents, as the parties had done, than in terms of levels of First Amendment scrutiny to be applied. The Third Circuit's opinion would track the government's approach.

Following a focused description of the wiretap statute allegedly violated by Vopper, and a synopsis of the proceeding thus far, the government summarized its argument: the First Amendment does not prohibit the application of the wiretap statute's "use prohibitions" to the defendants in this case. As applied, those provisions are "subject only to intermediate scrutiny under the First Amendment, rather than strict scrutiny, and the statute readily satisfies the requirements of intermediate scrutiny."[98] Thus, one argument among others suggested in the PSEA brief had become the foundation for the government's position.

The government argued that the statute's ban on disclosure had to be read as part of a comprehensive ban on all uses of intercepted material; thus, the prohibition did not single out speech for any special burden. Where that is so, where any burden on speech is merely incidental to the purpose of the law, First Amendment precedent dictates the application of intermediate, rather than strict scrutiny in determining its constitutionality. A statute satisfies intermediate scrutiny if it furthers an "important" or "substantial" governmental interest (in contrast to strict scrutiny's "compelling" interest); if that interest is unrelated to the suppression of free expression; and if the incidental restriction on speech is not unnecessarily great (in contrast to strict scrutiny's "no less restrictive alternative available").[99]

Intermediate scrutiny is also appropriate, the government said, where the prohibitions on the use of illegally intercepted communications are not related to the content of the communications. Pointing out that the appellants would be free to broadcast the very same tape if acquired lawfully, the government noted that such content-neutral restrictions on speech also require courts to apply intermediate, rather than strict, scrutiny in evaluating their constitutionality. The restrictions at issue in the *Landmark* line of cases asserted by the appellants required strict scrutiny because they singled out speech for special burdens and restricted speech because of its content, among other reasons.[100]

Having established the appropriateness of intermediate scrutiny, the government then proceeded to show how the wiretap statute satisfied that standard. The privacy interest to be protected is "manifestly substantial. Moreover, by protecting the confidentiality of communications, the regulations encourage, rather than suppress, free expression. And, finally, the regulations are tailored carefully enough that they would even satisfy a strict scrutiny standard.[101]

It was a powerful argument, invoking not merely competing analogies, but basic principles of First Amendment analysis; indeed, the Third Circuit adopted just such an approach. Writing for herself and Judge Robert Cowan, Judge Dolores Sloviter rejected Appellants' argument that *Landmark* was controlling, noting that the question before this court had been expressly reserved by the Supreme Court. "[W]e will resolve the present controversy not by mechanically applying a test gleaned from *Cox* and its progeny, but by reviewing First Amendment principles in light of the unique facts and circumstances of this case."[102] But Sloviter also rejected the District Court's application of *Cohen*. Expressing some doubt that the wiretap statute's disclosure provision was a law of general applicability, she pointed out that, even if it were, *Cohen* did not stand for the proposition that laws of general applicability are not subject to First Amendment scrutiny. Rather, the Supreme Court held only that "'enforcement of such general laws against the press is not subject to stricter scrutiny than would be applied to enforcement against other persons or organizations.'"[103]

As if to emphasize the importance of the United States as a party in this case, Sloviter's analysis all but ignores the original parties and addresses the government's brief directly. Briefly summarizing its argument for intermediate scrutiny, Sloviter proceeded to mock the government's assertion that the statute's ban on "disclosure" is merely an aspect of its ban on "use," that is, conduct, rather than speech, and thus meriting intermediate scrutiny. "A statute that prohibited the 'use' of evolution theory would surely violate the First Amendment if applied to prohibit the disclosure of Charles Darwin's writings."[104]

On the other hand, the court found the content-neutrality argument more persuasive, based on the Supreme Court's definition of content-neutral restrictions on speech as restrictions that "'are justified without reference to the content of the regulated speech.'"[105] Had the act's only purpose been to prevent the disclosure of private facts, Sloviter suggested, its content-neutrality might be doubted. But the government did not rely on that justification; rather, she said, insofar as the act's purpose was to deny the illegal interceptor a market for the "fruits of his labor," it was properly treated as content-neutral and intermediate scrutiny applied.[106]

After reviewing various interpretations of the intermediate scrutiny standard, Sloviter formulated the question before the court as "whether the government has shown that its proffered interest" – eliminating the demand for intercepted communications – is sufficiently furthered by imposing liability on the defendants in this case to justify the restrictions on their First Amendment interests.[107] Finding the connection "indirect at best," the court concluded that "it would be a long stretch indeed" to conclude that imposing damages here would even peripherally promote the government's effort to deter interception. Since the wiretap act already provides punishment for illegal interception, it would be more effective to enforce those provisions than to impose liability here.[108]

Writing in dissent, District Judge Louis Pollack agreed with the majority's analytical approach to the case, but not with its application. Pollack took issue with the court's assertion that the connection between prohibiting disclosure and preventing interception was "indirect at best," citing a recent decision, *Boehner v. McDermott*, from the U.S. Court of Appeals for the District of Columbia Circuit to the contrary. In that case, the court opined that, "[u]nless disclosure is prohibited, there will be an incentive for illegal interceptions... and the damage caused... will be compounded."[109] The majority distinguished *Boehner* on the ground that the newspapers reporting the intercepted conversation were not defendants in that case, and that defendant McDermott, who provided the tape to the newspapers, knew who had intercepted the conversation and had a political interest in its disclosure.[110]

Following the judgment, Bartnicki and Kane moved for a rehearing by the entire Third Circuit court. According to Brobst, the motion failed by only one vote, suggesting the case was much closer than the panel decision would indicate.[111]

D. Before the Supreme Court

1. New Counsel

On April 19, 2000, Bartnicki and Kane filed a petition for a writ of certiorari, asking the United States Supreme Court to review the Third Circuit decision.[112] Their original lawyer, Wilkes-Barre attorney Raymond P. Wendolowski, was still listed on the brief supporting their petition, but with the stakes now that much higher and the venue shifting to Washington, Wendolowski was no longer listed as counsel of record. That responsibility was assumed by Robert H. Chanin and Jeremiah A. Collins of the Washington, D.C., firm of Bredhoff & Kaiser, a 33-lawyer firm that specialized in representing unions. Collins had been part of the team that wrote the Pennsylvania State Education Association's amicus brief for the Third Circuit. The Bredhoff firm was far more experienced in Supreme Court litigation and styles itself "the voice of labor."[113]

Taking a cue from the dissent below, Bartnicki argued that the Supreme Court should review the case because the Third Circuit's decision conflicted with *Boehner*, setting up a conflict between two circuits that the Supreme Court ought to resolve.[114] That kind of argument is considered one of the most effective at this stage of the process. According to Perry, "Without doubt, the single most important generalizable factor in assessing certworthiness is the existence of a conflict of 'split' in the circuits."[115] Bartnicki also argued that the decision below not only struck down an important provision of a federal statute, but also called into question similar statutes enacted by a majority of the states.[116] The Third Circuit majority had disparaged that argument as hyperbole when raised by the dissent, pointing out that its "as applied" decision was expressly limited to the facts of this case.[117]

Finally, Bartnicki asserted that the Third Circuit opinion was just wrong as to an important question of constitutional law that had been reserved by the Supreme Court in prior decisions. The petition asserts that this case provides "an ideal vehicle" for determining whether "a statute that protects privacy interests by making it unlawful for a person to disclose information *unlawfully obtained by another* violates the First Amendment."[118] The following week, the United States weighed in, seeking certiorari on its own behalf as an intervenor in the case, with Solicitor General Seth P. Waxman listed as counsel of record.[119] The government's argument closely paralleled Bartnicki's.

When Vopper's brief in opposition to certiorari was filed on May 30, the radio host was also represented by new counsel. According to Donald Brobst, Vopper's employer, Keymarket of NEPA, the owner of radio station WILK, had been acquired by Sinclair Broadcast Group sometime during the pendancy of the case. While Sinclair initially kept Brobst on as outside counsel, he had what he describes as a "falling out with in-house counsel for Sinclair that had nothing to do with this case"[120] although part of the problem involved Fred Vopper.

In one case, Brobst said, Sinclair wanted him to defend Vopper in a case brought by a district attorney who also happened to be running for judicial office. One of the Rosenn, Jenkins & Greenwald partners was campaign treasurer, raising a potential conflict of interest for any lawyer in the firm. Another case involved Vopper's challenging the integrity of two judges before whom RJG had other cases pending. Sinclair's in-house counsel was "not happy about that," Brobst said, and the relationship started to go downhill. After another, unrelated dispute arose, "we decided to have a parting of the ways on all cases,"[121] and Brobst lost the chance to take *Bartnicki v. Vopper* to the U.S. Supreme Court.

Instead, that honor went to Lee Levine, even then a major star in the media law firmament, having founded his own Washington law firm – Levine, Sullivan & Koch, L.L.P. – only three years earlier.[122] This would be Levine's second argument before the Supreme Court; he had previously represented the newspaper defendant in *Harte-Hanks Communications, Inc. v. Connaughton.*[123] Levine also taught media law at Georgetown University Law Center and had co-authored a major treatise on newsgathering.[124] Brobst recalls that he had some initial contact with the new litigation team – "we sent them everything they wanted"[125] – then bowed out of the case.

Levine's brief in opposition to certiorari rejected all of the reasons for judicial review raised in the Bartnicki and United States petitions. The Third Circuit decision "constitutes an unremarkable assessment of whether the imposition of civil liability" on the media defendants under the Wiretap Acts "survives intermediate scrutiny. In making this fact-bound assessment," the brief asserted, "the Third Circuit expressly declined to address the 'important question of constitutional law' referenced by Petitioners, 'struck down' no provision of either statute, and applied the same standard of First Amendment scrutiny embraced by the majority of the District of Columbia Circuit in *Boehner*."[126]

Those arguments were echoed in respondent Yocum's brief in opposition,[127] but successfully rebutted in reply briefs from Bartnicki[128] and the United States.[129] On June 26, 2000, the United States Supreme Court granted the petition for certiorari.[130]

In contrast to the Third Circuit proceeding, amicus briefs began flowing into the Court in September; three of them were filed by litigants in cases representing nearly identical issues. Representative John Boehner (R-Ohio), whose victory in the D.C. Circuit had prompted Bartnicki's "split in the circuits" argument, argued for petitioners that "there is no First Amendment right to distribute someone else's pilfered speech."[131] Boehner's opponent, Representative James McDermott (D-Wash.), whose petition for certiorari was still pending at the time, argued that disclosure provisions of the wiretap statute should be subject to strict scrutiny.[132] WFAA-TV of Dallas, Tex., which was poised to file its own petition seeking review of an adverse Fifth Circuit decision,[133] sought to push the Court to the ultimate rule – further than any other participant:

> This case should be decided according to a simple, bright line rule: if a journalist breaks the law to obtain information, she is subject to whatever generally applicable legal penalties may be triggered by the act of misappropriation. However the journalist has obtained information, she may be punished only for any impropriety in obtaining it, and not for publishing it, absent a countervailing governmental interest of the highest order.[134]

Only one other amicus brief was filed on behalf of Bartnicki and Kane; the cellular telephone industry argued that ensuring the privacy of wireless communications would further federal policies favoring the free speech of cell phone subscribers and encouraging the industry's growth.[135] In addition to McDermott's and WFAA-TV's briefs, four briefs were filed on behalf of the media defendants. Both the American Civil Liberties Union and the Liberty Project argued that strict scrutiny, rather than intermediate scrutiny, was the appropriate standard to apply.[136] And *Wall Street Journal* owner Dow Jones, with a brief signed by Supreme Court veteran Theodore Olson, called for "straightforward application of the *Daily Mail* test" – essentially Brobst's argument in the district and circuit courts.[137]

But the media's principal amicus brief, with Floyd Abrams as counsel of record, was filed on behalf of more than 20 "media entities and organizations," including newspaper and magazine publishers, television and cable networks, and journalism trade and professional associations.[138] The list of attorneys representing the amici read like a "Who's Who" of media law. It is impossible to say with any certainty how much influence any brief may have had on the Court, but the similarity between the media entities' brief and the Court's majority opinion is striking.

2. Today's Media Defense Bar

Before discussing the content of the various briefs filed with the Court, a brief digression is warranted to explore the process through which the media bar participates as amici curiae in Supreme Court litigation today. According to Lucy Dalglish, executive director of Reporters Committee on Freedom of the Press, the process is an informal one.[139] For example, RCFP first got involved in the *Bartnicki* case in June 2000. Legal defense director, Gregg Leslie, had put out an email message to a number of prominent media lawyers, among them Laura Handman of Davis Wright Tremaine, Bruce Sanford of Baker Hostetler, and Lee Levine, asking, "Does anyone know of an amicus effort underway in *Bartnicki*? We've always been available to write one, or at least coordinate efforts, but I assume that there will be big companies willing to pay a firm for a brief now that it's before the high court. If you have any information that you're able to share, I'd be happy to hear it."[140]

Soon after, Adam Liptak, then in-house counsel for *The New York Times*, now its Supreme Court reporter, replied, "Gregg, yes, there is an amicus effort. The *Times* and others have asked Floyd Abrams to prepare a brief and I'm sure the Reporters Committee will be welcome [to join the brief] on the usual terms." By "usual terms," Liptak was referring to the informal arrangement through which signatories to the brief help the lead organization (here, the *Times*) pay for it. RCFP and other nonprofits usually ride along for free, and when RCFP lawyers write the brief, all others in the media world are invited to join at no charge. Typically, however, the private entities pay for the privilege. According to Dalglish, the cost can vary.[141]

"It depends on how much time it's going to take, how many people [the lawyers] think they need to do it. They've been cutting their rates a little bit lately. In the summertime, they want to do it more because they can use their summer associates if they have them. I'd say anywhere from $10,000 to $30,000 these days is what it would cost." Once the cost is established, the lead organization would begin "trolling" for signers. If, for example, the sign-on price is $1,500, Dalglish said, "if you get a whole pile of people to sign on, you're doing OK, but if you only get five, you've rolled the dice and you've lost."[142]

As to the content of the briefs, Dalglish said amici first figure out what the party they are supporting has already argued, then identify other issues that the party did not have room for. "Usually, what we try to do is present a national perspective, do some public policy stuff, or brief an issue that the parties would have loved to have briefed if they had time or space. Sometimes they will ask you specifically, could you do this issue." Other times, amici will suggest the focus of the brief. In either event, amici will try to avoid simply repeating the party's arguments. "No court wants to put up with that," Dalglish said. "I just have no interest in parroting back the party's brief."[143]

The relationship between amici and the parties varies somewhat depending upon the court hearing the case. Under Supreme Court rules,[144] and throughout the federal system,[145] all parties must consent to the filing of an amicus brief; where consent is withheld, amici may petition the court to receive the brief anyway. So there is always some communication between the amici and the party they are supporting. Dalglish described the typical process: "You let them know you're going to do it, and they say… that would be great… we'll sign the letter and give it to you."[146] On the other hand, Supreme Court rules require amici to disclose whether counsel for a party had a hand in writing the brief or paying for it.[147]

Still, the parties often ignite the amicus process. If the case gets to the Supreme Court, it has already been percolating through the media defense bar. By the time they have won or lost in the appellate courts, the parties will have talked about it in one of several forums where members of the media defense bar get together. Among these are the Practising Law Institute's annual Communications

Law Conference, founded and managed for some 35 years by James Goodale, now conducted by Lee Levine as Communications Law in the Digital Age;[148] the biennial conference and other meetings of the Media Law Resource Center, formerly the Libel Defense Resource Center, also based in New York;[149] the annual conference and various workshops of the American Bar Association's Forum on Communications Law;[150] and the annual Media and the Law Seminar at the University of Kansas.[151]

One of the most important of these forums is the District of Columbia Bar Association's Media Law Committee, which meets informally once a month for lunch at the offices of one of the participating law firms. The meetings were started by Davis Wright's Handman, who chaired them for two years. Lee Levine has also chaired the meetings, as have RCFP's Gregg Leslie, Covington & Burling's Kurt Wimmer, and Holland & Knight's Chuck Tobin. Lawyers from Washington and often New York come to talk about their strategy in cases that have been argued or to preview upcoming cases. They are not, Dalglish said, strategy sessions to plan how the bar might get involved.[152]

That happens more informally, Dalglish said. Frequently, *The New York Times* takes the lead, or *The Washington Post*, or the Associated Press. "They tend to sort of rotate. Sometimes it's the individual lawyer [who is interested in a particular case]... Sometimes it's geographic. Sometimes they have a similar case percolating and they want to jump on it.... Sometimes it's driven by who's interested in covering a story." Dalglish says the informal system works so well because the bar is so small. "It's a very small group of people. Very tight knit. ... So you're seeing these people frequently, and you're staying on top of things frequently. ... Everybody knows everybody else."[153]

As for the Reporters Committee itself, Dalglish noted that she has former fellows working all over the country. "I will hire a fellow [who] will spend a year working here. I will work [at] getting him a job at one of the firms. And then some of those folks end up going in house because they don't like the law firm atmosphere. Right now, I've got former fellows in house at *The Washington Post* [and] National Public Radio.... [In] the last couple of years, my folks have been snatched up by the government... as FOIA officers."[154]

Dalglish said RCFP used to be a lot more involved in direct litigation, pointing out that "the last time we were actually involved as a party was ... when we went in with the Center for National Security Studies... to get a list of the 1,500 or so foreign nationals who were snatched off the streets and put in detention centers" after Sept. 11, 2001. The U.S. Court of Appeals for the District of Columbia ultimately reversed an initially favorable decision by the district court.[155] During the past decade or so, since Dalglish has been executive director, RCFP has been doing more amicus briefs.[156]

"We look for cases that will have potential to have an impact on what journalists are able to do, either in their home state or on the federal level, and that can be in regards to an open meetings or open records violation… it can be getting involved in a libel case, or certainly in a reporter's privilege case. We tend not to get involved at the trial level," Dalglish said, citing lack of need, cost, and the potential to irritate trial judges. "That's not to say we haven't done it, but at the trial level we usually get involved if it is an issue that can be of great relevance to the media, but neither of the parties is a media entity…. We may look at some of the pleadings and decide that it may be of benefit to having a media lawyer write the brief and raise some issues that perhaps [another lawyer would see differently]."[157]

Dalglish said she also tries "not to get involved at the cert. petition stage at the U.S. Supreme Court, unless there's a compelling reason to, like if it's a case we really, really want them to take, or if a case that we know they're going to take and we want to get the issue teed up right away. And, quite honestly, there's one other very important factor, and that has to do with journalism politics. We want to stake our territory. We want to do a brief and show that the Reporters Committee is on top of it."[158]

"If [the case is] at the intermediate court level at the federal level, we're almost certainly going to get involved if it involves anything to do with the media. Sometimes, they slip by us." In *Bartnicki*, where no media amicus briefs were filed in the Third Circuit proceeding, Dalglish recalls that other, similar cases were being "teed up" at about the same time.[159] "Hopefully, we've gotten a little better at spotting them on the circuit level, but that doesn't mean we always catch them…. Certainly, when the Supreme Court took [*Bartnicki*], we got involved in force."[160]

3. The Arguments

In the *Bartnicki* case, most of the arguments in the parties' briefs had been auditioned in the courts below. Bartnicki and Kane began their argument for reversing the Third Circuit opinion by urging the Court to adopt an intermediate scrutiny standard – a point on which the Third Circuit agreed. It next walked the Court through an unremarkable analysis to show that the statutes, as applied, satisfy that standard.[161] The federal government's brief made essentially the same case.[162] For Vopper and the other media defendants, Levine argued that the case required application of the *Daily Mail* principle, another way of arguing for strict scrutiny, but he added that the statutes in question would not even satisfy intermediate scrutiny.[163] Yocum, who had by now retained his own Supreme Court specialist, Thomas C. Goldstein, made the same arguments in reverse order.[164] The petitioners' reply briefs broke little new ground.[165]

Floyd Abrams's amicus brief for the "media entities" also argued that the Third Circuit opinion should be affirmed on a *Florida Star* (i.e., *Landmark* or *Daily Mail*) analysis,[166] noting only in a footnote that the statute would fail intermediate scrutiny as well.[167] But Abrams prefaced his legal argument with a much broader policy appeal:

> From the time individuals first consider becoming journalists, two principles are drilled into them.
>
> The first is that telling the truth about matters of public interest is what journalism, at its best, is all about. ... [J]ournalists who read opinions of this Court find unsurprising this Court's repeated reference to "the overarching public interest, secured by the Constitution in the dissemination of truth." That public interest is directly imperiled in this case.
>
> So is the journalistic norm that in the course of gathering news, journalists should affirmatively seek the truth from those who have it.... For journalists, then, the notion that liability may be imposed upon them for doing nothing more or less than reporting truthfully about newsworthy events is deeply disturbing.[168]

Although the Third Circuit had viewed the government's interest in deterring unlawful interceptions as the most, albeit insufficiently, compelling justification for the statute's non-disclosure provisions, Abrams focused on the privacy interest. The privacy interests held insufficient in the *Florida Star* line of cases, he said, were no less powerful than the privacy interests in this case. "[W]hy, after all, is the right of a rape victim not to have her name disclosed less significant than that of a union official not to have a telephone call disclosed in which he threatened to engage in criminal conduct?"[169]

Abrams moved on to reject the notion, advanced by Bartnicki, that the *Florida Star* line of cases was limited to content-based restrictions on speech and, thus, not applicable to the content-neutral disclosure restrictions of the wiretap laws. Rather, he said, that line of authority is firmly grounded in the public interest in truth-telling. Abrams also made the seemingly unnecessary argument that the media defendants acted lawfully in obtaining the tape, then returned to balance of privacy and truth-telling interests. In the very last paragraph of the argument, almost as an afterthought, Abrams struck the precise theme that would dominate the Supreme Court's opinion:

> We offer the final thought that there is, in the end, a certain lack of equivalence between the First Amendment interests at stake here and the privacy interests that underlie the wiretapping statute. Both are important but only one is in the written Constitution. It should not be too late to assert that when the First

> Amendment's protection of truth-telling is pitted against an interest that was only first identified just over a century ago, some deference should be given to the Framer's expressed intentions.[170]

Oral arguments were held on Dec. 5, 2000. Collins led off for petitioners Bartnicki and Kane, and his responses to the Court's questions emphasized the content-neutrality of the anti-disclosure statutes. When a content-neutral statutory regime protects important governmental interests that would be harmed by disclosure, he said, "we believe and we have argued that that in essence exhausts the First Amendment concerns...."[171] Solicitor General Waxman, who argued next, contradicted Collins's "suggestion" that no heightened scrutiny is required here. "That's not our position," he said; "we submit that the appropriate level of scrutiny is intermediate scrutiny."[172]

Justice Anthony Kennedy and others expressed concern that the statutes created a class of speech that was forever tainted and could not be repeated by anyone. Waxman countered that, once the speech became publicly known, the statutes would no longer apply. Thus a newspaper was free to comment on the conversation once Vopper broadcast it.[173] Waxman also argued that enforcing the anti-disclosure statutes would deter unlawful interceptions.[174]

Levine began his oral argument by calling attention to the threat contained in the intercepted conversation, which led to a distracting colloquy with Justice John Paul Stevens and others about whether he wanted to win his case on that narrow ground or on principle. Insisting, as he was bound to do, that he would take the win "any way I can get it," Levine focused on the *Daily Mail* principle as the proper basis for decision.[175] Levine denied that the statutes' content neutrality would require an intermediate scrutiny analysis, but asserted that the anti-disclosure provisions would not survive even that modest test.[176]

The balance of Levine's time was taken up with an inconclusive discussion of the statutes' deterrence value, and that was where Yocum's counsel, Thomas Goldstein, began his appearance before the Court. "Even if [the anti-disclosure provisions] add some deterrent, that prohibition is too crude a weapon, effectively a thermonuclear bomb of sorts, to be sustained in the sensitive area of... free speech."[177] Goldstein endorsed the Third Circuit's intermediate scrutiny approach,[178] and took issue with Waxman's assertion that the statutes' effectively immunized down-stream commentary on the intercepted conversation.[179] Waxman, in a brief rebuttal, defended the deterrence argument and distinguished the *Daily Mail* line of cases.[180] At 12:03 p.m., Chief Justice Rehnquist declared the case submitted.[181]

E. Victory in the Balance

In his opinion for the Court, delivered May 21, 2001, Justice Stevens adopted the frame that Abrams had urged – a conflict between the "full and free dissemination of information concerning public issues" and "individual privacy." Stevens's formulation of the issue, however, labeled both interests "of the highest order," and he appeared to accept the idea, advanced by petitioners, that the disclosure provisions of the statute would "foster[] private speech."[182] Nevertheless, Stevens promptly declared that the disclosures made in this case were protected by the First Amendment.[183]

The opinion that followed was unusually disjointed, shifting from doctrinal analysis, to interrogation of precedents, and ultimately to ad hoc balancing. Stevens began by accepting petitioners' characterization of the disclosure provisions as "content-neutral law of general applicability."[184] Unlike the trial court, however, he did not find that dispositive. "On the other hand," he said, the "naked prohibition against disclosure… is a regulation of pure speech,"[185] as if that somehow negated or counterbalanced the general applicability doctrine as applied in *Cohen v. Cowles Media*.[186]

Seeming to reach a dead end with this doctrinal inquiry, Stevens shifted abruptly to interrogating precedent. Here, too, the analysis ended without resolution, with Stevens pointing out that neither the Pentagon Papers case,[187] nor the *Landmark-Daily Mail-Florida Star* line of cases,[188] resolved the question presented here. The only lesson Stevens seemed to take from these precedents was the need to balance, on the facts of this case, the interests served by the law against its restrictions on speech.

Like the Third Circuit, Stevens ultimately rejected the government's asserted interest in deterring interception of private conversations as a bona fide interest of the "highest order."[189] Unlike the Third Circuit, Stevens found the privacy interest compromised here to be a "valid independent justification for prohibiting such disclosures…."[190] Nevertheless, those privacy interests had to "give way when balanced against the interest in publishing matters of public importance."[191] Drawing principally on libel cases for support, Stevens held that a "stranger's illegal conduct does not suffice to remove the First Amendment shield from speech about a matter of public concern."[192]

In a concurring opinion, joined by Justice Sandra Day O'Connor, Justice Stephen Breyer emphasized the narrowness of the Court's holding.[193] Breyer, well known for his ad hoc balancing approach to First Amendment cases,[194] cautioned that this case was decided on the facts that the broadcasters acted lawfully in obtaining the information and the information involved the threat of physical harm to others. It did not signal a "significantly broader constitutional immunity for the media," Breyer warned.[195]

Breyer asserted that concepts like "strict scrutiny" are inappropriate to resolve competing interests.[196] Breyer also seemed to put far more value in the deterrent effect of the anti-disclosure provisions than either the majority or Third Circuit opinion.[197] But on these facts, Breyer said, the speakers had no "legitimate" interest in the privacy of a threat to harm others – even where the danger had passed.[198] Breyer also emphasized that Bartnicki and Kane were "limited public figures" with a "lesser" interest in privacy.[199]

Breyer concluded that the Court did "not create a 'public interest' exception that swallows up the statutes' privacy-protecting general rule." Rather, he said, these speakers' privacy expectations were unusually low, while the public interest in "defeating those expectations" was unusually high.[200] "I would not extend that holding beyond these present circumstances."[201]

Of course, the dissenters would not have gone even that far. Writing for Justices Antonin Scalia and Clarence Thomas, Chief Justice William Rehnquist correctly identified the contradiction in Justice Stevens's acknowledgment that the anti-disclosure provisions were "content-neutral laws of general applicability" and the outcome that Stevens ultimately reached.[202] But he inexplicably mischaracterizes Stevens's analytical approach as a kind of strict scrutiny derived from "the *Daily Mail* string of newspaper cases," which he proceeds to read as narrowly as possible.[203] As noted above, Stevens paid very little attention to that line of cases, and barely mentioned strict scrutiny doctrine. Breyer's characterization of a fact-bound balancing came far closer to the essence of the majority opinion.

Rehnquist also took issue with Stevens's rejection of the government's deterrence argument, calling "[r]eliance upon the 'dry up the market' theory ...both logical and eminently reasonable...."[204] And he emphasized the First Amendment right of Bartnicki and Kane to keep their conversation from the public domain.[205] Finally, he castigated the Court for relying on the Pentagon Papers case and "other inapposite cases" to subordinate the right to communications privacy "to the claims of those who wish to publish the intercepted conversations of others."[206]

F. Ten Years After

In assessing the impact of *Bartnicki* on future development of First Amendment doctrine, one may choose to adopt the expansive reading that the dissenters ascribed to the majority opinion or the narrow reading suggested by the concurring opinion. Ironically, the press would surely favor the former; indeed, they argued all along for strict scrutiny and the invocation of the constitutional privacy cases. The concurring opinion is far more problematic: can one broadcast an intercepted conversation that does not threaten physical harm? Stevens's opinion is so poorly crafted as to leave in doubt, not merely the answer, but even the proper analytical approach.[207]

To return to the hypothetical with which this book begins, consider the prospective case against WikiLeaks.com for publishing hundreds of thousands of classified military and diplomatic documents allegedly downloaded from a government database by a disaffected soldier.[208] As of this writing, no indictment had been handed up by a grand jury, but assuming *arguendo* that no one associated with WikiLeaks participated in the unlawful leaking except as beneficiary, there is only one difference between the case against WikiLeaks and the case against Fred Vopper: national security replaces personal privacy as the counterweight to disclosure of publicly important information.[209]

Thus, if one reads *Bartnicki* as imposing strict scrutiny when reviewing any restriction on the dissemination of unlawfully obtained, but publicly important information, where the disseminator did not participate in the unlawful acquisition, then WikiLeaks is home free. On the other hand, if one reads *Bartnicki* as a case of ad hoc balancing, then the Court will ultimately have to decide whether freedom to publish without fear of sanction is outweighed in this case by national security, as opposed to personal privacy, considerations.

So far, the lower courts' applications of *Bartnicki* have not been particularly helpful in that regard. Several cases have distinguished *Bartnicki* on the ground that the disclosures were not a matter of public concern.[210] Others have distinguished *Bartnicki* on the ground that the disseminator participated in the illegal conduct that led to disclosure.[211] Still others have distinguished *Bartnicki* where the disclosures involved trade secrets,[212] copyrights,[213] or data mining.[214] In no case reported to date has the holding in *Bartnicki* been applied to reach a similar conclusion in an analogous case.[215]

The scholarly literature has been rather more enlightening. In his article on *Information as Contraband*, published shortly after the Court issued its opinion in *Bartnicki*, and clearly inspired by that case, Rodney Smolla saw *Bartnicki* as an immediate victory for the press, but a longer term victory for privacy interests.[216] With a majority of justices (two concurring and three dissenting) accepting an effective intermediate scrutiny standard,[217] albeit with a "newsworthiness" safety-valve,[218] Smolla saw the case as elevating personal privacy to an interest of constitutional dimension on a par with freedom of speech and press.[219]

Nevertheless, Smolla drew exactly the opposite conclusion with respect to classified information. Hypothesizing a new "Official Secrets Act" of the kind enacted by Congress to punish journalists for disclosing leaked classified information, and vetoed by President Clinton,[220] Smolla drew a sharp distinction between the "steal" considered in *Bartnicki* and the "leak" contemplated by the new law. Quoting both Laurence Tribe[221] and Potter Stewart,[222] Smolla asserted that "[r]espect for the structural independence of the media contemplated by the Constitution prohibits courts from conscripting journalists as leak-police." Thus, to Smolla, even the narrowest reading of *Bartnicki* poses no danger for a Julian Assange – assuming his hands are otherwise clean and WikiLeaks is found to share that "structural independence."[223]

Of course, the Court has changed since Smolla wrote in 2002, and so has the temper of the times. It may be that the best that can be said for the *Bartnicki* decision is that, absent participation in the unlawful acquisition of newsworthy information, the press is as free to publish it as changing societal values will allow.

At the very least, the "content-neutral law of general applicability" no longer presents the insurmountable obstacle to First Amendment protection that it was under *Cohen v. Cowles Media.* The *Landmark-Daily Mail-Florida Star* line of cases has emerged none the worse for wear – Justice Rehnquist's crabbed reading garners only three votes. And, most importantly, Fred Vopper and his media allies got the outcome they wanted, if not the mandate, taking the press a small step closer to the ultimate goal of protection for all truthful information of public importance.

Chapter 10 – Analysis and Conclusions

The purpose of this final chapter is to analyze and draw some tentative conclusions as to what the foregoing narrative tells us about the role of the press in establishing and protecting its First Amendment rights by litigating in the U.S. Supreme Court. We have focused on four central questions:

1. How, when, and why did the press emerge as a constitutional litigator?
2. How has the press's approach to constitutional litigation evolved from emergence to the present?
3. How successful has the press been in persuading the Court to its own view of the First Amendment?
4. What accounts for the disparity between publishing and newsgathering cases in terms of outcomes favorable to the press?

In this chapter, we'll try to answer each of these questions in turn.

A. Emergence of the Press as Constitutional Litigator

This book argues, and the historical record shows, that the press did not emerge as a constitutional litigator until the second quarter of the twentieth century, notwithstanding the occasional reliance on First Amendment arguments in earlier political or business-related cases. The conditions necessary for that emergence included the transformation of the economic foundation of the press from partisan to commercial after the Civil War, the subsequent self-identification of the press with public service under the unifying principle of objectivity, the adoption of an expansive reading of the freedom of speech under the First Amendment during the World War I period, and the incorporation of the First Amendment that enabled constitutional litigation against state laws.

The story of Col. McCormick's vision and leading role in mobilizing the press to litigate what must have seemed then a remote, insignificant, and probably distasteful case out of Minnesota fully explains how and why the press took up constitutional litigation.

It is entirely possible, however, that even without the example and precedent of *Near v. Minnesota*, the American Newspaper Publishers Association would have arrived at the same point with the case of *Grosjean v. American Press* that followed immediately after *Near*. Indeed, *Grosjean* would have been a much easier starting point, since the press had an immediate business interest in the outcome and the facts so clearly favored the press's constitutional position.

The narrative shows two distinct phases in the evolution of the press's approach to constitutional litigation. The first phase begins in 1931 and includes the reluctant and parsimonious participation in *Near*, as well as the slightly more organized and enthusiastic involvement in *Grojean*. It also encompasses the contempt cases of the 1940s, the landmark libel cases of the 1960s, and the Pentagon Papers case in 1971. A handful of broadcast regulation and other business cases rounds out the first phase, which comprised 24 cases in all.

In this phase, press participation in the litigation – aside from the litigants themselves – was minimal. The American Newspaper Publishers Association was the most active early on; in addition to giving moral support to McCormick's lawyers in *Near*, ANPA filed briefs in *Grosjean*, all three contempt case and, later, in one antitrust case. The Radio-Television News Directors Association, a party in one broadcast regulation case, filed an amicus brief in another case raising the same issue, along with broadcasting networks NBC and CBS. The National Association of Broadcasters also filed one amicus brief in a broadcast regulation case, and the Magazine Publishers Association filed one in a subscription sales case. *The Washington Post* and *Chicago Tribune* filed amicus briefs in *New York Times v. Sullivan*, and the *Tribune* filed one in *Butts/Walker.* Otherwise, there were no press amici in any of the libel cases that followed *Sullivan* in the 1960s or in the Pentagon Papers case.

There is no doubt that the *Caldwell* case represented a wake-up call to the media bar. As the narrative shows, that case – which reached the Supreme Court as *Branzburg v. Hayes* – prompted the formation of the Reporters Committee for Freedom of the Press in 1970 as a powerful new litigation "engine." Soon after that case was decided in 1972, James Goodale launched the Communications Law Conference under the auspices of the Practising Law Institute as an unifying forum for the media defense bar. As a consequence of these and similar developments, press participation in constitutional litigation entered a second phase characterized by a steady increase in direct litigation and amici filings.

For example, the number of press-related First Amendment cases that reached decision in the Supreme Court in the thirty years after *Branzburg* totaled three times the number of cases that reached decision in the forty years between *Near* and *Branzburg*. There is a striking difference between press participation in the 1971 Pentagon Papers case, with no amicus briefs, and the next prior restraint case, *Nebraska Press Association*, in which roughly sixty media organizations filed or signed on to amicus briefs. That pattern of massive press participation has continued to this day.

Overall, the number of amicus briefs submitted by the press or urging the same position taken by the press was more than twice the number of amicus briefs taking the opposing position. Of the major press participants, the Newspaper Association of America (formerly the American Newspaper Publishers Association) was the most active, with thirty-five amicus briefs submitted or signed, followed closely by the Reporters Committee for Freedom of the Press, with thirty briefs and three appearances as named party.

Why have these organizations dedicated so much time, talent, energy, and, frankly, money, to the pursuit of favorable constitutional rulings before the United States Supreme Court? In the introduction to this book, I assert that the opinions of the Supreme Court on First Amendment issues are, with respect to the press, analogous to the laws and regulations that govern any other enterprise in this society. That view shines through the "Statements of Interest" that routinely appear in media amicus briefs. Floyd Abrams's brief in *Bartnicki* is typical:

> Amici are vitally interested in and deeply concerned about any ruling that could result in the imposition of sanctions against journalists for reporting truthful matters of public significance about which they become aware as a result of entirely lawful and wholly routine newsgathering efforts. This case raises that spectre and amici submit this brief to set forth their views as to why the judgment of the Court of Appeals for the Third Circuit should be affirmed.[1]

The press litigates because the decisions coming out of these cases directly affect the ability to gather and report the news.

B. Success of the Press in Persuading the Court

Of course, it is impossible to ascribe the outcome of a Supreme Court argument to any single factor, including the volume and quality of amicus briefs. The very best Supreme Court advocates take their share of losses, failing for any number of reasons to persuade a majority of justices that their arguments are better than their adversaries'. Statistics can only show correlations, not causation, but they are nevertheless instructive.

Overall, the facts suggest the press has done pretty well for itself in constitutional litigation. In an analysis of 101 Supreme Court decisions involving the institutional press,[2] the press has been successful more often than not, although by a relatively small margin, winning fifty-four and losing forty-seven. However, the press has been considerably more successful in dealing with content regulation/publishing cases than with newsgathering cases. Of the seventy publishing cases, the press won forty-three or 61%, while in the twenty-five newsgathering cases, the press won only seven or 28%. This certainly comports with other scholarship in this area, [3] although, alone, it says nothing about the reasons why this would be true.

The press was significantly more successful when it was a named party, winning forty-three or 56.6% of the seventy-six cases in which it was a named party, compared to only eleven or 44% of the twenty-five cases in which the press was represented only through amicus briefs. It did not seem to matter at all whether the press as party litigant was supported by additional press amici or not, although it was more common for press party litigants to have press amicus support than not, especially after *Branzburg*. While this in no way detracts from other scholarly findings on the importance of amicus briefs,[4] the statistics suggest some advantage to party status for which amicus briefs cannot compensate.

The media were also far more successful as or supporting petitioners than as or supporting respondents, winning thirty-eight of fifty-four cases or 70.4% as petitioner, compared to ten out of thirty-six cases or 27.8% as respondent, probably for reasons having less to do with characteristics of the press than with the theory that the Supreme Court is more likely to review decisions it wishes to reverse.[5] That notion finds some support in the fact that, in the eleven cases that reached the Court on direct appeal, the press won six of eight cases as or supporting appellees and lost all three cases as or supporting Appellants. In other words, the Court affirmed nine of eleven cases on direct appeal when it did not have the discretion to deny certiorari.

Much has been written about the American Civil Liberties Union as amicus,[6] and its presence in cases involving the institutional press certainly appears to have affected the outcome. The press significantly improved its winning percentage when the ACLU lined up on the same side, winning 75.8% of the time. Moreover the press lost five of the six cases in which the ACLU argued against the press position.

Ironically, press amici and the ACLU are rarely found on the same brief today. According to Reporters Committee's Dalglish, the ACLU requires other amici to yield all decision-making authority. "I've virtually gotten out of signing on [to ACLU briefs] except in extreme circumstances," Dalglish said, "because you basically sign over everything to them. They make all the decisions."[7]

Looking at the opposition, the press did much better against state and local agencies, including trial courts, winning twenty-three of thirty-four cases or 67.6%, than against the federal government, winning only eight of twenty-four or 33.3%. This certainly comports with Herbert Kritzer's findings that the federal government is, indeed, the proverbial 800-pound gorilla, but it does not reflect the considerably smaller advantage he attributes to state and local governments. The explanation may lie in the "linkage" Kritzer found between the success rate of state and local government entities and the resources of their opponents.[8]

Even most state attorneys general do not command the legal talent that the institutional press can assemble. The lawyers mobilized on behalf of the press, such as Floyd Abrams, James Goodale, Jane Kirtley, Bruce Sanford, Lee Levine, and others encountered in this study are among the best that the country has to offer. The press faced only a half-dozen non-governmental "repeat players"[9] and won four of the cases.

Perhaps the greatest surprise was the finding that the institutional press did only slightly better than even against thirty-seven so-called "one-shotters" (parties who do not regularly appear in court) that it faced in Court. This flies in the face of all the variations on the Galanter theme. Looking more closely at the individual cases, however, suggests two possible explanations. One explanation involves the five newsgathering cases,[10] where the 1-4 losing record might be expected in light of this study. The second is more complicated. The press won eleven libel cases against one-shotters and lost eleven, won three privacy cases and lost two, won two prior restraint cases and lost one, and won two other content-related cases.

Most of the libel cases were decided after 1964 when the Court revolutionized libel law in *New York Times v. Sullivan.* Nearly all of the cases that followed made important doctrinal refinements to answer constitutional questions raised by the *Sullivan* prescription: what is "actual malice"? who is a "public figure"? etc.

Thus, one suspects the libel cases, which account for twenty-two of the thirty-six one-shot cases, were accepted and resolved almost without regard to the litigants as the Court wrestled with very technical questions of pure law. Two of the non-libel cases, which sounded in privacy and intentional infliction of emotional distress, could also be explained as refinements of the *Sullivan* doctrine.

Yet another unexpected finding from this study was the relatively little difference in press case outcomes among the Warren, Burger, and Rehnquist Courts – the only Courts with enough press cases for comparison – despite the marked conservative trend from 1953 to 2005. Indeed, the press was most successful in the Rehnquist Court, winning sixteen of twenty-nine cases or 55.2%, and least successful in the Burger Court, before which the press won twenty-seven of fifty-two cases or 51.9%.

C. Disparity between Publishing and Newsgathering Cases

Why has the press fared so poorly in constitutional litigation involving newsgathering – other than access to courtrooms – despite striking successes in publishing cases? This book has already explored at some length the reasons for failure in access to government information cases, as well as the overwhelming influence of "generally applicable law" doctrine in *Branzburg, Zurcher, Cohen, Wilson,* and *Hanlon.* But there are some broader factors that separate newsgathering from publishing and operate to disfavor newsgathering; a few of these bear mention here.

At the most concrete level, it might be said that newsgathering cases affected working reporters more directly than editors and publishers; perhaps publishers put fewer resources into newsgathering litigation. Differences between reporters and their bosses were apparent in *Branzburg* and *Cohen*, not to mention in the formation of RCFP, but there is little evidence that the differences adversely affected the resources available for newsgathering litigation. Doctrinally, the difference is more striking. At the most abstract level, publishing cases turn on the right to speak – a right explicitly guaranteed by the Constitution – while newsgathering cases turn on the right to receive information, the right of the public to know, a far more attenuated, derivative, and, to some minds, completely imaginary right.[11] While the Court has recognized a "right to know" from time to time, it is a much weaker platform from which to mount constitutional litigation.

Gleason's study of nineteenth century contempt and libel cases links the failure of the press to gain expansive newsgathering privileges to a rejection of the "watchdog concept" of the press clause by the common law courts of that era. Gleason points out that the watchdog concept postulated that the duty of the institutional press "to gather the news in the public interest outweighed the harm caused by newspapers' transgressions."[12] Although Gleason uses the term "newsgathering" in a broader sense than has been used here, focusing on the recognition of practical problems inherent in newsgathering to mitigate culpability in libel cases, there is no reason why the analysis could not be extended to grant special privileges to reporters engaged in the newsgathering process. For a variety of reasons, however, "most courts continued to reject the watchdog claims of publishers."[13] A case like *Bartnicki* suggests that, had the concept been entrenched in constitutional thinking in the nineteenth century, instead of the mid-twentieth century, it might by now have evolved to protect newsgathering.

Margaret Blanchard attributes the disparity to the Court's refusal to extend any special privilege to the institutional press that is not available to the general public, a posture deriving from the historic idea that the press is merely an extension of speech.[14] Alternatively, Helle argues that the answer lies in the struggle between the press and the government for, respectively, access to and control of information.[15] Steven Helle's reading of the cases appears to be most compatible with interest group theory, with the government in these cases acting as an offsetting interest group.[16]

This dissertation has also raised two additional contributors to the disparity in outcomes between publishing and newsgathering cases that do not generally appear in the literature. One of those, discussed at some length in connection with *Branzburg* and the legacy cases, is Justice White's personal disillusionment with the institutional press. White was assigned to write the majority opinion in both *Branzburg* and *Cohen*, arguably the two most influential newsgathering cases.

Yet another reason for the disparity may lie in the press's history of claiming First Amendment protection for business practices that the Court did not tolerate in other industries. Such overreaching can be found in the labor-management, antitrust, tax, and copyright cases that are largely beyond the scope of this study. There is no doubt that some of the pre-*Near* litigation conducted by the ANPA employed First Amendment arguments which, in hindsight, we would find inappropriate today, and that practice continued well into the modern era. Two examples, pre- and post-*Near*, illustrate the point.

In August 1912, Congress enacted the Newspaper Publicity Law as a rider attached to the Post Office Appropriation Act.[17] Among other matters, the law required newspapers that availed themselves of second-class mailing privileges to file and publish a sworn statement listing average daily circulation, as well as the names of key editors, executives, and owners. It also required that all editorial matter published for money to be labeled "advertisement." [18] In September, the ANPA announced that "at the request of a great majority of our members our counsel are arranging to test the constitutionality of the law."[19] In October, ANPA Counsel Robert Morris and Guthrie B. Plante filed a law suit on behalf of the Lewis Publishing Co., publisher of the New York *Morning Telegraph*, the *Journal of Commerce*, and the *Commercial Bulletin*. They lost in district court, but were allowed to appeal directly to the U.S. Supreme Court on First and Fifth Amendment grounds.[20]

In his opinion for a unanimous Court, Chief Justice Edward D. White all but mocked the press's argument that the law abridged the freedom of speech guaranteed by the First Amendment.

> [I]t was and is in the power of Congress in "the interest of the dissemination of current intelligence" to so legislate as to the mails, by classification or otherwise, as to favor the widespread circulation of newspapers, periodicals, etc., even although the legislation on the subject, when considered intrinsically, apparently seriously discriminates against the public and in favor of newspapers, periodicals, etc., and their publishers. Although in the form in which the contentions here made by the publishers ... seem to challenge this proposition by suggesting that the power of Congress to classify is controlled and limited by conditions intrinsically inhering in the carriage of the mails, we assume that such apparent contention was merely the result of an unguarded form of statement, since we cannot bring our minds to the conclusion that it was intended on behalf of the publishers to generally assail as an infringement of the constitutional prohibition against the invasion of the freedom of the press the legislation which for a long series of years has favored the press by discriminating so as to secure to it great pecuniary and other concessions and a wider circulation and consequently a greater sphere of influence. If, however, we are mistaken in this view, then, we think, it suffices to say that the contention is obviously without merit.[21]

White went on to hold that the specific provisions of the act were merely incidental to the second-class privilege, and in no way infringed upon any right of the press.[22] As Emory wrote, "Thus the American Newspaper Publishers Association lost in its first appearance before the Supreme Court."

If the *Lewis Publishing* decision discouraged the ANPA from pursuing the publishers' business objectives through First Amendment litigation,[23] victories in *Near* and especially *Grosjean* – a tax case at bottom – seemed to restore its confidence.[24] Indeed, Emery points out that, by the mid-1930s, "the association leadership increasingly advanced the argument that business activities of newspapers either were exempted under the First Amendment from government regulation, or should be protected against any adverse effects of federal general business laws."[25]

With the advent of the New Deal, that argument was manifest in ANPA's insistence on an expansive "press freedom" exemptions in the National Industrial Recovery Act code of fair competition for daily newspapers and in the association's hostility toward unionization. [26] The NIRA and its industrial codes were ultimately struck down by the Supreme Court in 1935,[27] but the unionization issue did not reach the Court until after the conservative block had been broken in the aftermath of President Roosevelt's "court-packing" scheme.[28]

ANPA had initially welcomed the formation of the American Newspaper Guild in 1933; as publishers began resisting the Guild's collective bargaining efforts, however, the association began to formulate a First Amendment argument against unionization.[29] In 1935, an Associated Press staffer named Morris Watson was discharged for what he claimed were Guild-related activities.[30] Watson appealed to the new National Labor Relations Board, which ruled against AP the following year and ordered Watson's reinstatement. AP refused to comply with the order, and the NLRB won an enforcement order from the U.S. Court of Appeals for the Second Circuit.[31] With the support of ANPA,[32] the AP successfully petitioned for certiorari on First Amendment and Commerce Clause grounds.

But the balance of power on the Court had shifted, and, in a 5-4 decision, the Court declared the National Labor Relations Act constitutional and upheld the NLRB's finding. Writing for the Court, Justice Owen Roberts declared:

> The business of the Associated Press is not immune from regulation because it is an agency of the press. The publisher of a newspaper has no special immunity from the application of general laws. He has no special privilege to invade the rights and liberties of others. He must answer for libel. He may be punished for contempt of court. He is subject to the anti-trust laws. Like others he must pay equitable and nondiscriminatory taxes on his business. The regulation here in question has no relation whatever to the impartial distribution of news. The order of the Board in nowise circumscribes the full freedom and liberty of the petitioner to publish the news as it desires it published or to enforce policies of its own choosing with respect to the editing and rewriting of news for publication, and the petitioner is free at any time to discharge Watson or any editorial employee who fails to comply with the policies it may adopt.[33]

The so-called "Four Horsemen" of the old conservative block – Justices Sutherland, Van Devanter, McReynolds, and Butler – dissented,[34] but the idea that the First Amendment afforded the press no immunity from generally applicable laws was reinforced and, to this day, remains the greatest single obstacle to constitutional protection for newsgathering.

D. The Last Word – For Now

This study has only scratched the surface of what promises to be a goldmine of information that is as deep as it is wide. Vertically, the study should be expanded to include certiorari decisions, as well as decided cases, and federal and state courts at every level. Horizontally, further study might compare pure speech and non-mainstream press cases to see how the results might vary in the absence of a coherent interest group.

But there can be little doubt that the institutional press is an interest group to be reckoned with in the Supreme Court, any aversion to such a designation notwithstanding. Over the past century, and especially since 1964, the press has secured for itself the greatest legal protection available anywhere in the world. And while some of that protection has come from Congress, by far the greatest share has come from the Supreme Court's expansive interpretation of the First Amendment's Press Clause.

The hypothetical Wikileaks scenario that begins this book may or may not come to pass, but the challenges it represents are very real. We have already seen the Wikileaks controversy sink a prospective federal shield law,[35] and the differences among journalists promises even more mischief.[36] Will those differences, and other issues arising in the new digital environment, impair the press's ability to litigate or lobby effectively for First Amendment rights? Perhaps. But if this study has shown anything, it is that the press has developed a strong, though certainly not invincible, institutional mechanism for protecting its rights through litigation and a commitment to pursue that course whenever necessary.

NOTES

Chapter 1

[1] *See, e.g.*, Bill Keller, *Dealing with Assange and the Wikileaks Secrets*, N.Y. TIMES MAG., Jan. 26, 2011, *available at* http://www.nytimes.com/2011/01/30/magazine/30Wikileaks-t.html?pagewanted=1.

[2] Keller, who was executive editor of the *Times* when the newspaper published the Wikileaks revelations, reflects the ambivalence within the press:

> But while I do not regard Assange as a partner, and I would hesitate to describe what WikiLeaks does as journalism, it is chilling to contemplate the possible government prosecution of WikiLeaks for making secrets public, let alone the passage of new laws to punish the dissemination of classified information, as some have advocated. Taking legal recourse against a government official who violates his trust by divulging secrets he is sworn to protect is one thing. But criminalizing the publication of such secrets by someone who has no official obligation seems to me to run up against the First Amendment and the best traditions of this country.

Keller, *supra* note 1, at 8.

[3] ALEXIS DE TOCQUEVILLE, DEMOCRACY IN AMERICA 217 (Gerald E. Bavan trans., 2003)(1835).

[4] *Id.* at 602.

[5] *See* DAVID BICKNELL TRUMAN, THE GOVERNING PROCESS: POLITICAL INTERESTS AND PUBLIC OPINION 55 (1951).

[6] *See* MICHAEL EMERY & EDWIN EMERY, THE PRESS AND AMERICA 574-581 (6th ed. 1968).

[7] Craig v. Harney, 331 U.S. 367, 397 (1947).

[8] One notable exception is TIMOTHY W. GLEASON, THE WATCHDOG CONCEPT: THE PRESS AND THE COURTS IN NINTEENTH-CENTURY AMERICA (1990). Gleason writes that his study "is an attempt to examine the influence of the institutional press on the development of free-press case law and doctrine." *Id.* at 111. This study attempts to do the same, but focusing on constitutional law and doctrine in the twentieth century.

[9] The preamble to the Code of Ethics of the Society of Professional Journalists reads as follows:

> Members of the Society of Professional Journalists believe that public enlightenment is the forerunner of justice and the foundation of democracy. The duty of the journalist is to further those ends by seeking truth and providing a fair and comprehensive account of events and issues. Conscientious journalists from all media and specialties strive to

> serve the public with thoroughness and honesty. Professional integrity is the cornerstone of a journalist's credibility. Members of the Society share a dedication to ethical behavior and adopt this code to declare the Society's principles and standards of practice.

SPJ Code of Ethics, 1996.
[10] Jonathan Alter, *You Shield Us, We'll Shield You*, NEWSWEEK, July 11, 2005, at 55.
[11] Broadcasting, for example, is heavily regulated in many respects, although the government exercises no significant control over the content of broadcast news except with respect to political campaigns.
[12] U.S. CONST. amend. I.
[13] Both justices were widely considered First Amendment "absolutists." *See, e.g.,* N.Y. Times v. United States (The Pentagon Papers), 403 U.S. 713, 717-18 (1971) (Black, J., concurring, joined by Douglas, J.). Black quoted Solicitor General Erwin Griswold at oral argument: "Now, Mr. Justice [BLACK], your construction of . . . [the First Amendment] is well known, and I certainly respect it. You say that no law means no law, and that should be obvious. I can only say, Mr. Justice, that to me it is equally obvious that 'no law' does not mean 'no law,' and I would seek to persuade the Court that that is true. . . ."
[14] U.S. CONST. art. III, § 2, cl. 1 (the "case or controversies" clause).
[15] 283 U.S. 697 (1931).
[16] An earlier version of this case study was previously published as Eric B. Easton, *The Colonel's Finest Campaign: Robert R. McCormick and* Near v. Minnesota, 60 FED. COMM. L.J. 183 (2008). Copyright is held by the author.
[17] 408 U.S. 665 (1972).
[18] An earlier version of this case study was previously published as Eric B. Easton, *A House Divided: Earl Caldwell,* The New York Times, *and the Quest for a Testimonial Privilege*, 2009 UTAH L. REV. 1293. Copyright is held by the author.
[19] 532 U.S. 514 (2001).
[20] An earlier version of this case study was previously published as Eric B. Easton, *Ten Years After:* Bartnicki v. Vopper *as a Laboratory for First Amendment Advocacy and Analysis.* 50 U. LOUISVILLE L. REV. 287 (2011).

Chapter 2

[1] Then again, it would probably be wrong to push that image too far; as Attorney General of Pennsylvania, a member of the Provincial Council, and Speaker of the Assembly, Hamilton actively participated in the seditious libel prosecution of Andrew Bradford, publisher of Philadelphia's *American Mercury* for criticizing the colonial government. *See* Stanley Nider Katz, *Introduction*, in JAMES ALEXANDER, A BRIEF NARRATIVE OF THE CASE AND TRIAL OF JOHN PETER ZENGER 22 (Stanley Nider Katz ed., 1963) (1736); LEONARD W. LEVY, EMERGENCE OF A FREE PRESS 49 (1985).
[2] LEVY, *supra* note 1, at 17.
[3] Katz, *supra* note 1, at 36-38; BURTON ALVA KONKLE, THE LIFE OF ANDREW HAMILTON, 1676-1741: "THE DAY-STAR OF THE AMERICAN REVOLUTION" 108-109 (1941).

[4] *See, e.g.*, DWIGHT L. TEETER, JR. & BILL LOVING, LAW OF MASS COMMUNICATIONS: FREEDOM AND CONTROL OF PRINT AND BROADCAST MEDIA 35 (12th ed. 2008); MARC A. FRANKLIN, ET AL., MASS MEDIA LAW: CASES AND MATERIALS 3 (7th ed. 2005); DAVID KOHLER & LEE LEVINE, MEDIA AND THE LAW 4-5 (2009); T. BARTON CARTER ET AL., THE FIRST AMENDMENT AND THE FOURTH ESTATE: THE LAW OF MASS MEDIA 30-31 (8th ed. 2001); DONALD E. LIVELY ET AL., COMMUNICATIONS LAW: MEDIA, ENTERTAINMENT, AND REGULATION 3 (1997). The list could go on and on. This version of the story is based principally on Katz, *supra* note 1, but to a lesser extent on the worshipful biography of Hamilton by KONKLE, *supra* note 3, and the eyewitness account of the far-from-disinterested ALEXANDER, *supra* note 1.

[5] Katz, *supra* note 1, at 8.

[6] *Id.*

[7] *Id.* at 2.

[8] *Id.* at 4.

[9] *Id.* at 4-6.

[10] *Id.* at 8.

[11] *Id.*

[12] *Id.* at 17-18.

[13] *Id.* at 19.

[14] *Id.* at 20.

[15] KONKLE, *supra* note 3, at 69 n. 1.

[16] Katz, *supra* note 1, at 22.

[17] ALEXANDER, *supra* note 1, at 59.

[18] *Id.* at 62.

[19] *See* Stanley Nider Katz, *Notes*, to ALEXANDER, *supra* note 1, at 216 n. 22; *see also* De Libellis Famosis, 5 Coke Reps. 125a (1605), in 1 SIR EDWARD COKE, *THE SELECTED WRITINGS AND SPEECHES* (Steve Sheppard ed. 2003), *available at* http://oll.libertyfund.org /?option=com_staticxt&staticfile=show.php%3Ftitle=911&chapter=106331&layout= html &Itemid=27.

[20] ALEXANDER, *supra* note 1, at 62.

[21] *Id.* at 62-69.

[22] *Id.* at 69.

[23] *Id.* at 70-74.

[24] *Id.* at 74.

[25] *Id.* at 75.

[26] *Id.* at 99.

[27] KONKLE, *supra* note 3, at 105.

[28] *Id.* at 70.

[29] As to the conflict between law and practice in colonial journalism, see LEVY, *supra* note 1, at vii-xix.

[30] 4 WILLIAM BLACKSTONE, COMMENTARIES ON THE LAWS OF ENGLAND 151-152 (1765-69).

[31] During the Tudor period, the Court of Star Chamber was chiefly known for its criminal jurisdiction – including riot, fraud, forgery, perjury, libel and conspiracy – and harsh punishments, including heavy fines, imprisonment, the pillory, whipping, branding and mutilation. Torture was available as needed to extract confessions. The Star Chamber was abolished in 1641. DAVID M. WALKER, THE OXFORD COMPANION TO LAW 1174 (1980). For an accessible example of a seditious libel proceeding in the Star Chamber, *see* COKE, *supra* note 19.
[32] Libel (Fox's) Act, 32 Geo. III c. 60 (1792), *available at* http://www.statutelaw.gov.uk /content .aspx?activeTextDocId=1517268.
[33] Libel (Lord Campbell's) Act, 6 & 7 Vict. c. 96 (1843), *available at* http://www.opsi.gov.uk/acts/acts1843/pdf/ ukpga_18430096_en.pdf.
[34] JOHN FISKE, 2 THE DUTCH AND QUAKER COLONIES IN AMERICA 296 (1902) (quoted in Katz, *supra* note 1, at 1).
[35] LEVY, *supra* note 1, at 17.
[36] *Id.* at 77.
[37] Duties in American Colonies (Stamp Tax) Act, 5 Geo. III c. 12 (1765), *available at* http://ahp.gatech.edu/stamp_act_bp_1765.html.
[38] (Townshend) Revenue Act, 7 Geo. III c. 46 (1767), *available at* http://avalon.law .yale.edu/18th_century/townsend_act_1767.asp.
[39] *See* Julie Hedgepeth Williams, *The American Revolution and the Death of Objectivity*, in FAIR & BALANCED: A HISTORY OF JOURNALISTIC OBJECTIVITY 51 (Steven R. Knowlton & Karen L. Freeman eds. 2005).
[40] Resolution (Feb. 21, 1766), *available at* http://www.historycarper.com/resources/ docs/stamprep.htm.
[41] "*The Pennsylvania Journal*, published the day preceding that on which the stamp act was to take effect, was in full mourning. Thick black lines surrounded the pages, and were placed between the columns; a death's head and cross bones were surmounted over the title; and at the bottom of the last page was a large figure of a coffin, beneath which was printed the age of the paper, and an account of its having died of a disorder called the stamp act." ISAIAH THOMAS, THE HISTORY OF PRINTING IN AMERICA, WITH A BIOGRAPHY OF PRINTERS & AN ACCOUNT OF NEWSPAPERS 158 (Marcus A. McCorison, ed., Weathervane Books 1970) (1810).
[42] *See, e.g.,* LEVY, *supra* note 1, at 85 (recounting John Holt's adherence to the Sons of Liberty's threatening "suggestion" to continue publishing his New York *Gazette* without stamps).
[43] LETTERS FROM A FEDERAL FARMER NO. 16 (1788) (variously attributed to Richard Henry Lee or Melancton Smith or both), *available at* http://press-pubs.uchicago.edu /founders/documents/ v1ch14s32.html.
[44] *A Federal Republican: A Review of the Constitution* (Nov. 28, 1787), in 14 THE DOCUMENTARY HISTORY OF THE RATIFICATION OF THE CONSTITUTION 255-276 (John P. Kaminski & Gaspare J. Saladino eds. 1976), *available at* http://www.consource.org /index.asp?bid=582&documentid=1051.
[45] Madison's notes for Sept. 14, 1787, record the following dialog:

"Mr. Pinckney & Mr. Gerry, moved to insert a declaration 'that the liberty of the Press should be inviolably observed….'

"Mr. Sherman – It is unnecessary – The power of Congress does not extend to the Press. On the question, (it passed in the negative)."

JAMES MADISON, NOTES ON THE CONSTITUTIONAL CONVENTION OF 1787, *available at* National Heritage Center for Constitutional Studies, http://www.nhccs.org/Mnotes.html.
[46] THE FEDERALIST NO. 84, at 513-14 (Alexander Hamilton) (Clinton Rossiter ed. 1961)(1788).
[47] *Id.* at 514 (unnumbered footnote).
[48] Respublica v. Oswald, 1 U.S. 158 (1788) (quoting the Decl. of Rights § 12).
[49] *Id.* (quoting the PA. CONST., § 35).
[50] *Id.* at 158-159.
[51] *See, e.g.,* JEFFREY L. PASLEY, "THE TYRANNY OF PRINTERS": NEWSPAPER POLITICS IN THE EARLY AMERICAN REPUBLIC 100-101 (2001); *see generally* RICHARD N. ROSENFELD, AMERICAN AURORA: A DEMOCRATIC-REPUBLICAN RETURNS: THE SUPPRESSED HISTORY OF OUR NATION'S BEGINNINGS AND THE HEROIC NEWSPAPER THAT TRIED TO REPORT IT (1997).
[52] An Act to Establish a Uniform Rule of Naturalization; ch. 54, 1 Stat. 566; An Act Concerning Aliens; ch. 58, 1 Stat. 570; An Act Respecting Alien Enemies; ch. 66, 1 Stat. 577; An Act for the Punishment of Certain Crimes against the United States; ch. 74, 1 Stat. 596 (1798).
[53] 1 Stat. 596, *available at* http://memory.loc.gov/cgi-bin/ampage?collId=llsl&filename =001/llsl001.db&recNum =719.
[54] PASLEY, *supra* note 51, at 125.
[55] *See, e.g.*, PAUL STARR, THE CREATION OF THE MEDIA: POLITICAL ORIGINS OF MODERN COMMUNICATIONS 79 (2004); JOHN LOFTON, THE PRESS AS GUARDIAN OF THE FIRST AMENDMENT 35 (1980); GEOFFREY R. STONE, PERILOUS TIMES: FREE SPEECH IN WARTIME FROM THE SEDITION ACT OF 1798 TO THE WAR ON TERRORISM 63 (2004).
[56] ROSENFELD, *supra* note 51, at 232.
[57] STONE, *supra* note 55,at 48-66.
[58] *Id.* at 67.
[59] PETER CHARLES HOFFER, THE FREE PRESS CRISIS OF 1800: THOMAS COOPER'S TRIAL FOR SEDITIOUS LIBEL (2011).
[60] LOFTON, *supra* note 55, at 35.
[61] STONE, *supra* note 55, at 68.
[62] JEAN EDWARD SMITH, JOHN MARSHALL: DEFINER OF A NATION 282-289 (1996).
[63] STONE, *supra* note 55, at 62.
[64] 1 Cranch 137 (1803).

[65] SMITH, supra note 62, at 246-47. The text of the resolutions are available at http://www.constitution.org/rf/kr_1798.htm (Kentucky) and http://www.constitution.org/rf/vr.htm (Virginia).
[66] STONE, *supra* note 55, at 71-73.
[67] *Id.* at 46.
[68] EDWIN EMERY, HISTORY OF THE AMERICAN NEWSPAPER PUBLISHERS ASSOCIATION 49 (1950) (ANPA "early began to raise its voice whenever governmental regulation or legislation affected the business interests of publishers.").
[69] STONE, *supra* note 55, at 37.
[70] *Id.* at 40-41.
[71] *Id.* at 43-44.
[72] HOFFER, *supra* note 59, at 114.

Chapter 3

[1] People v. Croswell, 3 Johns. Cas. 337, 1804 N.Y. Lexis 175 (Feb. 13, 1804). *See also* RON CHERNOW, ALEXANDER HAMILTON 667-671 (2004); STARR, *supra* ch. 2, note 55, at 81; LEVY, *supra* ch. 2, note 1, at 340.
[2] *Croswell*, 1804 N.Y. Lexis 175, at 3.
[3] CHERNOW, *supra* note , at 572; LOFTON, *supra* ch. 2, note 55, at 25.
[4] *Croswell*, 1804 N.Y. Lexis 175 at 4. Callender died a few weeks before the trial actually began. CHERNOW, *supra* note 1, at 668.
[5] *Croswell*, 1804 N.Y. Lexis 175, at 5-8.
[6] *Id.* at 9. By this, the court did not mean the truth of the article, but rather whether its meaning was the same as charged in the indictment.
[7] *Id.* at 44.
[8] *Id.* at 38.
[9] *Id.* at 123-24; 1805 N.Y. Sess. Laws, Sess. 28, ch. 90 (April 6).
[10] *Croswell*, 1804 N.Y. Lexis 175 at 125-26.
[11] CHERNOW, *supra* note 1, at 708.
[12] *Croswell*, 1804 N.Y. Lexis 175 at 90.
[13] *Id.* at 90-91.
[14] GLEASON, *supra* ch. 1, note 8, at 4.
[15] *Id.* at 3.
[16] *Id.* at 58.
[17] *Id.* at 124 n. 2.
[18] LOFTON, *supra* ch. 2, note 55, at 48.
[19] *Id.* at 50-61.
[20] STONE, *supra* ch. 2, note 55, at 81.
[21] *See supra* notes 14-16 and accompanying text.
[22] The 1863 case of Copperhead Rep. Clement Vallandigham's trial under General Order No. 38 is a case in point. *See* STONE, *supra* ch. 2, note 55, at 98-120.
[23] LOFTON, *supra* ch. 2, note 55, at 83.
[24] STONE, *supra* ch. 2, note 55, at 95.

[25] EDWIN EMERY, HISTORY OF THE AMERICAN NEWSPAPER PUBLISHERS ASSOCIATION 13-14 (1950).
[26] EMERY & EMERY, *supra* ch. 1, note 6, at 117.
[27] Michael Schudson, *The Objectivity Norm in American Journalism*, 2 JOURNALISM 149, 156 (2001).
[28] *Id.* at 150.
[29] Maria Petrova, *Newspapers and Parties: How Advertising Revenues Created an Independent Press*, 105 AM POL. SCI. REV. 790, 805 (2011).
[30] *Id.*
[31] *Id.*
[32] Schudson, *supra* note 27, at 156.
[33] EMERY & EMERY, *supra* ch. 1, note 6, at 217; *see also* Donald L. Shaw, *News Bias and the Telegraph*, 44 Journalism Q. 3 (1967), and JAMES W. CAREY, COMMUNICATION AND CULTURE (1989).
[34] Schudson, *supra* note 27, at 160 (quoting EMERY & EMERY, *supra* ch. 1, note 6).
[35] Schudson, *supra* note 27, at 159-60.
[36] EMERY, *supra* note 25, at 30, 34.
[37] RICHARD C. CORTNER, THE KINGFISH AND THE CONSTITUTION: HUEY LONG, THE FIRST AMENDMENT, AND THE EMERGENCE OF MODERN PRESS FREEDOM IN AMERICA 130 (1996).
[38] *See infra* ch. 11.
[39] EMERY, *supra* note 25, at 49.
[40] *Id.* at 49.
[41] *Id.* at 50.
[42] N.Y. Times Co. v. Sullivan, 376 U.S. 254 (1964)(constitutionalizing libel law).

Chapter 4

[1] 268 U.S. 652 (1925).
[2] U.S. CONST. amend. I.
[3] STARR, *supra* ch. 2, note 55, at 74.
[4] *Id.* at 75.
[5] *Id.* Had the amendment passed, it would have been the fourteenth amendment in the original House resolution.
[6] For the time being, we can set aside the question as to whether this "freedom" was a right or a privilege (if those are different), or neither of those, but merely an immunity from Congressional action.
[7] U.S. Const. amend. V.
[8] Barron v. Baltimore, 32 U.S. 243 (1832).
[9] *Id.* at 247.
[10] *Id.* at 249.
[11] *Id.* at 250.
[12] *Id.*
[13] *See* MICHAEL KENT CURTIS, FREE SPEECH, "THE PEOPLE'S DARLING PRIVILEGE" 266-270, 366-67 (2000).

[14] Stanley Morrison, *Does the Fourteenth Amendment Incorporate the Bill of Rights? A Judicial Interpretation*, 2 STAN. L. REV. 140, 141 (1949-50).
[15] Curtis quotes a North Carolina statute making it a crime to circulate "any written or printed pamphlet or paper . . . the evident tendency whereof is to cause slaves to become discontented with the bondage in which they are held . . . and free negroes to be dissatisfied with their social condition." CURTIS, *supra* note 13, at 293. *See also* AKHIL REED AMAR, AMERICA'S CONSTITUTION: A BIOGRAPHY 371-72 (2005).
[16] U.S. Const., amend. XIV, § 1.
[17] This was the view of Rep. John A. Bingham (R-Ohio), principal drafter of the Fourteenth Amendment. CURTIS, *supra* note 13, at 360.
[18] Adamson v. California, 332 U.S. 46, 71-72 (1946) (Black, J., dissenting) (holding that the due process clause did not protect a criminal defendant's right against self-incrimination in state trials).
[19] Slaughter-House Cases, 83 U.S. 36 (1872). A year earlier, a federal circuit court had held that the First Amendment guarantee of free speech applied to the states through the privileges or immunities clause of the Fourteenth Amendment, but that view went nowhere. United States v. Hall, 26 F. Cas. 79, 81 (C.C.S.D. Ala. 1871).
[20] CURTIS, *supra* note 13, at 375-76. Curtis also cites with approval Richard L. Aynes, *Constricting the Law of Freedom: Justice Miller, the Fourteenth Amendment, and the* Slaughter-House Cases, 70 CHI.-KENT L. REV. 627 (1994).
[21] Morrison, *supra* note 14, at 171.
[22] *Id.* at 173.
[23] Charles Fairman, *Does the Fourteenth Amendment Incorporate the Bill of Rights? The Original Understanding*, 2 STAN. L. REV. 5 (1949-50).
[24] Morrison, *supra* note 14, at 168. "Substantive due process" is the notion that the Fourteenth Amendment's second clause quoted above, the "due process clause," provided something more than the procedural safeguards against arbitrary punishment suggested by the plain language and historical usage. By the early 1870s, legal arguments began to appear that interpreted the clause as protecting vested property rights and economic liberties against the regulatory powers of the states. Over the next several decades, conservative courts – including the U.S. Supreme Court – used this theory to strike down much progressive legislation until it was rejected in the wake of the New Deal after 1937. *See* ALFRED H. KELLY, WINFRED A. HARBISON & HERMAN BELZ, 2 THE AMERICAN CONSTITUTION: ITS ORIGINS AND DEVELOPMENT 386-91, 495-96 (7th ed. 1991).
[25] OLIVER WENDELL HOLMES, JR., THE COMMON LAW 5 (1881).
[26] *See* Walker v. Sauvinet, 92 U.S. 90 (1875) (civil jury trial); United States v. Cruikshank, 92 U.S. 542 (1875) (First and Second Amendments); Hurtado v. California, 110 U.S. 516 (1884) (indictment by grand jury); Presser v. Illinois, 116 U.S. 252 (1886) (right to bear arms); Speis v. Illinois, 123 U.S. 131 (1887) (right to impartial jury; resolved on other grounds); In re Kemmler, 136 U.S. 436 (1890) (cruel and unusual punishment); McElvaine v. Brush, 142 U.S. 155 (1891) (cruel and unusual punishment); O'Neil v. Vermont, 144 U.S. 323 (1892) (cruel and unusual punishment; resolved on other grounds).
[27] Morrison, *supra* note 14, at 151.
[28] O'Neil v. Vermont, 144 U.S. 323 (1892).
[29] *Id.* at 370.
[30] Chicago, Burlington & Quincy R.R. v. Chicago, 166 U.S. 226 (1897).
[31] Morrison, *supra* note 14, at 152.
[32] Maxwell v. Dow, 176 U.S. 581 (1900) (grand jury indictment, jury trial). Morrison

points out that pro-incorporation statements made during the debates on the Fourteenth Amendment were raised by counsel during this case, challenging Black's assertion that the legislative history had never been considered. Morrison, *supra* note 14, at 154.
[33] Twining v. New Jersey, 211 U.S. 78 (1908) (self-incrimination). In *Twining*, Harlan dissented on the grounds that compelled self-incrimination violated both the privileges or immunities clause and the due process clause.

> I am of opinion that as immunity from self-incrimination was recognized in the Fifth Amendment of the Constitution and placed beyond violation by any Federal agency, it should be deemed one of the immunities of citizens of the United States which the Fourteenth Amendment in express terms forbids any State from abridging—as much so, for instance, as the right of free speech....
>
> It is my opinion also that the right to immunity from self-incrimination cannot be taken away by any State consistently with the clause of the Fourteenth Amendment that relates to the deprivation by the State of life or liberty without due process of law.

Id. at 124-25 (Harlan, J., dissenting).
[34] DAVID M. RABBAN, FREE SPEECH IN ITS FORGOTTEN YEARS 125 (1997).
[35] *Id.* (quoting *A Plain Statement of the San Diego 'Free Speech' Fuss*, S.D. EVE. TRIB., Mar. 13, 1912, at 4. Such an editorial could be taken as evidence in itself that the press was not yet ready to act as an interest group with respect to First Amendment doctrine.
[36] *Id.* at 125.
[37] MARK A. GRABER, TRANSFORMING FREE SPEECH: THE AMBIGUOUS LEGACY OF CIVIL LIBERTARIANISM 8 (1991).
[38] *Id.*
[39] *See id.*
[40] RABBAN, *supra* note 34, at 209.
[41] *See* Schenck v. United States, 249 U.S. 47 (1919); Frohwerk v. United States, 249 U.S. 204 (1919); Debs v. United States, 249 U.S. 211 (1919); Abrams v. United States, 250 U.S. 616 (1919); Schaefer v. United States, 251 U.S. 466 (1920). *See infra* notes 77-94 and accompanying text.
[42] 254 U.S. 325 (1920).
[43] *Id.* at 332.
[44] *Id.* at 343 (Brandeis, J., dissenting).
[45] Prudential Ins. Co. v. Cheek, 259 U.S. 530, 543 (1922).
[46] Meyer v. Nebraska, 262 U.S. 390, 399 (1923).
[47] Gitlow v. New York, 268 U.S. 652, 666 (1925).
[48] *Id.* Of all the cited cases, only *Meyer* actually struck down a state statute on due process grounds. *See* 262 U.S. at 403. In another, *Patterson v. Colorado*, 205 U.S. 454, 462 (1907), the issue was explicitly left undecided.
[49] 268 U.S. at 672 (Holmes, J., dissenting) ("The general principle of free speech, it seems to me, must be taken to be included in the Fourteenth Amendment, in view of the scope that has been given to the word 'liberty' as there used, although perhaps it may be accepted with a somewhat larger latitude of interpretation than is allowed to Congress by the sweeping language that governs or ought to govern the laws of the United States.").

[50] KELLY, ET AL., *supra* note 24, at 518.
[51] 274 U.S. 357, 372 (1927).
[52] *Id.* at 373 (Brandeis, J., concurring).
[53] 274 U.S. 380, 386-87 (1927).
[54] Stromberg v. California, 283 U.S. 359, 368 (1931).
[55] *Gitlow*, 268 U.S. at 667. As we shall see in the next chapter, this more or less describes the conduct of which Jay Near would be accused in 1927.
[56] Ch. 30, 40 Stat. 217 (1917).
[57] *Id.* tit. I § 3.
[58] *Id.* tit. XII, § 1.
[59] *Masses*, 244 F. at 536. Each issue of the magazine was ready to mail during the first ten days of the preceding month. *Id.*
[60] *Id.*
[61] *Id.* at 539.
[62] *Id.* at 539-40.
[63] *Id.* at 540.
[64] *Id.* at 541-42.
[65] *Id.*
[66] *Id.* at 542-43.
[67] *Masses*, 245 F. 102, 106 (1917).
[68] *Masses*, 246 F. 24, 26 (1917).
[69] *Id.* at 33.
[70] *Id.* at 37.
[71] *Id.* at 27.
[72] *Id.* at 38.
[73] Gerald Gunther, *Learned Hand and the Origins of Modern First Amendment Doctrine: Some Fragments of History*, 27 STAN. L. REV. 719 (1974-75).
[74] Vincent Blasi, *Learned Hand and the Self-Government Theory of the First Amendment:* Masses Publishing Co. v. Patten, 61U. COLO. L. REV. 1, 5 (1990).
[75] *Id.* (citing 283 U.S. 697 (1931)). *See infra* ch. 5.
[76] Blasi, *supra* note 74, at 5.
[77] Ch. 75, 40 Stat. 553 (1918).
[78] *Schenck*, 249 U.S. at 52.
[79] *Id.*
[80] Debs, 249 U.S. at 217.
[81] *Frohwerk*, 249 U.S. at 209.
[82] *Debs*, 249 U.S. at 215; *Frohwerk*, 249 U.S. at 207.
[83] 250 U.S. 616, 627 (1919).
[84] *Id.* at 623.
[85] JOHN STUART MILL, ON LIBERTY (1859). *See also* JOHN MILTON, AREOPAGITICA (1644).
[86] *Id.* at 630.
[87] *See, e.g.*, David S. Bogan, *The Free Speech Metamorphosis of Mr. Justice Holmes*, 11 HOFSTRA L. REV. 97 (1982) and David M. Rabban, The Emergence of Modern First Amendment Doctrine, 50 U. CHI. L. REV. 1205 (1983).

[88] 251 U.S. 446, 482 (1920) (Holmes and Brandeis, JJ., dissenting from a decision affirming the convictions of German language newspaper publishers under the Espionage Act).
[89] 252 U.S. 239, 249 (1920) (Holmes and Brandeis, JJ., dissenting from a decision affirming the convictions of antiwar pamphleteers under the Espionage Act).
[90] 268 U.S. at 672.
[91] 274 U.S. 357, 372 (1927) (Holmes and Brandeis, JJ., concurring in a decision affirming the conviction of Communist Labor Party organizer Charlotte Anita Whitney under the California Criminal Syndicalism Act, Stats 1919, ch. 188).
[92] 283 U.S. 359 (1931) (reversing the conviction of a Young Communist League member for displaying a red flag in violation of a California statute prohibiting such displays, Cal. Penal Code § 43a).
[93] 301 U.S. 242 (1937) (reversing the denial of a writ of habeas corpus for a Communist organizer convicted of attempting to incite insurrection pursuant to Ga. Penal Code § 56).
[94] 299 U.S. 353 (1937) (reversing appellant's conviction under the Oregon Criminal Syndicalism Law, Or. Code §§ 14-3110 - 14-3112 (1930) (as amended), for conducting a meeting under the auspices of the Communist Party).
[95] 18 U.S.C § 11 (1946).
[96] 341 U.S. 494, 579, 582 (1951).
[97] *See* Gunther, *supra* note 73, at 751-52 for a discussion of Hand's role in *Dennis* and his regressive formulation of the clear and present danger test: "whether the gravity of the 'evil,' discounted by its improbability, justifies such invasion of free speech as is necessary to avoid the danger." *Dennis*, 183 F.2d 201, 212 (2d Cir. 1950).
[98] *See, e.g.,* Yates v. United States, 354 U.S. 298 (1957) (reversing the Smith Act convictions of 14 Communist Party organizers) and Scales v. United States, 367 U.S. 203 (1961) (reversing a Smith Act conviction for membership in the Communist Party). *See also* HARRY KALVEN, JR., A WORTHY TRADITION: FREEDOM OF SPEECH IN AMERICA (1988) for a discussion of the Smith Act cases.
[99] 395 U.S. 444 (1969) (reversing the conviction of a Ku Klux Klan organizer under the Ohio Criminal Syndicalism Act, Ohio Rev. Code Ann. § 2923.13).
[100] Gunther, *supra* note 73, at 754.
[101] 395 U.S. at 447.
[102] *See, e.g.,* LAUREN KESSLER, THE DISSIDENT PRESS: ALTERNATIVE JOURNALISM IN AMERICAN HISTORY (1984).
[103] MARGARET A. BLANCHARD, REVOLUTIONARY SPARKS: FREEDOM OF EXPRESSION IN MODERN AMERICA xi (1992).

Chapter 5

[1] Letter from Weymouth Kirkland, Partner, Kirkland, Fleming, Green & Martin, Chicago, to Col. Robert R. McCormick, Publisher, The Chicago Tribune (Sept. 14, 1928) (on file with Series I-60, Business Correspondence, 1927-1955, Tribune Archives at Cantigny, Wheaton, Ill. [hereinafter Tribune Archives]).

[2] 219 N.W. 770 (Minn. 1928).
[3] 283 U.S. 697 (1931).
[4] *See* EMERY, *supra* ch. 2, note 68, at 49.
[5] *Id.* at 138. *See also* PAUL ALFRED PRATTE'S GODS WITHIN THE MACHINE: A HISTORY OF THE AMERICAN SOCIETY OF NEWSPAPER EDITORS, 1923-1993 at 28 (1995) ("Involvement in the Minnesota case also marks the formal entrance of ASNE into the fight for freedom of information, which had been cited as a major reason for founding the society [in 1922]).
[6] FRED W. FRIENDLY, MINNESOTA RAG: THE DRAMATIC STORY OF THE LANDMARK SUPREME COURT CASE THAT GAVE NEW MEANING TO FREEDOM OF THE PRESS 3-28 (1981). Fred Friendly was always a great story teller, and his love of the Constitution and its First Amendment made him the perfect author to capture this story. McCormick's biographer calls it "the definitive history" of this episode. RICHARD NORTON SMITH, THE COLONEL: THE LIFE AND LEGEND OF ROBERT R. MCCORMICK 1880-1955 at 280 (1997). It is certainly more definitive than "the Colonel's" own version, which makes Near and Guilford seem like candidates for sainthood. *See* ROBERT R. MCCORMICK, THE FREEDOM OF THE PRESS 46-52 (Arno Press 1970) (1936); *see also* PHILIP KINSLEY, LIBERTY OF THE PRESS: A HISTORY OF THE CHICAGO TRIBUNE'S FIGHT TO PRESERVE A FREE PRESS FOR THE AMERICAN PEOPLE (1944).
[7] FRIENDLY, *supra* note 6, at 21.
[8] *Id.* at 22. Section 1 of the Act provided:

> Section 1. Any person who, as an individual, or as a member or employee of a firm, or association or organization, or as an officer, director, member or employee of a corporation, shall be engaged in the business of regularly or customarily producing, publishing or circulating, having in possession, selling or giving away.
>
> (a) an obscene, lewd and lascivious newspaper, magazine, or other periodical, or
>
> (b) a malicious, scandalous and defamatory newspaper, magazine or other periodical,
>
> is guilty of a nuisance, and all persons guilty of such nuisance may be enjoined, as hereinafter provided.
>
> Participation in such business shall constitute a commission of such nuisance and render the participant liable and subject to the proceedings, orders and judgments provided for in this Act. Ownership, in whole or in part, directly or indirectly, of any such periodical, or of any stock or interest in any corporation or organization which owns the same in whole or in part, or which publishes the same, shall constitute such participation.
>
> In actions brought under (b) above, there shall be available the defense that the truth was published with good motives and for justifiable ends and in such actions the plaintiff shall not have the right to report (*sic*) to issues or editions of periodicals taking place more than three months before the commencement of the action.

Near, 283 U.S. at 702 (quoting 1925 Minn. Laws 358 § 1).
[9] Paul L. Murphy, Near v. Minnesota *in the Context of Historical Developments*, 66 MINN. L. REV. 95, 135-36 (1980). Murphy notes without comment that the legislative history of the act is described in John E. Hartmann, *The Minnesota Gag Law and the Fourteenth Amendment*, 37 MINN. HIST. 161, 162 (1960). Hartmann, then a graduate student, acknowledges the "claim" that the act was directed against a particular editor but finds no substance in the legislative history pointing one way or the other. Introduced by a

Progressive-Republican from Minneapolis, the bill was apparently handled routinely, enacted without dissent, and signed by the governor without any fanfare with other end-of-session bills. *Id.* at 161.

[10] Murphy, *supra* note 9, at 137. Of that so-called "efficiency," McCormick writes, "The statute was cunningly devised not only to avoid the necessity of indictment by the grand jury, as had been done in the Zenger case, but to avoid a jury trial also and leave the newspaper at the mercy of a corrupt or politically controlled court." McCORMICK, *supra* note 6, at 46.

[11] *Newspaper 'Gag' Law is Assailed as 'Dangerous,'* CHI. TRIB., Mar. 26, 1929, at 17.

[12] Indeed, it seems they have been with us always. *See, e.g.*, Ralph Frasca, *The* Helderberg Advocate: *A Public-Nuisance Prosecution a Century before* Near v. Minnesota, 26 J. SUP. CT. HIST. 215 (2001).

[13] FRIENDLY, *supra* note 6 at 31.

[14] *Id.* at 32.

[15] *Id.* at 45-49. *See also* McCORMICK, *supra* note 6, at 47. McCormick's "spin" on Olson's decision to invoke the gag law is that "he would not risk" a libel action, implying that Near was telling the truth.

[16] McCORMICK, *supra* note 6, at 47; FRIENDLY, *supra* note 6, at 50. Friendly called the filing a "complaint," as does Hughes, but McCormick characterizes it as an "information," the kind of charging document used in the Zenger case to which McCormick had referred earlier. *Near*, 283 U.S. at 704.

[17] FRIENDLY, *supra* note 6, at 50.

[18] *Id.*

[19] *Id.* at 53. *But see* McCORMICK, *supra* note 6, at 47. The timeline here is somewhat unclear. Friendly says the TRO remained in force for twenty-six months but dates the permanent injunction at three months after an Oct. 10, 1928, hearing. That would make the duration of the TRO only fourteen months. McCormick dates the permanent injunction on Oct. 11, 1928, which may refer to an oral judgment that Friendly says was conveyed to the lawyers. None of the briefs or opinions provide clarification except by reference to the record extract.

[20] FRIENDLY, *supra* note 6, at 51.

[21] *Id.* at 51-52.

[22] *Id.* at 53.

[23] Minnesota *ex rel.* Olson v. Guilford, 219 N.W. 770, (Minn. 1928). Elsie Latimer is also listed as counsel for Near.

[24] *Id.* at 773.

[25] *See supra* note 19 and accompanying text.

[26] 1925 Minn. Laws 358 § 1.

[27] Murphy, *supra* note 9, at 134.

[28] *Id.* at 137 (citing LAMAR T. BEMAN, CENSORSHIP OF SPEECH AND THE PRESS 178 (1930)). *See also* SILAS BENT, BALLYHOO: THE VOICE OF THE PRESS (1927).

[29] FRIENDLY, *supra* note 6, at 63.

[30] *Id.* at 63-65. McCormick's version of the tale, at least in its published version, avoids any mention of the gangsters' religious affiliation or Near's anti-Semitism. McCORMICK, *supra* note 6, at 45-52.

[31] Letter from Kirkland to McCormick (Sept. 14, 1928).

[32] *Id.*

[33] *See* FRIENDLY, *supra* note 6, at 73.
[34] SMITH, *supra* note 6, at 175.
[35] *See* KINSLEY, *supra* note 6, at 28-34.
[36] *See* FRIENDLY, *supra* note 6, at 70-73.
[37] *Id.* at 72.
[38] SMITH, *supra* note 6, at 241-44.
[39] *Id.* at 243
[40] AM. NEWSPAPER PUBLISHERS ASS'N (ANPAREPORT OF THE FORTY-SECOND ANNUAL MEETING 146 (1928) (cited in EMERY, *supra* note ch.2, note 68, at 222 n. 5).
[41] Letter from Lincoln B. Palmer [hereinafter Palmer] ANPA General Manager, to McCormick (May 4, 1928), and reply (May 7, 1928).
[42] The committee also included Harry Chandler of the *Los Angeles Times*, William T. Dewart of *The (Los Angeles) Sun*, and James Kerney of the *Trenton Times*, according to an undated list of members (probably from 1928 or early 1929) in the *Tribune* Archives.
[43] Letter from McCormick to Samuel Emory Thomason [hereinafter Thomason] (Sept. 15, 1928).
[44] Letter from Thomason to McCormick (Sept. 17, 1928).
[45] FRIENDLY, *supra* note 6, at 79.
[46] *Id.* at 79-80.
[47] *Id.* at 80-81.
[48] *Id.* at 81.
[49] *Move to Repeal Minnesota Law Muzzling Press*, CHI. TRIB., Feb. 27, 1929, at 14.
[50] *Id.*
[51] *Id.* (emphasis added).
[52] *Solon Attacks Press Gag Law of Minnesota*, CHI. TRIB., Mar. 5, 1929, at 23.
[53] *Hearing Today on Newspaper Gag Law Repeal Bill*, CHI. TRIB., Mar. 18, 1929, at 24.
[54] *Id.*
[55] *Id.*
[56] Editorial, *A Monkey State Candidate*, CHI. TRIB., Mar. 19, 1929, at 14.
[57] *Id.*
[58] *Newspaper 'Gag' Law is Assailed as 'Dangerous,'* CHI. TRIB., Mar. 26, 1929, at 17.
[59] *Id.*
[60] *Bill to Repeal Press Gag Law is Set Aside*, CHI. TRIB., Mar. 27, 1929, at 22.
[61] *Id.*
[62] *Id.*
[63] Editorial, *Minnesota Joins the Monkey States*, CHI. TRIB., Mar. 28, 1929, at 14.
[64] *History of 2,300 Years Cited in "Gag" Law Brief*, CHI. TRIB., March 29, 1929, at 9.
[65] *Id.*, (quoting Petitioner's Brief in State ex rel. Olson v. Guilford, 228 N.W. 326 (Minn. 1929)).
[66] Letter from Palmer to McCormick (Mar. 6, 1929).
[67] Howard Ellis, *Resume of the Case of State versus Guildford* (Mar. 19, 1929) (transmitted to the Committee on Freedom of the Press of the American Newspaper Publishers Association).
[68] *Id.*
[69] *Id.* at 6.
[70] *Publishers Join in Fight on Law Muzzling Press*, CHI. TRIB., Apr. 25, 1929, at 11.
[71] *Minnesota Gag Law Target of New York Press*, CHI. TRIB., Apr. 26, 1929, at 16.

[72] *Id.*
[73] Editorial of the Day, *Minnesota's Gag Law*, CHI. TRIB., May 3, 1929, at 14 (reprinted from the *New York Herald-Tribune*).
[74] *Press-Gag Statute Assailed by Editor*, WASH. POST, Apr. 19, 1929, at 5.
[75] *Id.*
[76] *Id.*
[77] PRATTE, *supra* note 5, at 28.
[78] *Id.* (Pratte says the committee "provided mostly rhetoric in the fight for freedom and against censorship.")
[79] FRIENDLY, *supra* note 6, at 83-84.
[80] Letter from Near to McCormick (Dec. 14, 1929).
[81] *Id.*
[82] Minnesota ex rel. Olson v. Guilford, 228 N.W. 326, 326 (Minn. 1929).
[83] Indeed, the *Tribune's* coverage of the adverse decision carried the subhead, "Publishers Will Appeal to U.S. Tribunal," although the story was rather more modest. "It is expected sponsors of the action will take the case to the United States Supreme [C]ourt, as opponents of the law contend it is a violation of the right of freedom of speech." *Court Upholds Newspaper Gag Statute Again*, CHI. TRIB. Dec. 21, 1929, at 7.
[84] Letter from McCormick to Harry Chandler [hereinafter Chandler] (Dec. 23, 1929).
[85] *Id.*
[86] *Id.*
[87] *Id.*
[88] *Id.*
[89] Letter from Kirkland to McCormick (Dec. 24, 1929) (punctuation added).
[90] Letter from McCormick to Chandler (Dec. 24, 1929). It is not clear why Kirkland thought the United States Supreme Court would hear a challenge to the statute on the ground that it violated the state constitution. The state supreme court would have been the ultimate authority on that point.
[91] *Id.*
[92] Letter from Kirkland to McCormick, *supra* note 390.
[93] Telegram from McCormick to G.L. Burke (Dec. 26, 1929).
[94] *Id.* (pencil annotation on the telegram).
[95] Letter from Edward Butler [hereinafter Butler] to McCormick (Dec. 30, 1929).
[96] *Id.*
[97] *Id.*
[98] Letter from William T. Dewart [hereinafter Dewart] to McCormick (Dec. 30, 1929). On March 7, 1930, Dewart would write McCormick to say he had read that the United States Supreme Court lacked jurisdiction to hear the case on state constitutional grounds. "I should assume from this that the fight might better be based on the Fourteenth Amendment. However, I am not a Constitutional lawyer." Letter from Dewart to McCormick (Mar. 7, 1930).
[99] Letter from Thomason to McCormick (Jan. 2, 1930).
[100] Letter from Chandler to McCormick (Jan. 1, 1930).
[101] *Id.*
[102] *Id.*
[103] Letters from McCormick to Dewart, Thomason and Chandler (Jan. 16, 1930). McCormick had some of these published in the *Tribune*. Under the heading "Editorial of

the Day," he published editorials critical of the gag law from the *New York Herald-Tribune*, *The Minnesota Gag Law*, CHI. TRIB., Jan. 4, 1930, at 10, and the *St. Louis Post-Dispatch*, *The Minnesota Injunction Law*, CHI. TRIB., Jan. 27, 1930, at 12. Other clips in McCormick's file included two identical AP photos of himself, with the caption, "Col. Robert McCormick, publisher of the *Chicago Tribune*, as head of a committee of American newspaper publishers is leading a fight to nullify the Minnesota newspaper 'gag' law," from the Everett (Wash.) *Herald*, Jan. 17, 1930, and the Pocatello (Id.) *Tribune*, Jan. 18, 1930. The trade journal, *Editor & Publisher, The Fourth Estate*, had also sent McCormick a "rough early proof" of an article for its Jan. 18, 1930, issue entitled *Will Take 'Gag' Law To Supreme Court/Col. McCormick, As A.N.P.A. Committee Head, Will Be Leader in Fight to Prove Illegality of Minnesota Law.*

[104] Letters from McCormick to Dewart, Thomason and Chandler, *supra* note 103.

[105] Letter from McCormick to Butler, Jan. 18, 1930.

[106] Letter from James Kerney [hereinafter Kerney] to McCormick (Jan. 21, 1930).

[107] FRIENDLY, *supra* note 6, at 86-87.

[108] Letter from McCormick to Kirkland (Jan. 23, 1930).

[109] Letter from Kirkland to McCormick (Jan. 27, 1930).

[110] *Id.*

[111] FRIENDLY, *supra* note 6, at 86.

[112] Letter from Kirkland to McCormick, *supra* note 109.

[113] Arthur Evans, *Press Gag Law Called Blow at Basic Liberties*, CHI. TRIB., Feb. 4, 1930, at 5.

[114] Typical was a Jan. 23, 1930, letter from M.V. Atwood, secretary of the New York State Society of Newspaper Editors, who wrote McCormick to express his organization's appreciation for

> the brave and unselfish fight you are making of the freedom of the press in the matter of the Minnesota gag law. Because of the precedent it sets, this law is a menace to every newspaper in the United States and the editors of New York are indeed grateful that it is to be carried to the highest court by so fearless and distinguished a protector of free speech and the freedom of the press as yourself.

Letter from M.V. Atwood [hereinafter Atwood] to McCormick (Jan. 23, 1930).

[115] Letter from Palmer to Thomason (Feb. 11, 1930).

[116] *Id.*

[117] *Id.*

[118] Letter from Thomason to McCormick (Feb. 14, 1930).

[119] Letter from McCormick to Burke (Feb. 17, 1930).

[120] Telegram from McCormick to Thomason (Feb. 17, 1930).

[121] Telegram from Thomason to McCormick (Feb. 17, 1930).

[122] Letter from McCormick to Thomason (Feb. 18, 1930).

[123] *Id.*

[124] Letter from Thomason to McCormick (Feb. 1930) (date obscured).

[125] Telegram from Palmer to McCormick (Feb. 20, 1930), with reply telegram from Kirkland to Palmer (Feb. 22, 1930).

[126] Letter from Palmer to McCormick (Feb. 25, 1930).

[127] Telegram from McCormick to Palmer (Feb. 28, 1930).

[128] Letter from McCormick to Atwood (Mar. 10, 1930).

[129] *The Minnesota Gag Law*, CHI. TRIB., Mar. 11, 1930, at 14.

[130] Telegrams from McCormick to Palmer (Mar. 14, 1930); Palmer to McCormick (Mar. 15, 1930); McCormick to Palmer (Mar. 15, 1930). Letters from Palmer to McCormick

(Mar. 17, 1930); McCormick to Palmer (Mar. 19, 1930).
[131] Letter from Palmer to McCormick (Mar. 17, 1930).
[132] Letter from Palmer to McCormick (Mar. 18, 1930).
[133] Letter from McCormick to Palmer (Mar. 20, 1930).
[134] Letter from McCormick to Palmer (Mar. 21, 1930).
[135] Letter from Palmer to McCormick (Apr. 2, 1930).
[136] Letter from Palmer to McCormick (Mar. 20, 1930).
[137] Letter from McCormick to Palmer (Mar. 22, 1930).
[138] Letter from Palmer to McCormick (Mar. 22, 1930).
[139] Letter from McCormick to Palmer (Mar. 24, 1930).
[140] Letter from Palmer to Burke (Apr. 11, 1930) (including draft Report of Committee on the Freedom of the Press).
[141] *Id.* (quoting Report of the Committee on the Freedom of the Press).
[142] Seltzer v. Ohio ex Read, 1930 Ohio Misc. LEXIS 1116 (Ohio App. 8th Dist. March 6, 1930). For a description of the original contempt order, *see Press v. Bench*, TIME, Jul. 19, 1929.
[143] 1930 Ohio Misc. LEXIS 1116 (March 6, 1930).
[144] *Id.* at 20.
[145] *Id.* at 24.
[146] *See* Letter from Palmer to Burke, *supra* note 140.
[147] Letters from McCormick to Dewart, Kerney, Thomason, and Chandler (Apr. 14, 1930).
[148] Letter from Kerney to McCormick (Apr. 16, 1930).
[149] *Id.*
[150] *Id.*
[151] Letter from Dewart to McCormick (Apr. 16, 1930).
[152] Telegram from Ellis to McCormick (Apr. 18, 1930).
[153] Letter from Chandler to McCormick (Mar. 20, 1930).
[154] Letter from Chandler to McCormick (May 21, 1930) (quoting a letter from Palmer to Chandler without noting its date).
[155] Letter from Chandler to McCormick (May 21, 1930).
[156] Letter from McCormick to Kirkland (May 16, 1930). Kirkland noted the *Tribune* had already paid \$3,615.42 in the appellate process and incurred another \$949.21 still unpaid. He estimated the cost of printing the record and briefs at \$2,500. *Id.*
[157] Letter from Kirkland to McCormick (June 20, 1930).
[158] Letter from McCormick to Chandler (June 25, 1930).
[159] SMITH, *supra* note 6, at 282.
[160] Letter from McCormick to Kirkland (May 12, 1930).
[161] Letter from McCormick to Kirkland (May 26, 1930).
[162] Robert R. McCormick, Comments on the Minnesota Brief, May 27, 1930.
[163] Letter from McCormick to Kirkland (May 28, 1930). "'When a *woman* is habitually addicted to scolding at and before persons in general, on the highway, or in a populous neighborhood, so as to disturb passersby, *she* may be indicted as a common scold,'" Cmmw. v. Hamilton, 45 Pa. D. & C. 485, 489-90 (1945) (quoting Francis Wharton, Treatise on the Criminal Laws of the United States § 1715 (1846), and sentenced to a variety of punishments, including "ducking" in water.
[164] Letter from Kirkland to McCormick (May 29, 1930).

[165] Letters from McCormick to Kirkland (June 5, 1930 and June 11, 1930).
[166] "Give me but the liberty of the press and I will give to the minister a venal House of Peers. I will give him a corrupt and servile House of Commons. I will give him the full swing of the patronage of office. I will give him the whole host of ministerial influence. I will give him all the power that place can confer upon him to purchase up submission and overawe resistance: and yet, armed with the liberty of the press, I will go forth to meet him undismayed. I will attack the mighty fabric of that mightier engine. I will shake down from its height corruption and bury it beneath the ruins of the abuses it was meant to shelter." *Id.*
[167] *See, e.g.,* SMITH, *supra* note 6, at 291-299; LLOYD WENDT, CHICAGO TRIBUNE: THE RISE OF A GREAT NEWSPAPER 529-38 (1979); JOSEPH GEIS, THE COLONEL OF CHICAGO 86-100 (1979).
[168] By this time, McCormick had been asked to chair the freedom of the press committees for ASNE as well as ANPA, finally receiving ANPA Board permission to do both in October 1930. Letter from McCormick to Chandler (May 22, 1930); Letter from Palmer to McCormick (June 5, 1930); Letter from McCormick to Chandler (June 10, 1930); Letter from Palmer to McCormick (Oct. 15, 1930).
[169] Grosjean v. American Press Co, 297 U.S. 233 (1936). *See infra* Ch. 6, Pt. B.
[170] Letter from Philip Schuyler ("Schuyler") to McCormick (June 21, 1930).
[171] Letter from McCormick to Schuyler (June 25, 1930).
[172] *Minnesota Starts Movement to Repeal Newspaper Gag Law*, CHI. TRIB., Oct. 11, 1930, at 7.
[173] *Gov. F.B. Olson Asks Repeal of News 'Gag Law,'* CHI. TRIB., Jan. 9, 1931, at 5.
[174] Editorial, *The Minnesota Gag Law*, CHI. TRIB., Jan. 14, 1931, at 14.
[175] Editorial of the Day, *Minnesota Has a Governor [St. Louis Post-Dispatch]*, CHI. TRIB., Jan. 15, 1931, at 14.
[176] *Bill to Repeal Minnesota Gag Law is Offered*, CHI. TRIB., Jan. 16, 1931, at 26.
[177] *Minnesota "Gag" Law Repeal is Voted in House*, CHI. TRIB., Feb. 5, 1931, at 6; *Committee May Kill Minnesota Gag Law Repeal*, CHI. TRIB., Feb. 22, 1931, at 9.
[178] *See* Editorial of the Day, *Press "Gag" Law Doomed [Niagara Falls Gazette]*, CHI. TRIB., Jan. 24, 1931, at 10.
[179] *Severer Libel Law Considered for Minnesota*, CHI. TRIB., Feb. 7, 1931, at 14.
[180] *See Committee May Kill Minnesota Gag Law Repeal*, *supra* note 177.
[181] *Bill to Repeal 'Gag' Law Will Await Decision*, CHI. TRIB., Feb. 27, 1931, at 12.
[182] *Senate Blocks Minnesota Gag Law Repealer*, CHI. TRIB., Apr. 19, 1931, at 21.
[183] *Supreme Court Gets "Gag" Law Plea from Near*, CHI. TRIB., May 18, 1930, at 7.
[184] *See Minnesota Gag on Press Goes to High Court*, CHI. TRIB., Oct. 21, 1930, at 16.
[185] *Press Gag Law is Attacked in Supreme Court*, CHI. TRIB., Dec. 13, 1930, at 6; Appellant's Brief, Near v. Minnesota, 283 U.S. 697 (1931)(No. 91), 1930 WL 30038.
[186] *Minnesota Gag Law Defended in U.S. Court Brief*, CHI. TRIB., Jan. 20, 1931, at 6; Brief of Appellee, Near v. Minnesota, 283 U.S. 697 (1931) (No. 91), 1931 WL 30640.
[187] Appellant's Brief at 21, Near v. Minnesota, 283 U.S. 697 (1931)(No. 91), 1930 WL 30038.
[188] *Id.*
[189] *Id.* at 22.
[190] *Id.*
[191] *Id.* at 45-46.
[192] *Id.* at 46.
[193] 268 U.S. 652 (1925).
[194] *See supra* Ch. 4, Pt. A.

[195] 83 U.S. 36 (1872).
[196] *See supra* Ch. 4, Part A.
[197] Appellant's Brief at 65, Near v. Minnesota, 283 U.S. 697 (1931)(No. 91), 1930 WL 30038.
[198] Brief of Appellee at 8, Near v. Minnesota, 283 U.S. 697 (1931) (No. 91), 1931 WL 30640. That footnote refers to an article in the *Harvard Law Review* that continued to question incorporation, specifically whether the "liberty" referred to in the due process clause of the Fourteenth Amendment properly encompassed freedom of speech and of the press. *See* Charles Warren, *The New "Liberty" Under the Fourteenth Amendment*, 39 HARV. L. REV. 431 (1926).
[199] *Id.*
[200] *Id.*
[201] FRIENDLY, *supra* note 6, at 125-133 and accompanying note at 202.
[202] *Id.* at 126.
[203] *Id.* at 128.
[204] *Id.*
[205] *Id.*
[206] *Id.* at 129 (internal citations omitted).
[207] *Id.*
[208] *Id.*
[209] Note from Justice Louis D. Brandeis [hereinafter Brandeis] to HTA (presumably law clerk H. Thomas Austern) (Oct. 14, 1930) *in* the Brandeis papers at the Library of Congress.
[210] Note from Brandeis to HTA (Oct. 16, 1930).
[211] *Id.*
[212] Editorial, *Suppression Act Again Upheld*, MINN. J., Dec. 21, 1929, at 6.
[213] FRIENDLY, *supra* note 6, at 21.
[214] Editorial, *Minnesota's Press Gag*, WASH. POST, Jan. 12, 1931, at 6; *Expect Repeal of Newspaper 'Gag' Act in Minnesota*, LABOR, Jan. 27, 1931.
[215] *Brandeis Hints Minnesota's Gag Law is Invalid*, CHI. TRIB., Jan. 31, 1931, § 1, at 7.
[216] *Id.*
[217] FRIENDLY, *supra* note 6, at 130-31.
[218] 205 U.S. 454 (1907).
[219] FRIENDLY, *supra* note 6, at 132 (internal citations omitted).
[220] Letter from Near to McCormick (Feb. 4, 1931).
[221] *Libel Acquittal Adds Interest to Gag Law Case*, CHI. TRIB., May 8, 1930, at 3.
[222] Letter from Near to McCormick (Feb. 4, 1931).
[223] FRIENDLY, *supra* note 6, at 105.
[224] Smith points out that McCormick himself admitted that he would have lost if Taft had still been on the bench. SMITH, *supra* note 6, at 284.
[225] FRIENDLY, *supra* note 6, at 119.
[226] FRIENDLY, *supra* note 6, at 94.
[227] MERLO J. PUSEY, CHARLES EVANS HUGHES 268 (1951).
[228] *Id.* at 329.
[229] SAMUEL HENDEL, CHARLES EVANS HUGHES AND THE SUPREME COURT 23-35(1951).
[230] PUSEY, *supra* note 227, at 361.

[231] HENDEL, *supra* note 229, at 72-73; PUSEY, *supra* note 118, at 391-393.
[232] EMERY, *supra* ch. 2, note 68, at 60.
[233] HENDEL, *supra* note 229, at 68-77.
[234] *Id.* at 78. As usual, Friendly tells a far more colorful story of the selection of Hughes to succeed Taft. FRIENDLY, *supra* note 6, at 101-103.
[235] HENDEL, *supra* note 229, at 78-88. *See also* TREVOR PARRY-GILES, THE CHARACTER OF JUSTICE 50-55 (2006).
[236] HENDEL, *supra* note 229, at 91.
[237] *Id.* at 90-91. *See also* Trevor Parry-Giles, *Property Rights, Human Rights and American Jurisprudence: The Rejection of John J. Parker's Nomination to the Supreme Court*, 60 S. COMM. J. 57 (1994). Parry-Giles points out that Parker's rejection grew out of the tension between property rights and human rights championed by conservatives and progressives, respectively, in the Senate and "represented an ideological moment of profound importance for those struggling with the onset of the Depression." *Id.* at 60-61.
[238] *Near*, 283 U.S. at 701-03.
[239] *Id.* at 709-10.
[240] *Id.* at 703.
[241] *Id.* at 702-07.
[242] *Id.* at 706.
[243] *Id.* at 708.
[244] *Id.* at 708-09.
[245] *Id.* at 709.
[246] *Id.* at 710.
[247] *Id.* at 711.
[248] *Id.* at 712.
[249] *Id.* at 708.
[250] *Id.* at 713.
[251] *Id.* at 712-13.
[252] *Id.* at 713-14.
[253] *Id.* at 714.
[254] *Id.* at 714-15.
[255] *Id.* at 715.
[256] *Id.* at 715-16.
[257] *Id.* at 716.
[258] *Id.* at 715-16.
[259] *Id.* at 717.
[260] *Id.* at 718.
[261] *Id.* at 716-20.
[262] *Id.* at 720.
[263] *Id.* at 720-21.
[264] *Id.* at 712.
[265] *Id.* at 721.
[266] *Id.*
[267] *Id.* at 721-22 (internal quotations omitted).
[268] *Id.* at 722-23.
[269] *Id.* at 723 (Butler, J., dissenting).
[270] *Id.* at 723-24.

[271] *Id.* at 724.
[272] *See id.* at 724 n.1.
[273] *Id.* at 731.
[274] *Id.* at 732.
[275] *Id.*
[276] *Id.* (quoting 2 JOSEPH STORY, COMMENTARIES ON THE CONSTITUTION OF THE UNITED STATES: WITH A PRELIMINARY REVIEW OF THE CONSTITUTIONAL HISTORY OF THE COLONIES AND STATES BEFORE THE ADOPTION OF THE CONSTITUTION 635 (Melville M. Bigelow ed., 1994)).
[277] *Id.* at 733-34.
[278] *Id.* at 737-38.
[279] *Decision a Triumph for Free Thought, M'Cormick Says*, CHI. TRIB., June 2, 1931, § 1, at 7.
[280] Arthur Sears Henning, *Minnesota Act Quashed by U.S. Supreme Court*, CHI. TRIB., June 2, 1931, § 1, at 1.
[281] *Id.*
[282] *Governor Pleased by Decision Killing Minnesota Gag Law*, CHI. TRIB., June 2, 1931, § 1, at 7.
[283] *Editors Hail Gag Ruling as Press Victory*, CHI. TRIB., June 2, 1931, § 1 at 7.
[284] *Decision a Triumph for Free Thought, M'Cormick Says*, *supra* note 279.
[285] *Press Gag Decision Praised by Washington Officialdom*, CHI. TRIB., June 3, 1931, § 1, at 4.
[286] Arthur Sears Henning, *Supreme Court 'Liberalized' in Recent Months*, CHI. TRIB., June 3, 1931, § 1, at 4.
[287] Editorial, *The Background of the Gag Law*, CHI. TRIB., June 3, 1931, § 1, at 14.
[288] *See* Editorial of the Day, *Another Liberal Victory [St. Louis Star]*, CHI. TRIB., June 4, 1931, § 1, at 14; Editorial, *Freedom of the Press*, CHI. TRIB., June 14, 1931, § 1, at 14.
[289] Telegram from Dewart to McCormick (June 2, 1931).
[290] Letter from McCormick to C.B. Blethen (June 1931) (date obscured).
[291] This pamphlet was in the McCormick archives.
[292] Letter from Roger Baldwin [hereinafter Baldwin] "To the Editor" (April 4, 1931).
[293] Letter from Baldwin to McCormick (June 4, 1931).
[294] *Id.*
[295] Letter from McCormick to Baldwin (June 6, 1931).
[296] *Id.*

Chapter 6

[1] 297 U.S. 233 (1936).
[2] 303 U.S. 444 (1938).
[3] 380 U.S. 51 (1965).
[4] 384 U.S. 214 (1966).
[5] 384 U.S. at 219.
[6] 384 U.S. at 220-21 (Douglas, J., concurring).
[7] 403 U.S. 713 (1971).

[8] *See generally* SANFORD J. UNGAR, THE PAPERS AND THE PAPERS: AN ACCOUNT OF THE LEGAL AND POLITICAL BATTLE OVER THE PENTAGON PAPERS (1989) and DAVID RUDENSTINE, THE DAY THE PRESSES STOPPED: A HISTORY OF THE PENTAGON PAPERS CASE (1996). I've generally refrained from citing both sources for purely factual information; Rudenstine's book was published later and cites Ungar's book throughout.
[9] RUDENSTINE, *supra* note 8, at 33.
[10] *Id.* at 52-65.
[11] *Id.* at 79-81.
[12] *Id.* at 80.
[13] *Id.* at 99.
[14] *Id.* at 99-102.
[15] *Id.* at 102-105.
[16] *Id.* at 107.
[17] *Id.* at 139.
[18] *Id.* at 136. Chalmers Roberts, *Documents Reveal U.S. Effort in '54 to Delay Viet Elections*, WASH. POST, June 18, 1971.
[19] RUDENSTINE *supra* note 8, at 186-188.
[20] 446 F.2d 1322, 1324 (D.C. Cir. 1971).
[21] 446 F.2d at 1325 (Wright, J., dissenting).
[22] 328 F.Supp. 324, 331 (S.D.N.Y 1971).
[23] 444 F.2d 544 (2d Cir. 1971).
[24] *Id.*
[25] RUDENSTINE, *supra* note 8, at 212-213.
[26] 446 F.2d 1327, 1328 (D.C. Cir. 1971).
[27] RUDENSTINE, *supra* note 8, at 261-263.
[28] 403 U.S. at 713.
[29] *Id.* at 714 (citations omitted).
[30] *Id.* at 715 (Black, J., concurring).
[31] 403 U.S. at 763 (Blackmun, J., dissenting).
[32] *See, e.g.*, RUDENSTINE, *supra* note 8, at 250.
[33] The government tried Ellsberg for violations of the Espionage Act, but revelations of misconduct by White House officials prompted the trial judge to dismiss all charges on May 11, 1973. UNGAR, *supra* note 8, at 6-9. Thus, whether Ellsberg committed a crime in leaking the Pentagon Papers remains legally unsettled. *See also* PETER SCHRAG, TEST OF LOYALTY: DANIEL ELLSBERG AND THE RITUALS OF SECRET GOVERNMENT (1974).
[34] Goodale, along with Seattle attorney Cameron DeVore, launched a series of annual conferences on media law in 1973 under the auspices of the Practising Law Institute. Today, that conference is considered the unofficial headquarters of the media law bar. *See* Floyd J. McKay, *First Amendment Guerillas: Formative Years of the Reporters Committee for Freedom of the Press,* 6 JOURNALISM & COMM. MONOGRAPHS 105, 124 (2004). Abrams's involvement in media law cases is evident throughout this book.
[35] 408 U.S. 665 (1972).
[36] 427 U.S. 539 (1976).
[37] *See* MARK R. SCHERER, RIGHTS IN THE BALANCE: FREE PRESS, FAIR TRIAL & *NEBRASKA PRESS ASSOCIATION V. STUART* 19-30 (2008).

[38] *Id.* at 40.
[39] *Id.* at 42-43.
[40] *Id.* at 46.
[41] *Id.* at 43-45.
[42] *Id.* at 45
[43] *Id.* at 45.
[44] *Id.* at 48.
[45] *Id.* at 57.
[46] *Id.* at 58-62.
[47] *Id.* at 64.
[48] *Id.* at 70.
[49] *Id.* at 73.
[50] *Id.* at 78-79.
[51] *Id.* at 81-82.
[52] *Id.* at 94.
[53] *Id.* at 89.
[54] *Id.* at 96-97.
[55] *Id.* at 101-102.
[56] *Id.* at 102.
[57] *Id.* at 94-95
[58] *Id.* at 112.
[59] *Id.* at 125.
[60] *Id.* at 112. *See* Brief of the National Press Club as Amicus Curiae, Nebraska Press Ass'n v. Stuart, 427 U.S. 539 (1976)(No. 75-817), 1976 WL 181470 (Jan. 30, 1976); Brief of the Reporters Comm. for Freedom of the Press Legal Def. and Research Fund as Amicus Curiae, Nebraska Press Ass'n v. Stuart, 427 U.S. 539 (1976)(No. 75-817), 1976 WL 181469 (Jan. 26, 1976); Brief of the Wash. Post Co., Am. Broad. Cos., Inc., the Times Mirror Co., the Globe Newspaper Co., Newsday, Inc., the Miami Herald Publ'g Co., the Kansas City Star Co., the Houston Post Co., the Pulitzer Publ'g Co., Minneapolis Star and Trib. Co., Des Moines Register and Trib. Co., the Denver Publ'g Co., the Times Herald Printing Co., the Courier-Journal and Louisville Times Co., the Copley Press, Inc., the A. S. Abell Co., Times Publ'g Co., Tennessean Newspapers, Inc., Kearns Trib. Corp., Press-Enterprise Co., Sun Newspapers of Omaha, Inc., Keystone Printing Serv., Inc., the Consol. Publ'g Co., the Free Lance-Star Pub'g Co. of Fredericksburg, Va., the Susquehana Publ'g Co., and Herald Register Pub'g Co., Amici Curiae, in Support of Reversal, Nebraska Press Ass'n v. Stuart, 427 U.S. 539 (1976)(No. 75-817), 1976 WL 181471(Jan. 26, 1976); Brief for Trib. Co. as Amicus Curiae, Nebraska Press Ass'n v. Stuart, 427 U.S. 539 (1976)(No. 75-817), 1976 WL 181473 (Jan. 23, 1976); Brief of Nat'l Broad. Co., the New York Times Co., Philadelphia Newspapers, Inc., Chicago Sun-Times, Chicago Daily News, Dow Jones & Co., Inc., The Reader's Digest Ass'n, Inc., Pub. Broad. Service, CBS Inc., Parade Publications, Inc., Harte-Hanks Newspapers, Inc., Am. Soc. of Newspaper Editors, The Soc. of Prof. Journalists, Sigma Delta Chi, Associated Press Managing Editors Ass'n, Nat'l Ass'n of Broadcasters, Radio Television News Dirs. Ass'n and Nat'l Newspaper Ass'n As

Amici Curiae, Nebraska Press Ass'n v. Stuart, 427 U.S. 539 (1976)(No. 75-817), 1976 WL 181476 (Jan. 15, 1976); Brief Amicus Curiae of Am. Newspaper Publishers Ass'n, Nebraska Press Ass'n v. Stuart, 427 U.S. 539 (1976)(No. 75-817), 1975 WL 173724 (Oct. Term 1975).

[61] *See supra* ch. 5, note 6.

[62] McKay, *supra* note 34, at 125.

[63] *Id.* at 124.

[64] SCHERER, *supra* note 37, at 145-149; BOB WOODWARD & SCOTT ARMSTRONG, THE BRETHREN 499-503 (1979); BERNARD SCHWARTZ, THE ASCENT OF PRAGMATISM: THE BURGER COURT IN ACTION 171-73 (1990). Scherer had the benefit of all of these accounts as well as the notes of Justice Lewis F. Powell.

[65] SCHERER, *supra* note 37, at 146.

[66] WOODWARD & ARMSTRONG, *supra* note 64, at 500.

[67] SCHERER, *supra* note 37, at 147.

[68] WOODWARD & ARMSTRONG, *supra* note 64, at 501.

[69] 427 U.S. at 617 (Stevens, J., concurring in the judgment).

[70] *Id.* at 562 (quoting United States v. Dennis, 183 F.2d 201, 212 (2d Cir. 1950)).

[71] *Id.* at 562.

[72] SCHERER, *supra* note 37, at 176.

[73] *Id.* at 181.

[74] Butterworth v. Smith, 494 U.S. 624 (1990).

[75] 130 S.Ct. 876 (2010).

[76] *See* Supplemental Brief Amicus Curiae of The Reporters Comm. for Freedom of the Press in Support of Appellant, Citizens United v. FEC, 130 S.Ct. 876 (2010)(No. 08-205), 2009 WL 2219299, and Brief of Amici Curiae Cal. Broadcasters Ass'n, Ill. Broadcasters Ass'n, La. Ass'n of Broad., Me. Ass'n of Broadcasters, Mich. Ass'n of Broadcasters, Mo.Broadcasters Ass'n, Minn. Broadcasters Ass'n, Neb. Broadcasters Ass'n, N.Y. State Broadcasters Ass'n, And Tenn. Ass'n of Broadcasters iIn Support of Appellant, Citizens United v. FEC, 130 S.Ct. 876 (2010)(No. 08-205), 2009 WL 2365207.

[77] 130 S.Ct. at 895-96. Lucy Dalglish, executive director of Reporters Committee for Freedom of the Press, points out that most of the mainstream media did not want to have anything to do with the *Citizens United* case and that the *New York Times's* editorial position was "opposite ours." Dalglish said she thought the Court would raise a very narrow issue in that case, expressing concern that the law as it stood could be problematic for a fairly mainstream documentary maker because of the election calendar and the technologically evolving nature of the media. The Chief Justice, however, capitalized on the brief's argument that campaign finance laws could even limit publication of a book in the right circumstances. "I was taking a lot of grief for that," Dalglish said, as in "'what do you think you're doing?' I was taking all sorts of crap from people like [campaign finance reform activist] Fred Werthheimer… They were organizing media organizations just to counter our brief. I'd never seen anything like it." Interview with Lucy Dalglish, June 15, 2010 [hereinafter Dalglish Interview] (on file with author).

[78] Seattle Times v. Rhinehart, 467 U.S. 20 (1984).

[79] Regan v. Time, Inc, 468 U.S. 641 (1984).

[80] Hazelwood School Dist. V. Kuhlmeier, 484 U.S. 260 (1988).

[81] Miami Herald v. Tornillo, 418 U.S. 241 (1974).
[82] CBS v. FCC, 453 U.S. 367 (1981).
[83] CBS v. Democratic Nat'l Comm., 412 U.S. 94 (1973).
[84] FCC v. League of Women Voters of Cal., 468 U.S. 364 (1984).
[85] Red Lion Broad. Co. v. FCC, 395 U.S. 367 (1969).
[86] 400 F.2d 1002 (1968).
[87] *See* Brief of Am. Civil Liberties Union, Amicus Curiae, Red Lion Broad. Co. v. FCC, 395 U.S. 367 (1969) (Nos. 2 & 717), 1969 WL 120258; Brief for the Am. Fed'n of Labor and Cong. of Indus. Orgs. as Amicus Curiae, Red Lion Broad. Co. v. FCC, 395 U.S. 367 (1969) (Nos. 2 & 717), 1969 WL 136843 (Feb. 26, 1969); and Brief [amicus curiae] of: Office of Commc'n of the United Church of Christ, United Church Bd. for Homeland Ministries, Bd. of Nat'l Missions of the United Presbyterian Church in the U.S.A., Nat'l Div. of the Methodist Bd. of Missions, Gen. Bd. of Christian Soc. Concerns of the Methodist Church, The Nat'l Council of Churches Broad. and Film Comm'n, Nat'l Catholic Conf. for Interracial Justice, Nat'l Bd. of the Young Women's Christian Ass'n of the U.S., Red Lion Broad. Co. v. FCC, 395 U.S. 367 (1969) (Nos. 2 & 717), 1969 WL 136788.
[88] 418 U.S. at 257 n. 22.
[89] *See* Brief of the Times Mirror Co., Amicus Curiae, Miami Herald Publ'g Co. v. Tornillo, 418 U.S. 241 (1974)(No. 73-797), 1974 WL 185876 (Mar. 14, 1974); Brief of Amicus Curiae on Behalf of Publishers of the Following Fla. Newspapers: Today, Titusville Star Advocate, Melbourne Evening Times, Ft. Myers News-Press and Pensacola News-Journal, Miami Herald Publ'g Co. v. Tornillo, 418 U.S. 241 (1974)(No. 73-797), 1974 WL 185875; Brief for N.Y. News Inc., as Amicus Curiae, Miami Herald Publ'g Co. v. Tornillo, 418 U.S. 241 (1974)(No. 73-797), 1974 WL 185864; Brief of Amicus Curiae, the Nat'l Newspaper Ass'n, in Support of Appellant, Miami Herald Publ'g Co. v. Tornillo, 418 U.S. 241 (1974)(No. 73-797), 1974 WL 185865; Motion for Leave to File Brief Amicus Curiae and Brief Amicus Curiae of the Nat'l Ass'n of Broadcasters, Miami Herald Publ'g Co. v. Tornillo, 418 U.S. 241 (1974)(No. 73-797), 1974 WL 185866; Brief of Amici Curiae, the Am. Soc'y of Newspaper Editors and the Soc'y of Prof. Journalists, Sigma Delta Chi in Support of Appellant, Miami Herald Publ'g Co. v. Tornillo, 418 U.S. 241 (1974)(No. 73-797), 1974 WL 185867; Brief of the Nat'l Broad. Co., Inc., as Amicus Curiae, Miami Herald Publ'g Co. v. Tornillo, 418 U.S. 241 (1974)(No. 73-797), 1974 WL 185868; Brief of Amicus Curiae, the Am. Newspaper Publishers Ass'n, Miami Herald Publ'g Co. v. Tornillo, 418 U.S. 241 (1974)(No. 73-797), 1974 WL 185869; Brief of Dow Jones & Co., Inc. and the N.Y. Times Co., as Amici Curiae, Miami Herald Publ'g Co. v. Tornillo, 418 U.S. 241 (1974)(No. 73-797), 1974 WL 185870; Brief of the Wash. Post Co., Amicus Curiae, in Support of Reversal, Miami Herald Publ'g Co. v. Tornillo, 418 U.S. 241 (1974)(No. 73-797), 1974 WL 185871; Brief of the Am. Civil Liberties Union of Fla., Amicus Curiae, Miami Herald Publ'g Co. v. Tornillo, 418 U.S. 241 (1974)(No. 73-797), 1974 WL 185861; Amicus Curiae Brief for Times Publ'g Co., Miami Herald Publ'g Co. v. Tornillo, 418 U.S. 241 (1974)(No. 73-797), 1974 WL 185862; Brief for Radio Television News Dirs. Ass'n, as Amicus Curiae, Miami Herald Publ'g Co. v. Tornillo, 418 U.S. 241

(1974)(No. 73-797), 1974 WL 185863; Amicus Curiae Brief for Fla. Publ'g Co., Miami Herald Publ'g Co. v. Tornillo, 418 U.S. 241 (1974)(No. 73-797), Miami Herald Publ'g Co. v. Tornillo, 418 U.S. 241 (1974)(No. 73-797), 1974 WL 185874; Brief Amicus Curiae for Chi. Trib. Co., Gore Newspapers Co. and Sentinel Star Co. in Support of the Jurisdictional Statement, Miami Herald Publ'g Co. v. Tornillo, 418 U.S. 241 (1974)(No. 73-797), 1973 WL 172647; Brief of the Reporters Comm. for Freedom of the Press Legal Defense and Research Fund, Art Buchwald, Horance G. Davis, Jr., James J. Kilpatrick, Anthony Lewis, Robert D. Novak, Carl T. Rowan, Hugh Sidey, Thomas G. Wicker, and Jules J. Witcover as Amici Curiae, Miami Herald Publ'g Co. v. Tornillo, 418 U.S. 241 (1974)(No. 73-797), 1973 WL 172643. *Tornillo* also saw the emergence of a group of conservative anti-press amici who appear from time to time in press cases. *See* Brief of the Nat'l Citizens Comm. for Broad., Amicus Curiae, in Support of Affirmance, Miami Herald Publ'g Co. v. Tornillo, 418 U.S. 241 (1974)(No. 73-797), 1974 WL 185872, and Brief of Amicus Curiae Donald U. Sessions, Miami Herald Publ'g Co. v. Tornillo, 418 U.S. 241 (1974)(No. 73-797), 1974 WL 185877.

[90] Interview with Jane Kirtley, Silha Prof. of Media Ethics and Law, Univ. of Minn., and former executive director of Reporters Committee for Freedom of the Press.

[91] *See supra* ch. 5, note 252 and accompanying text.

[92] RICHARD C. CORTNER, THE KINGFISH AND THE CONSTITUTION: HUEY LONG, THE FIRST AMENDMENT, AND THE EMERGENCE OF MODERN PRESS FREEDOM IN AMERICA 2 (1996).

[93] *See supra* ch. 5, notes 169-71 and accompanying text.

[94] CORTNER, *supra* note 92, at 1.

[95] *Id.* at 4.

[96] *Id.* at 76.

[97] 297 U.S. at 240.

[98] CORTNER, *supra* note 92, at 77 (discussing La. Act No. 23 (1934)).

[99] *Id.* at 88.

[100] *Id.* at 91-92. The following year, Long completed his total takeover of the press in Louisiana by enacting legislation authorizing municipalities to impose a similar tax on newspapers, establishing a state printing board to approve which weekly newspapers would be "official printers" of government notices, creating a state board of motion picture censors with the power to censor newsreels, and even gagging the Louisiana State University student newspaper. *Id.* at 96-97.

[101] *Id.* at 99.

[102] *Id.* at 101 (quoting Deutsch memorandum titled "Memorandum and Discussion Relative to Validity of Act 23 of 1934 (Newspaper Advertising Tax) and Jurisdiction and Procedure to Set It Aside.")

[103] *Id.* at 103 (quoting Deutsch, quoting Marshall in McColloch v. Maryland, 4 Wheat. 316 (1819)). For an earlier version of this venerable quotation, see *supra* note 171 and accompanying text.

[104] *Id.* at 105.

[105] *Id.* at 106.

[106] EMERY, *supra* ch. 2, note 68, at 221.

[107] *Id.* at 222.

[108] CORTNER, *supra* note 92, at 107.
[109] *Id.* at 108-109.
[110] *Id.* at 86.
[111] *Id.* at 33-34.
[112] *Id.* at 126.
[113] *Id.* at 130.
[114] *Id.* at 125-126.
[115] *Id.* at 129.
[116] *Id.* at 141-143.
[117] *Id.* at 150.
[118] *Id.* at 155-156.
[119] *Id.* at 157.
[120] 297 U.S. at 242.
[121] *Id.*at 243-244.
[122] *Id.* at 245-249.
[123] *Id.* at 250.
[124] *Id.* at 250.
[125] *Id.* at 251.
[126] 460 U.S. 575 (1983).
[127] 460 U.S. at 580.
[128] Brief of Knight-Ridder Newspapers, Inc., and The Am. Newspaper Publishers Ass'n as Amici Curiae, Minneapolis Star & Trib. Co. v. Minn. Comm'r of Revenue, 460 U.S. 575 (1983) (No.81-1839), 1982 U.S. S. Ct. Briefs LEXIS 485. *See also* Brief of the Am. Civil Liberties Union, the Minnesota Civil Liberties Union, and the Minn. Coalition Against Censorship, Amici Curiae, Minneapolis Star & Trib. Co. v. Minn. Comm'r of Revenue, 460 U.S. 575 (1983) (No.81-1839), 1982 U.S. S. Ct. Briefs LEXIS 488.
[129] 481 U.S. 221 (1987).
[130] Brief of Amicus Curiae the State of Md., 1986 WL 727460 (Sept. 29, 1986), and Brief of the States of Am. Sam., Conn., Fla., Haw., Idaho, Iowa, La., Minn., Pa., Okla., S.C., S.D., Tex., Utah, and Vt. as Amici Curiae in Support of Appellee, Ark. Writers' Project v. Ragland, 481 U.S. 221 (1987)(No. 85-1370), 1986 WL 727461.
[131] Leathers v. Medlock, 499 U.S. 439 (1991).
[132] *Id.* at 249 (quoting *Near* at 716)(emphasis added).
[133] *Id.* at 248-250.
[134] *Near*, 283 U.S. at 715.
[135] 283 U.S. at 718.
[136] GLEASON, *supra* ch. 1, note 8, at 83.
[137] *Id.* at 83-84.
[138] BLACK'S LAW DICTIONARY 390 (4th ed. 1951).
[139] 4 Stat. 487 (1831). "The Act of 1789 (1 Stat. 73, 83) provided that courts of the United States "shall have power . . . to punish by fine or imprisonment, at the discretion of said courts, all contempts of authority in any cause or hearing before the same." Abuses arose, culminating in impeachment proceedings against James H. Peck, a federal district

judge, who had imprisoned and disbarred one Lawless [a lawyer] for publishing a criticism of one of his opinions in a case which was on appeal. Judge Peck was acquitted. But the history of that episode makes abundantly clear that it served as the occasion for a drastic delimitation by Congress of the broad undefined power of the inferior federal courts under the Act of 1789." Nye v. United States, 313 U.S. 33, 45 (1941).

[140] GLEASON, *supra* ch. 1, note 8, at 82, 84.

[141] LOFTON, *supra* ch. 2, note 55, at 215.

[142] GLEASON, *supra* ch. 1, note 8, at 85.

[143] *Id.* at 85.

[144] 205 U.S. 454, 1907 U.S. LEXIS 1380.

[145] *Id.* at 458-59.

[146] 1907 U.S. LEXIS 1380 at 2-5.

[147] 205 U.S. at 13-14.

[148] 1907 U.S. Lexis 1380 at 5-8.

[149] 1907 U.S. Lexis 1380 at 7-8.

[150] 205 U.S. at 462 (citing Massachusetts v. Blanding, 3 Pick. 304, 313, 314 (Mass. 1825), and Respublica v. Oswald, 1 Dallas 319, 325 (Pa. 1788).

[151] 205 U.S. at 462.

[152] *Id.* at 465 (Harlan, J., dissenting). *See supra* note 276 and accompanying text.

[153] *Id.* U.S. at 465-66.

[154] 247 U.S. 402, 411-14 (1918).

[155] *Id.* at 419.

[156] *Id.* at 419-20.

[157] *Id.* at 422, 426 (Holmes, J., dissenting; Brandeis, J., concurring in the dissenting opinion).

[158] *See supra* ch. 4, notes 85-91 and accompanying text.

[159] *See supra* Ch. 4, Pt. A.

[160] *See supra* Pt. B.

[161] *Nye*, 313 U.S. 33.

[162] 314 U.S. 252 (1941).

[163] *Id.* at 263.

[164] *Id.* at 272-73.

[165] 328 U.S. 331 (1946).

[166] GLEASON, *supra* ch. 1, note 8, at 218-19.

[167] 328 U.S. at 334.

[168] 328 U.S. at 350.

[169] *Id.* at 369-72.

[170] 331 U.S. 367 (1947).

[171] Kalven notes that, in 1962, the Court reversed a contempt citation issued by a Georgia court against a local sheriff for comments aimed at members of a grand jury, rather than a judge, in the midst of an election campaign. HARRY KALVEN, JR., A WORTHY TRADITION: FREEDOM OF SPEECH IN AMERICA 31 (1988) (citing Wood v. Georgia, 370 U.S. 375 (1962)).

[172] 331 U.S. at 397.

[173] LOFTON, *supra* ch. 2, note 55, at 230. Lofton was referring specifically to two important contempt cases – United States v. Dickenson, 476 F.2d 373 (5th Cir.), *cert. denied*, 414 U.S. 979 (1973)(declaring the contempt conviction of two Louisiana reporters for violating a judge's gag order unconstitutional but ordering them to pay fines of $300 nevertheless) and *In re* Farber, 394 A.2d 330 (N.J.), *cert. denied*, 439 U.S. 997 (1978) (*New York Times* and its reporter held in contempt for refusing to comply with a grand jury subpoena to turn over documents) – which the press lost. The United States Supreme Court denied certiorari in both cases, neither of which involved contempt by publication.
[174] 376 U.S. 254 (1964).
[175] Peck v. Trib. Co., 214 U.S. 185 (1909).
[176] Farmers Educ. & Coop. Union of Am. v. WDAY, Inc., 360 U.S. 525 (1959).
[177] In the *WDAY* case, both the ACLU and the National Association of Broadcasters filed amicus briefs in support of the broadcaster; neither argued the constitutionality of state libel law under the First and Fourteenth Amendments, but the ACLU did assert the unconstitutionality of enforcing state libel law by requiring the broadcaster to suppress the political speech in question. See Brief of the Nat'l Ass'n of Broadcasters, as Amicus Curiae, in Support of the Respondent, Farmers Educ. & Coop. Union of Am. v. WDAY, Inc., 360 U.S. 525 (1959) (No. 248), 1959 WL 101286; Brief of Am. Civil Liberties Union, Amicus Curiae, at 7, Farmers Educ. & Coop. Union of Am. v. WDAY, Inc., 360 U.S. 525 (1959) (No.248), 1959 WL 101285.
[178] The elements of libel law prior to 1964 remain elements of libel law today and thus are recounted in every media law textbook or casebook. For a better sense of the law prior to 1964, *see* WILLIAM G. HALE, LAW OF THE PRESS 41-128 (1948).
[179] ANTHONY LEWIS, MAKE NO LAW: THE SULLIVAN CASE AND THE FIRST AMENDMENT 32-33 (1991).
[180] *See supra* ch. 3, note 15-16 and accompanying text.
[181] 59 F. 530 (6th Cir. 1893).
[182] 98 P. 281 (Kan. 1908).
[183] *Sullivan*, 376 U.S. at 279-80.
[184] LEWIS, *supra* note 179, at 6-7. A reproduction of the advertisement appears at 2-3.
[185] *Id.* at 11-14.
[186] *Id.* at 36. Gene Roberts and Hank Klibanoff also discuss the use of libel suits as a weapon against the press during the civil rights era. "The Times had been fighting more than a half-dozen libel suits, totaling more than $6 million, for four years... By early 1964, public officials in three southern states had no fewer than seventeen libel lawsuits pending against newspapers, magazines, and a television station, seeking total damages that exceeded $288 million." GENE ROBERTS & HANK KLIBANOFF, THE RACE BEAT: THE PRESS, THE CIVIL RIGHTS STRUGGLE, AND THE AWAKENING OF A NATION 357 (2007).
[187] LEWIS, *supra* note 179, at 14-17.
[188] *Id.* at 28-30.
[189] *Id.* at 30-31.
[190] *Sullivan*, 376 U.S. at 287.
[191] LEWIS, *supra* note 179, at 32-33.

[192] *Id.* at 33.
[193] *Id.* at 43.
[194] *Id.* at 45.
[195] *Id.* at 107. Wechsler continued, "People were asking why it wasn't enough for the Times to 'stick to our established position that we never settle libel cases, we publish the truth, if there's an occasional error we lose and that's one of the vicissitudes of life' – that at a time when, I was told, the paper was barely making a profit and these judgments were mounting up." *Id.*
[196] *Id.*
[197] *See infra* Ch. 7.
[198] *Id.* at 106.
[199] *Id.* at 107-08.
[200] 371 U.S. 946 (1963).
[201] LEWIS, *supra* note 179, at 119-20 (citing Brief for the Petitioner, N.Y. Times v. Sullivan, 376 U.S. 254 (1964)(No. 39), 1963 WL 66441).
[202] *Id.* at 125 (citing Motion of the Wash. Post Co. for Leave to File a Brief as Amicus Curiae and Brief of the Wash. Post Co. as Amicus Curiae in Support of Petitioner, N.Y. Times v. Sullivan, 376 U.S. 254 (1964)(No. 39), 1963 WL 66441).
[203] *Id.* at 125 (citing Brief of Trib. Co. as Amicus Curiae, N.Y. Times v. Sullivan, 376 U.S. 254 (1964)(No. 39), 1963 WL 66444). The *Tribune* brief was signed by the same Howard Ellis who represented Jay Near.
[204] Brief of the Am. Civil Liberties Union and the N.Y. Civil Liberties Union as Amici Curiae, N.Y. Times v. Sullivan, 376 U.S. 254 (1964)(No. 39), 1963 WL 66443.
[205] LEWIS, *supra* note 179, at 124 (citing Brief for Respondent, N.Y. Times v. Sullivan, 376 U.S. 254 (1964)(No. 39), 1963 WL 105892). The Court had refused to review 44 libel cases in the past decade. *Id.*
[206] *Id.* at 131-32.
[207] 376 U.S. at 276.
[208] *Id.* at 279-80.
[209] *Id.* at 285-86.
[210] *Id.* at 284-85. *See* LEWIS, *supra* note 179, at 147-48.
[211] 376 U.S. at 293, 297 (Black, J., and Goldberg, J., concurring). Justice Douglas joined both concurring opinions.
[212] 379 U.S. 64 (1964).
[213] 343 U.S. 250 (1952).
[214] 379 U.S. at 82 (Douglas, J., concurring).
[215] 383 U.S. 75 (1966).
[216] *Id.* at 86.
[217] *Id.* at 88.
[218] *Id.* at 84.
[219] 385 U.S. 374 (1966).
[220] THE DESPERATE HOURS (Paramount Pictures 1955). The film was since remade with Mickey Rourke as the star. DESPERATE HOURS (Dino De Laurentiis Co. 1990).
[221] 385 U.S. at 376-78.
[222] *Id.* at 387.

[223] *Id.* at 398, 401 (Black, J., and Douglas, J., concurring).
[224] *Id.* at 402 (Harlan, J., concurring in part and dissenting in part).
[225] *Id.* at 411 (Fortas, J., dissenting). Chief Justice Warren and Justice Clark joined Fortas's dissent.
[226] *Id.* at 388.
[227] 388 U.S. 130 (1967).
[228] *Id.* at 133-45.
[229] *Id.* at 154. Writing for the Court, Justice Harlan said he "would hold that a 'public figure' who is not a public official may also recover damages for a defamatory falsehood whose substance makes substantial danger to reputation apparent, on a showing of highly unreasonable conduct constituting an extreme departure from the standards of investigation and reporting ordinarily adhered to by responsible publishers." That standard did not command a majority of the Court; public officials and public figures are held to the same "actual malice" standard.
[230] 389 U.S. 81 (1967).
[231] 390 U.S. 727 (1968).
[232] *Id.* at 731.
[233] 398 U.S. 6 (1970).
[234] *Id.* at 14.
[235] *Id.* U.S. at 23 (White, J., concurring).
[236] 401 U.S. 265 (1971). Edward Bennett Williams represented the paper.
[237] 401 U.S. 279 (1971).
[238] 401 U.S. 295 (1971).
[239] *Id.* at 301 (White, J., concurring).
[240] 403 U.S. 29 (1971).
[241] *Id.* at 63 (Harlan, J., dissenting).
[242] *Id.* at 60 (White, J., concurring in the judgment).
[243] 418 U.S. 323 (1974).
[244] *Id.* at 325-331.
[245] *Id.* at 350.
[246] *Id.* at 401 n. 43 (White, J., dissenting).
[247] *Id.* at 399-400 (White, J., dissenting).
[248] *See* Phila. Newspapers v. Hepps, 475 U.S. 767 (1986).
[249] *See supra* notes 81-89 and accompanying text.
[250] 418 U.S. at 263.
[251] 408 U.S. 665 (1972).
[252] 424 U.S. 488 (1976).
[253] 441 U.S. 153 (1979).
[254] *Id.* at 169-70.
[255] Brief Amicus Curiae of Am. Newspaper Publishers Ass'n, Herbert v. Lando, 441 U.S. 153 (1979) (No. 77-1105) 1978 WL 206692; Motion for Leave to File Brief Amicus Curiae and Brief Amicus Curiae of Time, Inc, Herbert v. Lando, 441 U.S. 153 (1979) (No. 77-1105) 1978 WL 206693; Brief of the N.Y. Times Co., the Miami Herald Publ'g Co., the

Wash. Post Co., Nat'l Broad. Co., Inc., the Times Mirror Co., Phila. Newspapers, Inc., Minneapolis Star and Trib. Co., Des Moines Reg. and Trib. Co., Chi. Sun Times, the Courier-Journal and Louisville Times Co., Dow Jones & Co., Inc., Globe Newspapers Co., the Bergen Evening Rec. Corp., Indianapolis Newspapers, Inc., Am. Soc'y of Newspaper Editors, Radio Television News Dirs. Ass'n, Nat'l Ass'n of Broadcasters, Reporters Comm. for Freedom of the Press, Amici Curiae in Support of Affirmance, Herbert v. Lando, 441 U.S. 153 (1979) (No. 77-1105) 1978 WL 206690.

[256] 443 U.S. 111 (1979). *See* Brief of Am. Soc'y of Newspaper Editors and Am. Newspaper Publishers Ass'n, Amicus Curiae in Support of Affirmance, Hutchison v. Proxmire, 443 U.S. 111 (1979) (No. 78-680), 1979 WL 199886.

[257] 443 U.S. 157 (1979). *See* Brief of Am. Soc'y of Newspaper Editors and Am. Newspaper Publishers Ass'n, Amicus Curiae in Support of Affirmance, Wolston v. Reader's Digest Ass'n, 443 U.S. 157 (1979) (No. 78-5414), 1979 WL 199759.

[258] 465 U.S. 770 (1984).

[259] *Id.* at 771 [brief unavailable].

[260] 465 U.S. 783 (1984).

[261] Brief Amicus Curiae of Reporters Comm. for Freedom of the Press, Calder v. Jones, 465 U.S. 783 (1984) (No. 82-1401) *1983 U.S. S. Ct. Briefs LEXIS 213.*

[262] 466 U.S. 485 (1984).

[263] *Id.* at 487 [briefs unavailable].

[264] 472 U.S. 749 (1985).

[265] Brief of the Wash. Post, Amicus Curiae, in Support of Reversal at 15, Dun & Bradstreet v. Greenmoss Builders, 472 U.S. 749 (1985) (No. 83-18) 1983 U.S. S. Ct. Briefs LEXIS 972. The *Post's* brief is also notable for its list of devastating libel verdicts against the press.

[266] Brief of Dow Jones Co., Inc., Amicus Curiae, in Support of Petitioner, Dun & Bradstreet v. Greenmoss Builders, 472 U.S. 749 (1985) (No. 83-18) 1984 U.S. S. Ct. Briefs LEXIS 398.

[267] Brief of Info. Indus. Ass'n, Amicus Curiae, in Support of Reversal, Dun & Bradstreet v. Greenmoss Builders, 472 U.S. 749 (1985) (No. 83-18) 1984 U.S. S. Ct. Briefs LEXIS 392.

[268] *Id.* at 9.

[269] *See, e.g.*, Cox v. Hatch, 761 P.2d 556, 559-60 (Utah 1988).

[270] 475 U.S. 767 (1986).

[271] *Id.* at 768-69.

[272] Brief of the Am. Civil Liberties Union, the Am. Civil Liberties Union of Pa., Am. Newspaper Publishers Ass'n, Ass'n of Am. Publishers, Dow Jones & Co., Inc., Gannett Co., Inc., the Soc'y of Prof'l Journalists, Sigma Delta Chi, and Time, Inc, as Amici Curiae in Support of Appellants at 4, Phila. Newspapers v. Hepps, 475 U.S. 767 (1986)(No. 84-1491), 1985 WL 670155.

[273] Brief Amicus Curiae of [41] Print and Broad. Media and Orgs. in Support of Appellants at 2-4, Phila. Newspapers v. Hepps, 475 U.S. 767 (1986)(No. 84-1491), 1985 WL 670154.

[274] Brief Amicus Curiae of Capital Cities Commc'ns, Inc., CBS Inc., Nat'l Broad. Co., Inc., Trib. Co., and Westinghouse Broad.and Cable, Inc., at 4, Phila. Newspapers v. Hepps, 475 U.S. 767 (1986)(No. 84-1491), 1985 WL 670150.

[275] 477 U.S. 242 (1986).

[276] Brief Amici Curiae of Am. Newspaper Publishers Ass'n, Am, Soc'y of Newspaper Editors, Ass'n of Am. Publishers, CBS Inc., Chi. Trib. Co., Dow Jones & Co., Inc., the Hearst Corp., the Mag. Publishers Ass'n, the Miami Herald Publ'g Co., Nat'l Broad. Co., Inc., Newsweek, Inc., the N.Y. Times Co., the Reporters Comm. for Freedom of the Press, Soc'y of Prof'l Journalists/Sigma Delta Chi, Time, Inc, Times Mirror Co., and Westinghouse Broad. and Cable, Inc., Anderson v. Liberty Lobby, Inc., at 3, 477 U.S. 242 (1986)(No. 84-1602), 1985 WL 669018.
[277] 477 U.S. at 265 (Brennan, J., dissenting).
[278] 485 U.S. 46 (1988).
[279] *Id.* at 47-49.
[280] Motion and Brief of the Reporters Comm. for Freedom of the Press, the Am. Soc'y of Mag. Editors, the Am. Soc'y of Newspaper Editors, the Newspaper Guild, and the Radio-Television News Dirs. Ass'n as Amici Curiae in Support of Petitioners, Falwell v. Hustler, 485 U.S. 46 (1988) (No. 86-1278), 1987 WL 864185, and Brief for the Ass'n of Am. Editorial Cartoonists, the Authors League of Am., Inc. and Mark Russell as Amici Curiae in Support of Petitioners, Falwell v. Hustler, 485 U.S. 46 (1988) (No. 86-1278), 1987 WL 864186.
[281] 485 U.S. at 56.
[282] *Id.* at 57 (White, J., concurring in the judgment).
[283] 501 U.S. 663 (1991).
[284] 491 U.S. 657 (1989).
[285] Brief Amici Curiae of Associated Press, Cable News Network, Inc., Capital Cities/ABC, Inc., CBS Inc., the Cincinnati Enquirer, Chronicle Publ'g Co., Dow Jones & Co., Inc., Globe Newspaper Co., the Hearst Corp., the Miami Herald, Nat'l Broad. Co., Inc., Nat'l Pub. Radio, the N.Y. Times Co., the Phila. Inquirer, Seattle Times Co., Time Inc., the Times Mirror Co., Trib. Co., Am. Civil Liberties Union, Am. Newspaper Publishers Ass'n, Am. Soc'y of Newspaper Editors, Ass'n of Am. Editorial Cartoonists, Nat'l Ass'n of Broadcasters, Nat'l Conf. of Editorial Writers, Nat'l Newspaper Ass'n, Newsl. Ass'n, Radio-Television News Dirs. Ass'n, Reporters Comm. for Freedom of the Press, Soc'y of Prof'l Journalists Sigma Delta Chi. at 3, Harte-Hanks Commc'n v. Connaughton, 491 U.S. 657 (1989)(No. 88-10), 1988 WL 1026349.
[286] *See supra* notes 262-63 and accompanying text. The *de novo* standard of review gives no deference to the the lower court, but requires the appellate court to review the case as though for the first time.
[287] *Id.* at 666.
[288] 388 U.S. at 155. Although Justice Harlan wrote the opinion for the Court, only Justices Clark, Stewart, and Fortas joined that part of the opinion defining the fault standard for public figure plaintiffs as "highly unreasonable conduct constituting an extreme departure from the standards of investigation and reporting ordinarily covered adhered to by responsible publishers." *Id. See supra* notes 227-29 and accompanying text.
[289] 491 U.S. at 664.
[290] 418 U.S. at 339-40. *See supra* notes 840-44 and accompanying text.
[291] 497 U.S. 1 (1990).

[292] 497 U.S. at 18-19.
[293] Brief Amici Curiae of Dow Jones & Co., Inc., the Am. Soc'ty of Newspaper Editors, Associated Press, Cable News Network, Inc., Capital Cities/ABC, Inc., CBS Inc., Gannett Co., Inc., the Hearst Corp., Mag. Publishers of Am., Inc., McClatchy Newspapers, Inc., the Miami Herald Publ'g Co., Nat'l Broad. Co., Inc., Newsday, Inc., Newsweek, Inc., the N.Y. Times Co., the Reporters Comm. for Freedom of the Press, Reuters Info. Servs. Inc., Seattle Times Co., Scripps Howard, Inc., the Soc'ty of Prof'l Journalists, Trib. Co., United Press Intern'l, Inc., the Wash. Post and Westinghouse Broad. Co., Inc., in Support of Respondents, at 2-3, Milkovich v. Lorain Journal, 497 U.S. 1 (1990) (No. 89-645) 1990 WL 10012805. *See also* Motion of Am. Civil Liberties Union, Am. Civil Liberties Union of Ohio, et al., for Leave to File Brief, with Brief Amici Curiae, in Support of Respondents, at 1, Milkovich v. Lorain Journal, 497 U.S. 1 (1990)(No. 89-645) 1990 WL 10012808.
[294] Brief of the Ohio Newspaper Ass'n, the Beacon Journal Publ'g Co., the Cincinnati Enquirer, Inc., the Dispatch Printing Co., Plain Dealer Publ'g Co., Thomson Newspapers, Inc., the Toledo Blade Co. and the Vindicator Printing Co. As Amici Curiae in Support of Respondents the Lorain Journal Co., the News Herald and J. Theodore Diadiun, at 4, Milkovich v. Lorain Journal, 497 U.S. 1 (1990)(No. 89-645) 1989 WL 1126997.
[295] 501 U.S. 496 (1991).
[296] 501 U.S. at 519.
[297] Brief Amicus Curiae of Certain Journalists and Academics in Support of Petitioner at 15, Masson v. New Yorker Mag., 501 U.S. 496 (1991) (No. 89-1799), 1990 WL 10012723. Signatories included free-lance writer Peter Collier, Prof. John DeMott of Memphis State University, Prof. Mark Fackler of Wheaton College, author Joseph C. Goulden, Prof. William E. Lee of the University of Georgia, Prof. Clark Mollenhoff of Washington and Lee University, Prof. Marvin Olasky of the University of Texas, *Reason* magazine publisher Robert Poole, Prof. Dwight L. Teeter, Jr., of the University of Wisconsin-Milwaukee, and *The American Spectator* editor Emmett Tyrrell, Jr.
[298] Brief of Amici Curiae Reporters Comm. for Freedom of the Press, Am. Newspaper Publishers Ass'n, The Soc'y of Prof'l Journalists, and Radio-Television News Dirs. Ass'n in Support of Respondents, at 10, Masson v. New Yorker Mag., 501 U.S. 496 (1991) (No. 89-1799), 1990 WL 10012725, and Brief of Amici Curiae the Time Inc. Mag. Co., Am. Soc'y of Newspaper Editors, Nat'l Ass'n of Broadcasters, the Authors Guild, Inc., the Point Reyes (California) Light, College Media Advisers, Inc., Student Press Law Ctr, Am. Civil Liberties Union, Newsl. Ass'n, Edmund Morris and David McCullough, at 30, Masson v. New Yorker Mag., 501 U.S. 496 (1991) (No. 89-1799), 1990 WL 10012729 (urging the Court to keep journalistic standards or ethics out of the First Amendment analysis). *See also* Brief Amici Curiae of Home Box Office, Inc., Buena Vista Pictures Distribution, Inc., Columbia Pictures Entm't, Inc., Orion Pictures Corp., Paramount Pictures Corp., and Twentieth Century Fox Film Corp. in Support of Respondents, at 29, Masson v. New Yorker Mag., 501 U.S. 496 (1991) (No. 89-1799), 1990 WL 10012726 (expressing concern that reversal would jeopardize the production of docudramas), and Brief of Ass'n of Am. Publishers, Inc. and Mag. Publishers of Am., Inc., as Amici Curiae, in Support of Respondents, Masson v. New Yorker Mag., 501 U.S. 496 (1991) (No. 89-1799), 1990 WL 10012727 at 29 (arguing that the defendant publishers had no reason to

doubt the accuracy of the quotations in question and thus lacked the requisite state of mind for actual malice).

[299] Samuel D. Warren & Louis D. Brandeis, *The Right to Privacy*, 4 HARV. L. REV. 193 (1890).

[300] William L. Prosser, *Privacy*, 48 CAL. L. REV. 383, 389 (1960).

[301] 385 U.S. 374 (1966) (citing N.Y. Civ. Rights Law §§ 50-51). *See supra* notes 816-23 and accompanying text.

[302] 419 U.S. 245 (1974).

[303] 433 U.S. 562 (1977).

[304] 420 U.S. 469 (1975).

[305] 420 U.S. at 489.

[306] 410 U.S. at 491.

[307] 410 U.S. at 501.

[308] 430 U.S. 308 (1977).

[309] 430 U.S. at 309-10.

[310] 430 U.S. at 311.

[311] Brief of Amicus Curiae Am. Newspaper Publishers Ass'n at 18, Okla. Publ'g Co. v. Dist. Ct. in and for Okla. County, 430 U.S. 308 (1977) (No. 76-867) 1977 WL 189322.

[312] 435 U.S. 829 (1978).

[313] Brief Amicus Curiae of Am. Newspaper Publishers Ass'n, Landmark Commc'n, Inc. v. Virginia, 435 U.S. 829 (1978) (No. 76-1450), 1977 WL 189715; Brief of the Nat'l Newspaper Ass'n, the Ariz. Newspapers Ass'n, the Louisiana Press Ass'n, the Maryland-Delaware-D.C. Press Ass'n, the Michigan Press Ass'n, the Neb. Press Ass'n, the Ore. Newspaper Publishers Ass'n, the Pa. Newspaper Publishers Ass'n, the Tex. Daily Newspaper Ass'n, the Tex. Press Ass'n, the Va. Press Ass'n as Amici Curiae in Support of Appellant, Landmark Commc'n, Inc. v. Virginia, 435 U.S. 829 (1978) (No. 76-1450), 1977 WL 189717; Brief of the Wash. Post Co., CBS Inc., Nat'l Broad. Co., Inc., Dow Jones & Co., Inc., the N.Y. Times Co., Field Enters., Inc., Newsday, Inc., the Globe Newspaper Co., Phila. Newspapers, Inc., the Miami Herald Publ'g Co., the Pulitzer Publ'g Co., Minneapolis Star and Trib. Co., Des Moines Reg. and Trib. Co., the Courier-Journal and Louisville Times Co., the Copley Press, Inc., Tennessean Newspapers, Inc., the Free Lance-Star Publ'g Co., and the Am. Soc'y of Newspaper Editors, Amici Curiae, in Support of Reversal, Landmark Commc'n, Inc. v. Virginia, 435 U.S. 829 (1978) (No. 76-1450), 1977 WL 189719; Motion of the Am. Civil Liberties Union and the Am. Civil Liberties Union of Va. for Leave to File Brief Amici Curiae, and Brief Amici Curiae, Landmark Commc'n, Inc. v. Virginia, 435 U.S. 829 (1978) (No. 76-1450), 1977 WL 189721.

[314] 435 U.S. at 838.

[315] 443 U.S. 97 (1979).

[316] Motion of the Am. Civil Liberties Union for Leave to File, and Brief Amicus Curiae, Smith v. Daily Mail, 443 U.S. 97 (1979)(No. 78-482), 1979 WL 213634; Motion of Chi. Trib. Co. for Leave to File Brief Amicus Curiae and Brief Amicus Curiae, Smith v. Daily Mail, 443 U.S. 97 (1979)(No. 78-482), 1979 WL 199841; Motion of Am. Newspaper Publishers Ass'n for Leave to File Brief Amicus Curiae and Brief Amicus Curiae, Smith v.

Daily Mail, 443 U.S. 97 (1979)(No. 78-482), 1979 WL 199845; Motion of Am. Soc'y of Newspaper Editors; Radio-Television News Dirs. Ass'n; Nat'l Newspaper Ass'n; Nat'l Ass'n of Broadcasters; the Soc'y of Prof'l Journalists, Sigma Delta Chi; Reporters Comm. for Freedom of the Press; Nat'l Press Club; Associated Press Managing Editors; W. Va. Press Ass'n; Ill. Press Ass'n; and Clarksburg Publ'g Co. for Leave to File Brief, Amici Curiae. In Support of Affirmance, and Brief Amici, Smith v. Daily Mail, 443 U.S. 97 (1979)(No. 78-482), 1979 WL 199839.
[317] 443 U.S. at 101-102.
[318] 443 U.S. at 103-104.
[319] *See Nebraska Press Ass'n*, 427 U.S. at 517 (White, J., concurring).
[320] 491 U.S. 524 (1989).
[321] *Id.* at 553 (White, J., dissenting).
[322] 491 U.S. at 541.
[323] Brief of Amici Curiae Am. Newspaper Publishers Ass'n, the N.Y. Times Co., the Miami Herald Publ'g Co., the Trib. Co., the Times Herald Printing Co., McClatchy Newspapers, Inc., and the Fla. First Amend. Found., Fla. Star v. B.J.F., 491 U.S. 524 (1989)(No. 87-329),1988 WL 1026321; Brief Amici Curiae of the Reporters Comm. for Freedom of the Press, Associated Press, Capital Cities/ABC, Inc., CBS Inc., Nat'l Ass'n of Broadcasters, Nat'l Broad. Co., Inc., Nat'l Newspaper Ass'n and Radio-Television News Dirs. Ass'n in Support of the Appellant, Fla. Star v. B.J.F., 491 U.S. 524 (1989)(No. 87-329), 1988 WL 1026323.
[324] 491 U.S. at 538-41. Ever since the Court's decision in Gertz v. Robert Welch, Inc., 418 U.S. 323 (1974), all libel plaintiffs had to prove at least some degree of fault (typically negligence or actual malice) on the part of the defendant. *See supra* note 243-47 and accompanying text.
[325] 532 U.S. 514 (2001).
[326] 408 U.S. 665 (1972).

Chapter 7

[1] Biographical information on Earl Caldwell comes from the Robert C. Maynard Institute for Journalism Education, where Caldwell is a founding director. Available at Earl Caldwell Directory, http://www.maynardije.org/news/features/caldwell/Biography-Earl Caldwell. Additional information comes from the author's interview with Earl Caldwell on Feb. 11, 2009 [hereinafter Caldwell Interview](notes on file with author).
[2] ROBERTS & KLIBANOFF, *supra* ch. 6, note 186, at 396.
[3] *Id.* at 365.
[4] Caldwell Interview, *supra* note 1.
[5] MAURICE VAN GERPEN, PRIVILEGED COMMUNICATION AND THE PRESS 37 (1979).
[6] Earl Caldwell, *Angry Panthers Talk of War and Unwrap Weapons*, N.Y. TIMES, Sep. 10, 1968, at 30.
[7] Earl Caldwell, *Declining Black Panthers Gather New Support from Repeated Clashes with Police*, N.Y. TIMES, Dec. 14, 1969, at 64.
[8] Caldwell Interview, *supra* note 1. *See also* VAN GERPEN, *supra* note 5, at 37-38.

[9] Caldwell Interview, *supra* note 1.
[10] Motion to Quash Grand Jury Subpoena, in Sup. Ct. App. of Records and Briefs for Branzburg v. Hayes, 408 U.S. 665 (1972) [hereinafter *Branzburg* App.], United States v. Caldwell, 408 U.S. 665 (1972)(No. 70-57) at 4. A subpoena *duces tecum* requires the respondent to bring prescribed documents to the hearing.
[11] *Id.*
[12] Caldwell Interview, *supra* note 1.
[13] Caldwell v. United States, 434 F.2d 1081, 1083 n. 2 (9th Cir. 1970).
[14] Subpoena to Testify Before the Grand Jury, in *Branzburg* App., *supra* note 10, *Caldwell*, 408 U.S. 665 (1972) (No. 70-57) at 4, 21.
[15] Motion to Quash Grand Jury Subpoena, *supra* note 10, at 4. James Goodale, then General Counsel of The New York Times Company, says the company intervened as owner of the work product of its reporter. James C. Goodale, Branzburg v. Hayes *and the Developing Qualified Privilege for Newsmen*, 26 Hastings L. J. 709, 735 (1975).
[16] Affidavits Attached to Motion to Quash, in *Branzburg* App., *supra* note 10, *Caldwell*, 408 U.S. 665 (1972) (No. 70-57), at 9-61.
[17] Memorandum in Opposition to Motion to Quash Grand Jury Subpoena, in *Branzburg* App., *supra* note 10, *Caldwell*, 408 U.S. 665 (1972) (No. 70-57), at 62-79 (includes two supplemental memoranda).
[18] Caldwell Interview, *supra* note 1.
[19] *Id.* Publicly, the *Times* editorialized against the subpoenas, but its support for Caldwell was equivocal:

> People whose jobs, associations, or reputations are at stake cannot be expected to speak freely on an off-the-record basis if they have reason to fear that both their identity and the totality of their remarks will be turned over to the police.
>
> The attendant and even more serious danger is that the entire process will create the impression that the press operates as an investigative agency for government rather than as an independent force dedicated to the unfettered flow of information to the public…
>
> ….
>
> This newspaper and all the mass media have the same duties as other organizations or individuals to cooperate in the processes of justice. But neither justice nor democracy will benefit if the subpoena power is misused to abridge the independence and effectiveness of the press.

Subpoenas on the Press, N.Y. TIMES, Feb. 4, 1970, at 42.
[20] Caldwell Interview, *supra* note 1.
[21] *Id.*
[22] *Id.*; *see also* Nadya Labi, *A Man Against the Machine*, The Law School: The Magazine of the New York University School of Law, Autumn 2007, at 15.
[23] *In re* Caldwell, 311 F. Supp. 358, 360 (N.D. Cal. 1970) (mem.).

[24] *Id.* at 362.
[25] *Caldwell*, 434 F.2d at 1083 n.2.
[26] *Id.*
[27] Caldwell Interview, *supra* note 1.
[28] *Caldwell*, 434 F.2d at 1083 n.2.
[29] Caldwell Interview, *supra* note 1.
[30] *Id.* Goodale says one of the reasons that Amsterdam decided to appeal the appearance issue after winning a qualified privilege in the district court was an apprehension that the government might possibly penetrate the privilege proposed there by Caldwell in some unknown respect, forcing testimony, albeit of an extremely limited nature, from Caldwell. Goodale, *supra* note 15, at 719 n.47 (citing personal correspondence from Amsterdam).
[31] *Caldwell*, 434 F.2d at 1089.
[32] Caldwell v. United States, 402 U.S. 942 (1971); *see also* Branzburg v. Hayes, 402 U.S. 942 (1971) and *In re* Pappas, 402 U.S. 942 (1971). Caldwell opposed the petition for certiorari on several grounds, none of which was or is particularly compelling. Indeed, the brief merely "suggests that this case presents an inopportune occasion for the exercise of the certiorari jurisdiction." Brief in Opposition to the Petition for a Writ of Certiorari to the United States Court of Appeals for the Ninth Circuit, Caldwell v. United States, 434 F.2d 1081 (9th Cir. 1970) (No. 26025).
[33] Affidavit of Paul M. Branzburg, in *Branzburg* App., *supra* note 10, Branzburg v. Hayes, 408 U.S. 665 (1972) (No. 70-85), at 51-52.
[34] Paul M. Branzburg, *The Hash They Make Isn't To Eat*, THE COURIER-JOURNAL, Nov. 15, 1969.
[35] *Id.* at 3-4.
[36] 408 U.S. at 667.
[37] *Id.* at 668.
[38] The statute provides that "No person shall be compelled to disclose in any legal proceeding or trial before any court, or before any grand or petit jury, or before the presiding officer of any tribunal, or his agent or agents, or before the General Assembly, or any committee thereof, or before any city or county legislative body, or any committee thereof, or elsewhere, the source of any information procured or obtained by him, and published in a newspaper or by a radio or television broadcasting station by which he is engaged or employed, or with which he is connected." KY. REV. STAT. § 421.100 (2009).
[39] Order, *In re*: 141087 in *Branzburg* App., *supra* note 10, *Branzburg*, 408 U.S. 665 (1972) (No. 70-85), at 6.
[40] Petition for Petition for Temporary and Permanent Restraining Order and Writ of Mandamus, in *Branzburg* App., *supra* note 10, *Branzburg*, 408 U.S. 665 (1972) (No. 70-85), at 8.
[41] *Id.*
[42] Order of the Court Granting Temporary Restraining Order, in *Branzburg* App., *supra* note 10, *Branzburg*, 408 U.S. 665 (1972) (No. 70-85), at 21.
[43] Opinion of the Court by Commissioner Vance Dismissing Petition for Writ of Prohibition and Writ of Mandamus, in *Branzburg* App., *supra* note 10, *Branzburg*, 408 U.S. 665 (1972) (No. 70-85), at 13.

[44] Motion to Reconsider, in *Branzburg* App., *supra* note 10, *Branzburg*, 408 U.S. 665 (1972) (No. 70-85), at 21.
[45] 434 F.2d 1081 (9th Cir. 1970).
[46] Opinion of the Court by Commissioner Vance, in *Branzburg* App., *supra* note 10, at 22.
[47] *Id.* at 24 n. 1. In that footnote, the court held that Branzburg had abandoned the constitutional argument and so limited its consideration to the statutory interpretation of protected "sources" under the Kentucky shield law. The United States Supreme Court would later reject that view, holding the constitutional question was properly preserved for appeal. *See* Branzburg v. Hayes, 408 U.S. 665, 671 n.6.
[48] Motion for an Order Staying the Effective Date of the Court's Order, in *Branzburg* App., *supra* note 10, *Branzburg*, 408 U.S. 665 (1972) (No. 70-85), at 29.
[49] Order (modified Jan. 22, 1971), in *Branzburg* App., *supra* note 10, *Branzburg*, 408 U.S. 665 (1972) (No. 70-85), at 29.
[50] Paul M. Branzburg, *Pot Problem Byproduct: Disrespect for the Law*, THE COURIER-JOURNAL & TIMES (Louisville, Ky.), Jan. 10, 1971; Paul M. Branzburg, *Rope Turns To Pot: Once an Industry, Kentucky Hemp Has Become a Drug Problem*, THE COURIER-JOURNAL & TIMES, Jan. 10, 1971.
[51] Franklin Circuit Court Grand Jury Subpoena, in *Branzburg* App., *supra* note 10, *Branzburg*, 408 U.S. 665 (1972) (No. 70-85), at 42.
[52] Motion to Quash Grand Jury Subpoena, in *Branzburg* App., *supra* note 10, *Branzburg*, 408 U.S. 665 (1972) (No. 70-85), at 43.
[53] Petition for Temporary and Permanent Restraining Order and Writ of Prohibition, in *Branzburg* App., *supra* note 10, *Branzburg*, 408 U.S. 665 (1972) (No. 70-85), at 47.
[54] Order (Jan. 18, 1971), in *Branzburg* App., *supra* note 10, *Branzburg*, 408 U.S. 665 (1972) (No. 70-85), at 45.
[55] Protective Order (Jan. 22, 1971), in *Branzburg* App., *supra* note 10, *Branzburg*, 408 U.S. 665 (1972) (No. 70-85), at 46.
[56] Order Denying Prohibition and Mandatory Relief, in *Branzburg* App., *supra* note 10, *Branzburg*, 408 U.S. 665 (1972) (No. 70-85), at 54.
[57] Opinion for the Court by Commissioner Vance Denying Petition for Order of Prohibition, in *Branzburg* App., *supra* note 10, *Branzburg*, 408 U.S. 665 (1972) (No. 70-85), at 55.
[58] *Id.* at 57-59.
[59] Motion for an Order Staying the Effective Date of the Court's Order and Motion for a Temporary Writ of Prohibition, in *Branzburg* App., *supra* note 10, *Branzburg*, 408 U.S. 665 (1972) (No. 70-85), at 61-62.
[60] Order, in *Branzburg* App., *supra* note 10, *Branzburg*, 408 U.S. 665 (1972) (No. 70-85), at 63.
[61] *Caldwell*, 402 U.S. 942 (1971) (mem.).
[62] *See* VAN GERPEN, *supra* note 5, at 39.
[63] *Branzburg*, 408 U.S. at 672.
[64] *Id.*
[65] *Id.*; *see also* VAN GERPEN, *supra* note 5 at 39.

[66] *Branzburg*, 408 U.S. at 673.
[67] Brief for Petitioner at 9, *In re* Paul Pappas, 402 U.S. 942 (1971)(No. 70-94).
[68] VAN GERPEN, *supra* note 5, at 40.
[69] Report of Superior Court for Bristol County, in *Branzburg* App., *supra* note 10, *In re Pappas*, 402 U.S. 942 (No. 70-94), at 8.
[70] *Id.*
[71] *In re* Pappas, 266 N.E.2d 297, 299 n. 2 (Mass. 1971).
[72] *Id.* at 301-02.
[73] *Id.* at 302.
[74] *Id.* at 304.
[75] *In re* Pappas, 402 U.S. 942, 942 (1971).
[76] Branzburg v. Hayes, 408 U.S. 665, 665 (1972).
[77] *See* Anthony L. Fargo, *What They Meant to Say: The Courts Try to Explain* Branzburg v. Hayes, 12 JOURNALISM & COMM. MONOGRAPHS 65 (2010); Rex X. Heinke & Galit Avitan, *Reconciling* Branzburg *and* Daily Mail: *A Proposal for a Qualified Reporter's Privilege*, 32 OHIO N.U. L. REV. 503, 503-07 (2006); Leila Wombacher Knox, Note, *The Reporter's Privilege: The Necessity of a Federal Shield Law Thirty Years After* Branzburg, 28 HASTINGS COMM. & ENT. L.J. 125, 137-44 (2006); Kristina Spinneweber, Comment, Branzburg, *Who? The Existence of a Reporter's Privilege in Federal Courts*, 44 DUQ. L. REV. 317, 318-22 (2006).
[78] Eric B. Easton, *Two Wrongs Mock a Right: Overcoming the* Cohen *Maledicta That Bar First Amendment Protection for Newsgathering*, 58 OHIO ST. L.J. 1135, 1149-50 (1997).
[79]*Branzburg*, 408 U.S. at 681 ("We do not question the significance of free speech, press, or assembly to the country's welfare. Nor is it suggested that news gathering does not qualify for First Amendment protection; without some protection for seeking out the news, freedom of the press could be eviscerated.").
[80] *Id.* at 712 (Douglas, J., dissenting).
[81] *Id.* at 747 (Stewart, J., dissenting).
[82] *Id.* at 710 (Powell, J., concurring).
[83] *See, e.g., In re* Roche, 448 U.S. 1312, 1315 (1980) (expressing the view that *Branzburg* stands for the proposition that the First Amendment provides some degree of protection for reporter's confidences); *see also* Goodale, *supra* note 938, at 709 (discussing Justice Powell's concurrence as supporting a "qualified newsman's privilege" judged on a case-by-case basis).
[84] *Branzburg*, 408 U.S. at 667 (White, J., joined by Burger, C.J., Blackmun, Powell & Rehnquist, J.J.).
[85] *See supra* notes 29-30 and accompanying text.
[86] *See supra* note 16 and accompanying text. John Bates of Pillsbury, Madison & Sutro represented the *Times*.
[87] Caldwell Interview, *supra* note 1.
[88] *Id.*
[89] *See, e.g.*, Brief of the N.Y. Times Co. et al. as Amici Curiae at 2-4, Caldwell v. United States, 402 U.S. 942 (1971) (No. 70-57) (arguing in favor of a qualified privilege); Brief for the Am. Newspaper Publishers Ass'n as Amicus Curiae at 4-5, Branzburg v. Hayes, 408 U.S. 665 (1972) (No. 70-85) (urging the Court to adopt an absolute privilege).

[90] *See, e.g.*, Eric B. Easton, *Public Importance: Balancing Proprietary Rights and the Right to Know*, 21 CARDOZO ARTS & ENT. L.J. 139, 141 (2003) (arguing that "the First Amendment's penumbral 'right to know' is the source of a 'public importance test'").
[91] *See* Murdock v. Pennsylvania, 319 U.S. 105, 115 (1943)("Freedom of press, freedom of speech, freedom of religion are in a preferred position.").
[92] BILL KOVACH & TOM ROSENSTIEL, THE ELEMENTS OF JOURNALISM 17(2001) ("The primary purpose of journalism is to provide citizens with the information they need to be free and self-governing.").
[93] Brief for Petitioner Paul M. Branzburg at 9, Branzburg v. Hayes, 408 U.S. 665 (1972)(No. 70-85).
[94] Brief of the N.Y. Times Co., et al., *supra* note 89, at 16.
[95] Brief for the Am. Newspaper Publishers Ass'n, *supra* note 89, at 8.
[96] Transcript of Oral Argument, Branzburg v. Hayes, 408 U.S. 665 (1972) (No. 70-85), reprinted in 74 LANDMARK BRIEFS AND ARGUMENTS OF THE SUPREME COURT OF THE UNITED STATES: CONSTITUTIONAL LAW 678 (Philip B. Kurland & Gerhard Casper eds. 1975).
[97] Petition for a Writ of Certiorari to the Supreme Judicial Court for the Commonwealth of Massachusetts at 12 n. 9, In the Matter of Paul Pappas, No. 70-94 (U.S. March 4, 1971).
[98] Affidavits Attached to Supplemental Memorandum of *The New York Times* and *Newsweek*, in *Branzburg* App., *supra* note 10, Caldwell v. United States, 408 U.S. 775 (1972) (No. 70-57) at 37-50
[99] *In re* Pappas, 266 N.E.2d 297, 303 n. 11 (Mass. 1971).
[100] The organizations were the American Broadcasting Co., American Newspaper Publishers Association, American Newspaper Guild, American Society of Newspaper Editors, Associated Press Broadcasters' Association, Associated Press Managing Editors Association, Association of American Publishers, Authors League of America, Columbia Broadcasting System, Chicago Daily News, Chicago Sun-Times, Chicago Tribune Co., Dow Jones, National Press Photographers Association, National Broadcasting Co., Newsweek, New York Times, Radio Television News Directors Association, Sigma Delta Chi, Washington Post Co. and a coalition of religious broadcasters, as well as the American Civil Liberties Union.
[101] *See, e.g.*, Brief of the N.Y. Times Co. et al., *supra* note 89, at 35 ("[R]equiring a reporter to disclose information obtained in confidence would chill…a substantial flow of news to the public.").
[102] SOCIETY OF PROFESSIONAL JOURNALISTS, CODE OF ETHICS (1996), http://www.spj.org/ethicscode.pdf ("Identify sources whenever feasible. The public is entitled to as much information as possible on sources' reliability. Always question sources' motives before promising anonymity. Clarify conditions attached to any promise made in exchange for information. Keep promises.").
[103] Brief for Radio Television News Dirs. Ass'n as Amicus Curiae Supporting Respondent, United States v. Caldwell, 408 U.S. 665 (1972) (No. 70-57) at *7 n. 4 (emphasis added).
[104] Cohen v. Cowles Media, 501 U.S. 663 (1991).
[105] Easton, *supra* note 78, at 1153-54.

[106] *Id.*
[107] *Id.*
[108] *Cohen*, 501 U.S. at 670.
[109] KOVACH & ROSENSTEIL, *supra* note 92, at 94, 112.
[110] Brief for the Am. Newspaper Publishers Ass'n, *supra* note 89, at 8-9.
[111] *Id.* at 9 (citing Caldwell v. United States, 434 F.2d 1081, 1086 (9th Cir. 1970).
[112] Brief for the Am. Newspaper Guild et al. as Amicus Curiae Supporting Respondents at 7, United States v. Caldwell, 408 U.S. 665 (1972) (70-57), and *In re* Pappas, 408 U.S. 665 (1972) (70-94).
[113] *Id.*
[114] Brief for the Am. Civil Liberties Union et al. as Amicus Curiae Supporting Respondents at 28-29, United States v. Caldwell, 408 U.S. 665 (1972) (70-57).
[115] *Id.* at 29.
[116] Pappas specifically told the Supreme Judicial Court of Massachusetts that he would file a petition for certiorari "[i]n view of the conflict between the decision of our court in the Matter of Paul Pappas and the decision of the Federal Court in the Matter of Caldwell vs. United States." Application for Stay of the Order of the Supreme Judicial Court, in *Branzburg* App., *supra* note 10, *In re* Pappas, 408 U.S. 665 (1972) (No. 70-94), at 24.
[117] 259 F.2d 545 (2d Cir. 1958).
[118] *Id.* at 547.
[119] *Id.* at 548.
[120] *Id.*
[121] *Id.* at 549 (quoting Blackmer v. United States, 284 U.S. 421, 438 (1932)).
[122] *Id.*
[123] *Id.* at 550.
[124] *See, e.g.,* Brief for Petitioner, *supra* note 93, at 39 (distinguishing *Garland*).
[125] Motion to Reconsider, in *Branzburg* App., *supra* note 10, *Branzburg*, 408 U.S. 655 (1972) (No. 70-85), at 21-22.
[126] Branzburg v. Pound, 461 S.W.2d 345, 346 n. 1 (Ky. 1971).
[127] Branzburg v. Meigs, 503 S.W.2d 748, 750 (Ky. 1971).
[128] Report of Superior Court for Bristol County, in *Branzburg* App., *supra* note 10, at 7.
[129] *Caldwell* is the focus of this discussion because it seems highly unlikely that either Branzburg or Pappas would have been motivated to pursue their cases by the ideology of their states' appellate courts. All seven justices who heard Pappas's case before the Massachusetts Supreme Judicial Court were appointed by Republican governors. *Compare* Supreme Judicial Court of Massachusetts, Justices of the Supreme Judicial Court, http://www. massreports.com/justices/alljustices.aspx (last visited Dec. 1, 2009)(listing the justices' respective appointment dates), *with* Former Governors of Massachusetts from 1780, http://www.netstate.com/states/ government/ma_formergov.htm (last visited Dec. 1, 2009) (listing the Governors of Massachusetts). Note, however, that according to the Justices of the Supreme Judicial Court Web site, Jacob Spiegel was appointed in 1960; however, his memorials state he was appointed in 1961, thereby making Governor Volpe the appointing governor. *Compare* Supreme Judicial Court of Massachusetts, Justices of the Supreme Judicial Court, http://www.massreports.com/justices /alljustices.aspx (last visited Dec. 1, 2009), *with* Supreme Judicial Court of Massachusetts, Memorials,

http://www.massreports.com/memorials/394ma1115.htm (last visited Dec. 1, 2009). The seven justices who heard Branzburg's case before the Kentucky Court of Appeals, the state's only appellate court at the time, were all elected. *See* Commonwealth of Kentucky, Court of Justices, http://courts.ky.gov/ courtofappeals (last visited Dec. 1, 2009) (noting that "fourteen judges, two elected from seven appellate court districts, serve on the Court of Appeals"). Having lost decisively at the trial court level, both Branzburg and Pappas were likely to pursue their appeals through the state courts regardless of actual or perceived ideological preferences.

[130] Federal Judicial Center, Biographical Directory of Federal Judges, http://www.fjc.gov/public/ home.nsf/hisj (search for Zirpoli) (last visited Dec. 1, 2009).

[131] *Id.*

[132] *Id.*

[133] Federal Judicial Center, *supra* note 130 (search for Merrill).

[134] *Id.* (search for Ely).

[135] *Id.* (search for Jameson).

[136] *See* LEE EPSTEIN & JACK KNIGHT, THE CHOICES JUSTICES MAKE 85 (1998) (suspecting that the Court is "reluctant to ignore disputes that the government wants them to resolve").

[137] *See* CHARLES M. LAMB & STEPHEN C. HALPERN, THE BURGER COURT: POLITICAL AND JUDICIAL PROFILES 110, 133 (1991).

[138] *Id.* at 68.

[139] *See id.* at 8, 193, 376.

[140] The identification of press-related cases was taken from Eric B. Easton, *The Press as an Interest Group: Mainstream Media in the United States Supreme Court*, 14 UCLA Ent. L. Rev. 247 (2007), Appendix. The voting records came from Congressional Quarterly, Inc., CQ Press Electronic Library, Supreme Court Collection, http://library.cqpress.com (last visited Dec. 1, 2009).

[141] Red Lion Broad. Co. v. FCC, 395 U.S. 367, 385 (1969)(upholding the personal attack and editorial reply rules of the FCC's "Fairness Doctrine" against challenge by broadcasters).

[142]Pickering v. Bd. of Educ., 391 U.S. 563, 583 (1968)(White, J., concurring in part, dissenting in part) (refusing to follow the Court's dictum suggesting that proof of harm would be required to fire a public school teacher who made intentionally or recklessly false statements about the school board), and Greenbelt Coop. Publ'g Ass'n v. Bresler, 398 U.S. 6, 22-23 (1970) (White, J., concurring in the judgment)(insisting that the press could be held liable for using words that might have both innocent and libelous meanings).

[143] 376 U.S. 254 (1964) (requiring public officials to prove actual malice to prevail in a libel suit).

[144] 381 U.S. 532 (1965).

[145] *Id.* at 615-16 (White, J., dissenting).

[146] *See, e.g.*, St. Amant v. Thompson, 390 U.S. 727, 731 (1968); Curtis Publ'g. Co. v. Butts, 388 U.S. 130, 173-74 (1967) (joining a dissent more favorable to the press than the majority opinion); Time v. Hill, 385 U.S. 374, 387-91(1967); Rosenblatt v. Baer, 383 U.S. 75, 80-81 (1966); Garrison v. Louisiana, 379 U.S. 64, 74-75 (1964).

[147] DENNIS J. HUTCHINSON, THE MAN WHO ONCE WAS WHIZZER WHITE: A PORTRAIT OF JUSTICE BYRON R. WHITE 449-50 (1998).
[148] *See, e.g.*, Gertz v. Robert Welch, Inc., 418 U.S. 323, 390-91 (1974) (White, J., dissenting) ("The communications industry has increasingly become concentrated in a few powerful hands operating very lucrative businesses reaching across the Nation and into almost every home. Neither the industry as a whole nor its individual components are easily intimidated, and we are fortunate that they are not. Requiring them to pay for the occasional damage they do to private reputation will play no substantial part in their future performance or their existence."); Miami Herald v. Tornillo, 418 U.S. 241, 263 (1974) (White, J., concurring) ("To me it is a near absurdity to so deprecate individual dignity, as the Court does in *Gertz*, and to leave the people at the complete mercy of the press, at least in this stage of our history when the press, as the majority in this case so well documents, is steadily becoming more powerful and much less likely to be deterred by threats of libel suits.").
[149] In addition to *Branzburg v. Hayes,* 408 U.S. 665 (1972), see White's majority opinions in *Cohen v. Cowles Media*, 501 U.S. 663 (1991) (holding promises of confidentiality from reporters to sources are enforceable against the press) , and *Zurcher v. Stanford Daily*, 436 U.S. 547 (1978)(holding neither First nor Fourth Amendment prohibited the government from using search warrants to recover evidence believed to be in newsrooms).White also joined majority opinions in *Houchens v. KQED*, 438 U.S. 1 (1978) (holding that the press has no greater right of access to government-held information than the general public), *Pell v. Procunier*, 417 U.S. 817 (1974) (same), and *Saxbe v. Wash. Post*, 417 U.S. 843 (1974) (same).
[150] 259 F.2d 545 (2d Cir. 1958).
[151] Caldwell Interview, supra note 1.
[152] *Id.* Caldwell points to a memo posted by Managing Editor Abe Rosenthal saying "'We all feel bad for Earl Caldwell and the difficult position *he* finds *himself* in.'" *Id.*
[153] *See* BLACK'S LAW DICTIONARY 1267 (8th ed. 2004).
[154] 8 JOHN HENRY WIGMORE, WIGMORE ON EVIDENCE § 2192 (John T. McNaughton rev. 1961).
[155] *See, e.g.,* Branzburg v. Hayes, 408 U.S. 665, 688 (1972); In re Pappas, 266 N.E.2d 297, 299 (Mass. 1971).
[156] KY. REV. STAT. ANN. § 421.100 (LexisNexis 2006). To this day, neither Massachusetts nor the federal government has enacted a similar statute.
[157] Petition for Temporary and Permanent Restraining Order and Writ of Mandamus, *in Branzburg* App., *supra* note 10, *Branzburg*, 408 U.S. 665 (1972)(No. 70-85), at 8-11.
[158] Branzburg v. Pound, 461 S.W.2d 345, 347-48 (Ky. Ct. App. 1970).
[159] *Id.* at 347-48.
[160] *Id.* at 348.
[161] *Id.*
[162] *Id.* (Hill, C.J., dissenting).
[163] *Id.* at 349 (Hill, C.J., dissenting) (quoting *In re* Taylor, 193 A.2d 181, 185-86 (Pa. 1963)).
[164] *In re* Pappas, 266 N.E.2d 297, 299 (Mass. 1971).
[165] *Id.* at 299-301.

[166] Caldwell v. United States, 434 F.2d 1081, 1092 (9th Cir. 1970) (Jameson, J., concurring). Jameson's comment regarding Congress's failure to enact a shield law was duly noted by Justice Cutter in his opinion for the Massachusetts Supreme Judicial Court in Pappas. 266 N.E.2d at 302.

[167] For a list of state shield laws at the time, see Branzburg v. Hayes, 408 U.S. 665, 691 n. 27.

[168] *Id.* (Louisiana, 1964; New Mexico, 1967; Alaska, 1967; Nevada, 1969; and New York, 1970.)

[169] *Caldwell*, 434 F.2d at 1091-92 n. 3 (Jameson, J., concurring) (quoting John N. Mitchell, Free Press and Fair Trial: The Subpoena Controversy, Address Before House of Delegates, American Bar Association. (Aug. 10, 1970)). The guidelines were formally published as United States Department of Justice Memorandum No. 692. 39 U.S.L.W. 2111 (Aug. 25, 1970). A complete copy was also published in *The New York Times*, Aug. 11, 1970, p. 24, and attached as an appendix to Levin v. Marshall, 317 F.Supp. 169, 173 (D. Md. 1970).

[170] LII/Legal Information Institute, Cornell University, Supreme Court Collection, http://supct.law.cornell.edu/supct/justices/rehnquist.bio.html (visited Dec 1, 2009).

[171] McKay, *supra* ch. 6, note 34, at 112.

[172] *Id.*

[173] The Reporters Committee for Freedom of the Press, *About the Reporters Committee for Freedom of the Press: A Short History*, http://www.rcfp.org/about.html (last visited Dec. 1, 2009).

[174] Brief for Petitioner, *supra* note 93, at 17; see also Brief for Nat'l Broad. Co. as Amici Curiae Supporting Petitioner at 10-11, *In re* Pappas, 408 U.S. 665 (1972) (No. 70-94).

[175] Brief of the N.Y. Times Co. et al., *supra* note 89, at 12.

[176] See Brief for Nat'l Broad. Co., *supra* note 174, at 9-10 (citing several similar lower court decisions around the same time, including People v. Rios, No. 75129 (Cal. Super. Ct. July 15, 1970); People v. Dohrn, No. 69-3808 (Cook Cnty., Ill., Cir. Ct. May 20, 1970); Transcript of April 6, 1970, at 18-24, 36, and Transcript of April 7, 1970, at 21, 38-39, 149-51, Air Transp. Ass'n v. Prof'l Air Traffic Controllers Org., No. 70-C-400-410 (E.D.N.Y.); and Transcript of Dec. 4, 1969, Alioto v. Cowles Comm., No. 52150 (N.D. Cal.).

[177] Some scholarship suggests that disproportionately strong amici support may be counter-productive. *See* Joseph D. Kearney & Thomas W. Merrill, *The Influence of Amicus Curiae Briefs on the Supreme Court*, 148 U. PA. L. REV. 743, 750 (2000). However, those findings are certainly counterintuitive and would probably have surprised the litigants here. My own research on press cases suggests that support from press amici has been largely irrelevant to the outcome. *See* Easton, *supra* note 140, at 256.

[178] My previous research shows that the press has been far more successful when supported by the ACLU than when opposed by the ACLU, winning 75% of its cases with the ACLU on board and losing 83% when opposed by the ACLU. Easton, *supra* note 140, at 257.

[179] The federal government, of course, was a party opponent in *Caldwell*, and amicus curiae in *Branzburg* and *Pappas*. In either capacity, the government is unquestionably the most formidable opponent the press could face. *See* Herbert M. Kritzer, The *Government*

Gorilla: Why Does Government Come Out Ahead in Appellate Courts?, in HERBERT M. KRITZER & SUSAN S. SILBEY, IN LITIGATION: DO THE "HAVES" STILL COME OUT AHEAD? (2003); Easton, *supra* note 140, at 257; Kearney & Merrill, *supra* note 177, at 829.

[180] *See, e.g.,* Cohen v. Cowles Media, Inc., 501 U.S. 663, 669-70 (1993) (citing *Branzburg* for the proposition "that generally applicable laws do not offend the First Amendment simply because their enforcement against the press has incidental effects on its ability to gather and report the news");
Houchins v. KQED, Inc., 438 U.S. 1, 10-11 (1978) (citing *Branzburg* for the proposition that "there is no First Amendment right of access to information...."); Zurcher v. Stanford Daily, 436 U.S. 547, 566 (1978) (citing *Branzburg* for the proposition that "it does not make a constitutional difference" whether search warrants or subpoenas served on reporters will result in the disappearance of confidential sources or cause the press to suppress the news); Pell v. Procurier, 417 U.S. 817, 834 (1974) (citing *Branzburg* for the proposition that "newsmen have no constitutional right of access to prisons or their inmates beyond that afforded the general public.").

[181] McKay, *supra* ch. 6, note 34, at 111,

[182] *Id.* at 112 (citing Curt Matthews, *Journalism's Full Court Press*, WASH. JOURN. REV. (March 1982) at 40). For a sense of the magnitude of the subpoena assault, see the list of 120 subpoenas served on reporters from NBC, CBS, and their wholly owned stations included as an Appendix to Brief of the N.Y. Times Co. et al., *supra* note 89.

[183] Caldwell v. United States, 311 F. Supp. 358,360 (N.D. Cal. 1970).

[184] *See* Brief in Opposition to the Petition for a Writ of Certiorari at 3, Caldwell v.United States, 408 U.S. 665 (1972) (No. 70-57).

[185] *Id.* at 3.

[186] *See* Brief for Respondent at 81, *Caldwell*, 408 U.S. 665 (1972) (No. 70-57).

[187] *Id.* at 82-84.

[188] Brief of the N.Y. Times Co. et al., *supra* note 89, at 8.

[189] *Id.* By "sumptuary" crimes, the *Times* was presumably referring to the violation of prohibitions imposed for moral, health, or social welfare reasons, such as illegal gambling. *See, e.g.*, Rushing v. United States, 381 A.2d 252, 256 (D.C. App. 1977).

[190] Brief for Chi. Trib. Co. as Amicus Curiae at 18, United States v. Caldwell, 408 U.S. 665 (1972) (No. 70-57).

[191] Brief for Radio Television News Dirs. Ass'n, *supra* note 103, at 10.

[192] Brief of the Authors League of Am., Inc., as Amicus Curiae at 7, *Caldwell*, 408 U.S. 665 (1972) (No. 70-57).

[193] Brief of Office of Commc'n of The United Church of Christ et al., as Amici Curiae at 22, *Caldwell*, 408 U.S. 665 (1972) (No. 70-57).

[194] Of course, there may be other, non-strategic reasons for advocating a qualified privilege, including a sincere belief that reporters should have to testify under some circumstances.

[195] Brief for the Am. Newspaper Publishers Ass'n, *supra* note 89, at 4.

[196] Brief of the Wash. Post Co. and Newsweek, Inc., as Amici Curiae in Support of Respondent at 4, *Caldwell*, 408 U.S. 665 (1972) (No. 70-57).

[197] Brief of the Am. Soc'y of Newspaper Editors et al. as Amici Curiae at 24, *Caldwell*, 408 U.S. 665 (1972) (No. 70-57).

[198] Brief of the Nat'l Press Photographers Ass'n as Amicus Curiae at 2, *Caldwell*, 408 U.S. 665 (1972) (No. 70-57).
[199] Brief of the Am. Civil Liberties Union et al., *supra* note 114, at 23.
[200] *See infra* Part D.2.
[201] Caldwell believes to this day that lukewarm support from the *New York Times* was responsible for the defeat. Caldwell Interview, *supra* note 1. He told the author that the late Fred Graham, then Supreme Court and Justice Department reporter for the *Times*, had evidence that William Rehnquist had prejudged his case while at Justice and that appropriate pressure from the *Times* would have forced Rehnquist to recuse himself from the case. *Id.*
[202] McKay, *supra* ch. 6, note 34, at 108. As chronicled by McKay, a member of the organization's steering committee from 1976 to 1986, the RCFP grew out of a 1970 meeting of 35-40 reporters at Georgetown University who gathered specifically to discuss the *Caldwell* case. *Caldwell* was seen as the most visible example of a dramatic increase in the use of subpoenas served on reporters in an effort to tap into the radical movements of the late 1960s and early 1970s. In the aftermath of *Branzburg*, the RCFP played a major role in advocating for an absolute federal shield law, and, in the view of some, its no-compromise stance was a major reason why no federal legislation was ever enacted. *See id.* at 126.
[203] Reply Brief at 13, *In re* Pappas, 408 U.S. 665 (1972) (No. 70-94). Blasi's study is treated at length in Vince Blasi, *The Newsman's Privilege: An Empirical Study*, 70 Mich. L. Rev. 229 (1971-72).
[204] Branzburg v. Hayes, 408 U.S. 665, 681-82 (1972).
[205] *Id.* at 683 (quoting Associated Press v. NLRB, 301 U.S. 103, 132-133 (1937)).
[206] 408 U.S. at 684.
[207] *Id.* at 685-86.
[208] *Id.* at 689.
[209] *Id.* at 690-91.
[210] *Id.* at 692.
[211] *Id.* at 693.
[212] *Id.* at 696.
[213] *Id.* at 707-708.
[214] *See infra* Part D.2.
[215] McKay, *supra* ch. 6, note 34, at 108.
[216] *Id.* at 109; *see also* Joe Holley, Obituary, Jack *Landau; Founded Reporter Group*, Wash. Post, Aug. 17, 2008, at C7 (describing the formation of RCFP).
[217] McKay, *supra* ch. 6, note 34, at 109.
[218] *See id.*
[219] *Id.*
[220] Although the new Reporters Committee was "emerging as the leading advocate of the 'no compromise' position on reporter confidentiality, McKay, *supra* ch. 6, note364, at 112, both the American Newspaper Publishers Association and the American Society of Newspaper Editors also urged an absolute privilege. *See supra* text accompanying notes

1007-1010. Later, however, ANPA would split with Reporters Committee to support compromise legislation.

[221] *See* McKay, *supra* ch. 6, note 34, at 112-13.

[222] Although a number of states had already enacted shield laws, and similar bills had been introduced unsuccessfully in nearly every Congress since 1929, VAN GERPEN, *supra* note 5, at 148, popular support for a shield law had never been higher than immediately after the *Branzburg* decision was handed down. McKay, *supra* ch. 6, note 34, at 115.

[223] Sam J. Ervin, Jr., *In Pursuit of a Press Privilege*, 11 HARV. J. LEGIS. 233, 251 (1973-74) (citing S.3552, 91st Cong. (1970)).

[224] *Id.* at 253 (citing S.1311, 92nd Cong. (1971)).

[225] *Id.* at 253-54. The government's certiorari petition in *Caldwell* was pending at the time.

[226] *Id.* at 254.

[227] In February, Attorney General John Mitchell issued a statement "regret[ting]" any misunderstanding arising from the issuance of subpoenas to the press and promising that, "in the future, no subpoenas will be issued to the press without a good faith attempt by the Department to reach a compromise acceptable to both parties." Ervin, *supra* note 223, at 251 (citing N.Y. TIMES, Feb. 6, 1970, at 40). Mitchell's press spokesman at the time was Jack Landau. McKay, *supra* note 514, at 112. At a press conference in May, President Nixon said he took a "very jaundiced view" of subpoenaing the notes of reporters or taking action requiring reporters to reveal their sources. Ervin, *supra* note 223, at 254 (citing The President's News Conf., 7 WEEKLY COMP. PRES. DOC. 703, 705 (May 1, 1971). Also in May, Mitchell told an interviewer he had no objection "to legislation protecting" reporters' notes. *Id.* at 252. Finally, in August, Mitchell's Justice Department issued restrictive guidelines to U.S. Attorneys regarding subpoenas for journalists. *See supra* notes 1098-1100 and accompanying text. As noted therein, the guidelines were originally drafted by Landau. *Id.*

[228] Ervin, *supra* note 120, at 254-55.

[229] *Id.* at 255.

[230] *See id.* at 254-55.

[231] Ervin, *supra* note 120, at 254-55 (citing S. 3796, 92nd Cong. (1972)).

[232] *Id.* at 256. The Joint Media Committee was a group of organizations pressing for shield legislation, including the American Society of Newspaper Editors, Associated Press Managing Editors Association, Sigma Delta Chi, National Press Photographers Association, and Radio Television News Directors Association. *Id.*

[233] *Id.* (citing S. 3932, 92d Cong. (1972)).

[234] *Id.* (citing H.R. 16527, 92d Cong. (1972)).

[235] *Id.* (citing S.3925, 92d Cong. (1972)).

[236] *Id.* (citing Hearings on Newsman's Privilege Before Subcomm. No. 3 of the House Comm. on the Judiciary, 92d Cong. (1972)).

[237] *Id.* at 256-57. Ervin is referring to Peter Bridge of the *Newark News* and William Farr of the *Los Angeles Herald Examiner*, who served twenty and forty-six days, respectively, for refusing to reveal confidential sources. *Id.*

[238] *Id.* at 258 (noting resolutions calling for enactment of an absolute privilege by American Society of Newspaper Editors, Sigma Delta Chi, Radio Television News Directors Association, and American Newspaper Publishers Association).

[239] *Id.*
[240] *Id.* at 258-59.
[241] *Id.*
[242] *Id.* at 261.
[243] *Id.*
[244] *Id.* at 261-62.
[245] *Id.* at 263.
[246] *Id.* at 267-68.
[247] *Id.* at 271 n. 132.
[248] *Id.* at 269.
[249] *Id.* at 270.
[250] *Id.*
[251] Cervantes v. Time, Inc, 464 F.2d 986, 992-93 (8th Cir. 1972) ("We are aware of the prior cases holding that the First Amendment does not grant to reporters a testimonial privilege to withhold news sources. But to routinely grant motions seeking compulsory disclosure of anonymous news sources without first inquiring into the substance of a libel allegation would utterly emasculate the fundamental principles that underlay the line of cases articulating the constitutional restrictions to be engrafted upon the enforcement of State libel laws. Such a course would also overlook the basic philosophy at the heart of the summary judgment doctrine.") (citations omitted).
[252] Baker v. F&F Investment Co., 470 F.2d 778, 784-85 (2d Cir. 1972) ("Manifestly, the Court's concern with the integrity of the grand jury as an investigating arm of the criminal justice system distinguishes *Branzburg* from the case presently before us. If, as Mr. Justice Powell noted in that case, instances will arise in which First Amendment values outweigh the duty of a journalist to testify even in the context of a criminal investigation, surely in civil cases, courts must recognize that the public interest in non-disclosure of journalists' confidential news sources will often be weightier than the private interest in compelled disclosure.")
[253] Ervin, *supra* note 223, at 272.
[254] *See* Democratic Nat'l Comm. v. McCord, 356 F. Supp. 1394, 1399 (D.D.C. 1973).
[255] Ervin, *supra* note 223, at 273.
[256] *Id.* at 274.
[257] *Id.* at 274-75.
[258] McKay recounts a story told by Jack Landau, when Landau solicited Marshall Field, publisher of the Chicago Sun-Times, for financial support for Reporters Committee for Freedom of the Press. After Landau's pitch, Field replied, "Well, Mr. Landau, I'm not really very comfortable funding a group that calls itself the *Reporters* Committee." McKay, *supra* ch. 6, note 34, at 122-23.
[259] Brief for Respondent at 48-49, Branzburg v. Hayes, 408 U.S. 665 (1972) (No. 70-57).

Chapter 8

[1] 381 U.S. 1 (1965).

[2] *Id.* at 4.
[3] 228 F.Supp. 65 (D. Conn. 1964).
[4] 381 U.S. at 20.
[5] *Id.* at 16-17.
[6] *See id.* at 3.
[7] *See* Potter Stewart, *Or of the Press*, 26 HASTINGS L.J. 631 (1975), and the response of Chief Justice Burger in First National Bank v. Bellotti, 435 U.S. 765, 797-802 (1978) (Burger, C.J., concurring).
[8] *Zemel*, 381 U.S. at 16.
[9] Branzburg v. Hayes, 408 U.S. 665, 728 n.4 (Stewart, J., dissenting) (quoting *Zemel*, 381 U.S. at 16-17).
[10] *Id.*
[11] 205 U.S. 454 (1907); *see supra* ch. 6, notes 144-53 and accompanying text.
[12] 205 U.S. at 462; *see also* C. THOMAS DIENES, LEE LEVINE & ROBERT C. LIND, NEWSGATHERING AND THE LAW 23 n. 12 (3d ed. 2005).
[13] 314 U.S. 252 (1941); *see supra* ch. 6, notes 162-64 and accompanying text.
[14] 314 U.S. at 281; *see also* DIENES, et al., *supra* note 12, at 23 n. 12.
[15] Holt v. United States, 218 U.S. 245, 248-51 (1910).
[16] 360 U.S. 310, 313 (1959).
[17] 366 U.S. 717 (1961).
[18] 373 U.S. 723 (1968).
[19] 381 U.S. 532 (1965).
[20] 384 U.S. 333 (1966).
[21] 384 U.S. at 358.
[22] 384 U.S. at 357-63. Specifically, Justice Clark called for trial judges to counteract the prejudicial effects of press coverage by adopting stricter rules governing the use of the courtroom by newsmen; insulating witnesses from the reporters; controlling the release of leads, information, and gossip to the press by police officers, witnesses, and the counsel for both sides; proscribing extra-judicial statements by any lawyer, party, witness, or court official which divulged prejudicial matters; requesting city and county officials to regulate dissemination of information by their employees; warning reporters as to the impropriety of publishing information not introduced at trial; and, if necessary, sequestering the jury.
[23] 384 U.S. at 358.
[24] 443 U.S. 368 (1979).
[25] *Id.* at 374-75.
[26] *Id.* at 376.
[27] *Id.* at 376-77.
[28] *Id.* at 394.
[29] *Id.* at 391.
[30] *Id.* at 392.
[31] *Id.* at 394 (Burger, C.J., concurring).
[32] *Id.* at 400-401 (Powell, J., concurring).
[33] *Id.* at 404-405 (Rehnquist, J., concurring).
[34] *Id.* at 433 (Blackmun, J., dissenting in part and concurring in part).
[35] *Id.* at 443 (Blackmun, J., dissenting in part and concurring in part).

[36] *See* Brief of the Am. Newspaper Publishers Ass'n and the Reporters Comm. for Freedom of the Press as Amici Curiae in Support of the Petition for a Writ of Certiorari, Gannett v. DePasquale, 443 U.S. 368 (1979) (No. 77-1301), 1978 WL 207247.
[37] *See* Brief Amici Curiae of the Reporters Comm. for Freedom of the Press [and] the Nat'l Ass'n of Broadcasters in Support of Petitioner, Gannett v. DePasquale, 443 U.S. 368 (1979) (No. 77-1301), 1978 WL 207259; Brief Amici Curiae of Am. Newspaper Publishers Ass'n and Am. Soc'y of Newspaper Editors, Gannett v. DePasquale, 443 U.S. 368 (1979) (No. 77-1301), 1978 WL 207258; Brief of the N.Y. Times Co. as Amicus Curiae, Gannett v. DePasquale, 443 U.S. 368 (1979) (No. 77-1301), 1978 WL 207257; Brief of Amici Curiae the Deadline Club, the N.Y.C. Chapter of the Soc'y of Prof'l Journalists, Sigma Delta Chi; and the Soc'y of Prof'l Journalists, Sigma Delta Chi, Gannett v. DePasquale, 443 U.S. 368 (1979) (No. 77-1301), 1978 WL 207256.
[38] Brief of Petitioner, Gannett v. DePasquale, 443 U.S. 368 (1979) (No. 77-1301), 1978 WL 207249.
[39] Brief Amici Curiae of Am. Newspaper Publishers Ass'n and Am. Soc'y of Newspaper Editors, *supra* note 36.
[40] Brief of Petitioner, *supra* note 38.
[41] Brief Amici Curiae of the Reporters Comm. for Freedom of the Press [and] the Nat'l Ass'n of Broadcasters In Support of Petitioner, *supra* note 37.
[42] Brief of the New York Times Co. as Amicus Curiae, *supra* note 37.
[43] Brief of Amici Curiae the Deadline Club, the N.Y.C. Chapter of the Soc'y of Prof'l Journalists, Sigma Delta Chi; and the Soc'y of Prof'l Journalists, Sigma Delta Chi, *supra* note 37.
[44] Brief of the Am. Civil Liberties Union and the N.Y. Civil Liberties Union as Amicus Curiae, Gannett v. DePasquale, 443 U.S. 368 (1979) (No. 77-1301), 1978 WL 207254.
[45] 448 U.S. 555 (1980).
[46] *Id.* at 559.
[47] *Id.* at 560, 560 n. 2 (citing Va. Code § 19.2-266 (Supp. 1980)).
[48] *Id.*
[49] *See* Brief Amici Curiae in Support of Appellants, The Reporters Comm. for Freedom of the Press, The Associated Press Managing Editors, The Nat'l Ass'n of Broadcasters, The Nat'l Newspaper Ass'n, The Nat'l Press Club, The Radio-Television News Dirs. Ass'n, The Soc'y of Prof'l Journalists, Sigma Delta Chi, The Va. Press Association, Richmond Newspapers v. Virginia, 448 U.S. 555 (1980) (No. 79-243), 1979 WL 199921; Brief Amici Curiae of Am. Newspaper Publishers Ass'n and Am. Soc'y of Newspaper Editors in Support of Appellants, Richmond Newspapers v. Virginia, 448 U.S. 555 (1980) (No. 79-243),1979 WL 199915; Brief of the Wash. Post, Am. Broad. Cos., Inc., CBS Inc., Nat'l Broad. Co., Inc., the N.Y. Daily News, the Wall Street J., the L.A. Times, The Chi. Sun-Times, The Detroit News, the S.F. Chron., Newsday, the Boston Globe, the Phila. Inquirer, the Kansas City Times, the Kansas City Star, the Hous. Post, Buffalo Evening News, the Minneapolis Star. Minneapolis Trib., the Des Moines Reg., Des Moines Trib., the Atlanta J., the Atlanta Const., the (Louisville) Courier-J., the Louisville Times, the San Diego Union, the (San Diego) Evening Trib., the Sacramento Bee, the (Baltimore) Sun, the

(Baltimore) Evening Sun, the (Jacksonville) Fla. Times Union, Jacksonville Journal, Wichita Eagle, Wichita Beacon, the Salt Lake Trib., the (Allentown, Pa.) Morning Call, (Allentown, Pa.) Evening Chron., the Albany Times-Union, the (Albany, N.Y.) Knickerbocker News, the Wis. State J., the (Madison, Wis.) Capitol Times, the (Riverside, Cal.) Press, the (Riverside, Cal.) Enterprise, St. Joseph (Mo.) Gazette, St. Joseph (Mo.) News-Press, the Decatur (Ill.) Herald, Decatur (Ill.) Daily Review, Jackson (Tenn.) Sun, the Anniston (Ala.) Star, Anchorage (Alaska) Daily News, the (Fredericksburg, Va.) Free Lance-Star, Waukesha (Wis.) Freeman, the (Bend, Ore.) Bull., Chippewa Herald-Telegram (Chippewa Falls, Wis.), the Greenwood (Miss.) Commonwealth, Omaha Sun, the (Havre De Grace, Md.) Record, Grinnell (Iowa) Herald-Register, Homer (Alaska) News, Amici Curiae, In Support of Reversal, Richmond Newspapers v. Virginia, 448 U.S. 555 (1980) (No. 79-243),1979 WL 199918.

[50] *Richmond Newspapers*, 448 U.S. at 564-72.

[51] *Id.* at 573.

[52] *Id.* at 575-76.

[53] *Id.* at 576.

[54] Id. at 580-81.

[55] *Id.* at 581-82 (White, J., concurring).

[56] *Id.* at 601 (Blackmun, J., concurring in the judgment).

[57] *Id.* at 605 (Rehnquist, J., dissenting).

[58] *Id.* at 600 (Stewart, J., concurring in the judgment.)

[59] *Id.* at 589 (Brennan, J., concurring in the judgment).

[60] 457 U.S. 596 (1982).

[61] *Id.* at 609.

[62] *See* Brief of Amici Curiae The Miami Herald Publ'g Co., Neb. Press Ass'n and Media of Neb., Okla. Publ'g Co., Landmark Commc'ns., Inc., Daily Mail Publ'g Co., Daily Gazette Co., Gannett Co., Inc., Richmond Newspapers, Inc., Dow Jones & Co', Inc., The L.A. Times, Advance Publications, Inc., Chi. Sun-Times, Detroit Free Press, Newsday, Phila. Inquirer, Des Moines Reg. and Trib. Co., Indianapolis Star and Indianapolis News, Courier-J. and Louisville Times Co., Ariz. Republic and Phx. Gazette, Seattle Times Co., Trib. Co., Bergen Evening Rec. Corp., San Jose Mercury and San Jose News, News and Sun-Sentinel Co., Chesapeake Publ'g Corp., Associated Press, Am. Newspaper Publishers Ass'n, Am. Soc'y of Newspaper Editors, Soc'y of Prof'l Journalists, Nat'l Newspaper Ass'n, New England Newspaper Ass'n, S. Newspaper Publishers Ass'n, Ala. Press Ass'n, and Mass. Newspaper Publishers Ass'n, Globe Newspapers v. Super. Ct. for the Cnty. of Norfolk, 457 U.S. 596 (1982) (No. 81-611), 1982 WL 608564; Brief of the Nat'l Broad. Co., Inc. as Amicus Curiae, Globe Newspapers v. Super. Ct. for the Cnty. of Norfolk, 457 U.S. 596 (1982) (No. 81-611), 1981 WL 389685; Brief Amicus Curiae of the Reporters Comm. for Freedom of the Press In Support of Appellant, Globe Newspapers v. Super. Ct. for the Cnty. of Norfolk, 457 U.S. 596 (1982) (No. 81-611), 1981 WL 389686; Brief of Amici Curiae, Am. Broad. Cos., Inc.; CBS Inc.; Nat'l Ass'n of Broadcasters; Radio-Television News Dirs. Ass'n; and the Wash. Post, Globe Newspapers v. Super. Ct. for the Cnty. of Norfolk, 457 U.S. 596 (1982) (No. 81-611), 1981 WL 389684.

[63] 464 U.S. 501 (1984).

[64] *Id.* at 510.

[65] *See* Brief Amicus Curiae of Cal. Newspaper Publishers Ass'n, Press-Enter. Co. v. Super. Ct. of Cal., Riverside Cnty., 464 U.S. 501 (1984) (No. 82-556), 1982 U.S. S. Ct. Briefs LEXIS 14; Brief of Amici Curiae in Support of Petitioner Filed on Behalf of USA Today and Oakland Trib. published by Gannett Satellite Info. Network, Inc.; Salinas Californian, Stockton Rec., and Visalis Times-Delta published by Speidel Newspapers Inc.; The Sun published by The Sun Co. of San Bernardino, Cal.; San Rafael Indep. J. published by Cal. Newspapers, Inc.; The Copley Press Inc., publisher of The San Diego Union and The (San Diego) Evening Trib.; McClatchy Newspapers, publishers of The Sacramento Bee, The Modesto Bee, and The Fresno Bee; The S.F. Examiner Div. of Hearst Corp., publisher of the S.F. Examiner; The Press-Telegram, published in Long Beach by Knight-Ridder Newspapers, Inc.; The Reg. (Santa Ana); San Jose Mercury News; Gannett News Serv., Inc.; Cal. Newspaper Publishers Ass'n; and the Cal. Freedom of Info. Comm., Press-Enter. Co. v. Super. Ct. of Cal., Riverside Cnty., 464 U.S. 501 (1984) (No. 82-556), 1983 U.S. S. Ct. Briefs LEXIS 28; and Brief Amici Curiae of The Soc'y of Prof'l Journalists, Sigma Delta Chi; Am. Newspaper Publishers Ass'n; Am. Soc'y of Newspaper Editors; Associated Press; Associated Press Managing Editors Ass'n; The L.A. Times; The Miami Herald Publishing Co.; Nat'l Ass'n of Broadcasters; Nat'l Newspaper Ass'n; The New York Times Co.; Radio-Television News Directors Ass'n; Reporters Comm. for Freedom of The Press; The S.F. Chron.; and The Wash. Post, Press-Enter. Co. v. Super. Ct. of Cal., Riverside Cnty., 464 U.S. 501 (1984) (No. 82-556),1983 U.S. S. Ct. Briefs LEXIS 30 (April 9, 1983).
[66] 467 U.S. 39 (1984).
[67] *Id.* at 47.
[68] Presley v. Georgia, 130 S. Ct. 721 (2010). *See* Brief Amicus Curiae of the Reporters Comm. for Freedom of the Press in Support of Petitioner, Presley v. Georgia, 130 S. Ct. 721 (2010) (No. 09-5270), 2009 WL 2481343.
[69] 478 U.S. 1 (1986).
[70] *Id.* at 4.
[71] *Id.* at 5.
[72] *Id.* at 6.
[73] Brief Amici Curiae of Am. Newspaper Publishers Ass'n; the Soc'y of Prof'l Journalists, Sigma Delta Chi; Am' Broad. Cos., Inc.; Am. Soc'y of Newspaper Editors; CBS Inc.; Chi. Trib. Co.; Chron. Publ'g Co.; the Concord Monitor; Dow Jones & Co., Inc.; Gannett Co., Inc.; Globe Newspaper Co.; the Hearst Corp.; the Miami Herald Publ'g Co.; Minneapolis Star and Trib. Co.; Nat'l Ass'n of Broadcasters; Nat'l Newspaper Ass'n; Nat'l Pub. Radio; the Phila. Inquirer; Phx. Newspapers, Inc.; Pub. Broad. Serv.; Radio-Television News Dirs. Ass'n; Reporters Comm. for Freedom of the Press; Richmond Newspapers, Inc.; Scripps Howard; Seattle Times Co.; and the Wash. Post, Press-Enterprise Co. v. Super. Ct. of Cal., Riverside Cnty., 478 U.S. 1 (1986) (No. 84-1560), 1985 WL 669954; Brief Amici Curiae of Cal. News Orgs. in Support of Petitioner Filed on behalf of The Copley Press, Inc.; The Associated Press; L.A. Times; Nat'l Broad. Co., Inc. (NBC); McClatchy Newspapers; S.F. Chron.; Freedom Newspapers; The John P. Scripps Newspaper Group; Trib. Co.; The Press Democrat; Santa Barbara News Press; Sparks Newspapers; McGraw-Hill, Inc.; The Sun

Co.; Marin Indep. J.; Visalia Times-Delta; Cal. Newspaper Publishers Ass'n; California Freedom of Info. Comm.; The Radio and Television News Ass'n of S. Cal.; Cal. Soc'y of Newspaper Editors; The East Bay Press Club; and Radio-Television News Dirs. Ass'n NorCal, Press-Enterprise Co. v. Super. Ct. of Cal., Riverside Cnty., 478 U.S. 1 (1986) (No. 84-1560),1985 WL 669961.

[74] *Press-Enterprise II*, 478 U.S. at 15 (Stevens, J., dissenting).

[75] *Id.* at 9.

[76] *Id.* at 13-14.

[77] *Id.* at 14.

[78] El Vocero v. Puerto Rico, 508 U.S. 147 (1993).

[79] Estes v. Texas, 381 U.S. 532 (1965); *see supra* note 19 and accompanying text.

[80] *Id.* at 552 (Warren, C.J., concurring).

[81] *Id.* at 587 (Harlan, J., concurring).

[82] *Id.* at 552.

[83] *Id.* at 588-89 (Harlan, J., concurring) ("The Estes trial was a heavily publicized and highly sensational affair. I therefore put aside all other types of cases . . . . The resolution of those further questions should await an appropriate case; the Court should proceed only step by step in this unplowed field. The opinion of the Court necessarily goes no farther, for only the four members of the majority who unreservedly join the Court's opinion would resolve those questions now.").

[84] *Id.* at 614 (Stewart, J., dissenting).

[85] *Id.* at 617 (Brennan, J., dissenting) (quoting Harlan's concurrence, *supra* note 1272).

[86] Brief of the Nat'l Ass'n of Broadcasters and The Radio Television News Dirs. Ass'n as Amici Curiae, Estes v. Texas, 381 U.S. 532 (1965) (No. 256), 1965 WL 130164 at *12.

[87] Brief of the American Civil Liberties Union and the Texas Civil Liberties Union, Amici Curiae, Estes v. Texas, 381 U.S. 532 (1965) (No. 256),1965 WL 115508 at *3; Brief of the American Bar Association as Amicus Curiae, Estes v. Texas, 381 U.S. 532 (1965) (No. 256),1965 WL 115507 at *10.

[88] 449 U.S. 560 (1981).

[89] *Id.* at 573-74.

[90] *Id.* at 582.

[91] *See* Brief of Cmty. Television Found. of S. Fla., Inc., the Pub. Broad. Serv., the Fla. Public Broad. Serv., Inc., and the Educ. Broad. Corp. as Amici Curiae, Chandler v. Florida, 449 U.S. 560 (1981) (No. 79-1260), 1980 WL 339586; Brief of Amici Curiae, Fla. News Interests on Dev. and Operation of Fla. Rule, Chandler v. Florida, 449 U.S. 560 (1981) (No. 79-1260), 1980 WL 339604; Joint Brief for Amici Curiae Radio Television News Dirs. Ass'n, Am. Broad. Cos., Inc., Am. Fed'n of Television and Radio Artists (AFL-CIO), Am. Soc'y of Newspaper Editors, Associated Press Broad., Inc. , Associated Press Managing Editors, Nat'l Ass'n of Broadcasters, Nat'l Broad. Editorial Ass'n, Nat'l Broad. Co., Inc., Nat'l Newspaper Ass'n, Nat'l Press Club, Nat'l Press Photographers Ass'n, Nat'l Public Radio, the Reporters Comm. for Freedom of the Press, and Soc'y of Prof'l Journalists, Sigma Delta Chi, Chandler v. Florida, 449 U.S. 560 (1981) (No. 79-1260), 1980 WL 339605.

[92] Stewart, *supra* note 7, at 709-10.

[93] 408 U.S. 665, 684 (1972).

[94] 417 U.S. 817 (1974).
[95] 417 U.S. 843 (1974).
[96] Brief Amicus Curiae for Chi. Trib. Co., Pell v. Procunier, 417 U.S. 817 (1974) (No. 73-918), 1974 WL 185822; Brief of Hous. Chron. Publ'g Co., Amicus Curiae, Pell v. Procunier, 417 U.S. 817 (1974) (No. 73-918), 1974 WL 185929; Brief of the Wash. Post Co., the Miami Herald Publ'g Co., the Minneapolis Star and Trib. Company, N.Y. News, Inc., and the Times Mirror Co., Amici Curiae, in Support of Reversal, Pell v. Procunier, 417 U.S. 817 (1974) (No. 73-918),1974 WL 185930.
[97] 364 F.Supp 196 (N.D. Cal. 1973).
[98] 417 U.S. at 826-27.
[99] 417 U.S. at 835 (Powell, J., dissenting).
[100] 417 U.S. at 854 n. 4 (Powell, J., dissenting) (The court received testimony from three experienced reporters, two academic journalists, and an attorney with special expertise in this area. The reporters were respondent Ben H. Bagdikian, a Washington Post reporter experienced in covering prisons and interviewing inmates; Timothy Leland, a Pulitzer prize winner who is Assistant Managing Editor of the Boston Globe and head of its investigative reporting team; and John W. Machacek, a reporter for the *Rochester Times-Union*, who won a Pulitzer prize for his coverage of the Attica Prison riot. The academic journalists were Elie Abel, Dean of the Graduate School of Journalism of Columbia University, and Roy M. Fisher, Dean of the School of Journalism of the University of Missouri and former editor of the Chicago Daily News. The sixth witness was Arthur L. Liman, an attorney who served as general counsel to the New York State Special Commission on Attica. In that capacity he supervised an investigation involving 1,600 inmate interviews, at least 75 of which he conducted personally.)
[101] Brief for the Reporters Comm. for Freedom of the Press Legal Defense and Research Fund as Amicus Curiae, Saxbe v. Wash. Post Co., 417 U.S. 843 (1974) (No. 73-1265), 1974 WL 186234. Amicus briefs for the Trib. Co. and the Hous. Chron., *supra* note 96, were filed for both cases.
[102] 438 U.S. 1 (1978).
[103] *Id.* at 7.
[104] *Id.* at 16.
[105] 438 U.S. at 16 (Stewart, J., concurring in the judgment).
[106] Motion for Leave to File Brief Amici Curiae and Brief Amici Curiae of the Reporters Comm. for Freedom of the Press Legal Defense and Research Fund, Am. Soc'y of Newspaper Editors and Radio-Television News Dirs. Ass'n, Houchins v. KQED, 438 U.S. 1 (1978) (No. 76-1310), 1977 WL 205226; Brief for Kearns-Trib. Corp. as Amicus Curiae, Houchins v. KQED, 438 U.S. 1 (1978) (No. 76-1310), 1977 WL 189697; and Brief of the Nat'l Newspaper Ass'n, the Ariz. Newspapers Ass'n, the Pa. Newspaper Publishers Ass'n, the S.D. Press Ass'n As Amici Curiae in Support of Respondents, Houchins v. KQED, 438 U.S. 1 (1978) (No. 76-1310), 1977 WL 189696.
[107] 438 U.S. at 19 (Stevens, J., dissenting).
[108] DIENES ET AL., *supra* note 12, at 413.
[109] 433 U.S. 425 (1977).

[110] Pub. L. 93-526, 88 Stat. 1695, note following 44 U.S.C. § 2107 (1970 ed., Supp. V).
[111] *Nixon*, 433 U.S. at 466.
[112] Brief of Appellees the Reporters Comm. for Freedom of the Press, Am. Historical Ass'n, Am. Pol. Sci. Ass'n, et al., at 75, Nixon v. Adm'r of Gen. Servs., 433 U.S. 425 (1977) (No. 75-1605), 1977 WL 189798 (quoting Grosjean v. Am. Press Co, 297 U.S. 233, 247 (1936)).
[113] 435 U.S. 589 (1978).
[114] *See, e.g.*, DIENES ET AL., *supra* note 12, at 244. We include it here because access to the tapes in the hands of the President was an issue well before the criminal trial which brought the case to the Supreme Court's attention, because of the deference to the executive shown by the courts throughout this proceeding, and by the Supreme Court's holding that the Presidential Recordings and Materials Preservation Act, which dealt explicitly with executive branch materials, was all but dispositive in this case.
[115] *Id.* at 595.
[116] *Id.* at 596.
[117] *Id.* at 603.
[118] 435 U.S. at 609.
[119] *Id.* at 611 (White, J., dissenting).
[120] *Id.* at 612 (Marshall, J., dissenting).
[121] *Id.* at 614 (Stevens, J., dissenting).
[122] 456 U.S. 615 (1982).
[123] 5 U.S.C. § 552 (2010).
[124] 5 U.S.C. § 500 et seq. (2010).
[125] 445 U.S. 136 (1980).
[126] *Id.* at 155 (1980).
[127] *Abramson*, 456 U.S. at 618-19.
[128] *See* Brief Amici Curiae of The Soc'y of Prof'l Journalists, Sigma Delta Chi; The Am. Soc'y of Newspaper Editors; The Nat'l Ass'n of Broadcasters; The Nat'l Newspaper Ass'n; The Radio-Television News Dirs. Ass'n; and The Reporters Comm. for Freedom of the Press in Support of Respondent, FBI v. Abramson, 456 U.S. 615 (1982) (No. 80-1735), 1981 WL 390061.
[129] *Abramson*, 456 U.S. at 631-32.
[130] 456 U.S. 595 (1982).
[131] *See* Brief Amici Curiae of the Am. Newspaper Publishers Ass'n; the Am. Soc'y of Newspaper Editors; the Nat'l Ass'n of Broad.; the Nat'l Newspaper Ass'n; the Reporters Comm. for Freedom of the Press; and the Soc'y of Prof'l Journalists, Sigma Delta Chi in Support of Respondent, U.S. Dep't of State v. Wash. Post, 456 U.S. 595 (1982) (No. 81-535), 1982 WL 608533.
[132] *Id.* at 602-603.
[133] 489 U.S. 749 (1989).
[134] *See* Brief of Amici Curiae the Am. Newspaper Publishers Ass'n, the Am. Soc'y of Newspaper Editors, Nat'l Ass'n of Broadcasters, the Miami Herald Publ'g Co., the Wash. Post and McClatchy Newspapers, Inc., U.S. Dep't of Justice v. Reporters Comm. for Freedom of the Press, 489 U.S. 749 (1989) (No. 87-1379), 1988 WL 1026013.
[135] *Id.* at 780.

[136] 541 U.S. 157 (2004).
[137] Brief of Amici Curiae Reporters Comm. for Freedom of the Press, Am. Soc'y of Newspaper Editors, Radio-Television News Dirs. Ass'n, Soc'y of Prof'l Journalists, Ass'n of Alternative Newsweeklies, Nat'l Press Club, Investigative Reporters and Editors, Inc., and Nat'l Freedom of Info. Coalition in Support of Respondent, Nat'l Archives and Rec. Admin. v. Favish, 541 U.S. 157 (2004) (No. 02-954), 2003 WL 22038397, and Brief of Amicus Curiae Silha Center for the Study of Media Ethics and Law in Support of Respondent Allan J. Favish, Nat'l Archives and Rec. Admin. v. Favish, 541 U.S. 157 (2004) (No. 02-954), 2003 WL 22019552 (Aug. 21, 2003).
[138] 542 U.S. 367 (2004).
[139] *See* Brief Amici Curiae of The Reporters Comm. for Freedom of the Press, Am. Soc'y of Newspaper Editors and Soc'y of Prof'l Journalists in support of Respondents, Chaney v. U.S. Dist. Ct. for D.C., 542 U.S. 367 (2004) (No. 03-475), 2004 WL 522595.
[140] Fed. Open Market Comm. v. Merrill, 443 U.S. 340 (1979). *See* Brief for Amici Curiae Reporters Comm. for Freedom of the Press and Freedom of Information Clearinghouse, Fed. Open Market Comm. v. Merrill, 443 U.S. 340 (1979) (No. 77-1387), 1978 WL 207107.
[141] U.S. v. Webber Aircraft Corp., 465 U.S. 792 (1984). *See* Brief of the Reporters Comm. for Freedom of the Press, et al. (FOI Service Center and the Texas Daily Newspaper Ass'n), as Amici Curiae, U.S. v. Webber Aircraft Corp., 465 U.S. 792 (1984) (No. 82-1616), 1983 U.S. S. Ct. Briefs LEXIS 610.
[142] L.A. Police Dep't v. United Reporting Publ'g Corp., 528 U.S. 32 (1999). *See* Brief Amici Curiae of the Reporters Comm. for Freedom of the Press, Am. Court and Commercial Newspapers, Inc., Am. Soc'y of Newspaper Editors, and the Nat'l Newspaper Ass'n in Support of Respondent, L.A. Police Dep't v. United Reporting Publ'g Corp., 528 U.S. 32 (1999) (No. 98-678), 1999 WL 513826, and Brief of Amicus Curiae Investigative Reporters and Editors, Inc., in Support of Respondent, L.A. Police Dep't v. United Reporting Publ'g Corp., 528 U.S. 32 (1999) (No. 98-678), 1999 WL 516060 (July 20, 1999).
[143] Reno v. Condon, 528 U.S. 141 (2000). *See* Brief Amici Curiae of the Reporters Comm. for Freedom of the Press, the Am. Soc'y of Newspaper Editors and the Soc'y of Professional Journalists in Support of Respondents, Reno v. Condon, 528 U.S. 141 (2000) (No. 98-1464), 1999 WL 688443.
[144] 130 S. Ct. 2811 (2010). *See* Brief Amici Curiae of the Reporters Comm. for Freedom of the Press, Gannett Co., Inc., Nat'l Newspaper Ass'n, Newspaper Ass'n of Am., The Radio-Television Digital News Ass'n, and Soc'y of Prof'l Journalists, in Support of Respondents, John Doe #1 v. Reed, 130 S. Ct. 2811 (2010) (No. 09-559), 2010 WL 1256466; Brief Amici Curiae of Nat'l and Wash. State News Publishers, News Broad. and News Media Prof'l Ass'ns in Support of Respondents, John Doe #1 v. Reed, 130 S. Ct. 2811 (2010) (No. 09-559), 2010 WL 1362079.
[145] U.S. Dep't of Justice v. Tax Analysts, 492 U.S. 136 (1989). *See* Brief Amicus Curiae of the Reporters Comm. for Freedom of the Press in Support of the Respondent, U.S. Dep't of Justice v. Tax Analysts, 492 U.S. 136 (1989) (No. 88-782), 1989 WL 1127764.

[146] Dep't of Interior v. Klamath Water Users Protective Ass'n, 532 U.S. 1 (2001). *See* Brief Amici Curiae of The Reporters Comm. for Freedom of the Press, Am. Soc'y of Newspaper Editors, and the Soc'y of Prof'l Journalists in support of Respondent, Dep't of Interior v. Klamath Water Users Protective Ass'n, 532 U.S. 1 (2001) (No. 99-1871), 2000 WL 1845932.

[147] Owasso Independent School Dist. No. I-011 v. Falvo, 534 U.S. 426 (2002). *See* Brief Amici Curiae of The Reporters Comm. for Freedom of the Press and The Student Press Law Ctr. Urging Reversal, Owasso Independent School Dist. No. I-011 v. Falvo, 534 U.S. 426 (2002) (No. 00-1073), 2001 WL 967496.

[148] Gonzaga University v. Doe, 536 U.S. 273 (2002). *See* Brief Amici Curiae of The Reporters Comm. for Freedom of the Press, The Student Press Law Ctr., Soc'y of Prof'l Journalists, and Security on Campus, Inc., in support of Petitioners, Gonzaga University v. Doe, 536 U.S. 273 (2002) (No. 01-679), 2002 WL 312502.

[149] Smith v. Doe, 538 U.S. 84 (2003). *See* Motion for Leave to File Brief Amicus Curiae, and Brief Amicus Curiae of The Reporters Comm. for Freedom of the Press, in Support of Petitioners, Smith v. Doe, 538 U.S. 84 (2003) (No. 01-729), 2002 WL 1269892.

[150] Conn. Dep't of Pub. Safety v. Doe, 538 U.S. 1 (2003). *See* Motion for Leave to File Amicus Curiae Brief and Brief Amicus Curiae of The Reporters Comm. for Freedom of the Press in support of Petitioners, Conn. Dep't of Pub. Safety v. Doe, 538 U.S. 1 (2003) (No. 01-1231), 2002 WL 1728586.

[151] Doe v. Chao, 540 U.S. 614 (2004). *See* Brief Amicus Curiae of the Reporters Comm. for Freedom of the Press in Support of Respondent, Doe v. Chao, 540 U.S. 614 (2004) (No. 02-1377), 2003 WL 22304854.

[152] Taylor v. Sturgell, 553 U.S. 880 (2008). *See* Brief of Amici Curiae the Nat'l Security Archive, the Reporters Comm. for Freedom of the Press, OpenTheGovernment.org, the Nat'l Whistleblower Ctr., and the Electronic Frontier Found. in support of Petitioner, Taylor v. Sturgell, 553 U.S. 880 (2008) (No. 07-371), 2008 WL 563433.

[153] *See* Reporters Comm. for Freedom of the Press, http://www.rcfp.org/news/documents/20100715-amicusbriefinsnydervphelps.pdf.

[154] 436 U.S. 547 (1978).

[155] *Id.* at 551.

[156] *Id.*

[157] *Id.* at 442. A subpoena *duces tecum* commands a witness to produce a specified tangible item at trial or deposition. BLACK'S LAW DICTIONARY (Bryan A. Garner ed. 2010).

[158] *Id.*

[159] *Id.* at 553.

[160] *See* Brief for Amici Curiae the Reporters Comm. for Freedom of the Press, the Am. Newspaper Publishers Ass'n, the Nat'l Newspaper Ass'n, the Nat'l Ass'n of Broadcasters, the Am. Soc'y of Newspaper Editors, the Associated Press Managing Editors, the Radio-Television News Dirs. Ass'n, the Student Press Law Ctr., the Soc'y of Prof'l Journalists (Sigma Delta Chi), the Newspaper Guild (AFL-CIO), the Am. Fed'n of Television and Radio Artists (AFL-CIO), the Cal. Newspaper Publishers Ass'n, Zurcher v. Stanford Daily, 436 U.S. 547 (1978) (No. 76-1484), 1977 WL 189749.

[161] *See* Brief for the United States as Amicus Curiae, Zurcher v. Stanford Daily, 436 U.S. 547 (1978) (No. 76-1484), 1978 WL 206910; Brief Amici Curiae Submitted by the States

of Alabama, Alaska, California, Georgia, Idaho, Illinois, Indiana, Maryland, Massachusetts, Mississippi, Nebraska, New Hampshire, New Mexico, Oregon, Pennsylvania, Utah and Virginia, Zurcher v. Stanford Daily, 436 U.S. 547 (1978) (No. 76-1484),1977 WL 189747; Brief of Amici Curiae, the Nat'l Dist. Att'ys Ass'n and the Cal. Dist. Att'ys Ass'n, in Support of Petitioners, Zurcher v. Stanford Daily, 436 U.S. 547 (1978) (No. 76-1484),1977 WL 189746; and Brief, Amici Curiae, of Ams. for Effective Law Enforcement, Inc. and the Intern'l Ass'n of Chiefs of Police, Inc., in Support of the Petitioners, Zurcher v. Stanford Daily, 436 U.S. 547 (1978) (No. 76-1484), 1977 WL 189745.

[162] *See* Brief of the Nat'l Ass'n of Criminal Defense Lawyers, Inc., Amicus Curiae, in Support of the Position of Respondents, Zurcher v. Stanford Daily, 436 U.S. 547 (1978) (No. 76-1484),1977 WL 189748.

[163] 436 U.S. at 564-65.

[164] *Id.* at 565.

[165] *Id.* at 570 (Powell, J., concurring).

[166] 436 U.S. at 574 (Stewart, J., dissenting).

[167] *Id.* at 577.

[168] 436 U.S. at 567.

[169] 42 U.S.C. 2000aa (2010).

[170] *Id.*

[171] 501 U.S. 663 (1991).

[172] *Id.* at 665. *See also* Bill Salisbury, *Burning the Source*, WASH. JOURNALISM REV., Sept. 1991, at 18. Much of this history and analysis is adapted from Easton, *supra* ch. 7, note 78.

[173] Salisbury, *supra* note 172, at 19-20. According to Salisbury, the *Pioneer Press* reporter involved, Cohen refused even to describe the information until he received a promise of confidentiality.

[174] *Id.* Associated Press reporter Gary Nelson and WCCO-TV reporter Dave Nimmer also received the information. Nelson's stories did not name Cohen, while Nimmer decided the story was not newsworthy. *Id.*

[175] *Cohen*, 501 U.S. at 665-66.

[176] Salisbury, *supra* note 172, at 21-22.

[177] *Cohen*, 501 U.S. at 666. Cohen said he was fired, and that position was adopted by the Supreme Court. According to Salisbury, his supervisor said he resigned. Salisbury, *supra* note 172, at 22.

[178] *Cohen*, 501 U.S. at 666.

[179] Cohen v. Cowles Media Co., 445 N.W.2d 248, 260 (Minn. Ct. App. 1989).

[180] Cohen v. Cowles Media Co., 457 N.W.2d 199, 203 (Minn. 1990).

[181] In a successful promissory estoppel action, one who makes, then breaks, a promise is prevented from denying the existence of contract, despite the absence of a contract formality. *See Cohen*, 501 U.S. 663 (1991).

[182] *Id.* at 205.

[183] *Cohen*, 501 U.S. at 667.

[184] Dissenting opinions were written by Justice Blackmun, joined by Justices Marshall and Souter, and Justice Souter, joined by Justices Marshall, Blackmun, and O'Connor. *Id.* at 672, 676.
[185] *Id.* at 668-69 (quoting Smith v. Daily Mail Publ'g, 443 U.S. 97, 103 (1979)).
[186] *Id.* at 669.
[187] 485 U.S. 46 (1988). *See supra* ch. 6, notes 278-83 and accompanying text.
[188] 501 U.S. at 671-72.
[189] 501 U.S. at 672-76 (Blackmun, J., dissenting).
[190] 501 U.S. at 676-679 (Souter, J., dissenting).
[191] Cohen v. Cowles Media Co., 479 N.W.2d 387 (Minn. 1992).
[192] ELLIOT C. ROTHENBERG, THE TAMING OF THE PRESS: *COHEN V. COWLES MEDIA COMPANY* 218 (1999). In the interest of full disclosure, Rothenberg cites my own ("A pro-media law professor") appraisal of this case as "cut[ting] short the natural evolution of First Amendment protection for newsgathering and set[ting] the stage for many wrongheaded opinions coming out of the lower courts today." *Id.* at 254 (quoting Easton, *supra* ch. 7, note 78, at 1153.
[193] ROTHENBERG, *supra* note 192, at 180. *See also* Brief of Amici Curiae Advance Publications, Inc., Am. Newspaper Publishers Ass'n, Am. Soc'y of Newspaper Editors, Associated Press, The Copley Press, Inc., Gannett Co., Inc., Newsletter Ass'n, the N.Y. Times Co., and the Times Mirror Co., in Support of Respondents, Cohen v. Cowles Media, 501 U.S. 663 (No. 90-634), 1991 WL 11007832.
[194] ROTHENBERG, *supra* note 192, at 180.
[195] *Id.* at 134 (quoting Theodore L. Glasser, *Reporters Seen as Winners in* Cohen *Verdict*, MINN. J., Oct. 4, 1988, at 1).
[196] *Id.* at 166.
[197] *Id.* at 214 (quoting Floyd Abrams, *Battles Not Worth Fighting*, WASH. POST, June 13, 1991, A21).
[198] 526 U.S. 603(1998).
[199] 526 U.S. 808 (1998).
[200] Linda Greenhouse, *Police Violate Privacy in Home Raids with Journalists*, N.Y. TIMES, May 25, 1999, available at http://query.nytimes.com/gst/fullpage.html?res=9B05E1D81231F936A15756C0A96F958260 &sec=&spon=&pagewanted=all.
[201] Cable News Network, Inc. v. Berger, 526 U.S. 1154 (1999) (denying certiorari).
[202] *Hanlon*, 526 U.S. at 810.
[203] Brief Amici Curiae of ABC, Inc., et al. in Support of Petitioners in No. 97-1927 and Respondents in No. 98-83. A.H. Belo Corp.; Allied Daily Newspapers of Wash., Inc.; Am. Soc'y of Newspaper Editors; The Associated Press; Cal. Newspaper Publishers Ass'n; CBS Broad. Inc.; The Copley Press, Inc.; Dow Jones & Co., Inc.; Fox Television Stations, Inc.; Gannett Co., Inc.; The Hearst Corp.; King World Prods., Inc.; The L.A. Times; Mag. Publishers of Am., Inc.; The McClatchy Co.; Nat'l Ass'n Of Broadcasters; Nat'l Broad. Co., Inc.; Newspaper Ass'n of Am., Inc.; The N.Y. Times Co.; The Orange County Reg., A Div. of Freedom Commc'ns, Inc.; The Reporters Comm. for Freedom of the Press; Trib. Co.; Univision Communications, Inc.; The Wash. Post; and Washington State Ass'n of

Broad., Wilson v. Layne, 526 U.S. 603 (No. 98-83), Hanlon v. Berger, 526 U.S. 808 (No. 97-1927), 1998 WL 901781 (Dec. 28, 1988).
[204] Brief for Respondents Cable News Network, Inc., Turner Broad. Sys., Inc., Robert Rainey, Donald Hooper, and Jack Hamann in Support of Petitioners, Hanlon v. Berger, 526 U.S. 808 (No. 97-1927), 1998 WL 901783.
[205] 526 U.S. at 613.
[206] 526 U.S. at 614.
[207] 532 U.S. 514 (2001).

Chapter 9

[1] 532 U.S. 514 (2001). This chapter is adapted from Eric B. Easton, *Ten Years After:* Bartnicki v. Vopper *as Laboratory for First Amendment Analysis and Advocacy,* 50 U. Louisville L. Rev. 287 (2011).
[2] Federal Omnibus Crime Control and Safe Streets Act of 1968, 18 U.S.C. § 2511(1)(2010) ("Except as otherwise specifically provided in this chapter, any person who (c) intentionally discloses, or endeavors to disclose, to any other person the contents of any wire, oral, or electronic communication, knowing or having reason to know that the information was obtained through the interception of a wire, oral, or electronic communication in violation of this subsection; ... shall be punished...."); Pennsylvania Wiretapping and Electronic Surveillance Control Act, 18 PA. CONS. STAT. § 5703 (2010) ("Except as otherwise provided in this chapter, a person is guilty of a felony of the third degree if he (2) intentionally discloses or endeavors to disclose to any other person the contents of any wire, electronic or oral communication, or evidence derived therefrom, knowing or having reason to know that the information was obtained through the interception of a wire, electronic or oral communication....").
[3] *Id.* at 535 ("...a stranger's illegal conduct does not suffice to remove the *First Amendment* shield from speech about a matter of public concern.").
[4] *See infra* Part B.
[5] *See infra* Part C.
[6] *See infra* Part D.
[7] 283 U.S. 697 (1931).
[8] *See supra* ch. 5.
[9] 408 U.S. 665 (1972).
[10] *See supra* ch. 7.
[11] *Id.* at 525.
[12] 18 U.S.C. § 2520(a)(2010)("... any person whose wire, oral, or electronic communication is intercepted, disclosed, or intentionally used in violation of this chapter may in a civil action recover from the person or entity, other than the United States, which engaged in that violation such relief as may be appropriate."); 18 Pa. Cons. Stat. § 5725(a)(2010)("Any person whose wire, electronic or oral communication is intercepted, disclosed or used in violation of this chapter shall have a civil cause of action against any

person who intercepts, discloses or uses or procures any other person to intercept, disclose or use, such communication….").

[13] *Wyoming Valley*, http://en.wikipedia.org/wiki/Wyoming_Valley.

[14] *Wyoming Valley West School District*, http://en.wikipedia.org/wiki/Wyoming_Valley_West_School_District.

[15] *Id.*

[16] *Union Head: Furlough Slips Add Tension to WVW Contract Talks; Teachers and Board Directors in the Wyoming Valley West School District Returning to Bargaining Table This Week*, TIMES LEADER (Wilkes-Barre), Oct. 19, 1992, available at http://www.timesleader.com/archive/6865272.html.

[17] *Volunteer Work Halted by Teachers at WVW; Activities and Chaperoning are Falling Victim to a Contract Dispute Between Teachers and the School District*, TIMES LEADER (Wilkes-Barre), March 19, 1993, available at http://www.timesleader.com/archive/6865272.html.

[18] *Teachers at WVW Threaten to Strike; The Situation Appears 'Bleak,' A School Director Concedes*, TIMES LEADER (Wilkes-Barre), May 22, 1993, available at http://www.timesleader.com/archive/6865272.html.

[19] *Id.*

[20] *Contract Offer Best We Can Do, Says WVW Board Member; Under the Proposal, Teachers would receive a 3-Percent Raise Each Year for the Next Three Years*, TIMES LEADER (Wilkes-Barre), June 7, 1993, available at http://www.timesleader.com/archive/6865272.html.

[21] *WVW Could See Strike in Exam Week; Salary Increases and a Health Insurance Plan are the Two Chief Points of Contention, the Head of the Teachers' Union Says*, TIMES LEADER (Wilkes-Barre), May 29, 1993, available at http://www.timesleader.com/archive/6865272.html.

[22] *Id.*

[23] *Striking Wyoming Valley West Teachers Picket the High School Friday in Plymouth While Seniors File into the Cafeteria; Economics Lesson; Valley West Strike to End Tuesday, But Battle Over Contract Will Continue*, TIMES LEADER (Wilkes-Barre), June 6, 1993, available at http://www.timesleader.com/archive/6865272.html. The teachers picketed on Friday and Monday, then went back to school on Tuesday in compliance with a state statute. *Id.*

[24] A transcript of the conversation between Bartnicki and Kane was prepared by WILK Radio, one of the defendant's in *Bartnicki v. Vopper*, and a copy of the transcript is attached to the Media Defendants' Answer (29a-30a) and their Motion for Summary Judgment, as Exhibit "A" (315a-326a). Amended Brief of Appellants, Bartnicki v. Vopper, 200 F.3d 109 (3d Cir. 1999) (No. 98-7156), 1998 WL 34082380 at *8. The exact date of the conversation is not in the record.

[25] *Id.* at *3.

[26] *Id.*

[27] *Id.* at *8.

[28] *Id.* at *6.

[29] *Id.* at *7 (citing Yocum's deposition).

[30] *Id.*

[31] *Id.* Yocum also gave copies to Rob Neyhard at WARM Radio, and Kane's deposition states that copies were given to the *Times Leader* and *Citizens' Voice* newspapers, as well as television stations WNEP-TV and WBRE-TV. Only Yocum, Vopper, and the two radio stations that carried Vopper's program were named as defendants in the subsequent lawsuit. *Id.* at *7-8.
[32] *Id.*
[33] *Id.* at *8.
[34] *Arbitrator Suggests Raises at WVW; The Negotiator Says Teachers Should Receive their Requested Salary Increase, but Directors Seem Unwilling to Sway from their Offer,* TIMES LEADER (Wilkes-Barre), Sept. 28, 1993, available at http://www.timesleader.com/archive/6865272.html. The Supreme Court opinion says the parties accepted the arbitrator's proposal, 512 U.S. at 519, but the contemporaneous news reports seem more reliable on this point.
[35] 512 U.S. at 519.
[36] Brief of Appellees, Bartnicki v. Vopper, 200 F.3d 109 (3d Cir. 1999), 1998 WL 34083465 at 5. Indeed, the District Attorney for Wilkes-Barre testified that Vopper and WILK were so irresponsible that his office refuses to send press releases to WILK. Brief of Pennsylvania State Education Association as Amicus Curiae in Support of Plaintiffs-Appellees, Bartnicki v. Vopper, 200 F.3d 109 (3d. Cir.1999) (No. 98-7156), 1998 WL 34083460 at *3.
[37] *Alleged Threat by Union Heightens WVW Friction; Those Who Have Heard the Tape Allege Someone Says School Directors Could Suffer Property Damage At Their Homes if They Do Not Make Contract Concessions*, TIMES LEADER (Wilkes-Barre), Oct. 3, 1993, available at http://www.timesleader.com/archive/6865272.html.
[38] Jim Van Nostrand, *DA Will Probe Alleged Threats Upon WVW; Several Directors Say They Will Ask Fellow Board Members to Formally Request an Investigation, Perhaps at Tonight's Meeting*, TIMES LEADER (Wilkes-Barre), Oct. 2, 1993, available at http://www.timesleader.com/archive/6865272.html.
[39] Amended Brief of Appellants, Bartnicki v. Vopper, 200 F.3d 109 (3d Cir. 1999) (No. 98-7156), 1998 WL 34082380 at *7.
[40] Interview with Donald Brobst of Rosenn, Jenkins & Greewald, L.L.P., June 25, 2010 [hereinafter Brobst Interview] (on file with author).
[41] *The Battle Ends; Valley West Board OKs Pact on 5-4 Vote*, TIMES LEADER (Wilkes-Barre), Nov. 4, 1993, available at http://www.timesleader.com/archive/6865272.html.
[42] One section of the Federal Omnibus Crime Control and Safe Streets Act of 1968 provides that "any person whose wire, oral, or electronic communication is intercepted, disclosed, or intentionally used in violation of this chapter may in a civil action recover from the person or entity which engaged in the violation such relief as may be appropriate." 18 U.S.C. § 2520(a)(2009). Similarly, one section of the Pennsylvania Wiretapping and Electronic Surveillance Control Act provides that "Any person whose wire, electronic, or oral communication is intercepted, disclosed or used in violation of this chapter shall have a civil cause of action against any person who intercepts, discloses or uses or procures any

other person to intercept, disclose or use, such communication.... 18 Pa. Cons. Stat. § 5725(a)(2009).
[43] Amended Brief of Appellants, Bartnicki v. Vopper, 200 F.3d 109 (3d Cir.1999) (No. 98-7156), 1998 WL 34082380 at *3.
[44] *Id.*
[45] *Id.* at *4.
[46] *Id.*
[47] *Id.*
[48] Memorandum & Order, Bartnicki v. Vopper, Civ. No. 3:CV-94-1201 (M.D. Pa. 1996), 1996 U.S. Dist. LEXIS 22517 at *12.
[49] Amended Brief of Appellants, Bartnicki v. Vopper, 200 F.3d 109 (3d Cir. 1999) (No. 98-7156), 1998 WL 34082380 at *5. The court ruled that the orders denying summary judgment involved "controlling questions of law as to which there is substantial ground for difference of opinion and that an immediate appeal... will materially advance the ultimate determination of this litigation." *Id.* As articulated by the Third Circuit, those questions were:

> (1) whether the imposition of liability on the media Defendants under the [wiretapping statutes] solely for broadcasting the newsworthy tape on the Defendant Fred Williams' radio news/public affairs program, when the tape was illegally intercepted and recorded by unknown persons who were not agents of the Defendants, violates the First Amendment; and (2) whether imposition of liability under the aforesaid [wiretapping statutes] on Defendant Jack Yocum solely for providing the anonymously intercepted and recorded tape to the media Defendants violates the First Amendment.

200 F.3d at 113-114.
[50] Amended Brief of Appellants, Bartnicki v. Vopper, 200 F.3d 109 (3d Cir. 1999) (No. 98-7156), 1998 WL 34082380 at *2.
[51] *Id.*
[52] *See* Brief of Appellees, Bartnicki v. Vopper, 200 F.3d 109 (3d Cir. 1999) (No. 98-7156), 1998 WL 34083465 and Addendum, 1998 WL 34082372; Brief on Behalf of Appellant Jack Yocum, Bartnicki v. Vopper, 200 F.3d 109 (3d Cir. 1999) (No. 98-7156), 1998 WL 34082376; and Amended Brief of Appellants, Bartnicki v. Vopper, 200 F.3d 109 (3d Cir.1999) (No. 98-7156), 1998 WL 34082380.
[53] *See* Brief of Pennsylvania State Education Association as Amicus Curiae in Support of Plaintiffs-Appellees, Bartnicki v. Vopper, 200 F.3d 109 (3d. Cir.1999) (No. 98-7156), 1998 WL 34083460.
[54] Brief for the United States, Bartnicki v. Vopper, 200 F.3d 109 (3d Cir.1999) (No. 98-7156), 1998 WL 34082480 at *1.
[55] 200 F.3d at 129.
[56] 530 U.S. 1260 (2000).
[57] Brief in Support of Media Defendants' Motion for Summary Judgment, Bartnicki v. Vopper, Civ. No. 3:CV-94-1201 (M.D. Pa. 1996), 1966 U.S. Dist. LEXIS 22517, at *18.
[58] *Id.* at 22.

[59] Brobst Interview, *supra* note 40.
[60] Brief in Support of Media Defendants' Motion for Summary Judgment, *supra* note 57, at *12-18. For a discussion of this line of cases, see *supra* ch. 6, pt. F.
[61] Memorandum & Order, Bartnicki v. Vopper, Civ. No. 3:CV-94-1201 (M.D. Pa. 1996), 1996 U.S. Dist. LEXIS 22517 at *10.
[62] Brobst Interview, *supra* note 40.
[63] Memorandum & Order, Bartnicki v. Vopper, Civ. No. 3:CV-94-1201 (M.D. Pa. 1996), 1996 U.S. Dist. LEXIS 22517 at 11 (quoting Cohen v. Cowles Media Co., 501 U.S. 663, 669 (1991).
[64] As applied to First Amendment claims, the doctrine goes back at least as far as *Grosjean*, which contained Justice Sutherland's dictum that owners of newspapers are not "immune from any of the ordinary forms of taxation for the support of government." Grosjean v. American Press, 297 U.S. 233, 250 (1936).
[65] Memorandum & Order, Bartnicki v. Vopper, Civ. No. 3:CV-94-1201 (M.D. Pa. 1996), 1996 U.S. Dist. LEXIS 22517 at *10.
[66] *Id.*
[67] *See, e.g.,* Turner Broadcasting System, Inc. v. FCC (Turner I), 520 U.S. 180, 185 (1997)(upholding legislation requiring cable television operators to carry local broadcast signals…) & Turner Broadcasting System, Inc. v. FCC (Turner II), 512 U.S. 622, 661-62 (1994) (but only after imposing "the intermediate scrutiny applicable to content-neutral restrictions that impose an incidental burden on speech.").
[68] *See supra* ch. 6, pt. F.
[69] *Florida Star*, 491 U.S. 524, 535 n. 8 (1989):

> The *Daily Mail* principle does not settle the issue of whether, in cases where information has been acquired unlawfully by a newspaper or by a source, government may ever punish not only the unlawful acquisition, but the ensuing publication as well. This issue was raised but not definitively resolved in New York Times Co. v. United States, 403 U.S. 713 (1971), and reserved in Landmark Communications, Inc. v. Virginia, 435 U.S. 829 (1978). We have no occasion to address it here.

[70] Memorandum & Order, Bartnicki v. Vopper, Civ. No. 3:CV-94-1201 (M.D. Pa. 1996), 1966 U.S. Dist. LEXIS 22517 at *12.
[71] Media Defendants' Brief in Support of Their Motion for Reconsideration, Memorandum & Order, Bartnicki v. Vopper, Civ. No. 3:CV-94-1201 (M.D. Pa. 1996), July 1996, at 6 (on file with author).
[72] *Id.* at 7.
[73] Brobst Interview, *supra* note 40.
[74] Amended Brief of Appellants, Bartnicki v. Vopper, 200 F.3d 109 (3d Cir.1999) (No. 98-7156), 1998 WL 34082380 at *10.
[75] *Id.* at *19.

[76] *Id.* at *20. One could argue the opposite position, of course: that the government's interest in protecting government speech is lower than its interest in protecting private speech, albeit private speech on a public matter. *But see* Boettger v. Loverro, 597 A.2d 712, 720-21 (Pa. 1991) ("Thus, the legislature intended for the public interest in a free press to supersede the interests of an individual whose private conversation regarding his illegal activities had been lawfully intercepted and lawfully obtained by a newspaper.").
[77] Amended Brief of Appellants, Bartnicki v. Vopper, 200 F.3d 109 (3d Cir.1999) (No. 98-7156), 1998 WL 34082380 at *22 (citing Peavy v. New Times, Inc., 976 F. Supp. 532 (N.D. Tex. 1997)). The following year, however, the Peavy decision would be reversed in pertinent part by the United States Court of Appeals for the Fifth Circuit, which applied an intermediate scrutiny test. Peavy v. WFAA-TV, Inc., 221 F.3d 158,193 (1999).
[78] Amended Brief of Appellants, Bartnicki v. Vopper, 200 F.3d 109 (3d Cir.1999) (No. 98-7156), 1998 WL 34082380 at *25.
[79] *Id.* at *25-26.
[80] Brief of Appellees, Bartnicki v. Vopper, 200 F.3d 109 (3d Cir. 1999) (No. 98-7156), 1998 WL 34083465 at *11.
[81] *Id.* at *11-12 (citing Natoli v. Sullivan, 606 N.Y.S.2d 504 (N.Y. Sup. Ct. 1993), *aff'd*, 616 N.Y.S.2d 318 (N.Y. App. 1994)).
[82] Brief of Appellees, Bartnicki v. Vopper, 200 F.3d 109 (3d Cir. 1999) (No. 98-7156), 1998 WL 34083465 at *17.
[83] *Id.* at *20.
[84] *See supra* note 1467.
[85] Brief of Appellees, Bartnicki v. Vopper, 200 F.3d 109 (3d Cir. 1999) (No. 98-7156), 1998 WL 34083465 at*21.
[86] *Id.* at *13.
[87] *Id.* at *15.
[88] Brief on Behalf of Appellant Jack Yocum, Bartnicki v. Vopper, 200 F.3d 109 (3d Cir. 1999) (No. 98-7156), 1998 WL 34082376 at *15 (citing 408 U.S. 665 (1972)).
[89] Brief of Appellees, Bartnicki v. Vopper, 200 F.3d 109 (3d Cir. 1999) (No. 98-7156), 1998 WL 34083465 at *28-29.
[90] Brief of Pennsylvania State Education Association as Amicus Curiae in Support of Plaintiffs-Appellees, Bartnicki v. Vopper, 200 F.3d 109 (3d. Cir.1999) (No. 98-7156), 1998 WL 34083460 at *15 n. 7 (discussing Boehner v. McDermott, 1998 U.S. Dist. LEXIS 11509 (D.D.C. July 27, 1998), which held that "protecting the privacy of electronic communications is not of sufficiently 'high order' to justify punishing publication of such communications.").
[91] Brief of Pennsylvania State Education Association as Amicus Curiae in Support of Plaintiffs-Appellees, Bartnicki v. Vopper, 200 F.3d 109 (3d Cir.1999) (No. 98-7156), 1998 WL 34083460 at *7-8.
[92] *Id.* at *14, *18-19.
[93] *Id.* at *16.
[94] Brief for the United States, Bartnicki v. Vopper, 200 F.3d 109 (3d Cir. 1999) (No. 98-7156), 1999 WL 34082480.
[95] 28 U.S.C. § 2403 (a).
[96] Brobst Interview, *supra* note 40.

[97] Brief for the United States, Bartnicki v. Vopper, 200 F.3d 109 (3d Cir. 1999) (No. 98-7156), 1999 WL 34082480 at *10.
[98] *Id.* at *11.
[99] *Id.* at *10.
[100] *Id.* at *11.
[101] *Id.* at *11-12.
[102] 200 F.3d at 117.
[103] *Id.* at 118 (quoting *Cohen*, 501 U.S. at 669).
[104] 200 F.3d at 121.
[105] *Id.* at 122 (quoting Renton v. Playtime Theatres, Inc., 475 U.S. 41, 48 (1985).
[106] *Id.* at 123.
[107] *Id.* at 125.
[108] *Id.* at 126.
[109] *Id.* at 133 (Pollock, J., dissenting) (quoting Boehner v. McDermott, 191 F.3d 463, 470 (D.C. Cir. 1999)).
[110] *Id.* at 128.
[111] Brobst Interview, *supra* note 40.
[112] Petition for Writ of Certiorari, Bartnicki v. Vopper, 532 U.S. 514 (2001) (No. 99-1687 & -1728), 2000 U.S. S.Ct. Briefs LEXIS 1059.
[113] *See* http://www.bredhoff.com.
[114] Petition for Writ of Certiorari, Bartnicki v. Vopper, 532 U.S. 514 (2001) (No. 99-1687 & -1728), 2000 U.S. S.Ct. Briefs LEXIS 1059 at *20.
[115] H.W. PERRY, DECIDING TO DECIDE: AGENDA SETTING IN THE UNITED STATES SUPREME COURT 127-28 (1991).
[116] Petition for Writ of Certiorari, Bartnicki v. Vopper, 532 U.S. 514 (2001) (No. 99-1687 & -1728), 2000 U.S. S.Ct. Briefs LEXIS 1059 at *24.
[117] 200 F.3d at 128.
[118] Petition for Writ of Certiorari, Bartnicki v. Vopper, 532 U.S. 514 (2001) (No. 99-1687), 2000 U.S. S.Ct. Briefs LEXIS 1059 at *25-26 (emphasis in the original).
[119] Petition for Writ of Certiorari, Bartnicki v. Vopper, 532 U.S. 514 (2001) (No. 99-1728), 2000 U.S. S.Ct. Briefs LEXIS 1063.
[120] Brobst Interview, *supra* note 40.
[121] *Id.*
[122] Levine's biography shows just how plugged into the media defense bar he is:

> Mr. Levine has served as Chair of the American Bar Association's Forum on Communications Law, as President of the Defense Counsel Section of the Media Law Resource Center, as Chair of both the Media Law Committee and the Publications Committee of the District of Columbia Bar, ... and as an ABA Advisor to the Uniform Defamation Act Drafting Committee of the Conference of Commissioners on Uniform State Laws. He currently serves as co-chair of the Practising Law Institute's annual Communications Law conference, as a member of

> the Board of Directors of Fred Friendly Seminars, Inc., ... and as a member of the Advisory Board of the Bureau of National Affairs' *Media Law Reporter.*

Levine, Sullivan, Koch & Schultz, L.L.P., http://www.lkslaw.com/bios/llevine.htm.
[123] 491 U.S. 657 (1989). *See supra* text accompanying notes 284-89.
[124] DIENES, ET AL., *supra* ch. 8, note 12.
[125] Brobst Interview, *supra* note 40.
[126] Brief in Opposition, Bartnicki v. Vopper, 532 U.S. 514 (2001) (No. 99-1687 & -1728), 2000 U.S. S.Ct. Briefs LEXIS 1060 at *7-8.
[127] Brief in Opposition, Bartnicki v. Vopper, 532 U.S. 514 (2001) (No. 99-1687 & -1728), 2000 U.S. S.Ct. Briefs LEXIS 1061.
[128] Reply Brief for Petitioners, Bartnicki v. Vopper, 532 U.S. 514 (2001) (No. 99-1687 & -1728), 2000 U.S. S. Ct. Briefs LEXIS 1062.
[129] Reply Brief for the United States, Bartnicki v. Vopper, 532 U.S. 514 (2001) (No. 99-1687 & -1728), 2000 U.S. S. Ct. Briefs LEXIS 1064.
[130] 530 U.S. 1260 (2000).
[131] Brief for Amicus Curiae Representative John A. Boehner in Support of Petitioners, Bartnicki v. Vopper, 532 U.S. 514 (2001) (No. 99-1687 & -1728), 2000 U.S. S.Ct. Briefs LEXIS 492 at *4.
[132] Brief Amicus Curiae of Rep. James A. McDermott in Support of Respondents, Bartnicki v. Vopper, 532 U.S. 514 (2001) (No. 99-1687 & -1728), 2000 U.S. S.Ct. Briefs LEXIS 548 at *6.
[133] Peavy v. WFAA-TV, Inc., 221 F.3d 158 (5th Cir. 2000).
[134] Brief of Amici Curiae WFAA-TV and Robert Riggs in Support of Respondents, Bartnicki v. Vopper, 532 U.S. 514 (2001) (No. 99-1687 & -1728), 2000 U.S. S. Ct. Briefs LEXIS 578 at *6.
[135] Brief Amicus Curiae of the Cellular Telecommunications Industry Association in Support of Petitioners, Bartnicki v. Vopper, 532 U.S. 514 (2001) (No. 99-1687 & -1728), 2000 U.S. S. Ct. Briefs LEXIS 493.
[136] Brief Amicus Curiae of the Am. Civil Liberties Union and the ACLU of Pennsylvania in Support of Respondents, Bartnicki v. Vopper, 532 U.S. 514 (2001) (No. 99-1687 & -1728), 2000 U.S. S. Ct. Briefs LEXIS 577 at *10; Brief Amicus Curiae of the Liberty Project in Support of Respondents, Bartnicki v. Vopper, 532 U.S. 514 (2001) (No. 99-1687 & -1728), 2000 U.S. S. Ct. Briefs LEXIS 547 at *8-9.
[137] Brief Amicus Curiae of Dow Jones & Co., Inc., in Support of Respondents, Bartnicki v. Vopper, 532 U.S. 514 (2001) (No. 99-1687 & -1728), 2000 U.S. S.Ct. Briefs LEXIS 546 at *11.
[138] Brief Amici Curiae of Media Entities and Organizations in Support of Respondents, Bartnicki v. Vopper, 532 U.S. 514 (2001) (No. 99-1687 & -1728), 2000 U.S. S.Ct. Briefs LEXIS 579.
[139] Dalglish Interview, *supra* ch. 6, note 77.
[140] *Id.*
[141] *Id.*
[142] *Id.*

[143] *Id.*
[144] SUP. CT. R. 37.2.
[145] FED. R. CIV. P. 29.
[146] Dalglish Interview, *supra* ch. 6, note 77.
[147] SUP. CT. R. 37.6.
[148] Floyd Abrams, *James Goodale Passes the Torch at PLI Communications Law Conference*, MLRC MEDIA LAW LETTER, Nov. 2007, p. 6. *See also* http://www.pli.edu/Content.aspx?dsNav= Rpp:1,N:4294963947-167&ID=60604.
[149] *See* http://www.medialaw.org/Template.cfm?Section=Home.
[150] *See* http://new.abanet.org/forums/communication/Pages/default.aspx.
[151] *See* http://www.continuinged.ku.edu/programs/media_law/.
[152] Dalglish Interview, *supra* ch. 6, note 77.
[153] *Id.*
[154] *Id.*
[155] Ctr. for Nat'l Security Studies v. U.S. Dept. of Justice, 331 F.3d 918 (2003).
[156] Dalglish Interview, *supra* ch. 6, note 77.
[157] *Id.*
[158] *Id.*
[159] Referring to Boehner v. McDermott, 191 F.3d 463 (D.C. Cir. 1999) (upholding the disclosure provisions of the wiretap act where the defendant congressman allegedly knew the interceptors and promised them immunity for their illegal conduct) and Peavy v. WFAA-TV, Inc., 221 F.3d 158 (5th Cir. 2000) (upholding the disclosure provisions where the defendant television station not only knew the interceptions were illegal, but participated in their acquisition).
[160] Dalglish Interview, *supra* ch. 6, note 77.
[161] Brief for Petitioners Gloria Bartnicki and Anthony F. Kane, Jr., Bartnicki v. Vopper, 532 U.S. 514 (2001) (No. 99-1687 & -1728), 2000 U.S. S.Ct. Briefs LEXIS 494 at *25-32.
[162] Brief for the United States, Bartnicki v. Vopper, 532 U.S. 514 (2001) (No. 99-1687 & -1728), 2000 U. S. S.Ct. Briefs LEXIS 491at *22-31.
[163] Brief for Respondents Frederick W. Vopper, Keymarket of NEPA, Inc., and Lackazerne, Inc., Bartnicki v. Vopper, 532 U.S. 514 (2001) (No. 99-1687 & -1728), 2000 U.S. S.Ct. Briefs LEXIS 581 at *29-39.
[164] Brief for Respondent Jack Yocum, Bartnicki v. Vopper, 532 U.S. 514 (2001) (No. 99-1687 & -1728), 2000 U.S. S.Ct. Briefs LEXIS 580 at *15-23.
[165] Reply Brief for Petitioners Gloria Bartnicki and Anthony F. Kane, Jr., Bartnicki v. Vopper, 532 U.S. 514 (2001) (No. 99-1687 & -1728), 2000 U.S. S.Ct. Briefs LEXIS 659 and Reply Brief for the United States, Bartnicki v. Vopper, 532 U.S. 514 (2001) (No. 99-1687 & -1728), 2000 U.S. S. Ct. Briefs LEXIS 658.
[166] Brief Amici Curiae of Media Entities and Organizations in Support of Respondents, Bartnicki v. Vopper, 532 U.S. 514 (2001) (No. 99-1687 & -1728), 2000 U.S. S.Ct. Briefs LEXIS 579 at *15-19.
[167] *Id.* at *48 n.34.
[168] *Id.* at *8-14.

[169] *Id.* at *29.
[170] *Id.* at *30.
[171] Oral Argument, Bartnicki v. Vopper, 532 U.S. 514 (2001) (No. 99-1687 & -1728), 2000 WL 1801619 at *11.
[172] *Id.* at *16-17.
[173] *Id.* at *21-23.
[174] *Id.* at *22.
[175] *Id.* at *26-27.
[176] *Id.* at *30.
[177] *Id.* at *39.
[178] *Id.*
[179] *Id.* at *42.
[180] *Id.* at *52-55.
[181] *Id.* at *55.
[182] Bartnicki v. Vopper, 532 U.S. 514, 518 (2001).
[183] *Id.*
[184] *Id.* at 526.
[185] *Id.*
[186] 403 U.S. 713 (1971). *See supra* notes 63-74 and accompanying text.
[187] *See supra* ch. 6, notes 7-33 and accompanying text.
[188] *See supra* note 60-62 and accompanying text.
[189] *Bartnicki*, 532 U.S. at 532.
[190] *Id.* at 533.
[191] *Id.* at 534.
[192] *Id.* at 535.
[193] *Id.* (Breyer, J., concurring).
[194] *See, e.g.*, James C. Goodale, *Caught in Breyer's Patch*, N.Y. L.J. , July 23, 1996, at 1; Bruce Ennis, *Courtside*, COMM. LAWYER, Fall 1999, at 14, available at A.B.A. FORUM ON COMM. L., http://www.abanet.org/forums/communication/comlawyer/fall99/courtside.html.
[195] *Bartnicki*, 532 U.S. at 536.
[196] *Id.*
[197] *Id.* at 537.
[198] *Id.* at 539.
[199] *Id.*
[200] *Id.* at 540.
[201] *Id.* at 541.
[202] *Id.* at 544 (Rehnquist, J., dissenting).
[203] *Id.* at 545-49.
[204] *Id.* at 552-53.
[205] *Id.* at 553.
[206] *Id.* at 555-56.
[207] *See* Rodney A. Smolla, *Information as Contraband: The First Amendment and Liability for Trafficking in Speech*, 96 NW. U. L. REV. 1099, 1118 (2002) ("Astonishingly, at no point in Justice Stevens's opinion does the Court come right out and say what standard of review or doctrinal test it is applying to the laws before it.")

[208] *See* Charles Savage, *U.S. Weighs Prosecution of WikiLeaks Founder, but Legal Scholars Warn of Steep Hurdles*, N.Y. TIMES, Dec. 1, 2010.
[209] There are no legally meaningful differences between the web site and the radio station as platforms or between Assange and Vopper as communicators, absent Assange's complicity in the unlawful leaking of the information.
[210] *See, e.g.,* Quigley v. Rosenthal, 327 F.3d 1044 (10th Cir. 2003) (distinguishing *Bartnicki* where intercepted conversations regarding one family's anti-Semitic remarks about another family in the neighborhood were not matters of public concern); Trans Union Corp. v. FTC, 267 F.3d 1138, 1140 (D.C. Cir. 2001) (distinguishing *Bartnicki* where speech at issue – target marketing lists comprising names, addresses, and financial information – involved only matters of private concern); Doe v. Luster, 2007 Cal. App. Unpub. LEXIS 6042 at *16 (2007) (distinguishing *Bartnicki* where speech at issue – a videotape of woman being raped – is not a matter of public concern); M. G. v. Time Warner, Inc., 107 Cal. Rptr. 2d 504, 512 (Cal. Ct. App. 2001) (distinguishing *Bartnicki* where speech at issue – photo of team coached by child molester – was not a matter of public concern).
[211] *See, e.g.,* Boehner v. McDermott, 441 F.3d 1010, 1017 (2006), *aff'd en banc*, 484 F.3d 583 (2007) (defendant's actual knowledge of the circumstances of the illegal interception made this case distinguishable from *Bartnicki*); Bowens v. Ary, 2009 Mich. App. LEXIS 2000 at *20-21 (2009) (distinguishing *Bartnicki* where the defendant directed the recording of a private conversation without consent); Wisconsin v. Baron, 769 N.W.2d 34, 48 (2009) (distinguishing Bartnicki where the defendant illegally accessed the email account of a public official to disseminate truthful information about him).
[212] *See* DVD Copy Control Ass'n v. Bunner, 75 P.3d 1, 15 (Cal. 2003) (*Bartnicki* inapplicable, by its own terms, where disclosure in question involved trade secrets).
[213] *See* Barclay's Capital, Inc. v. Thyeflyonthewall.com, 700 F. Supp. 2d 310, 354 n. 15 (2010) (distinguishing *Bartnicki* where cause of action is copyright infringement and misappropriation of hot news).
[214] *See* IMS Health Inc. v. Ayotte, 550 F.3d 42, 51 (1st Cir. 2008) (*Bartnicki* inapplicable where disclosure and use of personally identifiable information by a data mining company was found to be conduct, not speech).
[215] Indeed, in *SEC v. Rajaratnam*, the court quoted Bartnicki for the proposition that "'disclosure of the contents of a private conversation *can be an even greater intrusion on privacy than the interception itself*.'" 622 F.3d 159, 169 (2010) (quoting *Bartnicki*, 532 U.S. at 533 (emphasis added)).
[216] Smolla, *supra* note 207, at 1149-50.
[217] *Id.* at 1119.
[218] *Id.* at 1170.
[219] *Id.* at 1150.
[220] *Id.* at 1166-67.
[221] *Id.* at 1167 ("There may be some rough 'law of the jungle' notion at work here: even if no sweeping right to know will be recognized as a limit on government's power to try to keep matters bottled up, an outsider who manages to obtain otherwise confidential

information cannot then be prevented from disseminating it - or punished for having done so." LAURENCE H. TRIBE, AMERICAN CONSTITUTIONAL LAW 965 (2d ed. 1988)).
[222] *Id.* at 1168 ("So far as the Constitution goes the autonomous press may publish what it knows, and may seek to learn what it can." Stewart, *supra* ch. 8, note 7, at 636.
[223] *Id.* at 1168.

Chapter 10

[1] Brief Amici Curiae of Media Entities and Organizations in Support of Respondents, *supra* ch. 9, note 138, at *3.
[2] This analysis is adapted from Easton, *The Press as an Interest Group, supra* ch. 7, note 140. In this study, some member of the institutional press was either a party to the litigation, participated as a friend of the court, or both, in all 101 cases analyzed.
[3] *See infra* notes 14-15 and accompanying text.
[4] *See, e.g.,* Joseph D. Kearney & Thomas W. Merrill, *The Influence of Amicus Curiae Briefs on the Supreme Court*, 148 U. PA. L. REV. 743, 750 (2000).
[5] PERRY, *supra* ch. 9, note 115, at 280.
[6] *See, e.g.*, Charles Epp, *External Pressure and the Supreme Court's Agenda*, in SUPREME COURT DECISION-MAKING: NEW INSTITUTIONALIST APPROACHES 265 (Cornell W. Clayton & Howard Gillman eds. 1999); SAMUEL WALKER, IN DEFENSE OF AMERICAN LIBERTIES: A HISTORY OF THE ACLU (1990).
[7] Dalglish Interview, *supra* ch. 6, note 77.
[8] Herbert M. Kritzer, The *Government Gorilla: Why Does Government Come Out Ahead in Appellate Courts?*, in HERBERT M. KRITZER & SUSAN S. SILBEY, IN LITIGATION: DO THE "HAVES" STILL COME OUT AHEAD? (2003).
[9] Marc Galanter, *Why the "Haves" Come Out Ahead: Speculations on the Limits of Legal Change*, 9 L. & SOC. R. 95 (1974). Galanter used the terms "repeat players" and "one shotters" to distinguish entities that litigated frequently from those who rarely appeared in court. The former, including the press, "has had and anticipates repeated litigation, ... has low stakes in the adjudication of any one case, and ... has the resources to pursue its long-run interests." In theory, these "repeat players" should have a far better record in court than the "one-shotters."
[10] The cases were *Estes v. Texas*, 381 U.S. 532 (1965) (cameras in courtrooms); *Chandler v. Florida*, 449 U.S. 560 (1986) (cameras in courtrooms; the only victory of the five); *Cohen v. Cowles Media*, 501 U.S. 663 (1991) (broken promise of confidentiality); *Wilson v. Layne*, 526 U.S. 603 (1998) and *Hanlon v. Berger*, 526 U.S. 808 (1998) (police ride-alongs).
[11] *See* Easton, *Public Importance*, *supra* ch. 7, note 90, at 154-58.
[12] GLEASON, *supra* ch. 1, note 8, at 69.
[13] *Id.* at 65.
[14] Margaret Blanchard, *The Institutional Press and its First Amendment Privileges*, 1978 SUP. CT. R. 225, at 226.
[15] Steven Helle, *The News-Gathering/Publication Dichotomy and Government Expression*, 1982 DUKE L.J. 1, at 1.
[16] *See* Kritzer, *supra* note 8, at 257.

[17] 37 Stat. 539, c. 389, § 2 (Aug. 24, 1912).
[18] *Id.*
[19] EMERY, *supra* ch. 2, note 68, at 115 (quoting Don Seitz, chairman of ANPA's committee on second-class postage, in *Bulletin 2753*, Sept. 27, 1912).
[20] Lewis Publishing Co. v. Morgan, 229 U.S. 288, 297 (1913).
[21] *Id.* at 313-14.
[22] *Id.* at 315-16.
[23] CORTNER, *supra* ch. 6, note 92, at 130 ("The ANPA had been largely oblivious to free-press issues prior to the 1920s and had concentrated its energies instead on the economic problems facing newspapers across the country.").
[24] *Id.* at 132 ("A victory for the press in the *Grosjean* case was apparently perceived as important to strengthening the hand of publishers in resisting the unionization of editorial employees.").
[25] EMERY, *supra* ch. 2, note 68, at 223.
[26] *Id.* at 224.
[27] A. L. A. Schechter Poultry Corp. v. United States, 295 U.S. 495 (1935).
[28] *See generally* JEFF SHESOL, SUPREME POWER: FRANKLIN ROOSEVELT VS. THE SUPREME COURT (2010).
[29] CORTNER, *supra* ch. 6, note 92, at 132.
[30] Associated Press v. NLRB, 301 U.S. 103, 123 (1937).
[31] *Id.* at 124.
[32] EMERY, *supra* ch. 2, note 68, at 234-35. ANPA Counsel Elisha Hanson filed an amicus brief in support of AP asserting that unionization of editorial employees under government compulsion destroyed freedom of the press. *Id.*
[33] *Associated Press*, 301 U.S. at 132-33. Following the decision, *Time Magazine* wrote: "Exultant in his private office which one enters through the anteroom to the men's toilet in Manhattan's Ritz Theatre, Morris Watson made plans to return, at least long enough to collect the accumulated back pay due him under the Labor Board's ruling that the AP must compensate him for the difference between his WPA pay, $200 monthly, and his $295 AP salary. Pleased at his victory and at receiving $1,710, Morris ("Gandhi") Watson was not sure that he wished to abandon what has begun to be a successful theatrical career as director of the WPA's 'Living Newspaper' project." *The Press: Guilded Age*, TIME, April 19, 1937.
[34] *Associated Press,* 301 U.S. at 133 (Sutherland, J., dissenting).
[35] *See, e.g.*, Kristin Rasmussen, *Detroit Free Press Reporter's Subpoena Battle With Former Terrorism Prosecutor Nears End; Federal Shield Law That Likely Would Have Protected David Ashenfelter Unlikely Anytime Soon,* NEWS MEDIA & THE LAW, Spring 2011, at 21 ("the August 2010 publication of 75,000 Afghanistan war documents by WikiLeaks was perhaps the bill's death knell").
[36] *See, e.g.,* Floyd Abrams, *Why Wikileaks is Unlike the Pentagon Papers*, WALL ST. J., Dec. 29, 2010.

CASES

Index

www.ingramcontent.com/pod-product-compliance
Lightning Source LLC
LaVergne TN
LVHW080034210926
848481LV00011B/3181